CITIZENSHIP IN COLD WAR AMERICA

A VOLUME IN THE SERIES

Culture, Politics, and the Cold War

edited by

Christian G. Appy and and Edwin A. Martini

OTHER TITLES IN THE SERIES

James T. Fisher, *Dr. America: The Lives of Thomas A. Dooley, 1927–1961*

Daniel Horowitz, *Betty Friedan and the Making of "The Feminine Mystique": The American Left, the Cold War, and Modern Feminism*

Tom Engelhardt, *The End of Victory Culture: Cold War America and the Disillusioning of a Generation*

Christian G. Appy, ed., *Cold War Constructions: The Political Culture of United States Imperialism, 1945–1966*

H. Bruce Franklin, *Vietnam and Other American Fantasies*

Robert D. Dean, *Imperial Brotherhood: Gender and the Making of Cold War Foreign Policy*

Lee Bernstein, *The Greatest Menace: Organized Crime in Cold War America*

David C. Engerman, Nils Gilman, Mark H. Haefele, and Michael E. Latham, eds., *Staging Growth: Modernization, Development, and the Global Cold War*

Jonathan Nashel, *Edward Lansdale's Cold War*

James Peck, *Washington's China: The National Security World, the Cold War, and the Origins of Globalism*

Edwin A. Martini, *Invisible Enemies: The American War on Vietnam, 1975–2000*

Tony Shaw, *Hollywood's Cold War*

Maureen Ryan, *The Other Side of Grief: The Home Front and the Aftermath in American Narratives of the Vietnam War*

David Hunt, *Vietnam's Southern Revolution: From Peasant Insurrection to Total War*

Patrick Hagopian, *The Vietnam War in American Memory: Veterans, Memorials, and the Politics of Healing*

Jeremy Kuzmarov, *The Myth of the Addicted Army: Vietnam and the Modern War on Drugs*

Robert Surbrug Jr., *Beyond Vietnam: The Politics of Protest in Massachusetts, 1974–1990*

Larry Grubbs, *Secular Missionaries: Americans and African Development in the 1960s*

Robert A. Jacobs, *The Dragon's Tail: Americans Face the Atomic Age*

Andrew J. Falk, *Upstaging the Cold War: American Dissent and Cultural Diplomacy, 1940–1960*

Jerry Lembcke, *Hanoi Jane: War, Sex, and Fantasies of Betrayal*

Anna G. Creadick, *Perfectly Average: The Pursuit of Normality in Postwar America*

Kathleen Donohue, ed., *Liberty and Justice for All? Rethinking Politics in Cold War America*

Jeremy Kuzmarov, *Modernizing Repression: Police Training and Nation Building in the American Century*

Roger Peace, *A Call to Conscience: The Anti–Contra War Campaign*

Edwin A. Martini, *Agent Orange: History, Science, and the Politics of Uncertainty*

Sandra Scanlon, *The Pro-War Movement: Domestic Support for the Vietnam War and the Making of Modern American Conservatism*

Matthew W. Dunne, *A Cold War State of Mind: Brainwashing and Postwar American Society*

Patrick Hagopian, *American Immunity: War Crimes and the Limits of International Law*

David Kieran, *Forever Vietnam: How a Devisive War Changed American Public Memory*

CITIZENSHIP IN COLD WAR AMERICA

The National Security State and the Possibilities of Dissent

Andrea Friedman

UNIVERSITY OF MASSACHUSETTS PRESS
Amherst and Boston

Printed in the United States of America

ISBN 978-1-62534-068-9 (paper); 067-2 (hardcover)

Designed by Sally Nichols
Set in Adobe Garamond Pro
Printed and bound by Sheridan Books, Inc.

Library of Congress Cataloging-in-Publication Data

Friedman, Andrea.
Citizenship in Cold War America : the national security state and the possibilities of dissent / Andrea Friedman.
pages cm. — (Culture, politics, and the Cold War)
Includes bibliographical references and index.
ISBN 978-1-62534-068-9 (paper : alkaline paper) — ISBN 978-1-62534-067-2 (hardcover : alkaline paper) 1. Citizenship—United States—History—20th century. 2. Citizenship—Social aspects—United States—History—20th century. 3. Dissenters—United States—History—20th century. 4. Internal security—United States—History—20th century. 5. National security—United States—History—20th century. 6. Cold War—Political aspects—United States. 7. Political culture—United States—History—20th century. 8. Cold War—Social aspects—United States. 9. United States—Politics and government—1945–1989. 10. United States—Social conditions—1945– I. Title.
JK1759.F85 2014
323.60973'09045—dc23

2014011263

British Library Cataloguing-in-Publication Data
A catalogue record for this book is available from the British Library.

Portions of this book were published previously in different form as "The Strange Career of Annie Lee Moss: Rethinking Race, Gender, and McCarthyism," *Journal of American History* 94, no. 2 (2007): 445–68 (copyright Organization of American Historians); "Sadists and Sissies: Anti-pornography Campaigns in Cold War America," *Gender and History* 15, no. 2 (2003): 213–39 (copyright Blackwell Publishing Ltd.); "Ruth Reynolds and the Struggle for Puerto Rican Independence," *MaComère* (The Journal of the Association of Caribbean Women Writers & Scholars) 12, no. 2 (2010): 95–103 (copyright MaComère/ACWWS).

For Corey, Oscar, and Marsha
and in memory of my parents

CONTENTS

ACKNOWLEDGMENTS

As Etta James sings, at last! This book has followed a long and sometimes torturous path to completion, and I am happy, finally, to be able to thank the friends, colleagues, students, administrators, audiences, archivists, and sundry others who shepherded it and me along the way. Their encouragement, critiques, and occasional admonishments improved it immeasurably; its remaining flaws are, of course, wholly my own.

This started out as a very different project, born out of the pre-tenure need to show I did in fact have another idea in my head. The idea was, alas, somewhat underdeveloped. That this book has taken the shape it has, indeed that it was finished at all, I owe to many wonderful colleagues at Washington University and around the country. In its earliest days, Derek Hirst and Linda Nicholson were enthusiastic supporters. Linda provided the important advice that I not simply give it up and move on to other, seemingly more tantalizing subjects. Annie Valk brought Ellen Knauff to my attention and pointed me to important sources. Many years ago Eileen Findlay encouraged me to write about Lolita Lebrón. I didn't listen to her then but remembered her advice later, and am so glad I did. I owe my fascination with Annie Lee Moss to an undergraduate student in a U.S. history survey I taught a lifetime ago at the University of California, Santa Cruz. I'm not sure I ever knew her name, but she went out of her way to share with me her sense that Edward R. Murrow's anti-McCarthy broadcasts deserved a closer look. Her generosity in that moment sustained me through many years of research. If nothing else, through writing this book I have come to know in a new way that serendipity rules the lives of historians.

My ideas have been shaped and sharpened by very smart people who heard me present pieces of this book in lectures, workshops, and colloquia at Washington University, the University of Connecticut, and the New York University Center for the United States and the Cold War, and at meetings of the Organization of American Historians, the Berkshire Conference on Women's History, the American Historical Association, and conferences at Smith College and the University of Michigan. I am particularly grateful to those who commented on presentations or read chapters along the way, including Liz Borgwardt, Howard Brick, Marie Cruz Soto, Eileen Findlay, Lessie Jo Frazier, Maggie Garb, Sonia Lee, Laura McEnaney, Joanne Meyerowitz, Margaret Power, Christine Skwiot, Lori Watt, and participants in the Washington University history department's Faculty Writing Workshop. Thank you as well to Mary Helen Washington for writing me about Annie Lee Moss, and to Margot Canaday and Anne Macpherson for delightful conversations in the archives. My wonderfully supportive, and challenging, writing sisters—Flannery Burke, Deborah Cohen, and Laura Westhoff—read nearly every word I wrote, often multiple times. Special thanks to them, as well as to Chris Appy, Laura McEnaney, and Jean Allman, who each read the entire book in manuscript and offered excellent advice on how to make it better. I am also indebted to members of the Intimate Histories of the Cold War and Decolonization Faculty Seminar (funded by the Center for the Humanities at Washington University) for broadening my perspective and stimulating my thinking in many ways.

I was able to navigate this research process only because others were willing to guide me. Margot Canaday, Dennis Doyle, Eileen Findlay, Vernon Pederson, Margaret Power, Susan Smith, Landon Storrs, and Don Ritchie very kindly shared sources, research tips, insights, and their own forthcoming work. Special thanks are owed to Heming Nelson, who provided access to Mary Stalcup Markward's FBI file, my starting place for unraveling the mystery of Annie Lee Moss's political life. Many, many archivists helped me find my way through their collections, searched out materials for me, or facilitated access to unprocessed materials. I am especially grateful to Bill Davis at the National Archives and Records Administration for his patience with my many requests; to staff at the Department of Special Collections at the University of North Dakota, the Dwight D. Eisenhower Presidential Library, the Franklin D. Roosevelt Presidential Library, the Schlesinger Library, and the Syracuse University Library for combing their collections on my behalf; and to David Fort and Mary Kay Schmidt at the National Archives for assisting me with Freedom of Information Act requests. Thank you as well to Barbara Heyman, who graciously housed and entertained me while I visited archives in New York City.

I must pay special tribute to those who helped a novice with few Spanish-language skills conduct research on Puerto Rico. Pedro Juan Hernández at the Archives of the Puerto Rican Diaspora, housed at Hunter College, and Julio E. Quirós Alcalá and Dax Collazo at Archivo Luis Muñoz Marín in San Juan helped me find sources I could use, provided access to staff, and allayed my anxieties about encroaching on the territory of experts in Puerto Rican history. At a very late stage, Pedro Aponte Vázquez graciously helped me identify images. Eileen Findlay and Margaret Power were always encouraging. They answered my questions, connected me to resources, shared their own work in progress, and, along with Deborah Cohen, alerted me to egregious errors of interpretation and language. Megan Havard and Luimil Negrón provided excellent and timely translations. Finally, my deepest appreciation to Professor Antonio Fernós, president of the Dr. Antonio Fernós Isern Educational Foundation, for sharing with me documents, memories of his father, and insights into the "status problem." I will always be grateful for his bountiful hospitality and his continuing interest in my work.

For institutional support, I thank the Washington University Center for the Humanities for a faculty fellowship that afforded time to write and, just as important, an expanded intellectual community with whom to share ideas. Dean of Arts and Sciences Barbara Schaal made available much-appreciated assistance with publication costs, and former dean of Arts and Sciences Ed Macias provided access to various forms of research support. As a result I have been able to work with a series of undergraduate and graduate research assistants whose contributions have been essential to this project and its development over time, including Julia Baskin, Bill Bulman, Sally Cohen, Joanna Franks, John McCurdy, Michelle Repice, Jenny Slosar, and particularly Tanya Roth and Kevin Wooten. My work on this book has spanned the terms of three Department of History chairs and two Directors of Women, Gender, and Sexuality Studies, and all of them—Derek Hirst, Hillel Kieval, Jean Allman, Linda Nicholson, and Mary Ann Dzuback—have been immensely supportive. Jean, in particular, made it possible for me to find time for research and writing. Her administrative creativity and her intellectual comradeship have sustained me these last few years.

Everyone with whom I've worked at University of Massachusetts Press has been unfailingly enthusiastic and helpful. To call Chris Appy and, especially, Clark Dougan "patient" does justice neither to the grace with which they tolerated my penchant for renegotiating deadlines nor to their active shepherding of this project. Carol Betsch and Mary Bellino answered numerous questions as we moved toward production; they helped make my obsessiveness manageable. Amanda Heller was a careful, judicious, and wise copy editor. Many more than three cheers to Jill Storm, who, at various moments, whipped the manuscript into shape. Her sensible interventions and hard work made an enormous difference.

Finally, a few people whose contributions to this book defy easy categorization. Annie Lee Moss's former student Bill Dickens contacted me after learning of my early foray into her life. His continuing conversations with me sustained my faith in my intuition while also pointing me in new research directions and toward new insights. I remain inspired by friends and colleagues who now live far away but nonetheless have made their mark on this work and my life. Howard Brick, Laura McEnaney, and Leisa Meyer have each in their own way kept me going. A special shout-out to Laura, who has been my greatest cheerleader and my companion in thinking about both Cold War history and the difficulties of second projects. Leslie Brown and Annie Valk offered day-to-day and intellectual support through much of my work on this book; you are sorely missed. Spread across four different states, my siblings, aunt, and uncle nonetheless keep me attached to my roots. I am grateful as well to the Sanguinette clan for welcoming me into the California branch of the family. Closer to home, Mary Ann Dzuback, Mary Carpenter, Maggie Garb, Lawrence Lewis, Susan Nanny, and Lisa Mandel, Ruth Heyman, and the other members of my Shabbat group have offered sage counsel, respite from parenting, fiction recommendations, and witty repartee about national politics, life in St. Louis, and the ridiculousness of academia. Jean Allman has become a good friend as well as mentor. Thank you for getting me out of my house.

Last, but in no way least, Corey, Oscar, and Marsha all came into my life near the beginnings of my work on this book, and just as I lost both my father and my mother. My partner, Marsha Sanguinette, and our sons anchor me to the world and make it possible for me to do my work. Despite this project's tendency to pull me away, they have pulled me back so that we could find our way toward being a family. Thanks for your patience with me, and for your impatience, too.

CITIZENSHIP IN COLD WAR AMERICA

INTRODUCTION.
Citizenship Stories in Exceptional Times

IN 1955 THE SOCIOLOGIST SAMUEL A. STOUFFER PUBLISHED HIS LANDMARK study *Communism, Conformity, and Civil Liberties.* Based on a massive survey of public opinion conducted in the summer of 1954, it sought to trace U.S. citizens' reactions to "two dangers. One, from the Communist conspiracy outside and inside the country. Two, from those who in thwarting the conspiracy would sacrifice some of the very liberties which the enemy would destroy."[1] Stouffer's main paradigm for assessing attitudes toward these related dangers was that of "tolerance." Which Americans were most tolerant of the rights of nonconformists to live undisturbed—to speak, to work, to move freely among their fellow citizens? What was the prospect for increasing tolerance in the future?

Stouffer's findings were potentially troubling to those concerned about the threat to civil liberties. Even though few survey respondents ranked Communism among the most important problems facing the nation, they were widely committed to depriving Communists of their citizenship rights. Asked about their attitudes toward admitted Communists, suspected Communists, socialists, and atheists, many were eager to punish nonconformists. Admitted Communists were least tolerated of all. More than 65 percent of respondents would deny Communists the right to speak or publish. The proportion who would fire Communists working in defense plants or as educators hovered around 90 percent, but 68 percent believed that even a Communist store clerk should be dismissed, figures suggesting that a substantial majority thought Communists had no right to earn a living. Three-quarters favored depriving Communists of U.S. citizenship, and half thought all Communists should be jailed. Fully 95 percent believed that it was impossible to be both a Communist and a loyal American.[2]

Nonetheless, Stouffer found hope for civil liberties, pointing to growing pockets of tolerance among young or highly educated individuals, a relatively strong level of tolerance among civic leaders, and the basic goodness of the American people, who believed in "fair play" and "truth" and cared about the welfare of their nation. He argued for a concerted campaign of education by the media and local and national leaders in order to provide a more accurate picture of the dangers posed by Communism and to make citizens more invested in policies that seemed abstract and distant. Since the survey showed that personal acquaintance with Communists and concrete knowledge about the anti-Communist crusade fostered tolerance, "dramatizing" the twin threats of Communism and repression was most likely to lead to the lessening of political apathy and greater respect for civil liberties.[3]

Although Stouffer's framework and methods came in for some criticism both at the time and since, he identified important inconsistencies within Cold War political culture. What did it mean that, while they backed draconian measures to deprive Communists of the right to speak or work, a majority of Americans simultaneously endorsed "letting people say anything they want to in a public speech"? Why were so many willing to support the repression of civil liberties for a range of nonconformist thinkers even though few saw political subversion as one of the greatest dangers facing the nation? What do these incongruities suggest about Cold War–era understandings of U.S. citizenship? Did they point to the basic goodness of Americans, as Stouffer would have it? Or did they reveal more fundamental contradictions in U.S. political culture?[4]

Just five years before Stouffer published his study, Supreme Court Justice Robert H. Jackson articulated these contradictions in a different way. His colleagues had just upheld the federal government's power to deny entry to Ellen Knauff, the foreign-born and stateless wife of a U.S. veteran, without disclosing the reasons for her exclusion from the country. This was a power, the justices determined, warranted by the continuing state of emergency posed to the nation by a hostile world. Along with several of his peers, Justice Jackson dissented vigorously from that decision. Memorably, he invoked two of the keywords of

American political culture in the Cold War era. The government had contended that Knauff's admission would pose a "hazard to internal security"; but, Jackson insisted, "security is like liberty in that many are the crimes committed in its name."[5] The concordance between security and liberty, he suggested, was both more complex and more troubling than Cold War platitudes might admit.

Ellen Knauff's exclusion was one of those moments when the power and reach of the national security state was made palpable to many U.S. citizens. They could identify with the aspirations and fears of a war bride, particularly one who was attractive, educated, and a refugee from German atrocities. It was hard to believe that such a woman posed a threat to U.S. security, even though the attorney general, the chief of the Immigration and Naturalization Service, even J. Edgar Hoover himself claimed to have secret evidence that she was not to be trusted. The civic leaders and media figures to whom Stouffer accorded so much responsibility for shoring up tolerance swung into high gear, waging a campaign for Knauff's admission into the country. Their insistence that security ought not preempt liberty succeeded. With their help, Knauff successfully asserted her right to be included within the nation—her right, as Hannah Arendt framed it, to "have rights." She died a U.S. citizen.

Ellen Knauff was not the only individual to push back against the national security state. There was also Annie Lee Moss, accused of membership in the Communist Party (CP), who faced down Senator Joseph R. McCarthy and his chief aide, Roy Cohn, on national television. A middle-aged African American widow who had worked her way up from humble beginnings in the South to middle-class status as a Pentagon employee, Moss fought back when McCarthy's allegations endangered her job. Despite the fact that there was substantial evidence that she had been involved with the CP, she too garnered help from powerful champions who presented her as a symbol of government repression gone wrong and defended her right to earn a living. Like Knauff, Moss was perceived as a "little woman," the kind of vulnerable individual who most needed the protection of the state, and this made her experience a compelling illustration of the threats posed by a national security regime to the rights and freedoms it was meant to defend. She kept her job at the Pentagon until she retired in 1975.

In their ability to gain such widespread public support and to persuade government officials at the highest levels to concede defeat, Ellen Knauff and Annie Lee Moss were perhaps exceptional, but their efforts to realign national security with principles of freedom and equality were hardly so. For example,

North Americans and Puerto Ricans like Ruth Reynolds and Lolita Lebrón worked to challenge Cold War policies that they believed subjugated Puerto Rico to U.S. empire. They argued that official "reform" of the Puerto Rican-U.S. relationship did nothing more than disguise the state violence—an amalgam of economic exploitation, political repression, military might, and nuclear technologies—that stripped Puerto Ricans of their liberties and rights. Deprived of their own liberty for their efforts, they nonetheless situated themselves as heirs to American political traditions to argue for Puerto Rico's total independence. Similarly, the prominent social psychiatrist Fredric Wertham is remembered today as a censorious foe of the comic book industry, but his anti–comic book crusade was part of a broader effort to redefine national security. He maintained that the state was responsible for protecting its most vulnerable citizens more from the pervasive everyday violence of racial, economic, and gender inequality than from the imagined violence of subversives. But, as with critics of U.S. violence in Puerto Rico, his attack on the broader structures of power that made a national security state both possible and necessary was illegible to an American public that saw itself endangered by the "total" power of the Soviet Union. Even if most citizens were unreceptive to these more sweeping analyses of the ways that national security impeded rather than fostered freedom, it matters that critics found in the Cold War moment the opportunity to ask such questions.

Episodes like the ones recounted here exposed the gap between democratic ideals and national policies. It is perhaps no real surprise that policies which undermined civil liberties and inhibited social equality in the name of defending "America" yielded disquietude and dissent; but the breadth of that disquietude has not yet been recognized. Puerto Rico's emergence as a supposedly decolonized "Free Associated State," and the violence surrounding that transformation, has rarely been considered in the light of U.S. Cold War policy, nor has Wertham's redefinition of national security. But these are fundamentally stories about Cold War contradiction. Some critics of U.S. policy, like Knauff and Moss, successfully drew attention to "unfair" impediments to liberty and rights. Reynolds, Lebrón, and Wertham, who focused on structural and state violence, were less successful. Still, each of these struggles demonstrates the myriad ways in which the paradox of condoning limitations on freedom in freedom's name was at the heart of Cold War politics.

These stories both confirm and complicate understandings of U.S. political culture in the early Cold War years. During the long 1950s, the sense that the United States was endangered by subversion from within as well as aggression from without fueled the expansion of a national security state that justified the abridgment of individual rights and freedoms as an indispensable strategy for protecting the supposed core values of economic and political liberty. Repression in the United States operated through executive order, administrative fiat, law, and judicial pronouncement, as well as government propaganda, self-regulation within the communications and entertainment industries, and public opinion. It was enacted at the local, state, and national levels and approved by many Americans as necessary to secure the future of freedom. And it was rationalized by psychological analyses which purported to demonstrate that Communists and other dissidents were incapable even of being American. It decimated the CP, severely hobbled a range of efforts to achieve social and economic equity and justice, and spilled over to many aspects of domestic life.[6]

Still, intentionally repressive strategies do not simply and solely create repressive outcomes. Michael Sherry has noted the "characteristic American form" of the Cold War national security state: "Pluralistic, civil libertarian, and antistatist traditions, like bureaucratic rivalries, ruled out the operation of any monolithic machine. A political system that both practiced repression and denied the intent to do so allowed authority to scatter in all sorts of directions, which only encouraged its capricious use."[7] This capriciousness did not go unnoticed, even at the time. I argue that the scattershot nature of Cold War repression had unintended effects, not only limiting the possibilities for dissent—although that certainly was its impact at many moments and in many settings—but also sometimes opening them up. The repressive apparatus and nationalist ideologies of the national security state ironically created opportunities for interrogating the very meanings and scope of U.S. citizenship.

States of Exception in Cold War America

For many years, the framework of containment dominated analyses of the early Cold War era. Deriving from the ideas of diplomat George F. Kennan, who suggested that postwar officials should adhere to "a policy of firm containment, designed to confront the Russians with unalterable counter-force at every point where they show signs of encroaching on the interests of a peaceful and stable world," the metaphor of containment has been taken up by scholars to explain both the domestic politics of the second red scare and the politics of domesticity. Elaine Tyler May coined the term "domestic containment" to describe the parallels between political and personal conformity, suggesting that Americans wanted "secure jobs, secure homes, and secure marriages in a secure country."[8] This framework was used by many to illuminate the ties between private and public life, domestic and foreign policy, culture and politics, as well as their relation to hierarchies of gender, race, and sexuality.[9]

Despite its handiness, containment was always simply a metaphor. As such it flattened out the complexities of foreign policy, domestic politics, and personal experience.[10] Indeed, the metaphor of containment makes sense only when it is placed in tension with the idea of consensus, for it suggests the effort to control matter and forces that had logics of their own—logics that threatened to seep through or overflow their boundaries. The desire for conformity always bumped up against the specter of rebelliousness; the security imperative emboldened some to question what security meant or how it could be attained. As a trope, then, containment has been used to overstate the extent of consensus and to minimize the contradictory nature of American political culture in the postwar years. And as scholars have increasingly recognized that "the Cold War was no monolith," they have identified the ways in which Cold War discourses enabled critique and questioning while reinforcing the sense that unity—consensus—was crucial to the nation's defense.[11]

From another perspective, the rhetoric of containment might be said to minimize the significance of this period as a whole. Senator Joseph McCarthy's campaign as a Communist hunter lasted only four years, but his name has become identified with the broad range of antisubversive policies that were created during the fifteen years following the end of World War II. Why are Americans so loath to dispense with the notion of the "age of McCarthyism"? Perhaps because this popular moniker works to label the entire era exceptional. The "age of McCarthyism" is a moment out of American time, explicable as a manifestation of one man's irrationality and recklessness. The anxiety over national security that temporarily overwhelmed the nation's traditions of respect for due process and freedom of conscience and speech, such an account would have it, was anomalous. Perhaps some of the repressive policies that were institutionalized by presidents, legislators, and judges and endorsed by many civic groups and citizens were necessitated (or seemed so) by Soviet aggression; but even so, they were quickly contained, and their repudiation restored the nation to its customary commitment to freedom and equality. Through such a narrative, exceptional moments of extreme illiberalism need not disturb the sense that the United States has a destiny to fulfill as leader of the free world.

Of course, the exceptionalism of McCarthyism has had many interlocutors.

Some have noted the breadth and depth of support for the senator's anti-Communist crusade. Others have illuminated the ways in which these policies reflected opposition to the New Deal, or continued a longer history of anti-communism, or even carried on a broader counter-subversive tradition rooted in the nation from its earliest years. In these analyses, the policies of the domestic Cold War are connected to much older tensions in U.S. political culture over economic liberty, the role of the state, and national belonging.[12]

Yet the sense of the early Cold War years as an aberration or anomaly remains pervasive. The political philosopher Giorgio Agamben's idea of the "state of exception" offers a good antidote to this interpretation. Agamben argues that states are founded on a contradiction, what he calls an "inclusive exclusion": the sovereign's ability to create law is rooted in his power to place himself outside of it. This "sovereign exception"—the assertion that "I, the sovereign, who am outside the law, declare that there is nothing outside the law"—is a paradox.[13] The sovereign's ability to exist both inside and outside the law has its parallel in his ability to decide to place others beyond the law as well (that is, to exclude by including them within his power to decide). The state of exception, then, is the "original structure in which law encompasses living beings by means of its own suspension," and it is *not* exceptional but fundamental to states and indeed, Agamben contends, to modern democracies composed of rights-bearing citizens.[14]

This formulation is cumbersome and complex, but nonetheless it can help us understand the nature of the U.S. national security state that was born in the first half of the twentieth century and strengthened during the Cold War (and, Agamben asserts, rejuvenated after 9/11). American officials claimed that their continued sovereignty—in fact, the sovereignty of the people and the very existence of the nation—depended on their ability and willingness to place some citizens beyond the law. This is the same power that underwrote the repressive apparatus of the Cold War state, depriving certain individuals of the rights that U.S. citizenship was understood to convey. Because it expressed a contradiction in democratic citizenship itself—that "rights" in fact enable the all-encompassing sovereignty of the state—the state of exception both consolidated governmental authority and raised questions about its legitimacy.[15] By its very nature, the early Cold War state of exception made more conspicuous the arbitrariness of government power and the inequalities preserved and even cultivated by that power.

Justified as a necessary response to the "state of emergency" created by Soviet ambitions and treachery, the U.S. state of exception was made legible via the ubiquitous contrast between the "free world" and the "slave state." These terms were so endemic to Western portrayals of the international scene, so taken for granted, that few scholars have seen fit to analyze them. Susan Carruthers's study of the uses of captivity narratives in Cold War culture is an important and welcome contribution. She notes that "metaphors of enslavement played a crucial role in transforming the Soviet Union and China from courageous wartime allies into barbarous foes implacably opposed to the 'free world.' This Cold War vision of a globe fractured between good and evil—half free, half slave—drew on a peculiarly American tradition of configuring any infringement of liberty as 'slavery.' "[16] Though the contrast between slavery and freedom has a long history as a political metaphor and had recently done yeoman duty in the framing of World War II, it was reconfigured to meet the specific contingencies of the early Cold War, translated into the opposition between totalitarianism and democracy. This rhetoric suffused the speeches of presidents and diplomats, the top secret analyses of foreign policy officials, the pronunciations of clerics, the writings of journalists and academics, newsreels and novels, and the letters of ordinary citizens.

"Slavery" and "freedom" operated to explain and legitimize American domestic and foreign policy on several levels at once. Most obviously, the contrast between the "free world" led by the United States and the "slave world" portended by Soviet expansion justified the decision to create a massive national security state based on the sustained expansion of U.S. military capacity; substantial military assistance to allies; the development and maintenance of intelligence, psychological warfare, and covert operations; and the creation of internal security programs.[17] This agenda of domestic and international militarization was necessary, wrote the author of the National Security Council report known as NSC 68, because "there is a basic conflict between the idea of freedom under a government of laws, and the idea of slavery under the grim oligarchy of the Kremlin. . . . The idea of freedom . . . is peculiarly and intolerably subversive of the idea of slavery."[18] According to this logic, the mere existence of a free world threatened the slave world, and the leaders of the Soviet Union could craft no other path but an unremitting war against freedom wherever it existed. To survive, the Soviet state would need to enslave the free world, and only a titanic commitment by the United States to protect the free world could secure the future of humanity. As we will see, this rhetoric did have its pitfalls, as the legacy of racial slavery in the United States facilitated counter-accusations by the Soviets that Americans were hardly trustworthy as guardians of freedom, but it remained "the controlling metaphor of the Cold War."[19]

Freedom, then, was the sine qua non of the American nation; its protection necessitated the Cold War, but the Cold War required that the nation-state sacrifice the freedom of its citizens. The very terms that explained the differences between democracy and totalitarianism were destabilized by practices and policies that made the liberty of American citizens tenuous and that made visible the calculus placing some individuals within the protections of the law and others outside. These exceptions were, perhaps, somewhat less troublesome when they were applied to members of the Communist Party in the abstract, or to those who could be cast as traitors and spies. But when they encompassed individuals who might be considered members of the American "family"—wives of veterans, hardworking widows, freedom-loving patriots, or vulnerable children—they gave some observers pause, while affording others the opportunity to question what it meant to be a citizen of the "leader of the free world." In the state of exception that was the early Cold War United States, the rights and obligations of Americans were less secure even as their symbolic significance increased.

Citizenship as a Contested Category

As the foregoing suggests, the domestic Cold War also raised questions central to the definition of citizenship: Who belongs to the nation? What rights and privileges does the nation-state protect? What is owed in return for those rights? Because the anti-Communist crusade embodied both a set of ideas about the worth of belonging to America and a collection of policies intended to guard that worth, it is useful to ask what it reveals about how mid-century citizenship ideals informed and were transformed by global pressures.[20] Such an inquiry illuminates the tensions *within* citizenship as well as the limits of consensus and dissent in the national security state.

Citizenship was strained in new ways by the Cold War, but it had always been a matter of contention. The ambiguity at the heart of U.S. citizenship was reflected in the nation's founding documents, for the term was barely mentioned and nowhere defined in the Constitution, which spoke of "persons" rather than "citizens." In part such vagueness may reflect a certain insignificance to the category of national citizenship vis-à-vis other sorts of statuses in distributing rights and responsibilities prior to the Civil War.[21] But it also may have expressed or at least enabled the paradoxes of a political system that hailed "liberty and justice for all" but excluded wide swaths of the population—as Judith Shklar has framed it, a system in which "the equality of political rights . . . was proclaimed in the accepted presence of its absolute denial."[22] As a result of both the ambiguity and the paradox, every aspect of American citizenship—membership, rights and obligations, and participation in self-governance—far from being self-evident, has been both historically contingent and continually challenged.

This was particularly true in the United States at mid-century. The aftershocks of World War II played an important role in framing citizenship as a matter of particular concern. Among these might be counted a massive Eurasian refugee crisis that generated attention to the problem of statelessness, the disruption of the European colonial order and the growth of independence movements in the global South, and the contributions of wartime rhetoric and experience to heightened expectations for racial and gender equality. More fundamentally, the long-standing contradictions of American democracy almost inevitably made citizenship one of the terrains on which the Cold War was fought. What the political scientist Elizabeth F. Cohen designates as the "myth of full citizenship"—the belief that in democratic nations, "a central function, perhaps the central function, of citizenship is to make members of a polity equal, and that it does so by fashioning a single, unitary political identity"—was essential to legitimating Cold War policy. By its very comparison with the "totalitarian" domination of the Soviet Union, "democratic" citizenship delineated the difference between an East that denied its inhabitants both autonomy and rights and a West that secured to all its people the highest levels of freedom, self-governance, and equality.[23]

Contrary to the myth, however, citizenship is at its most basic a category created to distinguish who does and who does not belong in order to classify populations for the purpose of governing them efficiently. Citizenship is itself a state of exception, and exclusions are woven into its fabric. It not only sorts people into those who are and those who are not members of, and therefore protected by, the nation; it also creates internal exclusions, allocating people more or less commodious bundles of rights and liberties on the basis of their position within hierarchies of race, gender, class, ethnicity, age, sexuality, and a host of other statuses. At times some of these hierarchies are portrayed (at least by those with social and political power) as natural, and they can be acknowledged without endangering the presumptions of fairness and equality embedded in U.S. citizenship norms. But at other moments—when those with less power are able to challenge their exclusion, or when terms like "fairness" and "equality" become laden with excess meaning—their recognition has more unsettling effects.[24]

The early Cold War era was one of those moments. Growing domestic demands for racial and gender equality, the emergence of national liberation movements in the global South, the intensifying conflict between East and West: all these and more collided with the national security state's modus operandi of defending the United States by sorting out those deserving of protection and rights from those undeserving of them. As a result, certain exclusions appeared especially weighty: the exclusion, for example, of a woman refugee whose marital status rendered her stateless, of Puerto Ricans denied the right to self-governance in a decolonizing world, of a hardworking widow fired from a government job, or of poor youth of color who were imagined to have no rights at all. In a context in which the continuing reality of unequal citizenship coexisted with an ever more urgent need to demonstrate the nation's commitment to full democracy, these citizenship stories overflowed with significance, and it was often those apparently most vulnerable who attracted attention and, sometimes, empathy. But their claims did not go unchallenged. Gender, race, class, and sexuality, so long and so deeply interlaced with hierarchies of status and authority, continued to provide means of communicating ideas about the naturalness of lingering hierarchies, about the ligatures of political attachment, and about the necessity of state power.[25]

As the stories gathered here show, the historically specific enmeshing of race, gender, and citizenship provided a conceptual framework for understanding the discord of the early Cold War years, wrought the continuing social and political inequalities that helped to produce that discord, and was instrumental in efforts to manage it. Together, these categories situated Communists and other dissidents and deviants as outside the bounds of U.S. citizenship while affording others its protections. Each of the individuals profiled in this book experienced the contradictions of early Cold War political culture. Although some were reluctant warriors, they challenged American democracy to live up to its ideals by extending to its Others rights to due process, to self-governance, to economic opportunity and protection from violence. As individuals, some met with greater success than others in making their claims to inclusion. Still, their very challenges exposed to a broader public, if briefly, the gap between the rhetoric of democracy and the practices of citizenship in the national security state.

It remains the case, however, that such challenges were often defused, as public officials and policy makers mobilized prevailing understandings of U.S. citizenship to resolve or suppress these conflicts. Often those who contested the states of exception that they confronted found themselves forced to narrate their struggles in terms that did injustice to the complexities of their lives. Indeed, superficially, each of these episodes can be read as evidence of the triumph of consensus during the early Cold War. But such an interpretation can be sustained only if we look past the lived contradiction, the struggle, and the resistance that created the necessity for reaction in the first place. If this was containment, it was only partial, and it could not last. Race and gender proved flashpoints in many of the episodes of the domestic Cold War. Soon they would become the battleground for a more fundamental—if still only partly successful—reassessment of the meanings of American citizenship.

This book tells citizenship stories that at first glance seem only loosely related, although a close reading will reveal the many ways they overlap and intertwine. Their diversity allows me to reveal the bonds and the ruptures between what Rogers Smith has called the "stories of peoplehood" told in the early Cold War, the policies of the national security state, and the opposition that those policies sometimes engendered.[26] Putting these stories together offers a more robust understanding of the reach and the limits of the national security paradigm. At the same time, a focus on individual episodes permits an engagement with a range of sources, encompassing FBI and immigration investigations; transcripts from loyalty board hearings and civil and criminal legal proceedings; congressional committee deliberations and court opinions; behind-the-scenes negotiations and widely noted political performances; and cultural texts including memoirs, film, and television shows, comic books, popular journalism, government propaganda, and theoretical tracts. Attending to diverse evidence across discrete cases allows us to pay close attention to the simultaneously intricate and mundane workings of national security policies, as well as to the specificity of the strategies individuals used to participate in the national debate about what citizenship meant. Finally, the stories presented here illuminate the deep impact of gender and race on discourses about and experiences of citizenship at mid-century while enabling a more fine-grained integrated analysis of the ways in which race, gender, and other categories (ethnicity, sexuality, age) work *together* to distribute citizenship unequally.

There were many other such episodes—the execution of the Rosenbergs comes to mind, or the lavender scare, which resulted in the persecution of thousands of gay men and women on national security grounds—but I have chosen to focus on stories forgotten or less familiar as a reminder of how the memory of this era has been shaped by insistence on a consensus and a coherence that may not have existed. Collectively, the stories told here expose a growing perception—sometimes inchoate, but nonetheless significant—of democracy's contradictions. These deep currents of unease were profoundly disturbing to many Americans who felt keenly the burdens of claiming to be the standard-bearer of democracy for the world.

Each of these divergent narratives of dissent in early Cold War America provides a distinct angle of vision on how citizenship has been imagined in the United States, and I employ a different lens for exploring the complexities of Cold War citizenship in each case. Chapter 1 uses the frame of psychological citizenship to examine how Communists were excluded from the democratic order that the Cold War was allegedly fought to protect. It explores the considerable power of Cold War–era psychoanalytic discourse to shape understandings of citizenship in ex-Communist memoirs, popular and academic "scientific" studies of Communists, and works of political theory, and notes the traces of these ideas in legal initiatives that institutionalized Communist exclusion as well. Psychological explanations of the connections between individual personality, human nature, and national political culture were articulated through ideas about gender, sexuality, and family, offering compelling portraits of what American citizenship looked like—and what it did not. At the height of its influence during these years, psychology helped strengthen the state of exception, but ironically, it also suggested that citizenship could be unmoored from embodiment, describing a democratic personality that any American could aspire to inhabit.

The next two chapters explore the diverse strategies used by two women to stake their claims to U.S. citizenship after each was confronted with the exclusionary power of the national security state. Chapter 2 follows the travails of the German Jewish war bride Ellen Knauff to investigate the emerging tension between notions of liberal citizenship predicated on membership in the nation-state and human rights paradigms, strengthened in the wake of World War II, which sought to disentangle basic protections for human liberty and dignity from national belonging. Focusing particularly on the ways in which the Cold War state of emergency was used to justify the denial of liberal rights such as due process, the chapter details how Knauff's statelessness allowed her to make citizenship claims both from the gendered position of devoted wife and from a universalist stance based on human decency. Unlike the Communists whose supposed psychological troubles and dysfunctional families placed them beyond the boundaries of national protection, Knauff ultimately succeeded in crossing the borders of the national security state to become a member of the American family, but she also helped to arouse a coalition of journalists, policy makers, and civil libertarians to question the efficacy and the justice of those borders.

Chapter 3 uses the lens of economic citizenship to explore the tensions between national security and U.S. claims of being a beacon of liberty and democracy, and describes how these tensions contributed to the opposition to "McCarthyism." Much recent literature on economic citizenship in the postwar United States has focused on consumption, but the struggle of Annie Lee Moss to keep her government job after being accused of CP membership returns us to the importance of the "right to earn a living" as a signifier of equal opportunity and racial justice. As an African American woman who had successfully struggled up from rural poverty to relative prosperity, Annie Lee Moss was a symbol of the promise of the American way of life, and when the national security state threatened that way of life, Senator Joe McCarthy took the fall. The public drama of Moss's confrontation with McCarthy demonstrates how racial liberalism undermined the most extreme anti-Communist practices while also shaping, for good and ill, the ability of African Americans to prove themselves worthy of full citizenship.

The remaining chapters focus on individuals who offered broader critiques of the state of exception, the forms of citizenship it enabled, and the violence on which it was based. These chapters also highlight the ways that race and gender shaped both these critiques and the national security state itself. In chapter 4 I use the political scientist Deborah Cohen's concept of semi-citizenship to investigate how the Cold War's postcolonial moment shaped debates about Puerto Rico's status as U.S. possession. U.S. and Puerto Rican officials responded to anticolonial pressures within the global South by seeking to reframe colonial semi-citizenship as self-determination. Activists in both North America and Puerto Rico, among them the radical pacifist Ruth Reynolds and the Puerto Rican nationalist Lolita Lebrón, sought to draw attention to the violence that undergirded these efforts, revealing Puerto Rico to be the archetypal state of exception. Each suffered the retaliation of a state that drew on both long-standing instruments of empire and the expanded security regime of the Cold War era. These domestic and global political conflicts, and the varying coalitions they made possible, were articulated through race- and gender-saturated languages of pathology and violence.

Chapter 5 returns to the influence of psychology in American life but highlights an alternative perspective on how to conceptualize the democratic personality. T. H. Marshall's notion of social citizenship provides an avenue for exploring the social psychiatrist Fredric Wertham's attempts to redefine national security for those left behind by democracy. I offer an interpretation of Wertham's infamous campaign against comic books that situates his concern with violence in comics alongside a longer career focused on the ways that poverty and racial inequality produce violence, both among individuals and within the state. Wertham proposed a different understanding of "national security," arguing that government ought to protect individuals from the violence they experienced in their everyday lives, and that such protection included access to a variety of social goods that would make true democracy possible. His advocacy of censorship, then, was only part—if the most illiberal part—of a broader agenda intended to question the state of exception that ruled certain Americans outside its bounds, especially poor youth of color.

In the mid-century expansion of the national security state, the liberty of individuals was always situated in relation to the security of the nation. It was the vulnerability of the collective that justified limits on individual rights, even as those limits were framed as a defense of individual freedom. The uneasy bond between the individual and the collective was at the center of ideologies about American citizenship. During the early Cold War, psychology provided a language for articulating both who the democratic citizen was and why some Americans did not qualify. In this way it enabled the consolidation of the Cold War state of exception. It is here—at the nexus between the individual and the political community that psychology described, which is the foundation of any notion of citizenship—that we begin.

CHAPTER ONE.

Internal Security, National Security

Psychological Citizenship in the Cold War Era

THE NATIONAL SECURITY COUNCIL REPORT NSC 68, APPROVED BY President Truman in 1950, was the ultimate expression of U.S. containment policy. Articulating the foundations of the battle between the free and slave worlds and laying out the need for a fully realized strategy for winning that battle, it opened with a disquisition on democratic and totalitarian attitudes toward the individual. Free societies, its author proclaimed, "valu[e] the individual as an end in himself, requiring of him only that measure of self-discipline and self-restraint which make the rights of each individual compatible with the rights of every other individual." In contrast, slave states seek paradoxically to subjugate individual will "in an act of willing submission, a degradation willed by the individual upon himself under the compulsion of a perverted faith." Although NSC 68 was confined largely to foreign policy, its rationale could also be applied to matters of internal security, for its author noted that totalitarianism was a "compulsion" that "demands total power over all Communist Parties . . . under Soviet domination," including, presumably, the Communist Party of the United States of America (CPUSA). These diametrically opposed attitudes toward the individual in relation to society, and the psychologies that they reflected and generated, constituted the ground on which, and the means by which, the domestic Cold War would be fought. This was psychological warfare at its most elemental level.[1]

The influence of psychology in American culture arguably reached its zenith in the early Cold War years, and unsurprisingly it left its mark on visions of citizenship. Its propensity to focus on the individual while always also placing that individual in a relational context made psychology a potent frame for conceptualizing interactions among self, community, nation, and state, and from there, international relations as well. Cold War–era psychology translated emotion and behavior into political terms, and as a particularly conservative rendition of psychoanalysis rose to prominence within the profession, it used rhetorics of gender and sexuality to popularize new understandings of the ideal democratic citizen and the totalitarian Other.[2]

Psychological concepts became fodder for a legion of political experts and commentators who sought to update long-standing citizenship norms for a modern age. Older presumptions about the necessity of economic and political independence to the constitution of a virtuous citizenry and polity—already weakened by the shift from a producer to a consumer economy—shaded into musings about whether Americans possessed the psychic strength to make democracy sustainable. Scholars and pundits declared that the advent of mass society created lonely, vulnerable individuals who were often unable to negotiate the frightening void between self and other. Personality, not virtue, was the watchword of the day.

Casting citizenship in psychological terms had diverse effects on the political culture of Cold War America. On the one hand, it justified broadening and strengthening the national security state, contributing to the intensification of a state of exception that placed dissenters outside the bounds of the law. How individuals confronted the loneliness produced by modernity determined their fitness for citizenship, establishing whether or not they ought to be trusted, whether or not they ought to have rights, and whether or not they belonged to the political community. This reasoning underlay numerous efforts to deny Communists (real or suspected) their status as American citizens. On the other hand, once citizenship became a matter of mind and personality, it lost some of its embodied, material quality. As distinctions among citizens on the basis of economic independence and dependence morphed into a concern with psychological maturity and health, the arena for demonstrating one's capacity for full citizenship also shifted, making a bit of room for those who had earlier been excluded.

Stories about psychological citizenship circulated in numerous contexts. Much has been written about the ways in which fiction—film, novels, even poetry—provided narrative structures for articulating the interior lives of democratic citizens and the void within the totalitarian anti-citizen. Here I focus on nonfiction, examining three distinct genres in which Americans encountered ideas about the psychology of Communists.[3] "Scientific" analyses of Communist psyches as well as theoretical meditations on the state of modern society provided meta-analyses of the role of psychology in structuring and suturing the political crisis of the early Cold War world. Memoirs penned by former Communists brought those broader analyses to life. Together, these works firmly linked national security to individual security.

"Really Alone Now"

Confessional Citizenship and the Ex-Communist Memoir

In the late 1940s, a new literary genre arrived on American best-seller lists: the ex-Communist memoir. Mostly penned by individuals who had come to public attention through their willingness to "name names" before congressional committees and courts, these narratives served most immediately as self-justifications, explaining both how their subjects had become entrapped by Communism and why they found themselves compelled to inform against others. The memoirs varied a great deal in their intellectual ambition and complexity. *The God That Failed,* a collection of essays by American and European ex-Communists and fellow travelers, offered a sympathetic and relatively subtle analysis of the attractions of Marxism and Communism for the "Western intellectual." Whittaker Chambers's elegiac *Witness* was similarly cerebral, surprisingly so, perhaps, in its assertion of the superiority of faith over reason. *This Deception,* penned by Hede Massing, who corroborated Chambers's accusations against Alger Hiss, focused more on emotional than intellectual motives, but it was well written and somewhat self-aware. By contrast, Louis Budenz's *This Is My Story* and Elizabeth Bentley's *Out of Bondage* had little literary value, although this did not diminish their popularity. Purporting to offer ordinary Americans an intimate glimpse of the hidden world of Soviet espionage (like the related genre of FBI informant memoirs such as Herbert Philbrick's *I Led Three Lives* and Matt Cvetic's *I Was a Communist for the FBI*), many of these books had a wide readership. Several were serialized, and a few were translated onto American screens, small and large.[4] While critical reception of the memoirs varied widely—mostly depending on the reviewer's political alignment—there was widespread agreement that the genre offered Americans "one of our primary sources of information about Communism."[5]

Ex-Communist memoirs were infused with the logic and the rhetoric of psychological citizenship. As a genre, they offered compelling stories about the dangers of Communism and provided case studies of the ideal Cold War citizen. The memoir's emphasis on the individual and the internal and its detailing of psychological dramas and journeys resonated with broader understandings of the postwar political crisis as emotional. As "reconversion narratives,"[6] or perhaps more appropriately reinclusion narratives, they explained both the flaws of American democracy—why had ex-Communists been drawn to Communism in the first place?—and its redeeming qualities, the reasons for the narrators' return. These books revealed their authors' unfitness for Communism as a prelude to demonstrating their fitness as American citizens. That citizen was made concrete through his or her contrast with the true Communist, and more specifically the Stalinist or "Russian." The confessions offered within the memoirs represented the final breaking away, the last act of disobedience to the CP. The very act of writing the memoir, then, became a demonstration that the author had freed himself or herself from Communist discipline and, through this act of self-mastery, become American again. The text was a plea to be readmitted to the original political community, the one that had been abandoned in a moment of youthful but tragic idealism. In this sense, the ex-Communist memoir was a talking cure; its publication accomplished the reunification of self and nation.

Because these texts were primarily meant as self-justifications, their authors had to maneuver a tortuous path: in order to reveal the ultimate evil of Communism, they had first to exhibit its attractiveness. Communism, in these renderings, appealed in three basic ways: it recognized continuing inequality and injustice, representing a path to a better world; it embodied Christian virtues of compassion and "brotherhood," offering an alternative faith for a modern age; and it provided kinship and love to those whose families had failed them. Each of these appeals, the texts taught, were illusions, but they nonetheless represented laudable impulses which, it would turn out, could be fulfilled only by American democracy and freedom.

Communism's promise of a better and more humane world was portrayed in distinct ways by these authors. Almost all emphasized that during the 1930s, the CP appeared to be at the forefront of the struggle against fascism. In his introduction to *The God That Failed,* for example, the British socialist Richard Crossman wrote that the "only link" between the six American and European authors who contributed to the volume was their willingness to "sacrifice 'bourgeois liberties' in order to defeat Fascism" in their despair over the failings of Western culture. For many of the essayists, their commitment to antifascism was strong enough to overcome any unease they might have felt about conditions in the Soviet Union or the CP's nondemocratic character, at least until the betrayal posed by the Nazi-Soviet Pact in 1939. More generally, memoirists stressed that Communism seemed to offer a path toward "a decent world where a man could work and live like a human being." The African American author Richard Wright saw in Communism "the possibility of uniting scattered but kindred peoples into a whole"; he was especially drawn to its vision of racial equality. Elizabeth Bentley, who captured nationwide attention in 1945 when she told the FBI that she had headed a Communist spy ring, explained that working with Communists in the League against War and Fascism in the 1930s had convinced her that they were "far better people than the average citizen; where others were out for themselves, they thought about the welfare of their neighbor." Although she'd hesitated to join the CP, wary of the sacrifices it entailed, when she finally made the commitment, Bentley felt she had come home: "At last I was where I had always belonged—with the people who were fighting for a decent society . . . a world in which there will be no suffering, no poverty, no pain!" By emphasizing that they were drawn to Communism by its seeming promise of justice and equality, ex-Communist authors invested themselves with precisely the sorts of characteristics that, it would be revealed, American citizens possessed—and Communists lacked.[7]

For Whittaker Chambers, whose monumental *Witness* was serialized in the *Saturday Evening Post,* Communism initially appeared the best choice a deeply committed humanist could make. Chambers had been a writer and an editor for Communist publications and, later, *Time* magazine, and was infamous as the man who accused Alger Hiss of being a Soviet spy. Like Richard Crossman, he believed that those who joined the CP were driven by their "despair" over the "crisis of history" that produced the poverty and warfare of the modern world. Unlike liberals, socialists, or other "men of good will," party members responded positively to Communism's question, "Have you the moral strength to take upon yourself the crimes of history so that man at last may close his chronicle of age-old, senseless suffering, and replace it with purpose and a plan?" When he decided to become a Communist in 1925, he recalled, he "made a choice against death and for life." It offered him "what nothing else in the dying world had power to offer at the same intensity—faith and a vision, something for which to live and something for which to die." Since Chambers begins his narrative with his break with Communism and describes its attractions only later, the reader knows that this is a fatal vision; still, his recollection of its seeming nobility loses none of its power.[8]

The overriding purpose of Chambers's book was to unmask Communism as a false faith, one that substituted "man" for God. Communism, he argued, appealed in its insistence that the world could be changed: it was "the vision of man's mind displacing God as the creative intelligence of the world. . . . Communism restores man to his sovereignty by the simple method of denying God." In this it shared much with modern capitalism, which was likewise founded on the bedrock of materialism; the "crisis of history" of which he wrote was a common crisis, and *Witness* functioned as a jeremiad portending the collapse of Western civilization absent a spiritual reawakening.[9]

Other ex-Communist memoirs may have lacked the religious fervor of Chambers's work, but they too explained Communism's attraction in spiritual terms. Richard Crossman described those who became Communists as "converts," emphasizing the similarities between the "Christian conscience" and the party's culture of personal sacrifice and commitment to equality. (Less positively, he suggested that Communism was akin to Catholicism in its requirement of the "surrender of spiritual freedom.") Similarly, Elizabeth Bentley saw Communism as "the Christianity of the future," congruent with the religious values with which she had been raised, and committed to "the brotherhood of man." The Hungarian-born British author Arthur Koestler, another contributor to *The God That Failed,* joined the party because he needed "a faith." Yet, tellingly, this was a faith without God, or one, as the title of the anthology so neatly conveys, that put itself in place of God.[10]

For many of these memoirists, their awakening to Communism's failings was accompanied by the return of God's presence to their lives, a return that enabled their break with the party. Elizabeth Bentley vacillated for weeks about whether to betray her former comrades to the FBI; as she yearned for "someone bigger than I am, someone to give me the strength to do what I have to do!" she serendipitously walked past a church, entered, and "tr[ied] to pray." Hede Massing, an Austrian actress who was a courier and recruiter for the Communist underground as she moved between Europe and the United States, also gradually acknowledged God's role in her life as she became disenchanted with the CP. Former *Daily Worker* editor Louis Budenz penned his memoir, *This Is My Story,* as a paean to the glories of Catholicism and its role in leading him from the false faith of Communism back to, as he put it, the "faith of my fathers."[11]

To Communism's apparent promise as a means to a more just and equal world and as a modern analog for religious faith, some authors added its appeal as a substitute for failing families. Hede Massing grew up a lonely child in a loveless family. Her mother, sunk in her own unhappiness, ignored her. Her father had a succession of mistresses, and Hede was "deeply ashamed" of him. As a young actress in Vienna, she was courted by a series of suitors who reassured her, she wrote, "that although my family did not love me, there were others who did." One of these was Gerhart Eisler, a party functionary who drew her into Communist circles. Massing commented that she was attracted to Eisler not simply because he loved her but because, as she put it, "he wanted to take me away from the misery and unhappiness of my own family and bring me to his sweet and gentle mother . . . and his shy and professorial father. They were to give me the feeling of a family that I had missed so deeply." She identified this impulse as "*the* important gesture of a Communist." The contours of Massing's CP affiliation were shaped by her relationships with a string of men, including her third husband, Paul Massing, whom she followed to the Soviet Union even though, she claimed, she had by then become disenchanted with Communism. It was not until after their return that she realized "how deeply, tragically" she had "missed parental love, the security of a normal family life, and how there was no substitute for it—ever."[12]

Bentley and Chambers similarly highlighted their alienation from family in explaining their desire for Communism. Bentley opened her account by emphasizing how adrift she was, describing her 1934 voyage back to the United States from a course of study in Italy. "I leaned on the deck rail," she remembered, thinking "what, really, was I coming back to? I had no home, no family. . . . Standing there on the deck, I felt alone and frightened." Chambers's parents, like Massing's, were trapped in a marriage so unhappy that it became distorted into something unrecognizable: "We were not a family. Our home was not a home. My father was not a father. My mother was not a mother. He was nothing. She was trying to be both father and mother." Chambers's escape from this family-which-was-not-one took him to Communism. But ultimately, he realized, this family "malady" was merely an expression of the soullessness that characterized the modern world. It was only when he turned away from Communism—a process that accelerated when he and his wife decided to have a child—that he could begin to create a real family. Indeed, Chambers's narrative was organized around the fundamental incompatibility of authentic family ties and the ideological "tie that binds" Communists worldwide, and

FIGURE 1. In *Witness,* Whittaker Chambers credited his wife's determination to have a child with enabling him to reject the false family of the Communist Party. Here, Esther and Whittaker Chambers relax after she testified at the Alger Hiss trial in 1949. (Bettman/CORBIS)

it was family, as much as faith in God, that fueled his abandonment of the party (fig. 1). The very structure of the book drives this home: Chambers opens *Witness* with a foreword addressed to his children, and he closes it with his hopes that his son, too, will bear witness for freedom.[13]

Some memoirists portrayed their attraction to Communism as an erotic one, using the language of romantic love and sexual desire either to justify or to condemn. Elizabeth Bentley's *Out of Bondage* purported to reveal "what a monstrous thing Communism is," but the book is most memorable for its passionate rendering of Bentley's intimate relationship with Jacob Golos, a founding member of the CPUSA, a Soviet spy, and her "handler" in the underground. In Bentley's account, Golos represented the "ideal Communist," a loyal, principled, generous, and compassionate "true revolutionary." His character was so untarnished that, when he realized how corrupt the Stalinist party had become, he could only die of a broken heart. It was her love for Golos—a love that blossomed *despite* the party (for as he reminded her, members of the Communist underground were "forbidden to . . . fall in love. You and I have no right, under Communist discipline, to feel the way we do about each other")—that explained her decision to remain a member of the underground even after his death, as she took up his efforts to protect her friends and comrades in the party from the brutal Stalinists who threatened them.[14]

If Bentley presented her life as a Communist spy as an uplifting heterosexual romance, Arthur Koestler portrayed his own party membership as a case of seduction or romantic enthrallment. He likened his encounter with the CP to falling in love with a woman, or "enter[ing] the womb of a church," an emotional rather than a rational event. Yet as he told it, this love was at first unrequited: "I was running after the Party, thirsting to throw myself completely into her arms, and the more breathlessly I struggled to possess and be possessed by her, the more elusive and unattainable she became." Apparently, however, the "stony" stance of the CP was merely a ploy to get him to participate in espionage. By the end of his dalliance with Communism, he offered a different story of seduction: "I served the Communist Party for seven years—the same length of time as Jacob tended Laban's sheep to win Rachel his daughter. When the time was up, the bride was led into his dark tent; only the next morning did he discover that his ardors had been spent not on the lovely Rachel but on the ugly Leah. I wonder whether he ever recovered from the shock of having slept with an illusion. I wonder whether afterwards he believed that he had ever believed in it." Koestler's bitterness is palpable, but it is somewhat softened by his parting thought: "I wonder whether the happy end of the legend will be repeated; for at the price of another seven years of labor, Jacob was given Rachel too, and the illusion became flesh."[15] Like Bentley, Koestler felt compelled to defend the principles that had drawn him to Communism, even if they were horribly distorted in practice.

These characterizations of the Communist Party as taking the place of family or lover were all specific articulations of a more general theme: Communism's attraction as a cure for or response to the unbearable loneliness of modern life. Ex–party members claimed to have found a kinship that reached beyond national borders, a realization of the idea of brotherhood that offered, in the words of Elizabeth Bentley, "peace, security, and a sense of doing something constructive." Richard Wright explored evocatively the visceral sense of community that brought people into the CP and kept them there. Reflecting on the party "trial" of one acquaintance, who confessed his guilt to the charges against him, Wright observed: "No one prodded him. No one tortured him. No one threatened him. He was free to go out of the hall and never see another Communist. But he did not want to. He could not. The vision of a communal world had sunk down into his soul and it would never leave him until life left him." Wright wrote movingly of how this "state of kinship" among Communists gave rise to "spectacle[s] of glory [and] of horror," including the Moscow show trials. In his contribution to *The God That Failed*, he emphasized his own loneliness as an African American intellectual, which propelled him into the CP but could not be overcome within it. The essay ended with an account of his ejection from a May Day parade, "really alone now," and with scant hope of finding comrades who could help him explore how to "live a human life." Hede Massing and Whittaker Chambers, too, wrote of the "annihilating loneliness" of the ex-Communist, especially when leaving meant betraying former friends.[16]

Abandoning the party was traumatic, but it was necessitated for the memoirists by their ultimate recognition of Communism's wickedness. Authors devoted a good deal of time to describing their discovery of Stalinist atrocities: the accommodation with fascism in the Nazi-Soviet Pact, the purges of the 1930s, the disappearance and presumed murder of recalcitrant comrades. But they also inscribed the evils of Communism within the Communist self. The mind and the character of the individual Communist were so twisted and corrupted—whether by personal inclination or, more often, by unremitting "discipline"—that he or she functioned as almost a distinct species, not human but machine, robot, automaton. These descriptions of how Communism rendered Americans unfit to be citizens also served to demonstrate that the author, in fact, never *belonged in* the CP, no matter the fact of membership (fig. 2).

Intellectually, Communists presented something of a puzzle, for they were depicted as both not rational enough and too rational. Sometimes authors tried to capture the "madness" or the "lunacy" of party members; a more common theme was that Communists were merely unthinking. They refused knowledge and gave up their "own powers of reason" in favor of party decisions. As Hede Massing wrote, Communists had "a gift for doing away with reality; of not wanting, or not needing to know, the facts, the truth." At the same time, though, CP members were characterized as thinking too much, privileging mind over both experience and emotion. Communism was ideological and therefore destructive. Whittaker Chambers's denunciation of Communism for elevating "reason and knowledge" over religion and the mystery of God was echoed in indictments of Communists for being too abstract. Massing criticized what

FIGURE 2. Through memoirs, ex-Communists showcased their escape from the party to reclaim not only their citizenship but their humanity as well. This 1948 photo was captioned "Elizabeth Bentley is happy to be herself once again." (Photographer, C. M. Steiglitz. Photo courtesy of the Library of Congress.)

she called the typical Communist attitude that "it is not the human being who counts, but the idea!" while Elizabeth Bentley described the "impersonal and detached mind that refused to be bogged down in petty problems and personal emotions." Writing in *The God That Failed* about Western intellectuals who joined the party, the British poet Stephen Spender argued that Communists took to new heights the "human . . . tendency to think abstractly," committing themselves to a "huge abstract calculation" that "cancelled out all experiential objections." Arthur Koestler agreed, declaring that it wasn't until he had "ceased to be a Communist" that he realized that "man is a reality, mankind an abstraction. . . . Men cannot be treated as units in operations of political arithmetic." This comfort with abstraction resulted in a multitude of sins, as the sacrifice of "man" for "mankind" validated "Communist morality," an ends-justifies-the-means ethics in which lying, cheating, spying, and even murder seemed right if they strengthened the CP or the Soviet state.[17]

Just as Communists were both too rational and not rational enough, they were both too willful and completely lacking in will. This is the paradox that was captured by that ubiquitous phrase "Communist discipline." Communist discipline signified the immense danger posed by the Communist Party, which was filled with individuals who had the will to change the world, who were strengthened by the belief that, as Whittaker Chambers put it, "there is almost nothing that is impossible," and who were committed to carrying out the dictates of party bosses. The decision to "submit" oneself to Communist discipline was a "Communist's pride," Chambers informed his readers, and because that discipline was "self-imposed," it was all the more effective. As Elizabeth Bentley allegedly was told at her first CP meeting, "That's the strength of the Party; it's composed of men and women who care enough about their principles to subordinate everything else to them." Yet as this statement foreshadowed, the keynote of Communist discipline was the surrender of will, of individual responsibility and freedom, of intellect, ethics, and compassion. Communists learned to substitute the CP's judgment for their own, to question nothing, to act without understanding. Richard Wright was incredulous that "when a man was informed of the wish of the Party he submitted, even though he knew with all the strength of his brain that the wish was not a wise one, was one that would ultimately harm the Party's interests." Like Wright, Hede Massing chafed at the demands of Communist discipline; when she discovered herself carrying out party orders even though, she claimed, she was "ashamed and uneasy about it," she began the long process of breaking away. Although Bentley admired the pragmatism and effectiveness of Communist discipline when she joined the CP, ultimately she realized that her decision "to trust the Party rather than [her] own judgment [was] the first step toward becoming a Communist in deed as well as in name. One of the first phases in transforming a young idealist into a hardened revolutionary is to imbue him with a terrific sense of his own inadequacy, to make him so humble that he refuses to use his own powers of reason and relies confidently on the decisions of the Party." Communist discipline, Richard Crossman wrote, "molded [individuals] into the life of the Party," and as a result, even the ex-Communist could "never again be a whole personality."[18]

Those who had accepted party discipline became "steeled Communists," and this oft-repeated metaphor suggests much about how Communism was understood. The steeled Communist, as Bentley suggested, was "hardened," ready to carry out any orders without question no matter how difficult or repugnant. Even more, he or she was an "automaton," a "robot," a "machin[e] for altering society." Made of steel and iron, not blood and bone, the Communist was "tempered" and "hammered" into an instrument of revolution; freedom, individuality, all that constituted humanity was surrendered in the process.[19]

One of the ways in which this sacrifice was made concrete in many of these memoirs was through the loss of a personal life. Communists gave over their most private selves to party discipline, including their decisions about love and marriage, childbearing and child rearing. We have already seen that Elizabeth Bentley and Jacob Golos kept their relationship secret, and indeed in Bentley's narrative the private and passionate nature of their love signified that neither she nor her beloved "Yasha" truly belonged in the party. The episode that brought about Golos's death revealed how twisted Communism was, and how it perverted private life. He had been ordered by his Russian bosses to "hand over" Mary Price, a young woman in the underground, for a "special job": to "set her up in an apartment, buy her fancy clothes, and let her use her wiles on men who would be useful to the cause." Golos's refusal resulted in an ultimatum. If he did not give up Mary Price, he would be branded a traitor and ejected from the underground. In the three days he was given to decide his course of action, Golos suffered a heart attack. As Bentley narrated it, Golos was a true revolutionary, a passionate soul detached from the terrible machine that was the Communist Party; he was so repulsed by what Communism had become that the only solution to his dilemma was death.[20]

The CP is seen to endanger American marriages, children, and families in a multitude of ways. Whittaker Chambers presumed that his wife would abort her first pregnancy, since, "as an underground Communist," he "took it for granted that children were out of the question." But she refused, and this decision to create a family, despite "the Communist Party and its theories," set him on a path toward a new faith. In his anti-Communist diatribe *Men without Faces,* Louis Budenz presented a whole series of cases describing how the CP dictated the personal lives of its female members. One woman couldn't decide whether to stay with her second husband, David, or return to her first. Her first husband had treated her better, but David was a better Communist, who "frowned upon the domestic arts. . . . David considered her petty party duties of such importance as to preclude any kind of family life in which she might play the part of housewife and mother." At the direction of party leaders, this woman stuck with David, despite her own knowledge that her life would be "more comfortable" if she left him. She forswore motherhood in order to do CP work until the party line changed in the 1940s: "Since the comrades were supposed to look and act like other Americans, they were to have families as other people did, too." Another female comrade had a different problem: her husband wanted her to "devote herself to her home and two children," but party leaders had other plans for her. "The next time he went to a meeting, she went too, leaving her children alone in the house. By such tactics she compelled her husband to yield to the desire of their branch that she do extensive party work." Soon she was taking her children along as she spoke on street corners, canvassed for the cause, and attended demonstrations. For Budenz, this was a clear case of parental neglect, an example of the "fanaticism" of "little people in the party [who] accept the discipline of the party [and] do what they are told, think what they are told." In the midst of the postwar baby boom and the cultural valorization of all things domestic, the willingness of even "humble" Communists to subjugate their family life to CP interests was the most visceral example of how Communist discipline dehumanized its adherents.[21]

Communist discipline also explained party members' willingness to spy for the Soviet Union or otherwise betray the United States. Memoirists frequently narrated the moment when they realized that their party membership—which they had originally conceptualized as an act of patriotism that would bring America to the realization of its founding ideals—in fact bound them to another nation. For Bentley, the dawning recognition that she had been made a pawn of Moscow (as well as her conviction that the Soviets were planning to kill her) persuaded her to confess her espionage to the FBI. Chambers suggested that Communists' allegiance was not "to any country [but] to a revolutionary faith and a vision of man and his material destiny which was given political force by international Communism" as it was represented in the Comintern and the Soviet Union. As a result, the question of loyalty or of treason was irrelevant to the American Communist: "Espionage . . . will not appear to him in terms of betrayal at all. It will, on the contrary, appear to him as a moral act." Other anti-Communist writers concurred. Budenz denounced CP members' "willingness to serve as tools for the destruction of their nation." When Communists spoke of "patriotism," he claimed, they meant "loyalty to Soviet Russia"; and when they spoke of "internationalism" they meant "loyalty to Soviet Russia" as well. J. Edgar Hoover went even farther in his 1958 best-seller *Masters of Deceit,* proclaiming, "Communists are not American."[22]

Communist discipline figured so prominently in these memoirs and other condemnations of the CP in part because it joined the personal and the political so neatly. Twinning the meta-rhetoric of slavery and freedom that purported to distinguish the totalitarian Soviet Union from the democratic United States, the notion of discipline marked CP members as enslaved by their subjugation to an ideology that celebrated their unfreedom, placing them outside the bounds of American citizenship. Significantly, this was an enslavement that was less *imposed* than *desired.* The belief that Communism was, in the end, an expression of mental or social pathology rather than political dissent was shared by many political commentators, including those who reviewed these books. Over and over again, they evaluated the memoirs on their "contribution toward solving the riddle of what constitutes the Communist mentality." Occasionally memoirists were criticized for too simply blaming their political deviance on dysfunctional families or personal tragedy, and female authors in particular came in for ridicule for being overly emotional and not sufficiently analytical; but more often commentators saw psychology, and especially early family life, as the key to the "riddle."[23]

In their memoirs, ex-Communists emphasized their ability to break from Communist discipline, but they also lamented the isolation incurred by such a move. They claimed that they were vilified and reviled for their past crimes, and so, paradoxically, leaving the party meant sacrificing belonging for loneliness, even as it represented an effort to regain one's place within the national community. It was the willingness to embrace that loneliness that, finally, marked the distinction between the democratic citizen and the Communist automaton. The emotional, spiritual, and political journeys that enabled the memoirists to return to the selves they had earlier abandoned stood in stark contrast to the Communist's psychological captivity, a theme that would be elaborated by other writers.

"Damaged Souls"
Loneliness, Neurosis, and Political Affiliation

The emphasis on loneliness as a political problem that suffused the ex-Communist memoirs also characterized more explicitly psychological studies of Communist affiliation published during these years. Two surveys—one written for a popular audience, another for academics and policy makers—presented primers on psychological citizenship, diagnosing the neuroses that attracted individuals to the CP. Co-authors Morris Ernst and David Loth surveyed nearly three hundred former Communists to discover why Americans joined the party and why they left. Despite their assertion that "there are no characteristics which mark [Communists] as totally different from other Americans," they offered a portrait of American Communists as psychologically wounded, "damaged souls" who might have the same high ideals of justice and equality as their fellow citizens but whose insecurities and emotional weaknesses propelled them into the party. The Princeton political scientist Gabriel Almond surveyed several hundred former Communists in France, the United Kingdom, and Italy as well as the United States. His research team concluded that while the CP in France and Italy was largely populated by working-class individuals who were motivated by real economic and political dislocations, British and American Communists were more likely to be middle-class neurotics. Although, like Ernst and Loth, Almond conceded that no "particular type of emotional maladjustment" could explain why a person became a Communist, his analysis of thirty-five psychoanalytic case studies and sixty-four questionnaires from American Communists and ex-Communists emphasized psychological dysfunction. Both sets of researchers contended that recruits to the CP were most commonly lonely individuals who lacked a sense of "belonging" or were "poorly related to others," often as a result of deficiencies in their sex-role adjustment. For such women and men, the "all-consuming" nature of the CP satisfied the emotional need for the connections that had been absent in the broader society.[24]

Just as in the ex-Communist memoirs, this sense of isolation most frequently originated in early childhood experiences. An unhappy childhood was not sufficient to make a Communist, but the abundance of stories of former Communists who had grown up in broken families, or with overly strict parents, and especially with dominant mothers and submissive fathers, communicated that Communists were more than partly "home made."[25] The parents of "Maureen," for example, had quarreled incessantly until, when she was still a young girl, her mother died. The party offered her the security that she had not found in her family of origin. "I never had a real family and, though you didn't have to like the CP family, at least you were all together against the world," she told her interlocutors. "Walter" had a manipulative, hysterical mother and a weak father. Even though he had many friends, his "dreadful need of being loved and approved by people" sent him to the party. "Alvin," too, became a Communist "out of loneliness." The son of Jewish immigrants, he represented a common pattern among the families of second-generation Americans who turned to Communism: a father who was unable to succeed in an unfamiliar economy, and a mother who emasculated her husband with incessant criticism. A boy raised in such a family would grow up to become a man who "had contempt for his father, and who distrusted his mother, who felt cheated by his family, and cheated by his society because of his foreign origin." In other words, he would become a man, completely isolated and consumed by loneliness, who would find succor in the CP. Overall, while both sets of researchers dismissed as too simplistic an oedipal theory of Communism that would draw a direct line from bad parenting to political extremism, they provided a wealth of stories that seemed to support such a theory.[26]

As the example of "Maureen" suggested, the party offered a substitute family for its adherents, but, in keeping with the conception of Communism as neurosis, this was a family that frustrated one's emotional needs at the same time that it met them. In the CP, members found surrogate parents who satisfied their infantile longing for authority and comfort, a "Papa Stalin" and a "mother Russia." They could remain children, reliving their childhood in a way that provided the security that had originally eluded them. Yet such relationships made authentic human connection impossible, because all personal ties were to be subordinated to the needs of the revolution. As one former party member put it: "Communism cannot thrive if personal attachments are really strong. There must be only one personal attachment and that is to the movement." This insistence on impersonality, particularly the breaking down of "family loyalty," molded the Communist into an individual who would "betray his family, his friends, his mate, and his country, if necessary."[27] Thus the decision to join the CP both resulted from emotional insecurity and intensified it into an absolute inability to fulfill the responsibilities of citizenship.

This analysis reduced Communists' political and economic critique to a matter of family dysfunction and their party membership to a crutch that relieved their emotional distress. Almond and his collaborators believed that the CP offered an outlet for the "chronic and unconscious hostility resulting from family and childhood experiences" felt by the 75 percent of American adherents they estimated to be neurotic. Party membership allowed Communists to displace the hostility they felt toward parents, siblings, and other inappropriate objects onto "impersonal" targets such as "capitalism, the ruling class and the like." The CP "dignified" and rewarded this hostility, providing its members with "the right to hate without guilt." Since many individuals isolated themselves in an effort to repress their hostility, finding the party provided welcome relief. But this sense of relief was false: "The party is not only a community, it is a hostile community, and it is a community for outcasts. In most of the cases of neurotic withdrawal, the party was the first real group which was joined. The party can offer such an individual the *illusion* of being related. . . . It helps him keep his hostile feelings in repression, by being hostile for him." Others internalized their hostility, rejecting their own class, ethnic, or gender identity for the inauthentic identity that Communism offered them. This was the case for middle-class intellectuals who escaped their bourgeois upbringing by claiming kinship with the proletariat. It also explained the "sex-role confusion" that could be found so often among party members.[28]

These studies' conclusions that the CP provided a refuge for gender deviants blended the conservatism that infused postwar American psychoanalysis with older interpretations of Communism as subversive of gender and sexual norms. Becoming a Communist supposedly offered relief for individual sex-role failings for both women and men, as Almond illustrated through the reports of psychoanalysts who had treated Communists and ex-Communists. "Frances," for example, grew up with the classic pattern of weak father and dominating mother. She translated her hatred of her mother into hatred of her own womanhood. Frances joined the CP, according to her analyst, because "the Communist doctrine of sexual equality helped her reject her femininity. Being a party member also meant that she could wear blue jeans, do common labor, in fact, do everything that was prohibited to middle-class girls. . . . It made it possible for her to think of herself as a strong male. . . . She sought to destroy herself—her social class and her sex—and bring the whole world down in the process." Another subject, "Arthur," grew up in the same sort of environment and became a Communist because the men in his family "were humiliated and dominated by women. He hated his mother for her domination and his father for permitting it. He felt helpless." Joining the party helped Arthur feel more masculine, giving him a sense of strength and providing him with new father figures—Lenin, Stalin, national party leaders—to whom he could be loyal.[29] Such psychoanalytic interpretations handily explained away Communist dissent as the result of either the individual inability to inhabit appropriate gender norms or the overriding desire to do so at any cost.

Indeed, for Herbert Krugman, who was primarily responsible for the Almond study's analysis of "neurotic need," one's history as a Communist came down to one's orientation toward maleness or femaleness. He posited that individuals joined the party to satisfy one of two needs: either to be ruthless and hostile, or to be submissive. The first of these he characterized as "a choice favoring maleness." The men in this category were trying to "remain men," while the women sought to "become men or something better." Whether male or female, such individuals were able to experience within the CP the masculine power that was otherwise inaccessible or tenuous for them. Those drawn to femaleness and submissiveness included men who were not "very successful in trying to be men" and women who identified as helpless victims and martyrs. These people subordinated their will to that of the party, as did all good Communists, and hence could be passive without guilt. All of these individuals, Krugman asserted, expressed in their political affiliation their inability to resolve what he called the "hostility syndrome," an active or passive orientation toward hostility that arose from their problematic sexual self-image. The vast majority of American members who were attracted to the CP out of neurotic need, then, were most often compensating for "some degree of homosexuality."[30]

Few other scholars asserted such a direct and causative link between Communism and homosexuality, but Krugman's analysis resonated with broader structures of thought about sexuality, gender, and politics. Most mid-century commentators understood homosexuality and Communism to flow from like sources—moral corruption, psychological immaturity, sex-role confusion—and to pose similar dangers to the nation. Both homosexuals and Communists were able to pass undetected among ordinary Americans. Homosexuals were too morally weak to remain loyal to the nation, and Communists had transferred their loyalty elsewhere; hence both groups constituted a risk to national security. In the early Cold War years, the similarities between these two forms of deviance had been suggested to the public in a number of settings, including tabloid publications, congressional investigations, media coverage of Alger Hiss's perjury trials, and the wholesale firing of homosexual government employees that historians have labeled the "lavender scare."[31] Krugman's more fully developed schema articulated the rich possibilities of psychoanalytic categories for linking gender norms, sexual neurosis, and political dissent in ways that nullified a variety of challenges to Cold War orthodoxies.

Although the foregrounding of gender and sexuality by Krugman, Almond, and Ernst and Loth reflected the presumptions of postwar psychoanalytic discourse, these concepts mapped more generally onto a broader concern with isolation and relationship in the modern world. Communists' gender and sexual perversions supposedly arose from their inability to attach to their families, just as their desire for the fictive kinship of party affiliation represented their (ultimately flawed) efforts to belong to a wider world that offered some meaning. Thus their emotional needs led them to link their fate to the international Communist conspiracy. Ernst and Loth concluded that if the most fanatical of them came "to the point of betraying their country, firm in the conviction that they [were] doing it to save the world," it was because, "by some psychological gymnastics, [the spy] convinces himself that the welfare of mankind is linked to the success of another country."[32] In other words, their loneliness, and their misguided efforts to deny it, unmoored them not just from their families but from their nation. This concern with loneliness also marked the work of those who sought to understand the broader political crisis of the twentieth century.

"Organized Loneliness"
The Psychology of Political Systems

The rise of fascism and the carnage of war yielded a substantial literature that sought to make sense of modern politics and society, and much of this work took a psychosocial approach. During the 1930s, for example, the critical theorists of the Frankfurt School began their interrogations into the relationship between family structure and authoritarianism. Their initial forays in this direction drew little attention in the United States, but *The Authoritarian Personality* (1950), by Theodor Adorno and colleagues, proved widely influential. It drew direct lines between economic transformation, marital roles and parenting practices, and psychological development to explain the emergence of "authoritarian" personalities that might leave a society vulnerable to fascist ideologies. Other scholars less firmly connected to the Frankfurt School also linked personality with politics. Two of the most important were German émigrés, the psychoanalyst Erich Fromm (originally affiliated with the Frankfurt School but, by the 1940s, marginal to it) and the philosopher Hannah Arendt. Fromm and Arendt shared the critical theorists' concerns with the conformity and unfreedom of mass society, but both spoke more directly to the sense that loneliness produced political crisis. Although they did not agree on much else, each identified loneliness as the fundamental problem in democratic as well as authoritarian (for Fromm) and totalitarian (for Arendt) societies. While both authors were widely read and influential, their ideas on loneliness were combined and popularized by Arthur Schlesinger Jr. in *The*

Vital Center. All three shaped understandings of the challenges to, and the promise of, American democracy.[33]

Fromm and Arendt approached the relationship between loneliness and politics in very different ways. Fromm emphasized biology and its social implications. In *Escape from Freedom* (1941) he traced the fundamental problems confronting "modern man" to the "very essence of the human mode and practice of life: the need to be related to the world outside oneself, the need to avoid aloneness." Originating in the human infant's dependence on his or her mother for care, the yearning for relatedness was nurtured by the requirements of living in society, essential to the very self-consciousness of a humanity that comprehended individual difference, and exacerbated in the modern world as industrialism and capitalism unmoored men and women from the "security" of "traditional status." All humans had no choice but to establish ties with the world beyond themselves, but modern political economy and social structure made it difficult to do so in a self-affirming way through "the spontaneity of love and productive work," what Fromm called positive freedom. As a result, individuals mostly found destructive ways to escape the fearful state of individuation.[34]

In fascist nations, Fromm argued, human loneliness fueled a propensity toward authoritarianism. The authoritarian character represented an effort to "fuse one's self with somebody or something outside of oneself in order to acquire the strength which the individual self is lacking." This desire for fusion gave authoritarianism its sadomasochistic quality.[35] Authoritarian individuals experienced masochistic and sadistic "strivings" that were rooted in their sense of their own insignificance and powerlessness. These strivings seemed to express contrary orientations, but in fact each had the same "symbiotic" aim: "the union of one individual self with another self (or any other power outside of the own self) in such a way as to make each lose the integrity of its own self and to make them completely dependent on each other. The sadistic person needs his object just as much as the masochistic needs his. Only instead of seeking security by being swallowed, he gains it by swallowing somebody else." Authority was not a thing to be possessed but a relationship, and its relational qualities made authoritarianism a mechanism of escape from unbearable aloneness.[36]

Arendt too identified loneliness as the source of political crisis in her writings on totalitarianism, including most prominently *The Origins of Totalitarianism* (1951), although she denied the value of psychology as a frame of analysis. Her interest was less in tracing origins than in describing the processes by which totalitarianism exploited, materialized, and intensified human isolation. For

Arendt, totalitarianism (in both its Nazi and its Soviet incarnations) was an entirely new political phenomenon, responding to a political vacuum occasioned by the decline of civil society. The masses who provided the primary support for totalitarianism, she argued, "grew out of the fragments of a highly atomized society whose competitive structure and concomitant loneliness of the individual had been held in check only through membership in a class. The chief characteristic of the mass man is not brutality and backwardness, but his isolation and lack of normal social relationships." They may not have been seeking to shed their selves in order to feel at one with the world, as Fromm would have it, but nonetheless the masses were "selfless," convinced that they did not matter except in their allegiance to the totalitarian movement, which connected them to something larger than themselves.[37] Arendt agreed with Fromm that loneliness was inevitable, "at the same time contrary to the basic requirements of the human condition *and* one of the fundamental experiences of every human life." She insisted that "totalitarian domination" manipulated this "experience of not belonging to the world at all, which is among the most radical and desperate experiences of man."[38] While loneliness made individuals open to totalitarianism, totalitarianism also required their complete isolation from "social ties to family, friends, comrades, or even mere acquaintances" in order to secure their "total, unrestricted, unconditional, and unalterable loyalty" to the movement. Paradoxically, then, totalitarianism organized the mass of "atomized, isolated individuals" into a "heterogeneous uniformity" that heralded the death of individuality and, ultimately, the "total domination" of human beings.[39]

Arendt's analysis paralleled more prosaic texts about CP membership not only in its emphasis on isolation but also in its identification of ideology as the machine that drove totalitarian regimes. The distinction between totalitarianism and democracy, according to Arendt, was the distinction between logic and thought. In its ability to operate as "the last support in a world where nobody is reliable and nothing can be relied upon," and to offer an "unwavering faith in a . . . fictitious world" in which "everything is possible," ideology was both the outcome of and the cure for the "lonely isolation" of modern man. But the "self-compulsion of ideological thinking" destroyed the possibility of creative thought and "ruin[ed] all relationships with reality." Although totalitarianism was marked by its senselessness, mobilizing men and women solely to demonstrate its own total power, it also existed to enact its "supersense," its explanation of the ends of human existence, subordinating "man" to its vision of "mankind."

Like the ex-Communist writers, therefore, Arendt located outside the bounds of democratic citizenship any individual who elevated mankind over man or who believed that everything is possible.[40]

According to Arendt, the camp was the proving ground of ideology, a "laboratory" for the production of totalitarian man. The concentration and extermination camps of Nazi Germany and the Soviet Union perfected the radical loneliness of totalitarianism through the enactment of "total terror," which "substitutes for the boundaries and channels of communications between individual men a band of iron which holds them so tightly together that it is as though their plurality had disappeared into One Man of gigantic dimensions." Individuality and spontaneity were destroyed, and "nothing then remains but ghastly marionettes with human faces, which all behave like the dog in Pavlov's experiments, which all react with perfect reliability even when going to their own death, and which do nothing but react." In this way the camp manufactured "the model 'citizen[s]' of a totalitarian state." Thoroughly atomized, completely passive, totally dominated in every aspect of their private and public lives, these "citizens" were made interchangeable "bundles of reactions" that existed only to forward the totalitarian movement. Totalitarianism, then, was the ultimate solution to human loneliness: it erased the human and created a "mere thing" that in "organized loneliness" was no longer able to experience itself as alone. It operated by destroying "psyche" while preserving the "physical man," and ended by producing "inanimate men . . . who can no longer be psychologically understood."[41]

Fromm did not share Arendt's insistence on totalitarianism's radical difference. In *Escape from Freedom* he diagnosed loneliness as the ill plaguing democracies as well. Instead of fostering authoritarian character, however, as it did under fascism, in democratic nations the flight from the aloneness of self resulted in the spread of "automaton conformity." This was, he argued, the situation of "the majority of normal individuals," who sacrificed their selves for the illusion of identity with the rest of the world. Analogizing from hypnosis, Fromm maintained that in modern democracies the individual, without knowing it, became "a reflex of other people's expectation of him." Democratic citizens were ignorant of the internalized constraints (such as public opinion or advertising) that substituted "pseudo" feelings, thoughts, and acts for original ones and resulted in the eventual replacement of the original self by a pseudo self. Believing themselves to be free, they gave up their freedom for conformity, becoming "automatons who live under the illusion of being self-willing individuals." But just as sadomasochistic strivings could never adequately compensate for the powerlessness and aloneness of modern life in fascist nations, so the loss of identity produced by conformity created a panic that made democratic citizens "ready to submit to new authorities."[42]

Fromm's concern with the rise of conformity as a response to the loneliness of late-capitalist life was shared by a host of others, from social scientists to filmmakers to the Beats, who bemoaned what K. A. Cuordileone has designated the "surrender of self."[43] Most of these commentators focused on men, since the gender norms of the time took for granted women's lack of an autonomous self. The oft-articulated anxiety about masculine conformity points to the absence of true consensus in American Cold War culture. But in most of the texts considered here, concerns about the lack of independence and individuality among American men were displaced onto the "robots" of totalitarianism, both in the Soviet Union and in the United States, who were mere cogs in the machine of the international Communist conspiracy. In these renderings, it was the Communists who were the conformists, fleeing their loneliness by enslaving themselves to an idea, a party, another nation, and an international movement dedicated to nothing so much as an irrational belief in human perfection. The democrats were the true individuals, able to embrace their individuality and their freedom while also maintaining their connection to the world.

This was the message of *The Vital Center.* Here Arthur M. Schlesinger Jr. brought together Arendt's and Fromm's theories for a wider audience while also broadcasting the psychosexual framework that would become so popular in explaining the attractions of Communism.[44] Schlesinger's totalitarians, too, sought shelter from the "loneliness and rootlessness" of modern life. He combined Arendt's emphasis on the threat of ideology and the inhumanity of "totalitarian man" with Fromm's "remarkable analysis" of the sadomasochism that underlay the rise of totalitarianism. The totalitarian had "no heart, no sympathy, no reason, no conscience," but he (there are no women in Schlesinger's political world) also actively desired the discipline that the totalitarian movement offered, and this was a desire that endangered the nation. Melding Arendt's work on the concentration camp with Fromm's work on sadomasochism, Schlesinger identified totalitarianism with sadomasochism, a yearning for "dominance and surrender" that reached its apex in the camp. "Even America," he wrote, "has its quota of lonely and frustrated people, craving social, intellectual and even sexual fulfillment they cannot obtain in existing society. For these people, party discipline is no obstacle; it is an attraction." Communist discipline provided a sense of belonging and the "release from individual responsibility in the affirmation of comradeship in organized mass solidarity."[45] CP members fled their selves for the false security of the party.

The Vital Center contrasted totalitarian man—whether found in Nazi Germany, in the Soviet Union, or in the United States as the Communist or the fellow-traveling "doughface" progressive at whom Schlesinger directed so much scorn—to "democratic man," best represented by the "radical democrats" with whom Schlesinger identified himself. Echoing Arendt's assertion that the belief that "everything is possible" was the cornerstone of totalitarianism, Schlesinger argued for the importance of a "moderate pessimism" about human nature, noting that the "gusto of democracy" was "a searching doubt about human perfectability." What distinguished radical democrats from the progressives—those "democratic men with totalitarian principles" who were open to "Communist permeation and conquest"—was precisely this disagreement about the possibilities of human perfection, what Arendt had characterized as the sacrifice of "men" for the "fabrication of mankind."[46] But even though democracy's strength was its "startling insight into the value of the individual," Schlesinger insisted that democracy could survive only if it answered the emotional needs for connection to which totalitarianism was a response. "For all the magnificent triumphs of individualism," he declared, "we survive only as we remain members of one another." His solution to the crisis of democracy, therefore, was to create a vibrant civil society, for "it is the disappearance of effective group activity which leads toward emptiness in the individual." Democracy would survive only if it found its own solution to the loneliness of modern life, "restor[ing] the center" in "fruitful union" between individual and community.[47]

Just as these critics echoed the concern with loneliness that was found in ex-Communist memoirs and psychological studies, they also shared the anxiety about Communist discipline. The concept of discipline had been part of the Communist movement since Lenin's day, but during the Cold War years it became a code word for Communism's queerness, rendering CP affiliation as the most fundamental sort of perversion. Erich Fromm's theories about the relationship between authoritarian character and sadomasochism paved the way for the common assertion that party members yearned for discipline.[48] Schlesinger quoted from a play by the Soviet writer Vladimir Kirshon to substantiate this claim: " 'The Party is a thong,' cries a character in Kirshon's play *Bread.* '. . . It often cuts into my flesh, but I can't live without it.' " Ernst and Loth similarly contended that "the [party] membership likes not only to punish, but it likes to be punished." They framed this desire for punishment as spiritual, akin to medieval practices of flagellation, as well as erotic. J. Edgar Hoover dedicated an entire chapter of *Masters of Deceit* to the concept of Communist discipline, which "means *conscious* and *voluntary* submission to the will of the Party. To obey Party instructions is regarded as a high ethical duty, to be undertaken joyously and willingly as an honor and privilege, never as bondage. . . . This is the terrifying danger of Communist discipline—that in the name of freedom, by appealing to the most noble qualities in man, the human being is pushed into deepest tyranny." In seeking party discipline, Communists enacted a sort of voluntary slavery. Willingly entering into bondage, they demonstrated not simply their disloyalty but, more fundamentally, their inability to *be* citizens in a free society.[49]

In sum, for all of these writers—those who were analyzing political systems, those who were diagnosing individuals, and those who were confessing sinful pasts—psychology provided a ready framework for distinguishing healthy political beliefs and institutions from those that were abnormal, even pathological. Communists were marked by their dysfunctional responses to the alienation and loneliness of modern life. They may have turned to the CP as a substitute for authentic social relations, but the party perfected their loneliness, offering them a place in a world apart that simply confirmed what Arendt called their "worldlessness," their lack of belonging "to a world in which they matter as individuals."[50] Providing the illusion of brotherhood, it exacted too high a price: the ability to think and to experience creativity and freedom, humanity itself. As a result, those who fell prey to Communism abdicated those characteristics and values that grounded their Americanness.

As those who could not be citizens, Communists lost what Arendt had famously called "the right to have rights." Certainly, by their membership in a party alleged to be controlled by Moscow and dedicated to the overthrow of the United States, Communists gave up their entitlement to civil liberties. As Attorney General Tom Clark declared, "Those who deny freedom to others cannot long retain it for themselves." According to such reasoning, if Communists ever accomplished their aim of world revolution, they would abolish all rights, all freedoms, all laws. Therefore it was necessary that they be denied their own rights to freedom of speech and assembly to prevent such an outcome. But more was required. As willing "twentieth-century slaves,"[51] Communists lacked the independence of thought and strength of character—the democratic personality—that entitled individuals to govern themselves. Not only their ideological commitments but also their mental and emotional pathology required that they be denied not just their rights but their very status as citizens. Psychology, then, justified the explicit creation of the Cold War–era state of exception.

"Sick with a Strange Malady"
Psychology and the State of Exception

The definition of Communism as voluntary slavery helped to legitimate myriad measures to abridge the citizenship rights of CP members, including state-level efforts to outlaw the party or to deprive Communists of the right to run for political office, as well as federal initiatives such as the Taft-Hartley Act's ban on Communist labor officials. It informed U.S. Supreme Court rulings that laws limiting the speech of CP members were needed to defend the nation against its enemies. For example, in *Dennis v. United States,* which upheld the Smith Act convictions of eleven CPUSA leaders on grounds of conspiring to advocate "the Marxist-Leninist principles of the duty and necessity of overthrowing and destroying the Government of the United States by force and violence," both the majority opinion by Justice Fred Vinson and a concurring opinion by Justice Robert Jackson (who had just the year before won praise for his principled stand in defense of individual rights in the Ellen Knauff case) referred to the "rigi[d] discipline" enacted by the party, which "denie[d] to its own members . . . the freedom to dissent, to debate, to deviate from the party line." Such discipline made the CP a completely different sort of opponent and justified extraordinary efforts to silence its members. Jackson went so far as to hint that Communist Party leaders did not qualify as "individual citizens" entitled to constitutional guarantees of liberty; his concern was instead with containing an "authoritarian dictatorship within a republic."[52]

Whereas the Smith Act had its origins in the prewar period and, at least theoretically, could be used against a variety of subversive individuals and organizations, legislators acted during the 1950s specifically to deprive Communists of the constitutional guarantees of free speech and association. The Internal Security Act of 1950 (also known as the McCarran Act or the Subversive Activities Control Act), requiring the registration of the CP and its members, included findings of fact that noted the "rigid and ruthless" nature of Communist discipline and rejected a view of Communists as free and independent individuals expressing their political beliefs. Four years later the Communist Control Act quoted Justice Jackson's opinion in *Dennis* to explain the dire threat presented by the CP:

> The Communist Party of the United States . . . constitutes an authoritarian dictatorship within a republic, demanding for itself the rights and privileges accorded to political parties, but denying to all others the liberties guaranteed by the Constitution. . . . Unlike political parties . . . the policies and programs of the Communist Party are secretly prescribed for it by the foreign leaders of the world Communist movement. Its members have no part in determining its goals, and are not permitted to voice dissent to party objectives. Unlike members of political parties, members of the Communist Party are recruited for indoctrination with respect to its objectives and methods, and are organized, instructed, and disciplined to carry into action slavishly the assignments given them by their hierarchical chieftains. . . . [The CPUSA] is the means whereby individuals are seduced into the service of the world Communist movement, trained to do its bidding, and directed and controlled in the conspiratorial performance of their revolutionary services. Therefore, the Communist Party should be outlawed.

The law did not explicitly make membership a criminal offense, but it placed the CP outside the Constitution, denying it "any of the rights, privileges and immunities attendant upon legal bodies." The legal scholar William M. Wiecek has suggested that laws such as these, and the federal courts' broad support for them, reflected a view of Communists as "something less than full humans, full citizens, fully rights-endowed."[53]

This view reached its apex in the Expatriation Act of 1954, which wrote into law the McCarran Act's "factual" observation that those who joined the CP thereby surrendered their allegiance to the United States. Passed at President Eisenhower's urging a mere ten days after the Communist Control Act, it established that, on conviction of "willfully" violating the Smith Act or "engaging in a conspiracy to overthrow, put down, or to destroy by force the Government of the United States," an individual would automatically lose his or her nationality as an American. Significantly, this law provided for the loss of nationality within the statutory framework of "voluntary expatriation." This was a position that had been foreshadowed in the McCarran Act four years earlier; its findings of fact had posited that "in the United States those individuals who knowingly and willfully participate in the world Communist movement, when they so participate, in effect repudiate their allegiance to the United States, and in effect transfer their allegiance to the foreign country in which is vested the direction and control of the world Communist movement." Yet U.S. statutes already made clear that those convicted of treason lost their citizenship. The brief "debate" over the bill (none spoke against it) when it was introduced in the House of Representatives demonstrated the logic of including those Communists who had not been or could not be convicted of treason. As Republican congressman Chauncey Reed of Illinois proclaimed, the law "would simply place the voluntary stooges of the international Communist conspiracy in the category of traitors to their own country." Harold Donohue, a Massachusetts Democrat, elaborated: "The grant of a personal right does not carry with it the unlimited privilege of abuse. . . . We have documentary evidence that the Communist doctrine is pledged to the accomplishment of the subjugation of all free peoples. . . . It has been too long obvious their intention and hope is to achieve our enslavement by the perverted use of the very freedoms and liberties we so proudly acclaim." His colleague Thomas Lane, also a Massachusetts Democrat, followed up by speculating on the sanity of any American plotting against the United States:

> How can people ever think of betraying freedom? Because they are sick with the strange malady that can do so much harm to others as well as themselves. It is diagnosed as the fanatical fever of Communism. How do they become its victims? In many ways. Perhaps through carelessness, not understanding the danger, as some unfortunates take to narcotics. Maybe their resistance was weak in the first place. Or possibly because they have a hidden and unsatisfied compulsion to revenge themselves upon others by dominating their lives. Whether they are impractical and misguided idealists, or the type who are incapable of meeting freedom's responsibilities and must have others live their lives for them, or whether they lust for absolute power, the end result is the same—they are a menace to the security of the United States and a danger to all of its people.

Lane laid bare the psychological presumptions of a law that purported to punish Americans for misusing their freedom.[54]

Punitive moves such as these threatened to blur the lines between the democratic United States and the totalitarian Soviet Union, as liberal commentators from George F. Kennan to Justice Felix Frankfurter cautioned.[55] Therefore, legislators were careful to frame anti-Communist laws in a way that highlighted the differences between the two systems. The champions of the Expatriation Act maintained that depriving convicted Communists of their nationality (and therefore their citizenship) actually demonstrated America's leadership of the free world. Using truly twisted logic, Republican representative Kenneth Keating of New York argued:

> The right of expatriation is itself something that distinguishes a slave-state from a free people. None of the dictatorships, including the vicious tyranny that is now settled upon so much of mankind for the Kremlin, has ever recognized the right of citizens or subjects to emigrate and renounce their ties. No tyranny could stand the enunciation and implementation of such a right. Yet we have always observed it fully. . . . In this light, it is nothing less than fair, that those who are convicted of trying to destroy this very structure of freedom, including the right to live in our midst, should be deprived of their nationality.

By the act of joining the CP, according to the Expatriation Act, Americans voluntarily subjugated themselves to the Soviet Union and hence sacrificed their citizenship. As a result of this law, they would, in effect, be rendered stateless. As one commentator critical of the law argued: "Expatriation represents a loss of the right to have rights—loss of membership in an organized community capable of guaranteeing any rights at all. The . . . stateless person [has] no right to stay anywhere on the face of the earth. . . . It must then be regretted that the United States, the world's leading proponent of human dignity, is today engaging in punitive denationalization causing an increase in statelessness, a practice long disfavored by civilized nations, and notoriously identified with the totalitarian States." Reversing the logic put forth by Keating, this critic disputed the fiction that the expatriation contemplated by the act was voluntary and quoted Hannah Arendt: "One is almost tempted to measure the degree of totalitarian infection by the extent to which the concerned governments use their sovereign right to denationalize." But this was a decidedly minority view. The vast majority of Americans—80 percent, according to one poll—endorsed the position that CP membership made one unfit for citizenship.[56]

The language of voluntarism embedded within the Expatriation Act had diverse origins and purposes. In part, it reflected concerns about the constitutionality of punitive expatriation.[57] It also was intended to sustain the vision of the United States as a nation committed to freedom and rights. But in addition, it was commensurate with understandings of Communist affiliation as an irrational and unnatural act of intentional submission. As Representative Lane put it: "There is no sane or plausible reason why anyone living here should plot to destroy our Government. For then he would be destroying himself."[58] The notion that CP members had willingly given up their national affiliation echoed the perception that they had willingly enslaved themselves, abandoning a political community that protected their liberty for one that rendered them without rights. Each of these gestures was, in a sense, incomprehensible, and each mandated exceptional responses by the state.

As individuals whose political desire was structured around the surrender of their individuality, Communists embodied a paradox that troubled the links forged in normative understandings of American citizenship—between citizen and nation, freedom and responsibility, independence and dependence. Liberalism invested individuals with the right to pursue their interests without interference from government, but their fitness for participating in the governance of themselves and others was predicated not only on their autonomy but also on their ability to ascertain and pursue a common good, to see themselves as members of a political community. Individualism and communalism existed in uneasy but necessary association. The framing of CP affiliation as the repudiation of self deprived Communists of their autonomy, dismissed their assessment of the common good, and made them not individual members of a political community but willing slaves to their masters in Moscow. It also deflected attention from the ways in which the instability at the heart of liberal democracy pervaded an emerging national security state that subordinated individual liberty to the sovereign nation. Envisioning Communist Party membership, and totalitarian systems more generally, as a psychological disorder, and particularly as the expression of a perverted sadomasochism, helped to suppress those contradictions while identifying the United States with the "normal" and "natural" human desire for freedom.

Casting dissent in psychological terms helped justify numerous policies of the national security state. The psychosexual dynamics that explained the attraction to the party also shaped the image of Communists as treasonous spies who combined sexual perversion and gender inversion with political subversion. This image facilitated some of the most notoriously repressive moves of the early Cold War, including the execution of Ethel Rosenberg.[59]

Morris Ernst, one of the prime popularizers of the view that Communists were "damaged souls," told FBI assistant director Lou Nichols that he had made "a psychological study" of the Rosenbergs and had "come to the conclusion that Julius is the slave and his wife, Ethel, the master." She was also depicted as an unnatural mother who had sacrificed her children to ideology. Explaining the decision to convict her, the jury foreman described her as "steely" and "the mastermind." Julius "was more human. She was more disciplined." This view influenced both J. Edgar Hoover and President Eisenhower to support her execution. As Eisenhower rationalized: "In this instance it is the woman who is the strong and recalcitrant character, the man who is the weak one. She has obviously been the leader in everything they did in the spy ring."[60] Ethel Rosenberg's execution, despite the lack of any evidence that she had engaged in espionage, even now stands out for many as the example par excellence of the out-of-control national security state.[61] But perhaps it is only the most egregious expression of how the psychological turn in conceptualizing citizenship made exceptional measures seem necessary.

The narrative presented in this chapter does little to disrupt the sense of the Cold War era as one of unremitting repression and consensus. At the height of its influence, psychology helped to turn Communists into democracy's Other, depriving them of belonging and rights. Still, psychology was a double-edged sword, and its emphasis on mind rather than body, on individuality rather than independence, and on personality rather than status could also make possible challenges to the state of exception that it helped to consolidate. Psychology was certainly an embodied framework for understanding human motivation and behavior: psychologists constructed some bodies (white, heterosexual, male) as more productive of a healthy, normative personality than others (dark, queer, female). But there was also a sense in which psychology liberated individuals from the burdens of embodiment. The emphasis on "the self" made it possible for a broader range of people to claim that they possessed the psychic health—the "democratic personality"—that not only was necessary to full citizenship but also made them the kinds of individuals whose rights the United States was beholden to protect. In training attention on both the universal and the particular, on the individual as well as on the communities in which she or he was embedded, psychology offered new ways of representing citizenship while also retaining the old. As the next chapter demonstrates, it was precisely this mix of universal and particular that helped the war bride Ellen Knauff outmaneuver the U.S. officials who tried to prevent her from becoming an American.

CHAPTER TWO.

The Case of the War Bride

Liberal Citizenship and Human Rights in the National Security State

On the morning of May 17, 1950, Ellen Raphael Boxhornova Knauff watched from the terminal as an American Airlines jet took off from Idlewild Airport for Frankfurt with sixty-six pounds of her luggage on board. Knauff, a thirty-five-year-old German war bride who had been held at Ellis Island for almost two years as she sought admission to the United States, had been scheduled for deportation on that plane. Twenty minutes before departure, immigration officials learned that Supreme Court Justice Robert H. Jackson had issued a stay.[1] Jackson was outraged that the Justice Department had moved to "bundl[e] this woman onto an airplane to get her out of this country" only hours after a court had denied her petition for habeas corpus, and despite a warning from the House of Representatives that it would consider such a move in contempt of Congress. He berated the executive branch for its haste: "It overtaxes credulity to believe that it would jeopardize the security of the United States to impart to coordinate branches of the Government some inkling of the charges against this woman. . . . To consummate [this removal] while the right to do so is still in litigation cannot be permitted. . . . To stand between the individual and arbitrary action by the Government is the highest function of this Court." Jackson's last-minute rescue was hailed by Knauff's advocates around the country. In contrast, New York District Commissioner of Immigration Edward Shaughnessy, frustrated yet again in his efforts to be rid of the war bride, could only sigh "I was afraid of that."[2]

Knauff had arrived in New York harbor in August 1948, the new wife of former U.S. soldier Kurt Knauff. They had met while working as civilian employees of the U.S. Army in occupied Germany. When she set sail for New York on the USAT *Comfort* with other women seeking entry under the auspices of the 1945 War Brides Act, her plan had been to establish residency, apply for naturalization, and return to her husband within two months.[3] Instead she found herself excluded from the United States as a security risk, denied not merely the opportunity to defend herself but even knowledge of the charges against her. A court battle resulted in a January 1950 Supreme Court ruling that the federal government had the power to exclude some aliens, a ruling from which Justice Jackson had dissented. But Knauff did not give up her struggle, and in November 1951 Attorney General J. Howard McGrath ordered her admitted to the United States. In 1963, long divorced from Kurt Knauff, Ellen Raphael Boxhornova Knauff Hartley finally became a citizen. How did she manage to triumph over the highest court of the land and the most powerful men in the U.S. Justice Department, including J. Edgar Hoover and two attorneys general?

Part of the answer is that Ellen Knauff was tenacious and savvy. The most remarkable aspect of her struggle to enter the United States may have been her ability to gather influential supporters who worked almost as hard as she did to challenge U.S. policy. During those three years, Ellen Knauff twice testified before Congress, built strong relationships with journalists who not only wrote about her case but also toiled behind the scenes to get government officials on her side, attracted support from civil libertarians and lawyers, dined with a senator, and wrote a book. She managed to mobilize men from all three branches of government on her behalf. Although some bureaucrats maintained that the Cold War state of emergency justified their departure from normal safeguards of due process, she was able to leverage quarrels within a developing national security state to call into question the legitimacy of the state of exception.

But she did so while also sustaining an image of herself as a doting and dependent wife, and this suggests that the tangled relations between immigration policy, domestic and international politics, and family ideology are also key to understanding Ellen Knauff's success. Domestic containment, as Elaine Tyler May has termed the neat fit between Cold War politics and a consensus favoring "marriage, parenthood, and traditional gender roles," cut both ways, working against the national security state as well as for it. This contradiction allowed

Ellen and her supporters to rally public opinion and force the government to allow her entry. Emphasizing the Knauffs' fight for "the right to live together," they broadened the debate about what, precisely, constituted national security.[4]

Knauff's particularities, as much as her ability to represent a generalized "war bride," made her a sympathetic figure. She was a tremendously attractive refugee—not just the loving wife of a veteran husband, but also an escapee from the horrors of the Holocaust, a soldier in the fight against totalitarianism, pretty, intelligent, and skilled. As a result of her marital history, she was also stateless. This combination of traits made Ellen Knauff a ready symbol of the promise and the limitations of Cold War citizenship. On the one hand, her ultimate victory signified the triumph of American values. In this sense, she was marked as what Bonnie Honig has called the foreign-founder, the immigrant who renews the nation and its democratic ideals.[5] On the other hand, the efforts to exclude her conveyed the dangers of a narrow conception of national citizenship. In a context in which liberal citizenship norms—the state's promise to defend individual liberties and rights against interference, especially but not only in the private sphere—figured so centrally in distinguishing American "democracy" from Soviet "totalitarianism," the government's refusal to protect Ellen Knauff's pursuit of her private happiness threatened to collapse that distinction.

In the early days of the domestic Cold War, Knauff's highly visible struggle for the opportunity to become an American illuminated the workings of the state of exception as well as the limits of a liberal citizenship dependent on the nation-state. Her initial exclusion from the United States limited her recourse to the due process guaranteed all "persons" by the Bill of Rights. But under normal circumstances, even excluded aliens received these protections.[6] Their denial in this case depended on the existence of an ongoing state of emergency apparently necessitated by the Communist threat. In using the language of national security to explain their power to place her beyond the usual protections of American law, government authorities laid bare the arbitrariness of that power. In the celebrated case of the war bride, liberal citizenship under the state of exception was tested and found wanting, suggesting the value of a more expansive definition of rights that transcended the citizen to include the human.

War Brides and Refugees at the Gates

When Ellen Knauff arrived in New York from Bremerhaven, Germany, on August 14, 1948, she had been many years in search of a safe berth. Born Ellen

Raphael in Dortmund, Germany, in 1915 to a prosperous Jewish couple, after graduating from high school she had been "swept off her feet" by a Czech named Edgar Boxhorn, and she married him against her parents' wishes. The couple moved to Prague, where Ellen discovered that her new husband was a philanderer, an extortionist, a bully, and, she later claimed, a (half-Jewish) anti-Semite. They were separated in 1934 and divorced in 1936, but she feared returning to Germany, so she stayed put until the Germans invaded Czechoslovakia in March 1939.[7] Ellen fled to London, where she worked as a private cook and Red Cross nurse. By 1943 she was serving in the British Women's Auxiliary Air Force as a map clerk. In 1946 she returned to Germany in search of her family, but she learned that except for three cousins and an aunt, all had perished in a concentration camp at Riga. She found work as a telephone monitor for the U.S. Occupation Forces' Civil Censorship Division, listening in on German citizens' phone conversations for evidence of black market activity. There she met Kurt Knauff, who had himself been born in Germany and migrated to New York City in 1929. Kurt was drafted into the U.S. Army in 1942 and naturalized as a citizen in 1943. He spent part of the war in Germany, where he continued to work for the army as a civilian employee after his discharge. Ellen and Kurt married in February 1948, after having obtained the required permission from military officials. Six months later, facing an impending deadline under the War Brides Act, Ellen set sail for the United States, alone.[8]

Ellen's status as a war bride was shaped by far-reaching changes in the nation's immigration and citizenship policies during the interwar years. The 1922 Cable Act, intended to grant U.S. women greater equality by disentangling their citizenship status from that of their husband, simultaneously denied immigrant women the naturalization through marriage they had earlier been granted. This left some women at risk of statelessness, because many other nations retained derivative citizenship, by which women acquired their husband's citizenship status. Women who over their lifetime entered into several marriages in different countries, as did Knauff, were especially affected. Ellen, for example, acquired Czech citizenship when she married Boxhorn; but under Czech law she lost it when she married Kurt, rendering her stateless.[9]

The War Brides Act of 1945 was intended in part to address this difficulty as well as the increased burdens that had been imposed by restrictive immigration laws passed in the 1920s. During World War I, women who married U.S. soldiers, if racially eligible, automatically became U.S. citizens. But this was not true during World War II, and GIs who married overseas encountered a cumbersome process for bringing their spouse home. Furthermore, because of gender inequalities that remained in immigration law, female military personnel were at a special disadvantage if they married abroad. The War Brides Act began life as an effort to foster equal treatment for "America's citizen girls" in the military. But as the army prepared to transport to the United States upwards of six thousand war brides monthly, it was trumpeted instead as a way to recognize and reward the dedicated service of male citizen-soldiers, who deserved to bring their wife home with them.[10]

These dual, and not completely compatible, purposes reveal some of the complexities of legislating marriage in the postwar era. The War Brides Act, and its companion the War Fiancées Act, were part of the social citizenship package extended to GIs in the postwar years, but a number of U.S. women objected that their own rights were being ignored. Some opposed these laws because they feared that encouraging marriage to foreign women would infringe their own "right" to marry. Others demanded that their own war service—in defense plants, for example—be recognized and rewarded. These female citizens registered unease about precisely what gender order was being guaranteed by federal legislation.[11]

The 1949 Howard Hawks film *I Was a Male War Bride* reveals something of the complexity of feeling about securing masculine marital prerogatives which surrounded the enactment of these laws. Cary Grant plays, rather unconvincingly, Henri Rochard, a French intelligence officer stationed in Germany during the postwar occupation, whose last assignment before leaving the military has him tracking down black marketeers. Ann Sheridan is Lieutenant Catherine Gates, a zany but very competent Women's Army Corps (WAC) translator assigned to accompany him. Despite Rochard's unruly hands (Gates has run into him before, apparently spending most of her time warding off his advances), his uncontrollable temper, and his obvious incompetence as a soldier and an intelligence officer, and despite Gates's impetuous, bossy personality and apparent disdain for Rochard and his work, the two fall in love. There ensues a race against time in which they encounter obstacle after obstacle as they seek to marry and obtain permission for Rochard to enter the United States. The comic complications arise first from the couple's inability to consummate their marriage, as at just the wrong moment Gates is ordered from their marriage bed to redeploy to the United States, and then from Rochard's efforts to negotiate the U.S. military bureaucracy as the atypical male war "bride." The unfortunate husband, who already has been emasculated several times by his too butch wife (confined to a motorcycle sidecar as she manfully drives them around the German countryside; jailed in a practical joke while she tracks down the black marketeer he has been assigned to contact), suffers the final humiliation when she disguises him as "Mrs. Henri Rochard" to get him aboard the ship that is transporting her unit home. These gender reversals are, of course, resolved in the end: after Rochard's unconvincing drag getup reveals him to be the man of the family, he locks himself and his bride in a cabin and throws away the key. He finally triumphs over the military's impressive, if accidental, ability to stop him from making love with his wife. Nevertheless, the state that was supposed to be facilitating men's sexual access to women was shown to have an uncanny tendency to interrupt that access—a theme that would be sounded in relation to Ellen and Kurt Knauff's travails as well.

The war bride story told in the film is anything but typical: the "war bride" in question is both a man and a soldier. Interestingly, Rochard/Grant's drag costume is a WAC dress uniform, snagged from a nurse's suitcase. Grant is in double drag—a British actor impersonating a French soldier impersonating an American military nurse—and the humorous incongruity of his portrayal lies not just in his purposefully unconvincing impersonation of a woman (and, it would seem, a Frenchman), but in the strangeness of the uniform itself: a dress shirt with a man's tie and suit jacket on top, skirt and heels on the bottom. So dressed, Rochard ceases to inhabit the position of the civilian alien war bride; and since he is so obviously a *man* in uniform, he comes to represent the American GI whose service the army seeks to reward by helping him exercise his right to couple and reproduce.[12] Although his ability to enter the United States derives only from his status as an "alien spouse of female military personnel en route to the United States under Public Law 271 of the Congress," as Rochard repeatedly intones as he seeks to navigate the military bureaucracy, the film reminds viewers that the law's primary function was to strengthen the marital rights of America's fighting men and thereby preserve heteronormative citizenship, even as the Grant-Sheridan relationship suggests the difficulties of such a task in an age when women, too, can be soldiers. In this way the film replicates the trajectory of the War Brides Act itself, from a law concerned with treating female soldiers equally with men, to one that reasserts the state's role in upholding male dominance.[13]

Despite some rumblings of discontent and doubt, the War Brides Act was a popular measure, allowing tens of thousands of war brides as well as a much smaller number of war husbands to enter the United States with a minimum of inconvenience. As the historian Susan Zeiger suggests, it was in tune both with assertions of enhanced U.S. engagement with and leadership of the postwar free world, and a general desire to restabilize gender and family relations.[14] White war brides were, in the main, welcomed in the postwar years, and the popularity of Ellen Knauff's crusade for admission reflected these positive feelings. There was much greater resistance to rolling out the welcome mat for war refugees, and in her guise as a Jew escaping genocide but tainted by her association with a Czechoslovakia that had gone Communist, Knauff was more troublesome.

The tension between a vision of the United States as a beacon of freedom and a restrictionist commitment to admitting only those considered "fit" for citizenship had long animated debates about immigration, and it intensified during World War II and the postwar years. Before and during the war, federal officials had obstructed efforts to facilitate the admission of Jewish refugees. Although before war's end the United States did accept several hundred thousand refugees from southern and eastern Europe, about two-thirds of them Jews, this assistance came almost in spite of, rather than because of, federal government efforts, which remained halfhearted and inept. And even these limited efforts threatened a backlash; as Leonard Dinnerstein has demonstrated, public perceptions that Jews had "too much power in the United States" increased steadily during the war years. Furthermore, as the world war morphed into the Cold War, restrictionist efforts focused on "subversives" as well, as immigration procedures that had been enacted to root out "enemy aliens" were adapted to the task of excluding Communists.[15]

As early as 1940, immigration was being reframed as a national security concern. In that year the Immigration and Naturalization Service (INS) was transferred from the Labor to the Justice Department, and Congress passed the Smith Act. Officially titled the Alien Registration Act, it is best remembered for outlawing the advocacy of the violent overthrow of the U.S. government, but it also required that all aliens be registered and fingerprinted, and added new classes of aliens subject to deportation. Upon declaring war, Congress enacted a provision that gave the president even greater power to police the entry and exit of aliens. Under that act, Franklin D. Roosevelt issued Presidential Proclamation 2523, authorizing the secretary of state and attorney general to exclude aliens whose entry they deemed "prejudicial to the interests of the United States" during the "national emergency." This law provided that if, in the opinion of federal officials, "the disclosure of the information upon which the exclusion was based would be prejudicial to the public interest," the reason for the exclusion might be kept secret, and a hearing was not required. These procedures were enacted as a wartime measure, but in 1946 President Truman moved to keep them in place; the Cold War apparently continued the state of emergency. (It was this provision that was used to deny Ellen Knauff any information about the charges against her.) As "enemy aliens" became conflated with an internationally organized Communist threat looming outside the nation's borders, anti-Semitism, anti-Communism, and xenophobia combined to make the Jewish war refugee a troubling figure, the more so since many Americans were also concerned about maintaining the nation's wartime image as a generous and valiant savior of the free world.[16]

Ellen Knauff was balanced precariously within this immigration system. Her marital history demonstrated the capriciousness of citizenship for women in a global world. As a woman without a country, she was simultaneously pitiable and unclassifiable, a stranger not just to the United States but to the institution of the nation-state. As a middle-class Jew, she was similarly puzzling: with her diminutive figure and girlish smile, she probably did not raise fears of "too much Jewish power" for most who followed her story; nor was she like the camp survivors who were so hard to place, the sort of Jewish refugee whose voracious needs so unsettled Americans' sense of themselves as a generous people. But many continued to associate Jews with Communists, and Knauff's former citizenship in what was now Communist Czechoslovakia may have heightened that association. Her German origins could also work against her, especially since German war brides—former enemy aliens—came in for extra suspicion. Marriage to German women was prohibited for a good part of the war; the German brides were extensively investigated, and they were disparaged as "fraternazis" and grasping "fraüleins" who used sex to leverage food, drink, and money from American GIs.[17] These multiple positionings helped shape responses to Knauff's petitions for admission and naturalization, allowing sharply contested understandings of her fitness to be an American citizen.

"It Leaves a Bad Taste"
Fissures in the National Security State

Although immigration officials did not reveal the charges against Ellen Knauff until quite late in their efforts to prevent her entry, the central issue involved whether she could be trusted as a Cold War–era citizen. Knauff first got a hint of the government's concerns after she had been held at Ellis Island for three months. Her cousin, maître d' at a fashionable Washington restaurant, asked one of his regular customers to use his influence to find out what was going on. The customer, former commissioner of the Internal Revenue Service Joe Nunan, spoke to Attorney General Tom Clark, who subsequently informed him that Knauff was "formerly a paid agent of the Czechoslovakian Government, and reported on American personnel assigned to the Civil Censorship Division in Germany. The Federal Bureau of Investigation feels that she would be a hazard to internal security."[18] Justice Department officials consistently refused to clarify or even acknowledge these vague charges, which Knauff's attorney shared with reporters and in court filings, or to provide any substantiation, citing the threat to national security and the need to protect confidential sources.

Even in the beginning, the charges against Knauff were contested within the federal government, portending the years of conflict that would follow. Knauff's entry to the United States was first opposed by Captain William Hacker, a special agent in the army's Counter Intelligence Corps in Germany. He had been given her name in early 1948 by Vaclav Victor Kadane, a Czech liaison to the army. According to Kadane, Knauff (then Boxhornova) had provided information to Colonel V. V. Podhora about a U.S. decoding machine and telephone-monitoring activities, as well as about the political beliefs of American personnel. Podhora was the Czechoslovakian consul general and, significantly, a Communist; even though these events occurred before the Communist takeover in Czechoslovakia, Knauff's alleged connection with him may have brought her own political commitments into question. Hacker argued that "since Boxhornova has revealed information of a classified nature to an agent of a foreign power . . . she would do the same thing again. . . . It is recommended that [she] not be permitted to enter the United States under any consideration." But officers at the European Command headquarters, who had already approved Knauff's application to travel under the War Brides Act, disagreed that she was a security risk and decided to allow her passage.[19] Nonetheless, shortly after her departure from Germany, intelligence personnel in the War Department forwarded Hacker's report to the FBI, at which time J. Edgar Hoover weighed in, writing on August 6 to the attorney general, the secretary of state, and the INS commissioner that Knauff's entry "raises a hazard to the internal security of the United States." It was at Hoover's urging that Clark decided to bar Knauff from the country.[20]

A quick sketch of the resulting controversy reveals that this one case grew to encompass significant segments of the U.S. government and civil society. The

Justice Department and its INS were unrelenting in their efforts to exclude Knauff, even after she hired immigration lawyer Gunther Jacobson to represent her and popular sentiment began to swing in her favor. Over the next three years, Knauff and Jacobson launched a defense that incorporated all three government branches, often playing one against the other. Jacobson filed numerous writs for habeas corpus on Ellen's behalf, appealing to a higher court or instituting a new proceeding each time he was rebuffed, and displaying great creativity when these tactics failed. After the Supreme Court ruled against her in January 1950, the INS attempted to deport her, notwithstanding the fact that, at Jacobson's behest, several bills had recently been introduced in Congress to admit her to the country. Such "private bills" were a time-honored method for circumventing the harshness of immigration regulations, and in most cases the INS ceased deportation proceedings while they were pending before Congress. Jacobson filed another writ contending that Knauff could not be deported while Congress was considering the private bills, and its (temporary) success forced INS officials to transport her back to Ellis Island from the dock where she was waiting to board the ship that would have taken her back to Germany. After further wrangling between Congress and the Justice Department, including a threat to hold INS officials in contempt of Congress, Knauff was brought to Washington to testify about her case. Following the hearing, Senator William Langer, who had introduced one of the private bills, communicated his displeasure with the INS by treating her to lunch in the Senate dining room. In May 1950 the House of Representatives unanimously approved a bill directing that she be admitted to the United States. They did so with virtually no information from immigration service officials, since the division had refused to disclose the evidence against her.[21]

This partial victory did not deter immigration officials from continuing their efforts, and when another of Jacobson's writs was denied by lower courts, they moved to fly Knauff out of the country, prompting Justice Jackson's dramatic rescue—the second time she was saved from deportation at the last minute. Jackson, it turns out, had been tipped off to Knauff's impending departure by journalists at the *St. Louis Post Dispatch*, who were also instrumental in bringing her dilemma to President Truman's attention. Their behind-the-scenes maneuvering had an impact, and soon Justice Department officials were fending off pressure not only from Congress and the press but from the White House as well. When, in early 1951, Kurt Knauff returned to the United States for a second time to try to secure Ellen's freedom, Attorney General J. Howard McGrath ordered that she be released to his custody while the INS looked further into the case. In March, after almost three years of arguing that granting Knauff a hearing would endanger national security, McGrath seemingly relented and scheduled a hearing before a Board of Special Inquiry, the customary first step for adjudicating immigration claims.[22]

Unlike other such hearings, this one was open to the press, and it was intended not to accord Knauff due process but to publicize the evidence against her and undermine the growing support for her. The government presented three witnesses, including Kadane, Hacker, and Anna Lavickova, a clerical employee of the Czech mission in Prague. All three were now resident in the United States, and Justice Department officials contended that secrecy was no longer needed to protect their safety.[23] They testified that Knauff had been a regular visitor to the Czech mission and that she had provided classified military information to Czech officials. Both men asserted that she had engaged in espionage under the code name "Kobyla," with Hacker describing her as a "trained espionage agent," although his earlier claim that she had been paid was dropped. Knauff did her best to defend herself, explaining her visits to the Czech mission as efforts to clear up passport difficulties that resulted from her statelessness and declaring her commitment to "freedom, honesty, truth . . . common decency . . . and God," but the next day newspapers throughout the country highlighted the charge that she was a Czech spy.[24] After the proceeding, even her staunchest supporters at the *Post-Dispatch* could only conclude that since Knauff had had her hearing, justice had been served.[25]

Although finally giving Knauff a hearing was a calculated move to seal the case against her, in the end it did not work. Once immigration officials opened the hearing process to her, Knauff earned the right to appeal. After another board scored the government's case and its procedures, McGrath issued a stunning reversal and ordered that Knauff be admitted to the United States, thirty-nine months after her arrival.[26] Displaying her customary mettle, she walked out of a 1953 citizenship hearing in which the allegations against her were resuscitated. Finally, a decade later—in 1963—she achieved her dream of becoming a U.S. citizen.

As this brief and much simplified summary of the efforts to exclude Knauff suggests, Cold War–era antisubversive policies could be hotly, and sometimes effectively, contested. Knauff's journey to citizenship demonstrates above all the instability of the national security state. How and whether it "worked" in any particular case was affected both by public opinion and by conflict *inside* the federal government. This conflict operated at every level, within the executive, judicial, and legislative branches, as well as among those branches. Sometimes it remained behind the scenes, but often it was played out in public, not only constraining national security policies but also enabling popular debate about their efficacy and legitimacy. Indeed, the relationship between secrecy, publicity, and national security was anything but straightforward, for the fact of secrecy might generate publicity. It also tended to produce space for misinformation, allowing Knauff to shape the debate in fundamental ways.

Disagreements over the reach of an emerging national security system were openly aired when the Supreme Court upheld Knauff's exclusion on January 16, 1950. The justices expressed contending understandings of the relationship between national sovereignty and individual rights in the Cold War era. The court split, 4–3; neither Justice Tom Clark, who had been the attorney general who ordered Ellen Knauff excluded from the United States, nor Justice William Douglass, recuperating from illness, participated. Writing for the majority, Justice Sherman Minton based his opinion on the federal government's fundamental sovereign power to decide who had the privilege of entering the country. It had long been held that this was a power that courts were severely constrained to disturb. But behind and beyond the question of sovereign power were two exceptional circumstances that made Knauff's case particularly compelling. The first was her status as an alien who had not yet been admitted to the United States; the second was the state of emergency that still formally prevailed in the postwar world.[27]

The distinction between exclusion and deportation, which may appear on the surface to be a distinction without a difference, in fact made an enormous difference to Knauff's case. Since the late nineteenth century, the Supreme Court had held that all U.S. residents, whether citizens or aliens, had many constitutional protections, including the right to guarantees of due process. Nevertheless, those who sought admission to the United States but were not yet on U.S. territory were denied these rights. These individuals "on the threshold" could challenge the decision of immigration officials to keep them out of the United States only if those officials had arbitrarily ignored existing statutes or regulations. "Non-admitted" aliens might include those who actually were (or had been) on U.S. soil, among them persons who were detained at Ellis Island, those who were "paroled" (i.e., released) while awaiting official action on their petition to enter, and resident aliens who were temporarily overseas. Thus, although Ellen Knauff had been living on Ellis Island for months, had been allowed to live and work in New York City while her case was before the Supreme Court, and had traveled to Kansas to meet her husband's relatives, she had not been "admitted" to the United States, and, according to the majority, the Court was powerless to validate her claims. As Justice Minton wrote: "Whatever the rule may be concerning deportation of persons who have gained entry into the United States, it is not within the province of any court . . . to review the determination of the political branch of the Government to exclude a given alien. . . . *Whatever the procedure authorized by Congress is, it is due process* as far as an alien denied entry is concerned."[28]

This, however, was a decision that rested on the existence of the state of exception as much as on the usual workings of congressional power. Under ordinary circumstances, Congress did extend the semblance of due process to non-resident aliens facing exclusion by providing them a hearing. It was only because the attorney general had found Knauff excludable under the terms of Presidential Proclamation 2523 that she was denied both a hearing and notice of the charges against her. Knauff contested this move to place her beyond normal safeguards, contending that the wartime emergency had ended, but the Court disagreed. "The national emergency has never been terminated. Indeed, a state of war still exists," ruled the majority, who concluded that these were not "ordinary" times, and that Knauff did not "stand the test of security." Up against the wall of both national sovereignty and national security, the war bride had to go.[29]

The dissents, penned by Justices Felix Frankfurter and Robert Jackson, with Hugo Black concurring in the latter's opinion, did not contest the majority's position that the federal government could exclude aliens at will. The dissenters objected, however, that Congress's intent to facilitate the admission of war brides, a reflection of "the dominant regard which American society places upon the family," was being ignored.[30] More to the point here, they warned that government secrecy endangered democracy itself. As Jackson wrote, the government's reliance on secret evidence against Knauff offered "a cloak for the malevolent, the misinformed, the meddlesome, and the corrupt to play the role of informer undetected and uncorrected. . . . The menace to the security of this country, be it great as it may, from this girl's admission is as nothing compared to the menace to free institutions inherent in procedures of this pattern." Knauff's treatment, he alleged, mirrored the tactics of a "police state." In what would become an oft-quoted phrase, he observed, "Security is like liberty in that many are the crimes committed in its name."[31] Keeping Ellen Knauff out of the country was a much greater threat to the nation than letting her in.

Jackson's own career made him a likely ally for Knauff. As a former attorney general, he might be expected to be friendly to the Justice Department's arguments, and as the Court's decision upholding the Smith Act in 1951 revealed, he was all too willing to limit rights in the name of national security. But often he was a strong defender of procedural due process and individual rights. In addition, he had served as chief U.S. prosecutor at the Nuremburg trials, where he vigorously pursued Nazi war criminals and was an important contributor to the development of an international human rights regime.[32]

Knauff's plight touched Jackson from the beginning, leading him to disregard his clerk's recommendation not to grant certiorari when the case first came before the Court and to order Knauff released on bond while it was being considered.[33] By the time he learned of the second attempt to deport her, he had lost patience, blasting Justice Department officials for keeping not only Knauff but also the courts and Congress in the dark about the charges against her. Later, apparently anticipating that the Court would refuse to grant certiorari when Jacobson again sought to bring her case before it, Jackson penned a remarkable draft opinion.[34] The passionate document reviewed Ellen's war service in the Royal Air Force, her experience in the United States, and his own role in saving her from deportation in May 1950. Condemning "the attorney general and his security sleuths" for subjecting Knauff to the same sort of persecution that "her people" had experienced in Germany under "Hitler's Gestapo," Jackson closed with a reflection on the broader meaning of the case: "She has done a great service to liberty loving people in the United States. Alone she has shown the hollowness and hypocrisy of the official ballyhoo about civil liberties. Alone she has taught us that it can happen here, that power corrupts Americans as it has others. She has taught the dangers of the secret condemnation on secret and untried evidence. . . . There is no water that will wash this damned spot out of the record."[35] The palpable emotion of this document suggests something of the intensity of Jackson's feeling on the issue.

Jackson and Frankfurter were not the only members of the judiciary to articulate their discomfort with the course of justice in the Knauff case. Gunther Jacobson's perseverance offered federal judges many opportunities to weigh her fate. When, in March 1950, he pleaded with a three-judge panel of the Court of Appeals to stay Knauff's deportation, the judges were clearly distressed by what they perceived as their lack of authority to restrain Justice Department officials. At the beginning of the hearing, Judge Learned Hand conceded, "There is nothing we can do," and his colleague Jerome Frank concurred, confessing: "My sympathies are with her. . . . I came very close to dissenting when the case was here before, but I didn't see how I could. . . . This is a very appealing case, but where is my power to act?" As the judges debated with government lawyers whether or not excluded aliens had rights that could be enforced in court, Frank confided that he was "disturbed" by the apparently "capricious" power exercised by immigration authorities: "Maybe there's nothing we can do about it but I want to reflect on it. It leaves a bad taste. It leaves me with considerable disquietude about this woman." In the end, a majority of the three-judge panel found a way to intervene. Apparently their irritation at the government lawyers' insistence that Knauff be deported that very day overrode their concerns about their limited powers.[36]

Although discomfort with the uses of government power fueled much of the conflict over the Knauff case, pride and jurisdictional disputes also came into play. This may explain the apparent disagreement within the army over whether to prohibit Knauff's entry in the first place. The reasons for the original decision to disregard Hacker's recommendation are not clear. Perhaps some army staffers, who had already investigated her prior to approving her marriage to Kurt, objected to the second-guessing of their decisions or were seeking to protect the reputations of those they regarded as their own. Or they may have viewed Knauff's alleged actions as indiscretions rather than serious violations of national security, a one-time event rather than a predictor of her capacity for loyalty. Nor is it apparent why, when one group of army personnel decided to facilitate Knauff's entry under the War Brides Act, another group alerted the FBI. Differences of opinion also erupted between Attorney General McGrath and his assistants in the Justice Department: after McGrath decided to admit Knauff in November 1951, members of the New York district attorney's office contemplated indicting her on espionage and perjury charges.[37] More visibly, the battle between the legislative and executive branches had all the markings of a turf war, as Justice Department officials sought to frustrate congressional investigations, and legislators denounced administrators as petty bureaucrats.

Indeed, the Knauff case occasioned a vigorous defense of civil liberties within all three branches of government, pointing to fissures in the national security system. In Congress, numerous legislators worked on Ellen's behalf, introducing multiple private bills, providing the Knauffs opportunities to testify, and even agitating for broader changes in immigration regulation. For example, Representative Franklin D. Roosevelt Jr., fresh from a stint as vice chairman of President Truman's Commission on Civil Rights and newly elected to Congress, was one of those alerted to the case by Knauff's lawyer. He moved from making relatively gentle statements about the importance of "balancing" national security interests with civil liberties, to insisting forcefully that Knauff's case "highlights a threat to the whole philosophy on which our Government is based—the system of checks and balances." To strengthen protections against arbitrary power, he introduced a bill mandating hearings for "all arriving aliens," essentially abrogating Proclamation 2523, which had been issued originally by his father. As a freshman representative affiliated with the Liberal Party, he had little clout, and the bill did not advance. Nonetheless, the editors of the *New York Times* praised his proposal because it would "guarantee to aliens the right of every free man" to a hearing. They called for reaffirming "the fundamental American belief in fair play—especially toward the weakest and the most defenseless."[38]

Less visible but just as vigorous were disagreements within the Truman administration. After the second attempt to deport Knauff was foiled, President Truman instructed an assistant, Stephen Spingarn, to "look into [the matter] and see if anything can be done to straighten it out." Spingarn, known to his colleagues as "our one-man civil liberties union," had already been asked to convey to Attorney General McGrath the president's sense that Justice Department support for legislation intended to facilitate deportation (unrelated to the Knauff case) betrayed an "excessive" concern with security and threatened to encroach "on the individual rights and freedoms which distinguish a democracy from a totalitarian country."[39] Now he launched a vigorous inquiry and "demanded" (as justice officials saw it) all of the evidence against Knauff, including FBI reports. After many months of persistent requests he got what he wanted, but he accused Justice Department officials of trying to stonewall his inquiries and wrote a highly critical memo blasting them for scant evidence and inadequate procedures: "I am not surprised that, despite the present intensive excitement about Communists, the House Judiciary Committee unanimously reported the bill to admit Mrs. Knauff to this country and the House unanimously passed it." Lecturing Assistant Attorney General Peyton Ford that "it is the right and duty of all citizens, as well as Government officials involved, to be vigilant that the use of absolute power such as that involved here is restricted to the most exceptional cases," he recommended that Knauff be afforded an "in camera [private] hearing by Justice Department attorneys outside the security services." Shortly after, Spingarn left the White House to take a position on the Federal Trade Commission, and his recommendations for a hearing were not enacted—at least not in the manner he had imagined. But Justice Department officials suspected that Spingarn was trying to embarrass them by leaking details of the investigation to the press. Apparently, when White House staff despaired of changing Justice Department practices through official channels, they found other ways to move the debate along.[40]

Finally, although top Justice Department and INS officials seem to have been united in their view of the case, INS administrative proceedings provided another site for disagreement. Despite the fact that members of the media were invited to attend Knauff's first hearing before the Board of Special Inquiry, it was organized around the presumption that a probe into the charges against her must be carefully circumscribed to guard national security. The hearing officers were all INS investigators, as was usually the case in such hearings. Knauff's attorney's vigorous objections that the testimony of government witnesses was hearsay and that he was not being permitted to cross-examine them were all overruled, as the board chair insisted that the rules of evidence governing deportation hearings did not apply in exclusion cases. In any event, since the burden was on Knauff to prove her admissibility—that is, to prove the negative, that she did not do what the witnesses suggested she had done—it was no surprise that the hearing panel voted unanimously to exclude her after deliberating for only an hour.[41]

Nonetheless, when the Board of Immigration Appeals (BIA) considered the case, two of its three members rejected the assertion of the special inquiry panel that it was "not bound by the rules of evidence." Staffed by Justice Department career lawyers, not INS personnel, the BIA overturned the decision to exclude Knauff, citing case law that permitted hearsay testimony in certain situations but ruled out "uncorroborated hearsay or rumor" as the "substantial evidence" required in administrative proceedings. They noted that, once the attorney general decided to accord Knauff a hearing, "the same standards appl[ied] as in any other case." Rejecting refuge in the state of exception that privileged national security above individual rights, while acknowledging "the extremely difficult task imposed on those who must investigate or prosecute security cases," they concluded that there was insufficient evidence that Knauff "would be likely to engage in activities subversive to the national security." Perhaps signaling continuing disagreement within the Justice Department, Attorney General McGrath waited more than two months before accepting the BIA's recommendation and authorizing Knauff's entry.[42]

DANGEROUS PATTERN OF THE ELLEN KNAUFF CASE

SUNDAY, FEBRUARY 5, 1950.

FIGURE 3. The *St. Louis Post-Dispatch* was Ellen Knauff's foremost champion. This cartoon by Daniel F. Fitzpatrick captured the editors' understanding of the situation: Knauff, an immigrant and a "little woman," encapsulated the dangers of a garrison state and government secrecy. (Editorial Cartoon Collection, The State Historical Society of Missouri)

These conflicts over Knauff's treatment within and among the three branches of government were generated, in part, by pressure from outside, especially from liberal newspapers and the American Civil Liberties Union (ACLU). In particular, journalists at the *St. Louis Post-Dispatch* worked hard to bring the case to the attention of Washington decision makers as well as the public, and they played a key role in keeping Knauff in the country. The *Post-Dispatch* was an early critic of what would come to be known as McCarthyism, and its editorial page editor, Irving Dilliard, was an attentive student of the Supreme

Court. Two days after the Court ruled against Knauff, Dilliard penned the first of several dozen editorials endorsing her cause, and within a week, publisher Joseph Pulitzer had agreed to "go to town" on the topic (fig. 3).

Going to town meant actively maneuvering behind the scenes, and at the highest levels. Washington bureau reporter Ed Harris not only talked Representative Roosevelt into speaking out on Knauff's behalf but persuaded the ACLU to draft Roosevelt's bill as well. He also waylaid President Truman after a White House news conference to lobby him on the issue. When, off the record, Truman responded, "Everyone is entitled to a hearing," Harris and another *Post-Dispatch* reporter conveyed these views to the attorney general. When their initial nudge of the president yielded no results, *Post-Dispatch* personnel asked Charlie Ross, Truman's press secretary and their own former editor, to intervene. Harris prepared a memo on the Knauff case for Ross, who passed it on to the president. Two days later Truman asked Spingarn to look into the matter. Furthermore, it was Dilliard who called Justice Jackson at home the night before Knauff was scheduled to be flown back to Germany to alert him to the impending deportation attempt and give him the chance to respond quickly to her lawyer's application for a stay.[43] Other journalists, especially the *New York Post*'s Fern Marja, also dedicated a good deal of time to publicizing Knauff's plight, but *Post-Dispatch* employees offered more than support and publicity, actively politicking to defend civil liberties against the incursions of the national security state.

All of this suggests that the Justice Department's decision to keep the evidence against Knauff secret and to deny her a hearing—justified in the name of national security and the state of emergency—in certain ways worked against them. In fact, the more they cited national security as the reason for secrecy about Knauff, the more critics questioned their competence to determine what constituted national security, particularly as information and misinformation about the government's case leaked out. For example, in September 1950 the *New York Post* published allegations that the government had named a former Czech general now living in the United States as the source of the accusations against Knauff, but when contacted by reporters, he denied ever having heard of her. In fact, this general had nothing to do with the case, but immigration and justice officials appeared paralyzed when journalists denounced the "hollow evidence" that kept Knauff captive. They also, remarkably, never countered Knauff's efforts to explain away the charges against her as resulting from either her naïve friendliness toward a casual acquaintance in the Civil Censorship

Division, or the vicious gossip of a jealous woman (or both). Their adamant silence on the case led Representative Francis E. Walter to encourage Knauff to "repeat gossip" when she testified before his committee, complaining, "We can't get facts—we get over-the-fence, over-the-back-fence gossip, which is the lowest form in the United States."[44] Anything she could tell Congress, even gossip, was preferable to the lack of information forthcoming from INS and Justice Department officials. Their insistence that revealing anything about the charges would jeopardize confidential sources and national security itself simply wasn't convincing, especially because it left Knauff a good deal of room to tell a different story—a domestic story—about her life.

The "Right to Live Together"
Domestic Security Meets National Security

Ellen Knauff's eventual triumph suggested a lack of congruence between national security policy and another foundation of early Cold War culture: marital unity. Strong marriages built on a blend of gender equality (the heterosexual couple whose common interests and mutual respect was signaled by the idea of "togetherness") and gender hierarchy (the husband's responsibility for providing for and protecting his dependents) were an important indicator of the benefits of the "American way of life." A whole range of social institutions dedicated themselves to defending these marriages. Churches and schools, medicine and psychiatry, the workplace, the marketplace, and the media, and an expanding array of federal policies linked morality, health, prosperity, and citizenship ever more firmly to normative heterosexuality.[45]

The threat of the national security state to the integrity of the nuclear family was at the center of the Knauffs' pleas for public support. Eliding the difference between the "privileges" extended to veterans by the War Brides Act and husbands' marital "rights," they framed the effort to keep Ellen out of the country as an attack on Kurt's rights first and foremost. It was Kurt who applied for the original writ of habeas corpus, a gesture that appealed to Justices Frankfurter and Jackson when they heard the case. Both pointed out that Ellen Knauff was not just any non-resident alien. She was the wife of a U.S. citizen; therefore it was Kurt's position as husband-citizen-soldier, rather than Ellen's as alien-in-waiting, that was determinative. Frankfurter asserted the import of attending to Congress's intent, arguing that in passing the War Brides Act, legislators "gave with a bountiful hand" not to the alien but to "the citizen who had honorably served his country" and in the process "acquired" a wife. This "beneficence" should not be disregarded and "the deepest tie that an American soldier could form . . . be secretly severed on the mere say-so of an official." Jackson also denounced the dismissal of Kurt Knauff's marital rights, noting that Ellen's exclusion posed the sort of choice that no citizen should ever be required to make: "Congress will have to use more explicit language than any yet cited before I will agree that it has authorized an administrative officer to break up the family of an American citizen or force him to keep his wife by becoming an exile. . . . He must abandon his bride to live in his own country or forsake his country to live with his bride." Reminders that Kurt had fought for his country and was now being forced to decide between that country and his wife ran rife in coverage of the case. It was because he refused to choose—because "he wanted both"—that the Knauffs found themselves taking on an array of officials in the federal government. The imposition of such a "choice" on Kurt demonstrated in the starkest of terms how a fetishized national security threatened both the tradition of martial citizenship and the domestic institutions on which the nation was founded.[46]

Ellen and Kurt emphasized the dangers to their family as well as to Kurt's citizenship that would ensue from such disregard for veterans' sacrifices. Should Kurt decide to "keep his wife" if Ellen was deported to Germany—and they conveyed little doubt that this would be his decision, for, as Ellen declared, "no administrative or court action can tear apart our marriage"—they would be marooned in a hostile country, "two people who are both of German origin, but who fought against Germany on the side of the Allies." As a naturalized citizen living outside the United States, Kurt would lose his American citizenship. If the prospect of returning permanently to Germany horrified Ellen, who saw herself as the "personal enemy" of the Germans who murdered her family, even more disturbing scenarios had the stateless and unprotected Ellen raped by Communist hordes who might invade West Germany. Alternatively, she might be deported to Czechoslovakia, where she would disappear behind the Iron Curtain.[47] These dire predictions did little to move Justice Department officials, who suspected that Ellen had married Kurt only to gain entry to the United States.[48] But they dramatized this couple's vulnerability before a state that had lost sight of the values it was supposed to guard.

The Ellen Knauff Story, begun by Knauff while she was interned on Ellis Island and published to acclaim in 1952, highlighted this conflict between family and national security. Opening with her approach to New York harbor on the *Comfort,* Knauff positioned her marital relationship with her husband at the very center of her story. His name is the first word in the tale ("Kurt had told me that the first glimpse I would get of the New World would be the parachute tower at Coney Island"), and she quickly explained the reason for her journey: she had recently had a debilitating miscarriage and Kurt decided that sending her to America was the best way to ensure they did not "start a family" too soon. This was a trip, Ellen implied, that was necessary to contain their sexual desire for each other, but she was careful to let her readers know that it was her protective husband who determined that the United States could preserve his wife's health. Theirs was a marriage both modern and traditional.[49]

Alas, the nation-state as guardian of this marriage was not to be. Nevertheless, it was not the United States writ large that was the villain here—the story is one in which, ultimately, American ideals and American institutions prevail—but INS and Justice Department officials, representatives of an out-of-control bureaucracy, who continually interfered with Kurt and Ellen's "right to live together." These misguided individuals made Kurt "feel he had to get rid of his wife to prove his loyalty to America," even urging him to divorce her.[50] Kurt may have sent Ellen to the United States to protect her from the effects of too much sex, but as time went by, he grew increasingly frustrated that the INS, in Ellen's words, "kept us from realizing our plan to settle down and raise a family." Justice Department staff interfered with the couple's coupling, just like the military officials in *I Was a Male War Bride,* or else they tried to use Ellen and Kurt's desire for each other to their own advantage. For example, in 1951 Attorney General McGrath offered to allow Kurt to live with Ellen at Ellis Island or, alternatively, to release her into his custody if she agreed to leave the country. After a few years, he suggested, she could reapply for admission from abroad. Kurt rejected the first option, and Ellen decided to stay at Ellis Island and continue the fight. Charging "first his subordinates prevent us from leading a normal life together, then we are offered the keys to the bedroom [just to] help the Justice Department to get rid of a hot potato," she sacrificed the possibility of satisfying her "thirst for this reunion" with her husband in order to display her commitment to democratic procedure and American justice. "If my husband were a citizen of Hell," Ellen wrote, "I would still consider it my duty to follow him there." But her higher duty was to fight arbitrary authority.[51] McGrath capitulated, temporarily releasing her into Kurt's custody.

Government officials' obsession with national security not only disrupted her marriage, it also aligned them with the familiar figure whom Ellen blamed for her troubles: the jealous woman. This was a rationale for the charges against her that Ellen had offered very early on, and it was fully elaborated in her memoir. As she recalled, Kurt had casually dated one "Eve," "a popular girl with the Army of Occupation" who "worked little and played hard." To readers of the time, Eve was immediately identifiable as a manipulative "fraülein." Eve viewed Kurt as her ticket to America until Ellen arrived on the scene, and, Knauff wrote, she angrily "promised . . . she would spoil my entry into the United States." Portraying her as a mean-spirited gossip, Knauff speculated that Eve had miscast her visits to the Czech mission (necessary to renew her passport) as evidence that she was a Czech spy, and had passed this information to another "favorite boy friend," an army intelligence officer and "self-styled FBI agent." The idea of a sexually out-of-control other woman who meant to destroy her marriage sustained the notion of Ellen's sexual and political innocence, and she was careful to distinguish her own sexuality, safely contained within conjugality, from that of the loose women like Eve who congregated at the base. As one sympathetic congressman responded when she told her story, "You know the expression that 'Hell hath no fury like a woman scorned,'" and of course *everyone* knew it. It was only Justice Department officials' gullibility, and their collusion with the other woman, their willingness to indulge in "over-the-back-fence gossip," that remained inexplicable.[52]

That Ellen Knauff was a Jew mattered to the chronicle in *The Ellen Knauff Story* as well as to others' versions of her story. It was a central theme in the press coverage of Knauff's case, which emphasized her vulnerability as a solitary individual confronted by the power of the state. The fate of her family at the hands of the Nazis was used to communicate her intense and continuing isolation as a "lone woman," weak and defenseless against the federal bureaucracy, which itself was identified with fascist Germany. For example, journalists described Justice Department officials as displaying "police state psychology" and using a "Fascist-like procedure" to persecute Knauff once more. Justice Jackson labeled "the story of her treatment here . . . sadly reminiscent of the Nazi world she had escaped," and columnist Max Lerner portrayed her as an anguished woman "who has somehow escaped the crematoria of the Nazis" only to meet the "familiar face" of "injustice" again in America.[53]

Knauff echoed these themes in her book, for example, in relating her first encounter with immigration officials at Ellis Island. Pulled from line by an inspector with a violent temper who would not tell her why she had been singled out, she offered him her documents. His shouted reply stunned her:

> "I am not interested. You know what's wrong with you. I am sending you to a place where they will look after you."
>
> How it happened I do not know, and perhaps it shouldn't have happened, but something exploded inside me. My mother and father were put to death in the extermination camp at Riga. . . . "We are sending you to a place where they will look after you." That's what the Jews were told when they were herded into open freight cars on the first lap of their journey to doom.
>
> I broke down for the first time in my life.

Her description of Ellis Island as a "concentration camp with steam heat and running water" reinforced the view of Ellen as a Jew experiencing anew the horrors of the war, but this time at the hands of agents of the U.S. government.[54]

Ellen's portrayals as lone, helpless woman and as loving wife and helpmate may seem to be in tension, but together they provided a deeply reassuring narrative. Having lost one family to the Nazis, she had found another. As she reflected when she first approached New York harbor:

> I felt suddenly chilled: I was alone, and here I was for the third time in my life seeking refuge in a new strange country.
>
> I tried to pull myself together. . . . Had I not repeated at my wedding ceremony Ruth's vow: "For whither thou goest, I will go; and where thou lodgest, I will lodge: Thy people shall be my people." I, too, was coming home. Kurt's country had become my own by virtue of this simple tradition established more than two thousand years ago.[55]

Ellen's marriage to Kurt made the American people her family; by joining him, she joined them, and was saved from life as a refugee. When, together, she and her husband triumphed over the narrow-minded officials who had let an "obsession with the negative side of security" derail their respect for the institution of marriage, they demonstrated all that was superior about the American system of justice. Their "long private war of hope against hope," Ellen concluded, was won because "the people of America despise tyrants, be they of the great or the petty variety, and they are fortunate to have inherited a system of protection which makes every little man master in his house and in his country."[56] The Ellen Knauff story was not just the story of two people in love; it was a comforting national family romance, as well as a cautionary tale about the dangers of forgetting the values that made American citizenship meaningful in the postwar world.

Thus, Knauff's entry was accomplished via the logic, if not the law, of derivative citizenship. Her relationship to the United States was premised on her relationship to her husband, and this enabled her to mobilize enough support to keep her cause alive even when the highest court in the land affirmed her exclusion. As a war bride, she was able to figure her loyalty to nation through her loyalty to her husband and refute the government's stance that she was incapable of loyalty. Knauff's story fit squarely within a gendered framework of citizenship that had old roots but was being retrofitted for the modern era. Claiming immigration and naturalization rights as her husband's wife was congruent with a broader reconfiguration of federal entitlements around men's family roles during the war and the postwar years, including benefits under the GI Bill facilitating men's ability to provide for their families as well as tax codes that rewarded husbands' economic dominance.[57] Domesticated through her relationship with Kurt, Ellen Knauff appeared to be precisely the sort of person who was desired as a citizen in the Cold War era.[58]

The connection between marriage and nationality that worked so well for Knauff both fit and furthered the strengthening of family reunification as a keystone of twentieth-century immigration policy. With its origins in the regulation of immigration from Asia in the late nineteenth and early twentieth centuries, the family reunification principle was embedded ever more firmly in a succession of immigration reforms, beginning with the National Origins Act of 1924 and continuing through the 1952 McCarran-Walter Act and the 1965 Hart-Celler Act. Reproducing the nation through those whom it already contained, family reunification palliated an exclusionary ethos, welcoming certain families while discouraging others.[59] During these same years, for example, about 200,000 Mexican men were admitted to the United States annually as guest workers under the bracero program; this temporary status was their only means of access, since U.S. borders were technically open to Mexican families, but almost all of these were excluded by means of the "likely to become a public charge" exception. At the same time, family reunification could make possible the entry of immigrants still deemed undesirable, as Mae Ngai has shown in her analysis of Chinese "paper sons," who circumvented exclusionary policies through invented claims to derivative citizenship.[60] An immigration system focused on the family was thus a double-edged sword for those who sought to guard the borders of the nation, and Ellen Knauff used this to her advantage.

Family reunification was not such a bedrock principle that it dictated legal outcomes, but it was compelling enough to help the Knauffs prevail.

Not all immigrants caught up by the national security system were able to turn family reunification arguments to their benefit. Gender mattered to the persuasiveness of such arguments, for some alien husbands had a harder time working family ties to gain entry to the United States. While on Ellis Island, for example, Ellen became acquainted with Frederick and Wilma Brauer. Fred, an immigrant from Germany who had been forced, he claimed, to join the German army before going on to serve with distinction in the U.S. military during the war, was excluded from the United States as an enemy alien. His American-born wife refused to abandon him; the couple lived at Ellis Island, together with their two children who were born there, until Fred was deported and the whole family accompanied him back to Germany. Similarly, the case of Ignatz Mezei suggests the greater difficulty sometimes faced by alien men. Mezei was an eastern European immigrant who arrived in the United States in 1923. He married a U.S. citizen and lived in Buffalo until 1948, when he attempted to travel to Romania to visit his dying mother. Prevented by Romanian authorities from entering the country, he remained overseas for more than a year; on his return to the United States, he was excluded on the grounds that he was a member of the Communist Party, a charge he denied. Since no other country would offer him safe harbor, Mezei was condemned to live out his life in limbo on Ellis Island. The Supreme Court, citing its ruling in the Knauff case, affirmed his exclusion. While some of Knauff's defenders also spoke out on Mezei's behalf, he had fewer advocates, and though his case, too, ultimately was heard by the Board of Immigration Appeals, he ended up "paroled" but not "admitted" to the United States, subject for the remainder of his days to possible removal at any moment. The family that deserved reunification under INS policy was headed by a husband, but the loyalty of men to their country of origin may have been perceived as harder to disrupt, weakening their claims of ties to their chosen country.[61]

But whatever the image of the Cold War–era American family, it was not the patriarchal family of common law, and the family reunification policy was not the derivative citizenship of yore. Ellen was a devoted and desiring wife, but she was neither submissive nor quiescent. She was "pert" and "plucky," a fighter on her own behalf, and this too was key to her appeal.[62] Even as Knauff herself situated her struggle within a domestic frame, she and her supporters also embraced individual rights arguments. But because the Supreme Court had ruled in her case that excluded aliens had no enforceable due process rights, and that the War Brides Act extended only a privilege, not a right, to her husband, any rights-based arguments she could offer had no grounding in the Constitution or in understandings of liberal citizenship established by a nation-state. Rather, appeals to "rights" on Knauff's behalf had to lean heavily on an emerging discourse of human rights.

"Decency Should Be Universal"
Toward a Rhetoric of Human Rights

Claims on the basis of "human rights" were not new, but this language became widespread during the 1940s, as it came to signify commitment to a variety of political, civil, and economic rights that inhered in individuals regardless of their membership in any particular nation-state. Inscribed as the foundation of a new international order in such documents as the 1941 Atlantic Charter and, the next year, the Allies' Declaration by United Nations, the human rights talk of the war years was explicitly linked to wartime aims, intended to signal "the so-called fundamental freedoms that differentiated the Allies from their totalitarian rivals." So, too, in postwar America, the embrace of human rights conveyed not just a belief in the "rights of man" or the creation of multilateral institutions to guard those rights, but also something about the character of the United States and its distinction from fascist and Communist states.[63]

Knauff's statelessness rendered human rights rhetoric particularly appropriate for her defense, but such rhetoric also had a commonsense meaning that made it useful in generating popular support. Claims on her behalf based in universal human rights neatly circumvented both the lack of a state to guard her interests and the acceptance, even among some of her fiercest defenders, that aliens "on the threshold" were positioned differently than resident aliens. Noting the "wisdom of the framers of the Constitution in providing that no person shall be deprived of life, liberty or property without due process of law," her supporters might acknowledge that she was not *legally* entitled to a hearing but still contend that denial of the right to defend herself violated the spirit of America.[64] In their comment on the Supreme Court ruling denying Knauff entry, for example, the editors of the *New York Times* opined that "this country stands for some important fundamental human rights, for its own citizens as for all peoples," and that "one of these is the right of every human being to have a chance to defend himself." They linked Justice Jackson's wisdom on this question to his service as chief prosecutor at Nuremberg. This view of the Knauff case as raising a "fundamental issue of human rights" was echoed by her allies among the press, Congress, and interested citizens. As the civil libertarian Arthur Garfield Hays asserted in his introduction to her book: "The principles of decent conduct . . . should be applicable to all human beings. Decency should be universal."[65]

Many commentators translated the denial of Knauff's "ancient" rights as a human being into the folksier idiom of "fairness." The ubiquity of this language might owe something to President Truman's advocacy of a "Fair Deal" for American citizens, by which he meant expanded economic opportunity and security, and some critics explicitly contrasted Truman's Fair Deal policy with his administration's treatment of the war bride. But more generally, fairness conveyed a sense of following established rules and providing equitable, unbiased treatment to all. Even as it was invoked to defend the "rights of every free man" regardless of membership in the nation-state, this vocabulary was also used to summon a particular view of "America." Keeping Knauff in the dark about the charges against her, according to one advocate, was "contrary to our spirit of fair play." As members of the ACLU wrote to senators, even though the Supreme Court had found—against the arguments of the group's amicus brief—that Knauff was not entitled to a hearing, she should nevertheless be granted one "in the name of elementary fairness." Invoking fairness, then, was simultaneously a way to evade the lack of constitutional protection while upholding a vision of a morally superior America. It also represented a popular rejection of the notion that citizens and aliens—including resident aliens and those "on the threshold"—ought to be treated differently, especially when the alien in question seemed more friend than stranger.[66]

Knauff's defenders cautioned that the handling of her case could have international repercussions, for resolving the "conflict between security and human rights" in favor of security threatened to collapse the distinction between democracy and totalitarianism that was so important to U.S. leadership in the postwar world. Echoing Justice Jackson's warnings that denying Knauff a hearing endangered America more than her presence possibly could, columnist Marquis Childs warned, "If in the pursuit of security we are to make ourselves over in the pattern of the totalitarians, then there will be little left to secure." Similarly, Irving Dilliard told *Post-Dispatch* readers that in refusing to reveal to Knauff the charges against her, "thus does our own Government wound the United States before the eyes of the world. It is a wound that no enemy could inflict. It is a hurt to democracy that no communist plot could impose." Many, including Knauff herself, fretted that European Communists were publicizing the case to make the United States look bad.[67]

Conversely, every moment when she seemed to triumph—for instance, when she was accorded a hearing by the House of Representatives, saved from deportation at the last minute, or finally admitted into the United States—revealed the U.S. Cold War position as the correct one. As the *New York Post* declared after Knauff had testified before the House immigration subcommittee: "In the 'new democracies' of Stalin's empire, Ellen Knauff would have been shot or imprisoned long ago and anyone who cried out in protest would have shared her fate. . . . The case of Ellen Knauff . . . embodies the heart of the difference between the slave states and the imperfect democracies. As we have said on other occasions, vive la difference." The ACLU similarly argued that passage of a private bill to admit Knauff "would be eloquent testimony that American democracy[,] unlike totalitarianism, respects the rights of all individuals. It would strengthen democratic anticommunist forces in the world-wide struggle for freedom." As one letter to the editor of the *Post-Dispatch* proclaimed, the very fact that the "abuse" of Knauff was "coming to light" demonstrated "the difference between 'Us' and 'Them.' . . . This is a great case for our system," the writer concluded. "Let's make the most of it."[68]

In fact, the Knauff case presented an opportunity for critics of the emerging national security state to try to rein it in. By emphasizing Ellen's status as a war bride—not merely a wife, but a reward for a citizen-soldier who had risked his life for democracy—and Kurt's compulsory "choice" between his adopted country and his wife, they dramatized the ways in which a single-minded concern with security endangered both the family and the nation. Over time, this morphed into an affirmation that Ellen Knauff stood for the individual whose rights were at the base of American democracy but also transcended the nation-state. The stateless Knauff came to represent the soul of American citizenship, for she appreciated and portended the promise of democracy to her compatriots both within and outside the nation. Those journalists who had taken up her fight most exuberantly summed up her role in regenerating the United States at a moment of crisis. "Once more," they opined in the *New York Post*, "this nation has been humbled—and exalted—by a stranger who had more faith in democracy than do many Americans." And Irving Dilliard chimed in: "This newcomer from Germany has earned her admission to citizenship many times over. *Would that 150,000,000 Americans might study, appreciate and apply the lesson of her amazing experience.*"[69]

Dilliard, along with some other journalists, was mistaken: Knauff was admitted to the United States but not to citizenship (fig. 4). She immediately applied for naturalization, under a provision that waived the two-year residency requirement for the spouses of federal workers living outside the United States. Ellen imagined that she and Kurt would be reunited in a few months. She passed her citizenship test in December 1951 (although she conflated the Atlantic Charter's Four Freedoms—somewhat more relevant to her own experience—with the freedom of religion, speech, press, and assembly when asked to recite the U.S. Constitution's guarantees of liberty). But the Justice Department opposed her application, and the process dragged on for years. In 1953 Knauff walked out on a citizenship hearing at which INS officials again raised accusations that she had spied for Czechoslovakia, this time adding allegations that she had once been spotted visiting the Czech Communist Party headquarters. The following year, justice officials investigated the possibility of prosecuting her for espionage or, failing that, perjury; but they got sidetracked when Puerto Rican nationalists attacked Congress, and their attention shifted to what seemed a more pressing assault on the nation's security. By 1956 the Knauffs had divorced, and Ellen soon married author William B. Hartley. The two lived in Miami, where they made a career co-writing books and magazine stories. In 1963, fifteen years after her first application for admission, Ellen Hartley finally was allowed to become a U.S. citizen. She and her third husband both died in 1980.[70]

It took immigration officials a long time to change their view that Ellen Raphael Boxhornova Knauff Hartley was "not the sort of person we want in this country." But "the sort of person" she was—and the sort of citizen she might become—was a matter of disagreement. Justice Department officials viewed Knauff as a woman without loyalties, ready to sell herself to the highest bidder. Privately they investigated her relationship with Kurt and shared their outrage that she had defied the government of the United States. In keeping with the long-held stereotype of women immigrants as tricksters, and perhaps suspicions about Jewish subversives, they perceived Knauff as someone whose past willingness to trade secrets for a passport cast doubt on her fitness to be a citizen.[71] Her lack of physical, emotional, or political attachment to *any* nation-state signaled her inability to belong to the United States.

But for many others, Ellen Knauff epitomized both the specifically embodied rights of husbands and wives to live together *and* the universal right of humans to be free from arbitrary government authority. She adeptly manipulated

Figure 4. "Pretty Mrs. Ellen Knauff" celebrates after leaving Ellis Island for the last time, "now free to become an American citizen." (Bettman/CORBIS)

expectations about the protections granted by U.S. citizenship to claim them for herself, even at a moment when the Cold War state of exception might have been expected to defeat those claims. Pushing U.S. officials to accord her the guarantees of liberal citizenship on the basis of human rights, she made visible the inclusive exclusion on which the national security state rested. If such a person as Ellen Knauff could be excluded from American freedom, then perhaps the legitimacy of the entire enterprise might be called into question.

Knauff, suspected of being willing to deal with Communists for her own selfish purposes, always claimed to hate Communism, but she believed that her experience offered a broader lesson for the developing national security state. In 1950 she confided to Irving Dilliard her hope that her "case will help to bring about a law in this country which permits every accused the right to face his accuser regardless of whether the accused is an alien asking for admission to this country, or Hazel Scott or Jean Muir." Both women—one black, one white—had just lost television contracts because of allegations they were Communists. Praising the decision to admit her to the United States, *New Republic* editor Jean Begeman would echo Knauff's words, noting that she "has helped secure the rights of all Americans, threatened by evidence based on rumor and hearsay."[72]

Of course, defending individual rights in the burgeoning national security state was a tall order even for Ellen Knauff, and the heyday of government by "rumor and hearsay" was still to come when she was admitted to the United States. Furthermore, legislative efforts to guarantee excluded aliens a right to a hearing failed, and the ruling in *Knauff v. Shaughnessy* remains the law of the land, even in the twenty-first century. But as the *Washington Post* observed, the case of the war bride drew attention to the extensive powers reserved to "the sovereign [during] the national emergency," causing many to deplore such "un-American practice[s]" as "abrupt and brutal." When J. Edgar Hoover, that supreme advocate of exceptional governmental capacities in the name of security, read this editorial, he responded that the "*Post* crowd" embraced a "queer philosophy," and perhaps, in the context of the state of exception that sacrificed liberty to security, they did. But it was a queerness domesticated by the story of the adoring war bride and her devoted husband, and as such, it moved a nation.[73]

Ellen Knauff became a symbol of the dangers posed by the national security state to American principles in part because she seemed so vulnerable, a "little woman" alone in a strange country and battered by powers she did not understand. Much of this portrait also characterized Pentagon employee Annie Lee Moss, also alone—a widow—and similarly threatened by the power wielded by Senator Joe McCarthy in his anti-Communist campaign. As we will see in the next chapter, Moss's plight, too, moved a nation to reconsider the contradictions of the Cold War state of exception.

CHAPTER THREE.

The Right to Earn a Living

Loyalty, Race, and Economic Citizenship

"I MAY BE STICKING MY NECK OUT AND I MAY BE WRONG. BUT I HAVE BEEN listening to you testify this afternoon, and I think you are telling the truth. . . . If you are not taken back into the Army . . . you come around and see me, and I am going to see that you get a job." The raucous applause greeting Missouri senator Stuart Symington's comments capped Mrs. Annie Lee Moss's testimony before Joe McCarthy's Permanent Subcommittee on Investigations (PSI). McCarthy and his chief aide, Roy Cohn, contended that Moss had been permitted to work in the U.S. Army Signal Corps code room even after loyalty hearings offered evidence that she was a member of the Communist Party. Seeking to make Moss another weapon in his campaign against the army, McCarthy pointed to her mysterious journey from "waitress to a code clerk" as one more demonstration of the government's criminal laxity over security matters.[1] Yet his efforts to portray Annie Lee Moss as a danger to national security backfired. When the eminent journalist Edward R. Murrow broadcast this hearing to millions of Americans, he helped to cement McCarthy's reputation as a bully and contributed to the senator's political demise. As indicated by the endless repetition, in media accounts and citizens' letters, of Symington's closing remarks, McCarthy's attack on the efforts of a middle-aged African American woman to make a decent living upset the presumptions underlying the domestic Cold War: that surveillance and repression were necessary to guarantee the prosperity, equality, and freedom of all Americans.

If Symington's comments were constantly invoked by contemporaries, McCarthy's encounter with Moss has been recounted again and again by historians and scholars as proof either of his evil and incompetence or of the rightness of his cause.[2] For many years, McCarthy's critics explained the episode as one of mistaken identity, citing Moss's claim that there were "three Annie Lee Mosses" living in Washington, while his defenders pointed to an FBI informant's testimony to substantiate his claims. But the question of whether the senator was right about Moss is misguided on several counts. First, it presumes that there is a simple answer regarding the matter of her political beliefs and affiliations—either she was a Communist or she was not—when the reality seems to be much more messy. Second, it ignores the question of how McCarthy's attack on Moss, while expressing the broader logic of the national security state, also exposed its workings. Finally, it neglects the far more interesting issue of why Moss's case was so compelling at the time. The causes of McCarthy's downfall were diverse, owing much to partisan politics, his own miscalculations about the risks of taking on the military, and the emerging role of television in national life. But it is no accident that one of the shoals on which he ran aground was a poor black woman whose upward mobility came to represent the nation's progress toward economic fairness and equal opportunity. Indeed, because Moss was such a potent symbol of what Gunnar Myrdal had so recently designated the "American Creed," President Eisenhower himself directed that she be restored to her government job.[3]

Examining the careers of Annie Lee Moss as a resident of the nation's capital, as a government worker, and as a public figure in the debates about McCarthyism illuminates the ways in which the Cold War opened up questions about race, gender, and economic citizenship. Anti-Communism had complicated and contradictory impacts on the postwar civil rights movement. U.S. officials, concerned about the nation's ability to compete with the Soviet Union for the allegiance of emerging independent nations in Africa and Asia, realized the necessity of presenting a convincing narrative of racial progress in order to defend their claims to world leadership in the face of unrelenting Soviet criticism of American racism. These foreign affairs coincided with a sea change already under way in American thinking about race, fueling the ascendancy of a politics of racial liberalism that identified white racism as the central challenge to American democracy, promoted integration as a solution, and invested government with responsibility for solving the nation's racial problems, primarily through the guarantee of "equal opportunity." This ideology, promulgated most famously in Myrdal's book *An American Dilemma,* was increasingly influential in national politics, even as it was sometimes bitterly contested at the local level.[4]

The perception of racial reform as a "Cold War imperative" reflected not just recognition of the enduring racial contradictions on which American democracy was founded (and foundering) but also a rising sense that these contradictions could not be sustained. This sentiment was detectable in the increase of black membership in the Communist Party, in the fivefold growth of the NAACP during the war years, and in the beginnings of a multiracial antiracist movement on the left. Nonetheless, because change in the racial order was both so threatening to many white Americans and so crucial to international legitimacy, the emerging national paradigm for racial reform privileged moderate goals and strategies that could be reconciled with the familiar modes of white paternalism and civility. Ironically, then, the internationalization of American race relations encouraged African American leaders to forswear the capacious language of "human rights" and an anticolonialist politics and embrace the more constrained rhetoric of civil rights, anticommunist politics, and incremental change.[5] As part of this shift, civil rights activists and their supporters intensified their emphasis on economic citizenship—the ability of African Americans to participate in the nation's growing prosperity, to access jobs and consumer goods—over radical transformation of economic and political structures.[6]

Washington, D.C., had a particularly significant role to play in the story of Cold War civil rights. Many have noted that as the nation's capital, it was a "portal into the practice of American democracy," but as its growing black population was shoehorned into an obdurately Jim Crow city, this portal offered a dismal view. A racially segregated Washington, President Truman's Committee on Civil Rights acknowledged, was "a graphic illustration of a failure of democracy." Grassroots activists were more acerbic, noting that the "eyes of the whole world" saw the city as "the capital of white supremacy." Surveys of postwar racial relations in the district lambasted segregation in education and housing, parks, restaurants and theaters, hotels, and hospitals. There were no laws mandating racial separation, but custom, poverty, and municipal and federal policy limited African Americans' access to jobs, health care, and schooling. As a result, one scathing study reported, black Washingtonians lived in homes that were about ten times as likely as those of whites to lack running water, central heat, or electricity; their infant mortality rates were twice those of local whites, while their maternal mortality rates were six times as high. And since residents had few tools to shape their destiny, lacking both home rule and national representation, it was up to the federal government to enact change. The National Committee on Segregation in the Nation's Capital, invoking the long shadow of slavery, declared: "At this moment the Federal government is holding more citizens in bondage than any single person or agency in the country. It is responsible because it, and it alone, has the power to break the chains that bar a quarter of a million Negroes in Washington from their equal rights as Americans."[7]

In this context, Annie Lee Moss's struggle to keep her job with the federal government drew the attention of a nation. Moss fought back against McCarthy's allegations that she was a CP member not by taking the Fifth Amendment, nor by admitting herself a former Communist or fellow traveler who had seen the light, nor even by defending her political activities as the efforts of a loyal citizen to participate in democracy, but by pretending to be someone she was not. In a way, then, this *was* a mistaken identity story. The Annie Lee Moss whose testimony before the PSI was broadcast to millions of Americans on Edward R. Murrow's *See It Now* television program was helpless, ignorant, bordering on illiterate. The Annie Lee Moss who lived in Washington and worked at the Pentagon was engaged, effective, and smart. The difference between these two Annie Lee Mosses expressed the gap between the ways in which the Cold War intensified racialized interpretations of national loyalty and the ways in which an upwardly mobile black woman enacted her rights and responsibilities as a citizen. Moss perceived that her record of activism in the black community, which brought her into proximity with members of the CP, might well rob her of the government job and middle-class status for which she had worked so hard. But she also sensed that Cold War politics required confirmation that America's black citizens had the same right to economic opportunity as white citizens. Certainly McCarthy's enemies, including Symington and Murrow, comprehended the advantages that would accrue to them, and the damage that would be done to him, if they proved themselves chivalrous defenders of Moss's right to participate in the American dream. And, indeed, their defense of her right to earn a living brought them accolades from across the nation.

Annie Lee Moss may have become a household name when she appeared before the McCarthy committee, but she was there only because she was already a subject of state surveillance by the federal government's loyalty-security program. The loyalty-security program is the point at which the domestic

Cold War touched Americans' economic rights most directly. Loyalty-security proceedings often lacked the high profile of congressional investigations, but they arguably had a deeper impact: millions of federal workers screened, along with state and local workers, federal contractors, and corporate employees; tens of thousands fired, pressured to resign, or intimidated into looking elsewhere for employment. The loyalty-security program offered grist for the mill of "naming names," enabled the FBI's intense and ongoing surveillance of many hardworking Americans, and facilitated the destruction of public worker unions. It chilled political dissent and intellectual freedom in the name of national security, shaping the federal bureaucracy in innumerable ways.[8]

Annie Lee Moss's tangles with the loyalty-security program offer a window into the threats posed by the Cold War–era state of exception to the individual rights and economic opportunity that were supposedly at the heart of the American way of life. Her experience reveals that the conflict between the obligation of loyalty and the "right" to opportunity was particularly troubled and troubling for African American citizens, whose continued inequality brought into question U.S. claims to leadership of the free world. Even after her clash with McCarthy, Moss remained under suspicion as FBI agents pored over every possible piece of evidence against her, the army suspended her yet again, and loyalty officials spent days in hearings and months considering her case. She may well have been a symbol of McCarthy's excesses, but her case also raised questions about the legitimacy of the national security state, the future of American race relations, and the role of the federal government in guaranteeing equal opportunity. As the "toast of the nation's capital," she drew Americans' attention to racial inequality even as she helped federal officials reassure the nation that equal opportunity was indeed possible in Cold War America.

"Who Is Annie Lee Moss?"

Before she was summoned by the McCarthy committee, Moss seemed to embody the promise of postwar America for the nation's black citizens. Her beginnings were humble. Born Annie Lee Crawford in 1905 in South Carolina, she was one of six children of tenant-farmer parents.[9] She began working in the cotton fields at age five while also pursuing an education that she later described as "scattered." Remarkably, though, Annie Lee stayed in school through the eleventh grade—quite an achievement for black women of her generation, who on average had less than seven years of schooling.[10] Nonetheless, after the family moved to North Carolina, she left school to follow a path familiar to Southern black women, working as a domestic servant and a laundress. Annie Lee married at age twenty-one, and she and husband, Ernest Moss, settled in Durham, where both found work in the racially segregated tobacco industry. Through the Great Depression years, she labored at the very dirty job of operating a stemming machine, for weekly wages of $18.[11] Times were hard for the Mosses, who, with their young son, moved five times between 1936 and 1941. Another child died in infancy.

The coming of war offered the family new opportunities, and they trekked northward to join Ernest's brother in Washington, D.C. Although Ernest got a construction job, helping to build the nation's defense capacities, Annie Lee's choices remained limited. She worked for a time in a commercial laundry, and then spent two years as a dessert cook in government cafeterias. But the war years offered the first real opportunity for African American women to enter both federal employment and white-collar work; during the 1940s, "government worker" became the second-largest occupational category for black women in Washington, after domestic service.[12] Early in 1945 Moss joined these ranks, obtaining a temporary appointment as a clerk in the General Accounting Office (GAO). The higher wages she received were especially important when her husband died in 1947 and Moss became the primary breadwinner for her family, including a brother who was a disabled veteran. Moss passed a civil service test, and although she was laid off in 1949, within a year she was able to secure a permanent position, this time as a machine operator in the Signal Corps. By 1954 she was making more than $3,300 a year, over twice the national median income for full-time black women workers. Annie Lee Moss, it seemed, was living proof of the possibility of achieving the American dream.[13]

Still, since Washington remained segregated and racially conservative, this was a dream accomplished only through struggle. The Mosses were part of an ever-accelerating stream of African American migrants to the city: during the 1940s, the black population increased by 50 percent, and those migrants found inadequate housing, public accommodations, and job opportunities. The Mosses' first residence was in one of the city's alley dwellings, infamous for a lack of sanitation and basic services, and they spent years in Washington's poorest neighborhoods. Furthermore, even though Moss was among the first black women to benefit from federal employment, she remained mired, like other African Americans, in the lowest of civil service classifications. But Moss proved herself more than equal to these trials. She managed to get her family into public housing, segregated but nonetheless a vast improvement over their previous accommodations. She took night and correspondence classes in arithmetic, English, typing, and shorthand. She obtained her real estate license and picked up some work as a realtor. And the coveted federal job promised an ever better life. Shortly before she was called before the McCarthy committee, Moss had moved out of the projects and bought a substantial home in the Brookland neighborhood, a stable middle-class area that welcomed Washington's African American elite.[14]

All of this was endangered in the spring of 1954 when Annie Lee Moss was summoned to appear before the PSI, but concerns over whether she was a good security risk had surfaced long before.[15] Moss was working for the GAO when President Truman issued an executive order mandating loyalty investigations for all federal workers. An FBI background check revealed that she had been named as a member of the Communist Party in 1944. The evidence against her consisted of about a dozen pieces of paper obtained from a CP informant and party files. The documents containing her name included a March 1943 list of CP recruits, which gave her age and race, occupation, and union affiliation, and noted that her initiation fee was paid to "Sadie." She was also identified as a member of several branches of the D.C. Communist Party and the Communist Political Association, and was recorded as having paid dues on a number of occasions, subscribing to the *Daily Worker*, and receiving CP membership books, numbers 37269 and 53395, in 1943 and 1944. Although occasionally the name was rendered differently (for example, "Anna" instead of "Annie"), the records showed three addresses for Moss, at all of which she had lived while employed in government cafeterias.[16]

This evidence triggered numerous investigations of Moss's loyalty. The standards and practices of federal loyalty-security programs were diverse and changing, with the result that an employee might have to defend herself many times. President Truman launched the first postwar program in 1947, establishing that an employee could be dismissed if "on all the evidence, reasonable grounds exist for belief that the person involved is disloyal to the Government of the United States." In 1951 he amended the standard to provide for dismissal on the less stringent grounds of "reasonable doubt as to . . . loyalty," permitting officials to reopen cases in which individuals had retained their jobs. A 1950 law accorded several federal agencies, including the departments of State, Justice, and Commerce, the power to summarily suspend any employee in the interests of national security, a system under which the military had already been operating.

This attention to security was extended to all federal employees by President Eisenhower's 1953 executive order, which made it possible to dismiss workers on the basis of "any criminal, infamous, dishonest, immoral, or notoriously disgraceful conduct, habitual use of intoxicants to excess, drug addiction, or sexual perversion," or any other situation that might conceivably influence them to act "contrary to the best interests of the national security."[17] Civilian employees were granted the right to a hearing and review before dismissal, but provisions stipulating that confidential informants need not be identified, as well as the lack of a right to cross-examine witnesses, often made it impossible for them to defend themselves.

Some of the evidence against Moss seems to have been secured by FBI break-ins, but a great deal of it came from a paid FBI informant, Mary Stalcup Markward. In 1943 Mary Stalcup was a soon-to-be-married hairdresser in suburban Virginia, a bright and attractive but otherwise undistinguished young white woman. Her life changed dramatically when an FBI agent approached her, seemingly out of the blue, and asked her to join the Communist Party as an informant. Markward loved her country and she had time on her hands—her fiancé was away at basic training—so she agreed. She was an exceptionally successful secret agent. She threw herself into party work and rapidly rose in the ranks, holding positions as membership director and treasurer; for a time she earned a small salary from the CP while simultaneously being paid by the FBI. From 1943 to 1949 she reported regularly, often daily, to the FBI, providing copies of party documents, membership lists, and detailed accounts of meetings and activities. In 1949 serious illness forced Markward to withdraw from CP activities, but her erstwhile comrades were already harboring suspicions about her loyalty to the cause, and in February 1951 she was denounced in the *Daily Worker* as a "stool pigeon." Just a week later she began talking, with the FBI's consent, to investigators from the House Committee on Un-American Activities (HUAC). Soon she was the star witness at a series of congressional investigations of Communist activities in Maryland and the District of Columbia.[18]

Attentive to detail and a hard worker, Markward took her job as an FBI informant seriously, sacrificing her own career and her social relationships to become, on the surface, a full-time crusader for the Communist cause. Her ability to lead the double life was really quite remarkable. Even as she was winning prizes for her successful recruiting efforts, she was secretly burning the Communist publications she could not bring herself to sell in her Sunday afternoon canvassing; even as she built what seemed to be intimate friendships with her party colleagues, she later told her daughter that she never met a Communist she didn't hate.[19] As a witness, Markward was poised, articulate, and relatively careful in her assessments. Unlike some "professional witnesses," she usually sought to distinguish between front organizations and the party itself. Nonetheless, there are reasons to be dubious about her testimony. Because she did not keep copies of the records and reports she sent the FBI from 1943 to 1949, she had to rely on her memory in many of her congressional appearances in the 1950s. At times she may have been coached by FBI agents or congressional investigators to "refresh" her memory, and this assistance could have resulted in misleading or oversimplified testimony. And of course as a woman deeply committed to the anti-Communist crusade, she was hardly unbiased. Markward named hundreds of individuals as Communists, names that were printed in local newspapers, and in the process she ruined reputations and careers. Yet in her encounter with Annie Lee Moss, it was Markward whose reputation suffered.[20]

The evidence provided by Markward placed Moss in the crosshairs of the national security state. When she first submitted records containing Moss's name, FBI agents conducted a pretext interview with Moss in her home, investigated her husband, and questioned her postal carrier. They were unable to document her active involvement in the CP and apparently dropped the investigation, but when Markward continued to submit records containing Moss's name, they reopened her file, preparing a "security index" card that denoted her Communist affiliation. When Truman's loyalty program was launched, the FBI conducted a full field investigation, interviewing Moss's employers, her neighbors and associates, and her Washington landlords. This evidence was forwarded to the GAO Loyalty Board in 1948, but Moss was cleared by the board after testifying at a hearing. Markward, then a confidential informant, was not available as a witness. In 1951, after the Truman administration changed the standards for judging loyalty from reasonable grounds to reasonable doubt, Moss was suspended as a security risk, but after another hearing she was reinstated with back pay. At that time J. Edgar Hoover notified army officials that Markward was available to testify about Moss's Communist ties, but they declined to reopen the case. Nonetheless, someone, whether in the army or in the FBI, must have thought her continued employment was a problem, for HUAC received a tip about her early in 1952, but did not pursue it. By November 1953 McCarthy staffers were seeking confirmation of Moss's Communist affiliations from the FBI, and early in 1954 both HUAC and the McCarthy committee questioned

Markward about her. Markward, as it turned out, was never able to identify Moss personally, acknowledging that she knew her only as a name in her records, and other witnesses who had told investigators that they knew Moss as a Communist ultimately retracted those assertions, saying only that they "seemed to remember" her name being mentioned. HUAC again determined that there was no reason to pursue the allegations. McCarthy, however, elected to hold public hearings.[21]

McCarthy's decision threatened to bring into public view a decade of surveillance that had largely remained secret. In early February the army got wind of his interest and transferred Moss to a less sensitive position as a supply clerk, but this effort at damage control did not succeed. On February 23 Markward appeared before the PSI and stated that she had absolutely no doubt that Annie Lee Moss, formerly a Pentagon cafeteria worker, was a "full-fledged" member of the Communist Party. Although Moss responded to a subpoena, she was too ill to testify. Two days later, army officials suspended her from her job once again, pending further investigation. Yet, while McCarthy claimed to have brought to light the dirty secret of Communist infiltration of the Pentagon's code room, much of the evidence concerning Annie Lee Moss remained hidden. By 1954 J. Edgar Hoover had determined that cooperation with McCarthy was not in the FBI's best interest, and agency officials were prohibited from sharing their information about Moss with McCarthy or his staffers.[22] Furthermore, army officials refused to provide loyalty files to the McCarthy committee. These decisions to keep the operations of the loyalty-security program as secret as possible in fact lessened the power of Markward's testimony and heightened Moss's ability to present herself as an innocent victim when she finally appeared before the McCarthy committee on March 11. The contours of this public performance of innocence owed a great deal to the racialized politics of the Cold War.

"I've Worked like a Dog for My Good Name"
Race, Loyalty, and the National Security State

White Americans' anxieties about black citizens' loyalty were not unique to the Cold War era. African American fidelity to the social order had long been a matter of concern to white Southerners, and black intellectuals and activists themselves had recognized a troubled relationship to Americanness. W. E. B. Du Bois wrote famously of the "twoness" of the American Negro, "two souls, two thoughts, two un-reconciled strivings; two warring ideals in one dark body."

For Du Bois this double consciousness was both a curse and a blessing. It forced African Americans to look at the world and themselves through the eyes of their oppressors, yet it also made possible a fuller understanding of that world, and the place of their nation in it. But to many white observers, the twoness of black Americans cast into doubt whether it was possible, as Du Bois put it, "for a man to be both a Negro and an American." The enmeshing of racial reform with Cold War politics made African American loyalty an issue of national and international import. As black loyalty to the nation, despite the inequities of its racial past, became accepted as proof of the rightness of gradualist reform, cases demonstrating its presence or absence took on exaggerated significance.[23]

These anxieties were exacerbated by the Communist Party's efforts to court African Americans. As early as 1919, right-wing politicians averred that Communists had targeted blacks for agitation and indoctrination. By the late 1920s, the CP had begun to develop a strategy for organizing in African American communities, and the hard times of the Great Depression yielded some rich results. Between 1931 and 1946, the proportion of party members who were African American doubled to 14 percent. Among the factors contributing to the CP's ability to attract a more racially diverse membership were its attention to issues of concern to working-class black folk, and substantial efforts to combat racism within the party itself.[24]

Nonetheless, while many black Americans flirted with party membership, they also had a particularly high turnover rate, apparently moving into and out of the party according to their own estimation of its effectiveness on the issues they cared about—racial as well as economic justice. These trends held true in Washington, where it was estimated that in the mid-1940s, a third of the party's membership was African American, a proportion equivalent to the black population of the district, but about 80 percent of black recruits dropped out within a year. Although critics accused the party of exploiting and misrepresenting American racial problems, of "deceiv[ing] and delud[ing] members of the Negro race" in order to weaken the nation by dividing it from within, the assessment of one black Communist was probably closer to the mark. He observed that, far from the party using African Americans, "it is probably more accurate to say that Negroes have used the Communist Party. It is the one party in which they feel free to speak and to act like Americans." In sum, the CP did have a degree of success in attracting black recruits, even if, for many black citizens, the party's avowed commitment to racial equality was not enough to maintain their long-term allegiance to its particular radical vision.[25]

The workings of the federal loyalty-security program reflected these racial tensions. In the nation's capital, individuals who had been active in left-leaning unions and the African American freedom struggle, especially members of the government employees' union, were particularly vulnerable in loyalty investigations.[26] The United Federal Workers of America (UFWA) was created by the Congress of Industrial Organizations in 1937; in 1946 it joined with a CIO organization of local and state workers to form the United Public Workers of America (UPWA). Members of the UFWA/UPWA were strong advocates of racial and gender equality as well as militant defenders of the rights of public employees to bargain collectively and strike, positions that earned them the enmity of many in Congress and led to the passage of the Hatch Act in 1939. The UFWA/UPWA organized both professional and less skilled workers, seeking particularly to include African American government employees. Indeed, after 1942 their largest local was the Cafeteria Workers' Union, which numbered almost four thousand black Washingtonians, mostly women, who served the rapidly growing federal bureaucracy. Annie Lee Moss was one of those women. The UFWA/UPWA included Communists and non-Communists in their membership and leadership, and union officials promoted a broad social justice platform, encompassing opposition to racial discrimination on the job, support for the Fair Employment Practices Commission (FEPC), and protest against Truman's loyalty programs. In 1950 the UPWA was expelled by the CIO as Communist-dominated. Although it sought to survive on its own, many of its leaders and members were investigated by Congress or lost their jobs after loyalty investigations; some were even jailed. Its president, Abram Flaxer, was convicted of contempt of Congress for refusing HUAC's demand that he turn over the union's membership lists. In 1953 the UPWA collapsed under the weight of this harassment.[27]

Government officials justified their scrutiny of the UPWA on the grounds that its leaders were "fanatic" Communists, but to a substantial degree it was members' advocacy of racial justice that got the unions in trouble. The UFWA and UPWA were prime examples of the milieu of left-unionism in which workers' rights advocates, antiracist activists, and Communists encountered and influenced one another. As one UPWA official later claimed, "Everything that happened in Washington, opening up the cafeterias to black people, breaking out of the counting rooms, beginning a consumer movement, hiring black bus drivers in the city, setting up the restaurant picket lines—that was our people." Certainly government worker unions were not responsible for "everything that happened"—Washington was home to a diverse civil rights community—but their members did play an active part in the city's movement for racial equality.[28] Their activism challenged the district's political culture in particular ways, as one union member recalled:

> You have to remember that Washington was a Southern town. . . . All of the government agencies had separate dining rooms or separate dining areas for blacks and whites. In a sense we were radicals in that we were breaking Southern traditions. . . . Suddenly there were picket lines all over the place. Here came all these people from all parts of the country, particularly New York Jews, to work for the federal government, people from union backgrounds, from the North and the West. . . . Everybody who's for equality has to be a Red: that was the attitude.

The relationship between loyalty investigations and advocacy of racial equality was recognized in the union's highest ranks. Union president Flaxer made the connection explicitly, informing President Truman that "practically all investigations of federal employees have been marked by questions dealing with the workers' attitude toward the problem of civil rights." He insisted that opponents of the president's civil rights initiatives would use the loyalty program as a shield for their bigotry, declaring, "We cannot have a Civil Rights Program and a Loyalty Order at the same time."[29]

United States Employment Service worker and local president Dorothy Bailey was perhaps the best-known UPWA member to lose her job after questions arose about her civil rights activism. Although Bailey was not a Communist, she was accused by anonymous informants of being a CP member, associating with Communists, and following the Communist "line" in her union work. During one of her hearings a member of the loyalty board asked Bailey, "Did you ever write a letter to the Red Cross about the segregation of blood?" Apparently the evidence gathered against Bailey included such a letter that had been furnished to the loyalty board by the Red squad of the Washington, D.C., police department. The question was justified, the interrogator later argued, because "objection to blood segregation is a recognized 'party line' technic" [*sic*] used to "inveigle Negroes into joining the Party."[30]

Bailey's experience was merely an infamous example of an endemic practice. Employees facing loyalty investigations were questioned as to whether they had friends of another race, owned Paul Robeson albums, or had "advanced" ideas about "discrimination, non-segregation of races, greater rights for Negroes, and so forth," as well as whether they read the *Daily Worker* or were interested in Russian culture. As one loyalty official notoriously maintained: "The fact that a person believes in racial equality doesn't *prove* that he's a Communist, but it certainly makes you look twice, doesn't it? You can't get away from the fact that racial equality is part of the Communist line."[31] Dorothy Bailey appealed her firing all the way to the Supreme Court, arguing that the loyalty program's reliance on anonymous informers—not even the board members hearing her case knew who had made the charges against her, or on what evidence—deprived her of due process of law. But the Supreme Court disagreed, letting stand a lower court ruling that due process guarantees did not apply because there existed no right to a government job.[32]

Some UPWA activists lost not just their jobs but their liberty as a result of their civil rights activism. Marie Richardson Harris was a union organizer and a graduate of Howard University. Reportedly she was the first black woman to hold national office in an American labor union. She was also active in several progressive organizations that came to be labeled Communist front groups, including the National Negro Congress. As executive secretary of that group's Washington branch, she campaigned for a permanent FEPC, for anti-lynching laws, and for home rule in the District of Columbia. In 1948, on her application for a position at the Library of Congress, she indicated that she was not a member of the Communist Party. Although she had held the job for only a few months, in 1951 Harris was indicted for falsifying her application for federal employment after HUAC urged the FBI to investigate her. Committee staff noted that, even though she had left government work "before any action could be taken" under Executive Order 9835, "this is one of the best cases from a prosecutive standpoint." Mary Markward was the primary witness against her, and Harris's defense team was prevented from introducing witnesses who would testify to her loyalty. She was convicted on eight counts and served four years in prison. At her sentencing, the judge contrasted the two women's loyalty in the starkest terms: Markward "deserves to take her place alongside of Molly Pitcher, Barbara Frietchie, and Clara Barton," but Harris, he maintained, had brought her fate on herself: "Your teachings at your mother's knee and your American father should not have permitted you to embrace such false doctrines. . . . If your country had been at war, and you had given material aid to a foreign government under our espionage statute, you too, like Mr. and Mrs. Rosenberg, might be sitting in death's row at Sing Sing Penitentiary, awaiting electrocution." Although Harris had never been accused of spying, the judge seemed to equate her alleged CP membership with treason. He was not alone. The committee that organized to defend her against these charges was denoted a subversive organization by the attorney general, and HUAC cited its publication of a pamphlet to raise funds on her behalf as evidence that the Communist Party was engaged in a nationwide conspiracy against the U.S. government (fig. 5).[33]

The exaggerated impact of the executive branch's loyalty-security program on both African American and white advocates for racial justice had its counterpart in another aspect of the national security state: the investigative hearings conducted by the legislative branch. Although these were not always public spectacles—McCarthy in particular was known for using the more private executive session to harass, intimidate, and rehearse witnesses—they were often ritualized occasions for the "stagecraft of statecraft" which communicated the complexity of racial politics in Cold War America. On the one hand, congressional hearings, like those of loyalty boards, warned of Communists' designs on and incursions into the black community, branding action on behalf of racial justice as subversive and working to discipline those who strayed beyond the "approved" boundaries of liberal racial reform. On the other hand, they offered object lessons in the "American way" of race relations. In these hearings, the racial meanings of loyalty were performed by witnesses and state officials alike.[34]

The 1949 furor over Paul Robeson's reported remarks to the World Peace Congress in Paris offered just one such opportunity for showcasing appropriate forms of black loyalty in Cold War America. Quoted as stating that it was "unthinkable that American Negroes would go to war [against the Soviet Union] on behalf of those who have oppressed us for generations," Robeson was harshly attacked by both the mainstream press and many African American leaders. The controversy provided an excuse for HUAC to hold a widely publicized set of hearings on "Communist infiltration of minority groups," a subject that had periodically commanded the committee's attention since its inception. Significantly, the hearings were dominated as much by protestations of faith in the unshakable loyalty of African Americans as they were by denunciations of Robeson. At the very outset of the hearings, HUAC investigator Alvin Stokes reported that, despite relentless "attempts to . . . recruit, capture, and control outstanding Negroes," the CP had failed miserably in its efforts to divide the American people, because "the Negroes of this country . . . realize that, despite certain inequalities and conditions which exist, the American

FIGURE 5. Loyalty-security policies enabled intensified persecution of individuals involved in the black freedom struggle. Marie Richardson Harris was particularly vulnerable as a union organizer and community activist. (Pamphlet in author's possession)

way of life provides ample opportunity to correct these conditions through democratic processes. The American Negro, down to the poorest sharecropper, is better off than the vast majority of Stalin's subjects." The representatives on the committee—from liberals to segregationists—fell over themselves to agree, averring that the "loyalty of the Negro race . . . is above reproach."[35]

The black men who testified before the committee also defended African Americans' loyalty against Robeson's reported comments while nonetheless reminding HUAC members of the necessity of struggling against racial inequality. Urban League director Lester Granger, for example, condemned the Communist Party as the Negro's "enemy" but nonetheless urged that there should be "less worry about Robeson and more concern for democracy." The most celebrated witness, Jackie Robinson, denounced Robeson's "siren song sung in bass," but he also censured those who worried about "Communists stirring up Negroes to protest." For "Negroes were stirred up long before there was a Communist Party," Robinson asserted, "and they'll stay stirred up long after the party has disappeared," as long as segregation, job discrimination, police brutality, and lynching were facts of American life. Still, while they ridiculed the notion that one could generalize about the loyalty of "the Negro," these men often did just that. For example, Fisk University president Dr. Charles Johnson declared that, while it made as much sense to ask about the loyalty of the Negro as about that of "Tennesseans, or Presbyterians . . . or American women, or persons with freckles," the nation's black citizens had consistently shown "not only an unshakable loyalty, but a persistent faith in the future and destiny of the Nation and all its people." George K. Hunton, director of the Catholic Interracial Council of New York, affirmed black loyalty unreservedly: "The Negro . . . is perhaps the only group in this country who has absolutely no background of memory of a fatherland or motherland. He is an American and nothing else." Such reminders of the "incomplete" nature of American democracy, uttered in tandem with reassurances about African American loyalty, provided a stronger defense of U.S. interests in the Cold War than if criticism of racism had been silenced: *despite* U.S. failings, black leaders had cast their lot with the nation.

HUAC members seemed equally eager to assuage fears about black loyalty, even as they excoriated black Communists. Perhaps their assurances that none of the congressmen doubted the fidelity of the nation's racial minorities were merely politic, a means of soothing balky witnesses. But they were also a testament to the importance of demonstrating black loyalty in defense of

American democracy for racial liberals and racial conservatives alike. Both John McSweeney of Ohio and John Wood of Georgia praised the nation's black soldiers, associating their service with the "unquestioned" loyalty of the race. McSweeney, a decorated veteran of both world wars, noted the "rapid rise" of the race since "the days of emancipation" and wondered aloud whether "the Unknown Soldier may be a Negro boy." Such an observation coming from a northern Democrat may have caused the witnesses relatively little discomfort. But when HUAC chair Wood, a Georgia Dixiecrat and a defender of the Ku Klux Klan, reminisced about "having had the privilege of association with the Negro race all of my life" and asked one witness to "carry back to your people that there never was any doubt on the part of this committee as to the patriotism of your race," it must have been harder to take.

It is because Robeson's purported comments went directly to an issue on which "race men" had long staked their own claims to full citizenship that African American leaders made the difficult decision to testify before HUAC, whose anticommunism they may have shared but whose ultraconservative politics they did not. From the earliest days of the black freedom struggle, the demand for "manhood rights" rested firmly on black men's readiness to shed their blood "freely and willingly in the cause of democracy." When Robeson said *something* that could be translated into the threat that black men might no longer be disposed to lay down their lives for their country, he eroded the foundation of these gendered claims to equal citizenship. Thus, much of the testimony of the race men (and they were all men) who spoke before HUAC referred to their own and their brothers' military service; indeed, one witness, C. B. Clark, was apparently chosen because the men of his family had fought "in every war since the Revolution," including in the Confederate Army.

If the HUAC hearings were ostensibly held to provide black leaders with the opportunity to prove their loyalty to the nation, Robeson functioned within this performance not just as the bad Negro in contrast to their good Negro but as an icon of disloyalty, a traitor to his race as well as his nation.[36] In his statement in Paris, investigator Stokes alleged, Robeson had spoken not for himself but in "the voice of the Kremlin." This image of the man who was famed for his forceful voice now speaking in a voice that was neither his own nor that of an "authentic" Negro was echoed by both black and white witnesses who claimed that Robeson's "betrayal" of "the masses of the Negro people" had robbed him of any claim to be a spokesman for his race. Manning Johnson, a black ex-Communist who was a frequent witness before investigative committees, and who went on in later years to claim that the civil rights movement was nothing but a Communist plot, told HUAC that Robeson had "sold himself to Moscow." The editors of the *New York Times* agreed, noting that by "attach[ing] himself to the cause of a country in which all men are equal because they are equally enslaved," Robeson had effectively made himself a slave to his Communist masters.[37]

The 1949 HUAC hearings, then, exposed the power of one strategy for asserting black loyalty to an America that had not yet achieved racial justice. The willingness of race men to lay their bodies and their lives on the line for the nation proved their entitlement to citizenship. Their expressions of impatience with the pace of racial reform were tolerated, even encouraged, by legislators who recognized that Cold War politics heightened the importance of demonstrating black loyalty. As C. B. Clark reminded them: "The American Negro holds it as his inalienable right to defend or fight for his country, for he and his ancestors have purchased a far greater share of it with their blood than many of the bigots who would deny them full participation in the fruits of their sacrifices. . . . They know that the United States is their heritage, far more so than many whites who are citizens of it." This, of course, was a strategy that was hardly available to women, black or white, at a time when inordinately few were afforded the opportunity for military service. And for those men who appeared before investigating committees not as carefully selected counters to the fear of black disloyalty but because their own allegiance was suspect, military service was hardly enough to clear their names.[38] Such women and men had to find other means to prove their loyalty to their interlocutors and the American public.

Some African Americans, both those famous and those less so, tried to distance themselves from Communist or progressive pasts. Writer Langston Hughes was called before the PSI as part of its investigation of "subversive" literature in overseas State Department information centers. In executive session he wrangled endlessly with Roy Cohn about the definition of Communism and the interpretation of literature and insisted on testifying at length to his own experiences of racism in his youth. By the time of his public appearance, however, he praised the "acceleration of improvement in race relations" in the United States and agreed that any of his books that "followed the Communist line" should not be in State Department libraries. Hughes's position toward the investigating committee had changed so much that Arkansas senator John McClellan praised him for his frankness about his "errors of the past."[39] Several years earlier, black labor activist Henry Thomas had struck a similar posture toward HUAC. Thomas, the president of Washington's Building Laborers' Local 74, was named a Communist by Mary Markward. He admitted that he had been a CP member until 1949, when he resigned in the wake of the passage of the Taft-Hartley Act so that he could sign a non-Communist affidavit. He cooperated with HUAC, naming other local Communists and repudiating the party for its "espionage, sabotage, spying and so forth." But he also tried to explain why he'd been drawn to the CP in the first place:

> When you are hungry and a man offers you something to eat, not only will you follow that man because you get more to eat, but you are thankful to him, and I was thankful to the Communist Party for taking me off the street and giving me a hot meal. . . . I went to the fifth grade in school. The Communists taught me quite a bit of what I know now; some I picked up myself. If I had had the opportunity to go to school maybe I wouldn't be sitting here today. I don't know what would have happened to me if I had graduated from school. I am sure I wouldn't be here. I probably would not have become a Communist.

Despite what could be interpreted as a veiled critique of the racial and economic injustice that prevented him from acquiring an education, presiding member Francis E. Walter praised Thomas for showing how well-meaning people could be "duped into becoming part of an international conspiracy" and for proving that he was "a good American."[40] Again, when black activists demonstrated their allegiance by denouncing the Communist Party, their criticism of U.S. racial inequality raised fewer hackles.

Others sought to avoid answering investigating committees' questions, whether by invoking the First Amendment's protections of individual belief to challenge the very right to ask them, or by citing the Fifth Amendment's protection against self-incrimination. Both of these strategies had their limitations: by the late 1940s it was apparent that courts were, by and large, not amenable to First Amendment limits on such investigations, while many Americans interpreted reliance on the Fifth Amendment as proof of disloyalty.[41] In fact, refusing to answer questions about their political beliefs cost many government employees their jobs, as Doris Walters Powell discovered. A black woman on maternity leave from her position as a clerk-typist in the Quartermaster Market Center, where she assisted with purchasing food for army personnel, Powell was one of

McCarthy's first targets in his investigation into army loyalty practices. Before working for the army, she had been a secretary at *People's Voice,* a progressive African American newspaper in New York City which in the mid-1940s was managed by Communists Doxey Wilkerson and Marvel Cooke. This affiliation brought her under suspicion in her new job, but army officials decided to wait until she returned from maternity leave to file loyalty charges against her. Shortly before her leave was due to expire, McCarthy subpoenaed her to testify in executive session. On her first appearance, Powell stated that she had gone to various meetings as part of her job, had been issued some sort of card so that she could attend required lectures, and had made donations to the paper, but that she was not a member of the Communist Party, at least not to her knowledge. She was recalled the next day, and this time, while denying CP membership in 1949 or after, she invoked her privilege against self-incrimination in response to questions about party membership while she was at *People's Voice.* Wilkerson and Cooke also took the Fifth when asked about Powell's membership as well as their own, but several ex-Communist witnesses claimed to know Powell as a "completely trustworthy Communist."[42] Although she did not testify publicly, her name was released by McCarthy, who confessed himself "shocked beyond words" that the army had not immediately fired an individual who refused to answer questions about her affiliation with the CP. Little more than a week later, she was suspended.[43]

Still, the Constitution retained its attraction for Americans who took seriously their rights to freedom of belief and association. Citing the Constitution provided a platform for asserting more nuanced visions of citizenship and could also legitimate a posture of defiance toward investigating committees. Paul Robeson's wife, Eslanda Robeson, proved herself a master of this strategy in her encounter with Joe McCarthy. McCarthy decided to question her because two of her books, including a biography of her husband, were included in State Department libraries. When asked if she belonged to the Communist Party, she confounded committee members by declining to answer under the protection of the Fifth and *Fifteenth* amendments. Instructed by McCarthy that "the Fifteenth Amendment has nothing to do with it. That provides the right to vote," she countered: "I understand it has something to do with my being a Negro and I have always sought protection under it. . . . I am a second-class citizen in this country and, therefore, feel the need of the Fifteenth. That is the reason I use it. I am not quite equal to the rest of the white people."[44] Robeson demonstrated how loyalty investigations especially disadvantaged African Americans, who needed a sort of super-constitutional protection against the current government. McCarthy, recognizing that this move called his legitimacy into question, lectured her: "Before this committee we do not have Negroes or whites. We do not have Catholics, Protestants, or Jews. We have American citizens. They all have the same rights and you have no special right because of your race." But Robeson would not back down: "I don't quite understand your statement that we are all American citizens. I have been fighting for this for all my 56 years. . . . I hope we will at some point get to a place where we don't have to [discuss race]. But in the meantime you are white and I am Negro, and this is a very white committee, and I feel I must sort of protect myself. I am sorry it is necessary." Although McCarthy proclaimed his unwillingness to proffer "special rights" on account of Robeson's race, her sex was apparently another matter: the senator told her he would not cite her for contempt for her refusal to answer his questions, but warned that "the first *man* who comes up before the committee and follows the same line" would not receive the same courtesy.[45]

Eslanda Robeson displayed considerable political acumen in her appearance before McCarthy, but the "special consideration" he extended her hints at the limits placed on women's political participation during these years. Many American women appeared before loyalty boards and legislative committees, lost their jobs and their social standing, and otherwise suffered for their political activities. Many more wholeheartedly endorsed anti-Communist efforts, joining community groups and national organizations, voting in elections, and writing to their representatives. Yet these women were taken less seriously than men as thinkers and activists, in large part because their public roles were so often comprehended in terms of their family responsibilities. Even into the 1960s, state and federal legislators often treated the women testifying before them not as political actors themselves but as sources of information about their husband's activities. Or, alternatively, women's allegedly subversive beliefs or behaviors could be explained in terms of their love for Communist men, their inability to "get" a man, or their lack of maternal instinct.[46] Similarly, women's patriotic work was deemed either a reflection of their responsibilities as wives and mothers or a remarkable exception to those responsibilities. A magazine profile of Mary Markward, titled "Secret Agent in Apron Strings," expressed the common understanding that women's domestic roles were incompatible with more obviously "political" activism:

> You've seen her, or her counterpart a thousand times. You've seen her at the supermarket, giving her child a ride in the cart as she buys the family groceries. You've seen her at PTA meetings, at Sunday school and church, at the American Legion Auxiliary—everywhere a typical, happy, young American housewife would be. The people in the committee room looked at each other and shook their heads in amazement as she told her story. They heard it from her own lips, and still it seemed unbelievable. For this pert young wife and mother was an undercover agent for the FBI![47]

Conceptualizing women as family members first and engaged citizens second was so pervasive that radical women themselves sometimes used that framework to build support for their activism, as, for example, when they emphasized the ways that the Smith Act harmed the children of accused Communists.[48]

In sum, the political scripts of the Cold War era offered limited options to those, like Annie Lee Moss, whose loyalty was questioned. Her choices were particularly constrained. Moss could not perform her loyalty by referring to her willingness to fight for her country, although her son's military service in the Korean conflict sometimes surfaced in sympathetic coverage of her struggle. Invoking constitutional protections to deflect investigators would very likely get her fired. Acknowledging a progressive past and distancing herself from it was only slightly more promising, and it shaded dangerously close to admitting that she was a "dupe," not really an attractive prospect. And as a working woman, a widow, and a mother whose son was already an adult, Moss had only a tenuous connection to familialist explanations for female activism.

Indeed, there were remarkably few ways for African American women to demonstrate their allegiance in a context in which the pursuit of racial and economic justice cast doubt on their loyalty. This may be why the black attorney Edith Sampson, who toured the world as a Cold War ambassador for the State Department and served on the U.S. delegation at the United Nations, offered such one-note defenses of American race relations. Although in private she claimed not to be a "stooge" for her country's racism and acknowledged the power of Communist-inspired statements about racial inequality, in public she vowed to "link arms with the worst Dixicrat [*sic*] on foreign policy" to save African Americans from the slavery that was certain under Communism. Sampson worked hard to avoid any criticism of U.S. race relations, telling an audience in India: "The question is, quite bluntly, 'Do Negroes have equal rights in America?' My answer is no, we do not have equal rights in all parts of the United States. But let's remember that eighty-five years ago Negroes in America were slaves and were 100 percent illiterate. And the record shows that the Negro has advanced further in this period than any similar group in the entire world." She touted her own professional achievements as an indication of the opportunities available to black Americans. The over-the-top quality of Sampson's denials of segregation and inequality, compared to the more nuanced positions taken by African American men representing the United States overseas, suggests the narrow limits within which black women who wished to weigh in on these matters had to maneuver.[49]

None of this is to say that black women were helpless in the face of the Cold War and domestic containment. Radical black women led the way in launching a wide-ranging critique of American racial, gender, class, and international politics. Indeed, Cold War repression may have incited more far-reaching analyses and opened up opportunities for women's leadership when their male comrades were jailed or went underground, even as their radical stance subjected many women to intensified state surveillance, unemployment, imprisonment, censorship, and deportation.[50] More broadly, black women across the political spectrum enacted their citizenship in a wide range of educational, social welfare, religious, economic, and political practices and institutions. Annie Lee Moss is a prime example. She was a committed community activist, doing her part to build a better world for Washington's black residents. "I've worked like a dog for my good name and to make life pleasant for others," she told a reporter. "I've held Christmas dances and plays to buy gifts for disabled veterans and baskets of food for the needy. I've taken boys from the Industrial Home School to the movies and to church and I've got a letter from the Fourth Precinct that says I've helped to prevent juvenile delinquency. I've worked with them all—the YWCA, the Syphax Recreation Center, the Boy Scouts, the Phelps PTA and the Friendship Baptist Church." But the sorts of community care activities that Moss enumerated rarely registered in the national consciousness as exercises of good citizenship, especially when performed by women, whose nurturing inclinations were presumed to make these extensions of their nature. And the more obviously "political" pursuits in which Moss engaged over the years—for example, her union membership in the early to mid-1940s, or her work on a campaign for the extension of the FEPC—were more likely to raise than to answer questions about whether she was a good citizen.[51]

In Cold War America even participation in liberal racial reform efforts threatened to cast doubt on the loyalty of African American citizens, as numerous black women and men discovered. Ralph Bunche, Mary McLeod Bethune, Josephine Baker all, at one time or another, found themselves called before investigating committees or otherwise under suspicion. Still, if active civic engagement could not be offered as proof of black allegiance to the nation, upward mobility could be.[52] The significance of African American economic opportunity and success to the Cold War debate about black loyalty was recognized, in very distinct ways, by Edith Sampson and Paul Robeson. In her addresses to foreign audiences, Sampson cited her own experience as a lawyer as she sought to offer "the truth" about race relations in America, but she also claimed that her experience was representative: "Today one and a half million Negroes belong to labor unions . . . with the right to receive the same pay, the right to strike and to bargain—equal rights with white workers in America. You should shed no tears for Negroes. They are getting along fine. They have savings in the United States of five billion dollars and purchasing power of seven billion. There are two hundred Negro insurance companies, with total assets of $100,000,000, and . . . two hundred Negro-controlled and owned newspapers and magazines." Their access to shining new cars, beautiful homes, and first-class educations made America a "glorious place" for its black citizens and secured their loyalty: "America is our homeland."[53] Paul Robeson, by contrast, warned of the dangers of confusing the achievements of one individual with the liberation of a people. Responding to the media coverage of the HUAC hearing at which he was excoriated for his disloyalty, he told a New York audience: "Personal success can be no answer. It can no longer be a question of an Anderson, a Carver, a Robinson, a Jackson, or a Robeson. It must be a question of the well-being and opportunities not of a few but for *all* of this great Negro people of which I am a part." Robeson claimed America for his homeland but challenged the nation to earn the allegiance of its black citizens. Nonetheless, while some African Americans raised their voices in criticism of Sampson's "propaganda with a capital P," most commentators praised her for offering "a refreshing antidote for the poison which Paul Robeson has been spreading."[54]

Annie Lee Moss lived these contradictions. She understood that a long history of activism on behalf of her family and community was less likely to win her vindication than reminding Americans that she represented the promise of equal opportunity, secured by white paternalism. This recognition shaped her appearance before the McCarthy committee, and the responses to it, in fundamental ways.

"This Doesn't Look Like I'm a Communist, Does It?"
Annie Lee Moss Explains Herself

Annie Lee Moss's appearance before the McCarthy committee was not the first time she had been called on to explain herself, of course. By the time McCarthy's aide Roy Cohn questioned her before the television cameras, she had testified before two loyalty boards and HUAC. Through all of these investigations, Moss protested her innocence, insisting that she didn't know "just what Communism means."[55] Yet her responses to the evidence against her were often inconsistent, suggesting she might have known more than she wished to admit. Although she professed ignorance about how her identifying information had made its way into CP records, her own testimony hints at the possibilities. It also reveals her awareness of the ever-narrowing range of acceptable political activities for black women during the Cold War.

In 1948 Moss was more forthcoming than she would be in later hearings. She told GAO loyalty board members that in the summer of 1944 she had been invited to a meeting by a white woman who lived in her neighborhood. Moss reported that she had expected it to be a "social affair" and that she'd be asked to clean up afterwards. Instead, she had been introduced to the group, listened to speeches about the FEPC and accounts of a recent Baltimore convention, and been given pamphlets by James Ford and "some man from Howard University, Wilkinson" (Doxey Wilkerson).[56] For a year after the meeting she received the *Daily Worker* in the mail and read it from time to time. She also got invitations to more meetings, invitations that were written on CP letterhead and, she admitted, "clearly labeled communications from the Communist Party." She concluded that her name might have ended up in CP records because of her attendance at this meeting, but she was unable to explain how it was listed in membership records as early as 1943, or why she would be recorded as paying for two months of the *Daily Worker* in 1945.[57]

The transcript from Moss's hearing before the army's loyalty-security board in 1951 does not survive, but we know that at that time she acknowledged attending this 1944 meeting. By 1954, however, she made no mention of it to HUAC and denied receiving notices of any Communist meetings. She did admit to attending "some kind of a social event" at a Northeast Washington church in 1943 while she was living with Hattie Griffin, a woman in whose home she boarded for several weeks. Griffin had also been named as a Communist by Markward, but Moss denied any knowledge that she was a party member and could remember nothing of substance about the meeting. Now she claimed that the *Daily Worker* had been brought to her house by a union acquaintance named Robert Hall, who told her it was a "good paper"; although she denied ever paying for it, the *Worker* began arriving in the mail after her family moved. She insisted that she was "not knowingly" a member of the Communist Party, and when asked how she could "unknowingly" have joined the CP she responded, "Maybe I could have, but I don't remember anything." Just a few weeks later, in her public testimony before McCarthy's committee, Moss became much more definitive. "I have never attended any Communist meetings," she testified; she had never attended any meetings in a church, she had never talked to Rob Hall about the *Daily Worker* (although her husband had), and she had never even read the paper. "I never had heard of Communism until 1948 when this first hearing came up, and I asked them then what was that?" All of the interactions of the mid-1940s were forgotten.[58]

Since she no longer admitted attending any suspicious meetings, Moss had to advance a new explanation for the mix-up about CP membership: her union. Moss was required to join the UFWA in 1942 when she got her cafeteria job. This was a union shop, and dues were automatically deducted from wages, but, it turned out, Moss went further than merely paying her dues. She attended "quite a few" monthly meetings and participated in a union-endorsed campaign demanding an end to racial discrimination in government employment. When HUAC staff asked her if she had "doubts" about any meetings she might have attended during the 1940s, she replied: "I'm kind of skeptical about this union [because] everything seems to center right around that period. Before there's nothing; afterward there's nothing. Everything seems to center right around that union."[59]

The inconsistencies in Moss's oft-retold story may reflect willful misrepresentation, a faulty memory, fear, or most likely all of these at once. They tell us as much about the messy margins between civil rights activism, the UFWA, and the left in wartime Washington, D.C., as they do about whether Annie Lee Moss was a "dues-paying, card-carrying" Communist. It would appear that Moss bumped up against Communists in numerous contexts, including her work life, but also as a member of her community. Despite her own efforts in loyalty hearings to minimize her activities, Moss was in fact not only vitally engaged in community work during the 1940s but also an energetic and effective leader. In addition to youth, church, and charity activities, she served several years as president of her public housing tenants' council. Newspaper articles described her as a "spark-plug" of neighborhood activism. Her interest in community improvement likely made her an attractive prospect for the CP organizers who focused on the neighborhood where she lived while employed at the Pentagon cafeteria. Party members would go door-to-door selling the *Daily Worker*, circulating petitions on police brutality, the FEPC, and anti-lynching legislation, and trying to gauge individuals' openness to the CP. The party also held meetings in this neighborhood, including at Unity Baptist Church, where Moss attended the "social event" with Hattie Griffin.[60]

That church offers a tantalizing clue to the puzzle of Moss's political inclinations. In 1953 Markward testified about CP overtures to African Americans before the Senate's Internal Security Subcommittee, along with ex-Communists Leonard Patterson and Paul Crouch. In a discussion of how black religiosity might affect Communist efforts, Markward told a story about a 1943 party meeting at Unity Baptist Church: "A Negro member of [the Northeast] club who had been recruited solely on the basis of non-discrimination, came and said after all of this talk, I think all we need is a prayer. She thought that if this group of people, a hundred or so in that room, would all get down and pray for God, we could solve some of the things that the Communists were haranguing themselves about." She told the same story to HUAC, at the 1954 session at which she named Annie Lee Moss as a Communist, remembering that at one meeting "a new member to the Party said she thought if we didn't talk about it so much and would all get down on our knees and pray, our problem would be solved quicker." This incident, Markward reminisced, "just floored everybody in the meeting." The pastor—not himself a Communist but willing to work with Communists to fight against discrimination—tried to smooth things over, suggesting that "perhaps this lady and himself felt they had an inside track with the Lord, and they would get home by praying, but the Communists would get home by doing." But "that member never attended any more meetings."[61]

Markward did not connect the devout woman with Annie Lee Moss, and perhaps they were not one and the same. Moss was indeed a deeply religious woman and a frequent preacher at community services. Lawyer and author Eleanor Bontecou, whose profile of Moss was never published, noted: "God slips in and out of her conversation. To pray to Him for help in time of need is as natural to her as breathing and she knows that her prayers are answered." Moss herself cited her spiritual beliefs as evidence that she could not be a Communist—"This doesn't look like I'm a Communist, does it?" she asked a reporter as she sat surrounded by Bibles and pictures of Jesus in her living room—but there is much evidence that, at least before the Cold War heated up, among working-class black activists religious faith and Communist work for racial equality were not merely compatible but synergistic. Whatever the identity of the woman Markward described, she may have been puzzled that individuals attending a meeting in a church were dubious about the power of prayer. Or she may have taken for granted that there were many paths toward racial justice and social equality, and was perhaps willing to collaborate with people who were working toward the same goals—whether by attending a meeting of the Communist Political Association in 1944, circulating petitions for the FEPC, or reading the *Daily Worker*. At that moment, the fact that they called themselves Communists may have seemed of relatively little import.[62]

In any case, in 1954, Moss implied that her name had become associated with the Communist Party without her knowledge or permission as a result of her union participation. Perhaps; but given the range of evidence of some sort of affiliation with the CP, it seems more likely that she was a casual recruit to the party, attracted by its politics of social and economic justice, and encountering party members in both her workplace and her neighborhood. Perhaps, during the war, while the United States and Soviet Union were allies and party membership was climbing, she did not perceive these as subversive activities. But perhaps, in the midst of the Cold War, Moss decided to leave such activities behind for the more acceptable civic work of scouting and neighborhood improvement. Or perhaps, like the 80 percent of black recruits who left Washington's Communist Party within a year, Moss discovered quickly that it was not what she had imagined. In later years, when her hard-won government job was threatened by reports of a dalliance with the CP, she believed it necessary to deny knowing even "just what Communism means."[63]

The Right to Earn a Living

Annie Lee Moss before the McCarthy Committee

Senator McCarthy was in the midst of his campaign against the Department of the Army when he learned about Markward's reports concerning Moss. One of McCarthy's primary targets was the army's loyalty-security program. He identified a number of minor personnel with suspicious backgrounds who had nonetheless received security clearances, blaming army brass for failing to protect the nation from Communist spies at the very heart of its defenses. Moss's case came to McCarthy's attention at the same time as another that ultimately served him well in this campaign: that of army dentist Irving Peress. By glossing over the facts of Moss's employment history, he could present the two cases similarly. His question "Who in the military, knowing that this lady was a Communist[,] promoted her from a waitress to a code clerk?" did not have the alliterative ring of "Who promoted Peress?" but it served to reinforce his claims about shoddy army security. After receiving a tip about Moss's case, the senator's staff began investigating her, and Roy Cohn interviewed both Moss and Markward. McCarthy must have envisioned a showdown between the two women that could only make him look good. Forgoing his usual practice of auditioning witnesses in executive session, he summoned them both to appear before his committee at a public hearing.[64]

The showdown did not go as intended. Markward played her part, testifying that she had "absolutely . . . no doubt" that the Annie Lee Moss who was now employed by the Signal Corps had been a "card-carrying, dues paying member" of the Communist Party in 1943 and 1944, and that the army knew of the evidence against her. But Moss, who was suffering from bronchitis and nervous exhaustion, arrived at the hearings looking so bedraggled that McCarthy deemed it prudent to delay her testimony. One imagines he thought her illness would invite public sympathy for her, but he sought to turn the situation to his own advantage, warning Moss and her attorney that he had no interest in allowing a sick woman, in no condition to use her best judgment, to perjure herself by denying that she was a Communist when "clearly, she has been a member of the Party." In subsequent weeks Moss, who was suspended from her job shortly after being subpoenaed, repeatedly requested a chance to testify, but the senator, who thought he had already gained the upper hand in his conflict with the army, seemed to have lost interest.[65]

But Moss was not without powerful friends, and on March 11 she had her hearing. In her dealings with the McCarthy committee, Moss was represented by George E. C. Hayes, one of Washington's most influential African American lawyers. His firm represented, on occasion, both Paul Robeson and W. E. B. Du Bois, and he had been counsel for Marie Richardson Harris at her perjury trial, where he had encountered Mary Markward. Hayes was also an important participant in the NAACP's campaign against school segregation. In 1955 he was nominated by President Eisenhower to serve on Washington's Public Utilities Commission, making him the most highly ranked black official in D.C. government. He and Moss apparently met during her tenure as tenants' council president, and although she had not sought legal advice in her earlier

FIGURE 6. An ill Annie Lee Moss and her attorney, George E. C. Hayes, before the Permanent Subcommittee on Investigations. Mary Markward is in the background. (Photographer, Hank Walter. Time & Life Pictures/Getty Images)

encounters with the government's loyalty-security program, she must have turned to Hayes when she was subpoenaed to testify before Congress. She chose well, for Hayes, media savvy and well connected, successfully worked behind the scenes to get Moss the "opportunity to be heard" (fig. 6).[66]

McCarthy's political instincts were surely failing him by late February 1954, but he had been right to try to prevent Moss's appearance: her testimony proved a calamity for him. Not because Annie Lee Moss was "innocent," for much less evidence had been needed to cast suspicion on others caught up in the anti-Communist purge. Nor because McCarthy—or the Democrats on the committee, for that matter—was taken by surprise by what she said. Other commentators have made much of the fact that McCarthy excused himself from the hearing early in Moss's testimony and left Roy Cohn to interrogate her. They suggested that, like a rat escaping a sinking ship, he sensed a disaster in the making. Weeks before Moss was sworn in on March 11, however, she had been questioned by Cohn, the transcript of her HUAC testimony had been made available to committee staff, and Democrat Henry Jackson (but not Cohn or McCarthy) had been briefed by FBI officials on the specific evidence against her—evidence that Jackson declared convincing. Also, prior to McCarthy's departure, Moss fulfilled Cohn's expectation that she would "play dumb" when she testified. She denied CP membership, payment of dues, attendance at Communist meetings, and subscribing to the *Daily Worker*, although she did admit that it was delivered to two of her addresses. In other words, Moss's testimony was so damaging to McCarthy not because it revealed truths previously unknown but because McCarthy's enemies staged her appearance in a way that accomplished the simultaneous goals of hurting him while sustaining the broader political and racial imperatives of the domestic Cold War.[67]

Much of the media coverage and many historical accounts of the hearing focused on its exposure of McCarthy's (and Cohn's) incompetence, as displayed by two stories of mistaken identity put forth by the committee's Democratic senators. The first concerned a man (or perhaps two) named Rob Hall, who had allegedly delivered the *Daily Worker* to Moss's home. The confusion pertained to whether he was a black union official or a white Communist, but the Democrats succeeded in using that question to undermine confidence in McCarthy's case against Moss. If Roy Cohn and Joe McCarthy didn't know the difference between a white man and a black one, they insinuated, how could they tell the difference between a Communist and a loyal American citizen?[68] The second mistaken identity story concerned Moss herself. Linking Markward's inability to identify Moss personally with the confusion over Rob Hall, Senator Symington asked the Signal Corps employee, "Isn't it possible that there are some other people named Moss, just like apparently there are some other people named Hall?" Her response—that "there are three Annie Lee Mosses" in Washington—became the allegedly definitive piece of evidence proving that McCarthy and Cohn were wrong about her. Although this exchange seemed to come as a complete surprise at the end of the hearing, it was likely choreographed by the Democrats, since in her HUAC testimony Moss had related a long story about being mistaken for other Annie Mosses when she ordered telephone service, when she applied for her real estate license, and while working in the cafeteria. In any case, none of the other Anne Mosses (or women with similar names) lived at the three addresses contained in the CP records—but this Annie Lee Moss lived at all of them.[69] Nonetheless, although McCarthy's conservative defenders in the media immediately drew attention to the weaknesses of the mistaken identity narrative, it persisted as a demonstration that McCarthy's carelessness threatened the rights of American citizens.[70]

The hearing was also orchestrated to showcase the Democratic senators as defenders of those rights, particularly the right to make a living. It may have served McCarthy's purposes to cast Moss's career moves as "sudden," but Senators Henry Jackson, John McClellan, and Stuart Symington emphasized the long hard road that Moss had taken to her job as a government clerk, a job uniquely evocative of the postwar opening of economic opportunity to the nation's black citizens. Under their questioning, she testified about her migration from South Carolina to North Carolina to Washington, her lack of education as a girl in the South, and her rise from low-paid cafeteria worker to her current position, which, she was encouraged to report, she got on her "own efforts [and] qualifications." This trajectory from poverty to self-sufficiency was jeopardized by McCarthy's investigation. Although it was the secretary of the army who had actually suspended Moss from her job, the Democrats laid the blame at McCarthy's feet. When Moss told Symington that if she couldn't regain her job soon, she would be "going down to the welfare," she invoked the specter of an America in which postwar progress was tenuous. And when Symington replied, "If you are not taken back in the Army, you come around and see me, and I am going to see that you get a job," he showed his own (and, by extension, his party's) commitment to fair treatment and upward mobility for loyal African American citizens.[71]

When, a week later, Edward R. Murrow featured the Moss hearing on his weekly television show *See It Now,* this upward mobility story was given a different cast. Murrow's program—appearing just as the dispute between McCarthy and army officials was heating up—brought Moss's testimony to 3.3 million homes, the largest audience for any of his McCarthy broadcasts.[72] In Murrow's hands, the mistaken identity narrative of the hearings was accentuated and simplified, but the story of the Annie Lee Moss who struggled up from poverty by her own efforts was transformed into the myth of an ignorant, illiterate, and incompetent victim. Indeed, Murrow's very introduction of Moss removed her from the mainstream of American life. Conjecturing that, until she was publicly named as a Communist, this Washington resident and Pentagon employee knew "very little about Senator McCarthy, General Zwicker, [or] Mr. Cohn," Murrow designated her a "little woman," oblivious to the events that were gripping the rest of the country.[73]

The core of the broadcast—film from the hearing—can be divided into four main segments. In the first, Moss denies any connection to the CP. The second segment presents, in simplified form, the confusion over the identity of Rob Hall, communicating McCarthy's and Cohn's ineptitude and drawing a clear boundary between the African American "Robert Hall" and Moss, on the one hand, and white Communists such as "Rob Hall" on the other. The third segment, departing most significantly from the upward mobility narrative of the hearings, portrays Moss as incompetent, even foolish. It features an interchange between Moss and Senator Symington. Under Symington's questioning, Moss seems to play the part of the clown, to the merriment of the Democratic senators and assembled observers. A rare voiceover by Murrow prepares us to interpret a series of failings, as Moss stumbles over words while reading her suspension notice and then, to frequent laughter and indulgent smiles, claims not to recognize the name Karl Marx and must ask her lawyer the meaning of the word "espionage."[74] Framed by this performance, Moss's insistence that she is a "good American" becomes an admission that she hasn't the wit or skills to be a bad American. If, in the overall narrative of the hearing, Annie Lee Moss emerged as a hardworking, ambitious woman whose entry into the mainstream of American society was menaced by McCarthy's unsubstantiated accusations, in the Murrow broadcast she is presented as a dullard who couldn't possibly be a threat to the country. The final segment focuses on the Arkansan McClellan, who passionately denounces "hearsay evidence," trumpets Moss's citizenship rights, and condemns McCarthyism as "evil," returning Murrow to his purported central theme of due process. Still, it is Symington who has the last word. He delivers the verdict in what has become a mock trial: "I have been listening to you testify this afternoon, and I think you are telling the truth." In finding Moss "innocent," he renders McCarthy and Cohn guilty of something akin to an attempted lynching.

The responses to this broadcast and other reports of the hearing reveal the power of the twinned discourses of black upward mobility and white paternalism to make Annie Lee Moss legible in Cold War America. Ordinary citizens wrote hundreds of letters, condemning McCarthy for "pillorying" the hapless victim Moss and praising the Democrats as her chivalrous defenders.[75] They echoed Murrow's introduction of the broadcast as a "little picture about a little woman," lauding Senators Symington and McClellan for defending the "little people."[76] But their responses went beyond acknowledging that Moss was simply an ordinary citizen, no match for a powerful senator like McCarthy, describing her in terms that were belittling: "weak," "pitiful," "helpless," "bewildered," "defenseless."[77] Most strikingly, these citizens almost universally referred to her as "poor": "that poor woman," "the poor soul," "this poor person," "that poor Mrs. Moss," "a poor Negro," "the poor colored lady," "that poor old colored woman," "that poor old colored lady."[78] Even if they used this term in a general sense, its ubiquity also suggests the possibility that they understood Moss's victimization by McCarthy as somehow related to her economic insecurity. Media pundits echoed such appraisals while being even more disparaging of Moss's capacities. For example, critic Marya Mannes, to whom CBS gave access to some of the letters to Murrow, characterized their sentiments: American citizens were "sickened" at McCarthy's abuse of "this elderly, soft-spoken 'nobody' (who could hardly read English, let alone code)." And in a widely circulated column, John Crosby concluded a listing of Moss's illiteracies with the observation "I greatly doubt whether Annie Lee Moss knows she has any rights. Yet, they were being so clearly violated in front of our very eyes that she won every heart."[79] In all of these accounts, Moss was immobilized and pathetic; it was Symington and McClellan, aided by Murrow, whose defense of a persecuted woman restored faith in democracy.[80]

Commentators on the case—whether journalists or ordinary citizens—seemed particularly troubled by the denial of economic opportunity that Moss's job suspension represented. Almost without fail, media accounts stated Moss's salary to the dollar—everyone in America, it seemed, knew that the job from which she had been suspended paid $3,335 per year—and just as regularly Symington's promise to get her a job himself figured prominently in news stories. Citizens' letters betrayed the same concern. As one letter writer put it, "After serving a long life in cafeterias and having worked up to the glorious heights of teletyping for the army for just enough money to keep body and soul together in dignity, she was to be canned in disgrace."[81] Columnist John Crosby used more sweeping terms. Quoting the second paragraph of the Declaration of Independence, he asserted: "When Thomas Jefferson wrote it, the phrase 'pursuit of happiness' meant simply the right to hold a job, the right to earn a living. The American people fought a revolution to defend, among other things, the right of Annie Lee Moss to earn a living, and Senator McCarthy now decided she had no such right. It's about time McCarthy was labeled for what he is—a subversive who is trying to undermine the very cornerstone of our country." He praised those who "wanted to *give* a woman a job, not to take it away," to "help a woman, not to hurt her."[82] Symington, McClellan, and Murrow were the heroes of this story, and many citizens agreed. They interpreted the condescension of Moss's defenders, on full display in the hearings, as "kindness" and "decency," proof to the world that "chivalry still lives and breathes in our beloved land." Restored to her job in late March, Moss became a symbol of how white paternalism would ensure the continuing "loyalty of the Negro."[83]

But there were other lessons that could be learned from Moss's story. For some, especially those in the African American press, Moss was the hero of her own life. Her loyalty did not spring from her rescue by white benefactors; it was organic. Black journalists abjured references to a "poor old colored woman," offering a portrait, instead, of a "perfectly loyal American citizen," active in her community and surrounded by supporters. They foregrounded her relationships with her son, a Korean War veteran, and her pastor at the Friendship Baptist Church, who attested that she was both a "staunch Christian and a good American." In these accounts, Moss's upward mobility was the result of her own struggle, including her efforts to continue her education, which had given rise to the "comparative security" of a civil service job. Moss's role as a community leader, her charitable activities, and her record as a long-standing supporter of the Democratic Party were also featured. In describing Moss's appearance before McCarthy's committee, these accounts emphasized her firm voice, calm demeanor, and composure. And while her good name may have been "sacrificed on the altar of McCarthyism," she was also portrayed as a worthy foe to the senator, the "toast of the nation's capital" who got "the upper hand" on McCarthy and Cohn. Her "triumphant session" before the committee was heralded as "the stumbling block in the insane quest of McCarthy to rule."[84] The differences between the dominant portrayal of Moss and this more respectful portrait can be summed up by comparing two photographs. *Time* accompanied a brief report of her testimony with a photo of a worried-looking Moss speaking into a sea of microphones; "Karl Marx? Who's that?" was the caption. The *Washington Afro-American,* by contrast, featured a formal head shot of Moss, well-groomed, determined looking, and gazing directly out of the photograph, with the legend "The truth shall prevail" (fig. 7a and b).[85]

Once again, we are left with two Annie Lee Mosses. And just as Moss claimed before the McCarthy committee, it seems there was a third. Even as his reputation came crashing down, Senator McCarthy had his passionate defenders, and whenever Moss made it back into the news—for example, in August 1954, when the army suspended her yet again, or in 1958, when a ruling of the Security Activities Control Board in a related case was misreported as proving that she was a Communist—citizens' letters disclosed yet another interpretation of her life.[86] This was the story of a devious and disloyal black woman who, taught as a Communist to lie, and inheriting "colored folks' [native] cunning," had fooled the Democratic senators into believing that "there must be another ANNIE LEE MOSS hiding somewhere in the woodpile."[87] The ugly

FIGURE 7a and b. Two images of Annie Lee Moss after her testimony before the Permanent Subcommittee on Investigations. (*Time,* March 22, 1954; *Washington Afro-American,* March 13, 1954, used with permission from the Afro-American Newspapers Archives and Research Center)

racism contained in much of this correspondence was echoed in an unsigned editorial by William F. Buckley Jr., writing in the *National Review* in 1958. Annie Lee Moss, he said, "is one of the symbols of our age. A middle-aged, sad-faced, distracted, harassed colored woman, plucked from the obscurity of her government job and publicly terrorized by Senator McCarthy . . . accused, would you believe it? of being a Communist. Have you read the writings of Karl Marx, Senator Symington asked her? Karl Marks? I don't believe ah know who he is, suh, she said sadly. . . . From that moment, Mrs. Moss became a symbol, here and abroad, of the typical victim of the ruthless wanton human destructiveness of the McCarthy machine."[88]

The grain of truth in this analysis is that the racial discourse ascendant in the United States in 1954 overdetermined the response to Annie Lee Moss, who was transformed from a community leader and productive citizen into a passive victim of the "McCarthy machine." As such a victim, she exposed how an extremist anti-Communism lay beyond the bounds of the political mainstream; her rescue confirmed that the American way was the best path toward racial equality. Even John McClellan, who built a political career on the bulwark of racial segregation, was committed to economic opportunity and due process for all citizens, black or white.[89] Annie Lee Moss's testimony before the PSI revealed the tenuousness of that opportunity and suggested how anti-Communist policies risked the nation's progress toward racial equality, but when McCarthy's critics defended Moss's right to earn a living, they preserved the fiction that the national security state nourished civil liberties and furthered democracy.

Unlike Doris Walters Powell, unlike Marie Richardson Harris, unlike untold numbers of other American citizens—black and white, women and men—who lost their livelihoods, and sometimes their freedom, Annie Lee Moss kept her government job until she retired in 1975. Her ability to do so owed more to luck and to the fact that she was a convenient symbol for the evils of the national security state run amok—that is, the evils of "McCarthyism"—than to any evidence exonerating her. In fact, even after the senator's fortunes declined, suspicions about her allegiance persisted. When in the summer of 1954 his Senate colleagues began discussing the possibility of censuring McCarthy, his "abuse" of Annie Lee Moss was listed as one of the counts, but it had disappeared by the time formal charges were filed. None too soon: in August 1954 the army suspended Moss again, supposedly on new information regarding her CP membership.[90] This time the investigation dragged on for months, while Moss remained at home, without pay. Finally, in late January she received a letter from Secretary of Defense Charles Wilson permitting her to return to work, despite the existence of "certain derogatory information" about her. The *New York Times* reported that Secretary Wilson had, "under somewhat mysterious circumstances," circumvented Secretary of the Army Robert Stevens and "reached in" to resolve the case. The *Times* reporter perhaps did not know that, several weeks before, President Eisenhower had taken time during a cabinet meeting to express his concern that Wilson ensure a "just outcome" in the case. Moss and her lawyer pronounced themselves delighted, but the editors of the *Times* did not agree. "The ending is not really a happy one for those who believe in fair play," they wrote. Wilson's "strange letter . . . leaves her . . . in a kind of never-never land in which no American citizen ought to be compelled to dwell."[91]

This "never-never land" was produced by a state of exception that predicated Americans' right to earn a living on their subjection to extensive surveillance and their ability to demonstrate loyalty to a government-approved racial order. It was also, in part, a place of Moss's own making. Whether or not she ever "knowingly" joined the Communist Party, she knew more about it than she pretended. But she also knew a great deal about how to survive in the racist milieu of the nation's capital, and she drew on well-learned lessons about racial etiquette as well as her political skills and community connections to respond successfully to the attack on her livelihood. What appeared to be ignorance was really an effective act of self-preservation, and it meshed well with the desire of many policy makers and opinion shapers to demonstrate that the United States jealously guarded the economic rights of its African American citizens. Indeed, it is not in the least surprising that presumptions of African American ineptitude shaped both the presentation and the reception of Moss's testimony,[92] for those presumptions enabled some white citizens to reconcile proclamations of U.S. dedication to democracy and equal opportunity with the massive evidence that many African Americans were particularly targeted by national security policies and excluded from full citizenship. Nonetheless, Annie Lee Moss continued to live out her own American citizenship as robustly as she could. In the wake of her encounter with McCarthy, and long after she retired from government service, she used the Baptist Church as her platform for community activism, organizing a training school for youth leaders, working on neighborhood safety issues, and staying well connected to Washington's black political elite. Her own role, she believed, was to raise up a new generation of African Americans ready to take on the challenges of citizenship.[93]

Moss's experience attracted so much attention precisely because the citizenship status of African Americans endangered the claims of the United States to lead the free world. Her economic mobility was understood to signal the distance from slavery to freedom, providing evidence of racial progress in a way that the continued discrimination, injustice, and violence experienced by many black women and men did not. But America's position vis-à-vis the Soviet Union was also threatened by the fact that the United States remained a colonial power. As a result, debates about the status of Puerto Rico acquired intensified significance during these years, offering an opportunity for both defenders and critics of U.S. policy to weigh in on the meanings of American citizenship. It is to those debates, and the ways they were affected by the national security state, that we now turn.

CHAPTER FOUR.

"A Dependent Independence and a Dominated Dominion"

Empire and Semi-Citizenship on the Cold War Stage

EARLY ON THE MORNING OF MARCH 1, 1954, DELORES "LOLITA" LEBRÓN, Irving Flores Rodriguez, Andrés Figueroa Cordero, and Rafael Cancel Miranda, all members of Puerto Rico's Nationalist Party (NP), left their homes in New York City to board a Washington–bound train. After a quick lunch near Union Station, they proceeded to the House of Representatives and seated themselves quietly in the Ladies' Gallery. In the midst of a debate about a Mexican guest worker program, Lebrón rose and unfurled a Puerto Rican flag, a signal for the four to begin spraying the House floor with gunfire. In the chaos that ensued, five congressmen were wounded, one critically.

None died as a result of the incident, but the dramatic action was met by the combined force of the Puerto Rican police and the U.S. Department of Justice (fig. 8). The four Nationalists were quickly brought to trial and received maximum terms of fifty to seventy-five years. Hundreds of Puerto Ricans were summoned to appear before grand juries, and dozens were arrested in New York City and Chicago. Thirteen of them, including Lebrón and the other shooters, were convicted of attempting to overthrow the government of the United States and sent to federal prisons. The evidence against them came, in large part, from an FBI informant within the NP as well as Lebrón's brother, a Nationalist leader in Chicago who cooperated with the prosecution. In Puerto Rico,

FIGURE 8. Lolita Lebrón, Rafael Cancel Miranda, and Andrés Figueroa Cordero after being seized by Capitol police. (Corbis)

officials arrested scores of known Nationalists and leftists, and several activists were convicted of attempting to overthrow the government of Puerto Rico.[1]

Also questioned by the grand jury in New York City were North American supporters of the Puerto Rican independence struggle. Two of them, Ruth Reynolds and Thelma Mielke, were each summoned dozens of times, and both lost their jobs after FBI agents visited their employers. This was not the first time that Reynolds's solidarity work had gotten her in trouble. She had been in Puerto Rico during a Nationalist-led uprising in 1950, was arrested for promoting the overthrow of the Puerto Rican government, and served nearly two years in prison there. Thousands of Puerto Ricans were detained, and many received harsh sentences, some up to four hundred years. The political repression unleashed on Nationalist supporters in 1950 and 1954 decimated the party both on the mainland and in Puerto Rico.[2]

The turmoil in Puerto Rico during the early 1950s was intimately connected to the territory's importance in the global Cold War, both as a symbol of U.S.

commitment to (or violation of) principles of freedom and equality, and as a staging ground for the atomic-era military. U.S. and Puerto Rican officials tried to make it an exemplar of the promises offered by U.S.-style development to emerging nations as well as a signifier of American support for decolonization. But making Puerto Rico a "showplace of democracy" in a decolonizing world required finesse, for residents of Puerto Rico—nominally citizens of both Puerto Rico and the United States—lacked many of the rights of self-governance. They were, to use the political scientist Elizabeth Cohen's term, semi-citizens, and a massive effort involving Puerto Rico's ruling Popular Democratic Party (PPD), many departments of the U.S. government, and even the United Nations was required to sustain the illusion that they were something else. This was an effort that was opposed by both the Nationalists and their North American allies. Indeed, American claims to leadership of the free world enabled the criticism of U.S. imperialism and semi-citizenship, facilitating the birth of a homegrown solidarity movement that paved the way for broader protests against U.S. foreign policy in the 1960s.[3]

The debates over Puerto Rico's status that raged on both island and continent during the early Cold War focused attention on the failures of American democracy and on the myth of full citizenship that underwrote U.S. policies and ideologies. Efforts to sustain that myth ranged from legislative reframings of the relationship between Puerto Rico and the United States to discursive reframings of nationalism as madness, colonialism as brotherhood, and continued political subordination as freedom. Rhetorics of gender and race featured centrally in these initiatives.[4] In turn, Nationalists and their allies sought to make visible the many forms of violence that underlay the national security state in both its domestic and its foreign operations. Although their numbers remained small, their struggles revealed that in these years Puerto Rico *was* the inclusive exclusion, the prototypical state of exception, a place where U.S. citizens were denied the rights of citizenship even as they were declared "part of the independence of the United States."[5]

"Is That the Kind of Citizenship You Offer Us?"
Semi-Citizenship and Anti-Imperialism

When the United States acquired Puerto Rico at the end of the Spanish-American War, Congress declared its residents citizens of "Porto Rico" but dictated that they would have only the most limited rights of self-government. Unlike previous territories, this one was not meant for statehood.[6] In a group of early twentieth-century legal cases that have come to be known as the Insular Cases, the Supreme Court endorsed this position. Creating a distinction between "incorporated" and "unincorporated" territories, a majority of justices agreed that Puerto Rico was "foreign in a domestic sense," a territory that was "owned by" but not included within the United States. Puerto Ricans were entitled to the natural rights due all individuals—freedom of religion and speech, due process, and individual liberty—but the Constitution did not extend to them those "rights to citizenship, to suffrage, and to the particular methods of procedure . . . which are peculiar to Anglo-Saxon jurisprudence." Puerto Ricans, U.S. officials agreed, were too different to be extended the full panoply of rights associated with American democracy.[7]

Subsequent developments affirmed that Puerto Rico was the "inclusive exclusion" par excellence. In 1917 the Jones Act declared island residents U.S. citizens and provided enhanced rights to elect members of the local legislature, but Puerto Rican leaders recognized the limits of this "progress." Summing up their doubts over the benefits of U.S. citizenship, Resident Commissioner Luis Muñoz Rivera had told members of Congress in 1914: "If you wish to make us citizens of an inferior class; . . . if we can not be one of your States; if we can not constitute a country of our own, then we will have to be perpetually a colony, a dependency of the United States. Is that the kind of citizenship you offer us? Then, that is the citizenship we refuse." In 1922 the Supreme Court confirmed their fears, ruling that even the Jones Act did not serve to incorporate Puerto Rico into the nation. As a result, residents of Puerto Rico were entitled to move to the mainland, but as long as they remained on the island, they were denied many of the rights to which other U.S. citizens were at least theoretically entitled, including trial by jury and representation in the federal government. Those who lived in Puerto Rico remained semi-citizens of the United States.[8]

Its anomalous status enabled U.S. corporations to penetrate Puerto Rico's economy thoroughly, generating increasing discontent when the Great Depression hit the island economy especially hard. During the 1930s Puerto Rico was roiled by strikes and political unrest, including growing support for independence.[9] Two pro-independence leaders who came to prominence would play critical roles in postwar Puerto Rico. Luis Muñoz Marín, son of former resident commissioner Luis Muñoz Rivera and well-connected to U.S. officials who sought to bring the New Deal to the island, advocated charting a path toward independence through economic and land reform. By 1938 Muñoz Marín's *independentista* leanings led him to help found the Popular Democratic Party, which he would go on to head for many years. Arguing for more immediate independence was Pedro Albizu Campos. A man of humbler beginnings, Albizu Campos was reportedly the first Puerto Rican to attend Harvard University, doing so on a scholarship. He served in the U.S. military during World War I, studied law, and returned to Puerto Rico in the early 1920s, where he became active in insular politics. In 1930 he was elected president of the Nationalist Party, which had been founded as a pro-independence political party in 1922.[10]

While Muñoz Marín focused his efforts on establishing himself and building support among the Puerto Rican electorate and federal officials, Albizu Campos quickly abandoned electoral politics to advocate direct action to expel the United States, arguing that its possession of the territory amounted to nothing more than illicit military occupation.[11] Soon the NP was organizing quasi-military local units and calling for armed struggle—if necessary—against the United States. U.S. officials' efforts to suppress the party produced even greater political turmoil and violence. In the wake of the assassination of a police commissioner and the police murder of two Nationalists, the federal government tried eight NP leaders for "conspiring to overthrow the government of the United States." Albizu Campos was sentenced to ten years in the federal penitentiary in Atlanta.[12]

When U.S. officials decided to incarcerate Albizu Campos on the mainland, they could not know that this would provide the spark for an organized pro-independence solidarity movement in North America. Since the late 1930s, pacifists, liberals, and leftists across the United States had occasionally raised their voices in favor of a resolution of the status problem, but an active movement dedicated to ending colonialism in Puerto Rico emerged first in New York City, where Albizu Campos had been transferred to a hospital after falling ill in prison.[13] He was something of a celebrity, and many well-known progressive New Yorkers sat at his bedside during these months. Among those who visited him were members of the Harlem Ashram, a center for radical pacifists founded in 1940 by former Methodist missionary Jay Holmes Smith. He had been ejected from India for his support of the pro-independence movement there, and his political commitments helped shape ashram members' advocacy. The radical Christian peace activists who lived and congregated at the ashram dedicated themselves to antiracist and anticolonialist causes. One of the residents of this intentional community was Ruth Reynolds, who would become the Nationalist Party's staunchest mainland ally.[14]

Ruth Reynolds was an unlikely convert to the cause of militant nationalism. Born in 1916 in the mining town of Terraville, South Dakota to an upwardly mobile Methodist family, she trained as a teacher. Unable to find steady work, she pursued a master's degree in English at Northwestern University. While there, Reynolds "fell in" with a group of pacifists, and in 1941 she moved to New York City to take a "training course in total pacifism" offered by the Fellowship of Reconciliation (FOR) at the Harlem Ashram. She settled in as one of five or six permanent residents, living an ascetic life of prayer, Bible study, discussion of Gandhianism, and activism. Reynolds participated in an interracial march from Harlem to the Lincoln Memorial, walked in picket lines protesting British imperialism, and did "volunteer social work" in the ashram's largely Puerto Rican neighborhood. And she became acquainted with many of those at the center of the pacifist and burgeoning civil rights movements, among them Ernest Bromley, Dave Dellinger, Jim Farmer, lawyer Conrad Lynn, A. J. Muste, and Bayard Rustin.[15]

It was not until Puerto Rican associates challenged ashram residents to examine imperialism in their own backyard that they began to pay attention to Puerto Rico. Shortly after Albizu Campos's arrival in New York, an ashram member brought Nationalist activist Julio Pinto Gandía to dinner. Both draft resisters (Gandía, in accordance with an NP policy of noncooperation with the U.S. government, had refused induction into the army), they had met in prison. At Gandía's urging, Jay Holmes Smith visited Albizu Campos, and, Reynolds recalled, soon he was "spending all his time down there in that hospital room."[16]

As a result, by January 1944, New York pacifists decided to incorporate the cause of Puerto Rico in their anti-imperialism work. For years they had picketed the British consulate on Indian Independence Day, a day dedicated by the Indian National Congress to work for India's self-rule. This year, the Free India Committee joined with the Fellowship of Reconciliation, the March on Washington Movement, the Congress of Racial Equality, and others to include Puerto Rican independence in their demands. Smith was away, and so it fell to Reynolds, who by now was assistant director of the ashram, to lead the demonstration. After marching through Harlem, the group took the subway to the British consulate, where about a dozen were arrested. Reynolds's picture made the paper, and Albizu Campos asked that she come to see him. Reynolds later remembered, "Within a month or so of knowing Don Pedro, I really felt that I had to commit myself to the struggle for the independence of Puerto Rico, and that it had to be primarily with North Americans, who, like myself, felt

. . . the holding of Puerto Rico to be an outrage to any principles we have."[17] By October 1944 she was meeting with a group of New Yorkers who were active in the pacifist, civil rights, civil liberties, socialist, labor, and internationalist movements to discuss the possibility of creating a permanent organization to focus on Puerto Rico's political status, and in early 1945 the American League for Puerto Rico's Independence (ALPRI) was born. Pledged to work for federal recognition of the island's independence, immediate amnesty for political prisoners, and "full and speedy reparations," its members sought to bring NP grievances to the attention of U.S. policy makers and the public.[18] Their numbers were small, but this group and its successors offered an important witness against the violence of empire and the national security state in the midst of the Cold War.[19]

"The Great Harshness of Our Destiny"

Dependence, Independence, and Reform

Ironically, at the very moment when North American activists were beginning to organize in support of independence, Luis Muñoz Marín, now the dominant figure on Puerto Rico's political landscape, chose to move away from that stance. Insisting that the island must remain tied to the United States for the foreseeable future, he emphasized that Puerto Rico's privileged position as a trading "partner," as well as federal largesse in the form of the New Deal, made complete independence a chimera.[20] But foremost among the PPD leader's justifications for rejecting independence was Puerto Rico's alleged "overpopulation" problem. He joined a host of commentators who cited overpopulation as an intractable barrier to independence. In one widely reviewed book, for example, the anthropologist Vincenzo Petrullo argued that the island would need "a large subsidy for many years to come, as well as freedom to emigrate" to the United States, since "the root of the Puerto Rican economic problem" was its "golden-skinned babies, whose nakedness so often decorates the front yards of the cabins."[21] Muñoz Marín echoed these thoughts, telling the Puerto Rican people in 1948 that the question of political status had to be decided in light of "the great harshness of our destiny." He continued:

> The condition of Puerto Rico is in its very nature an extremely unfavorable and difficult one. Puerto Rico is a very small island with a great many people. Puerto Rico has a little land and a great many people. Every year

> there are more people, but there is not more land. This great number of people must live off the little land there is. With the nature of the condition of Puerto Rico so difficult in itself, the only thing which allows it to live . . . is precisely the fact of its having such a favorable relationship with the richest market in the world.

As the repetitive structure of this speech reveals, by the postwar years, "too many people, not enough land" had become a mantra that rationalized continuing the United States' rule over Puerto Rico.[22]

These assertions of Puerto Rico's continuing dependence were problematic in the context of the emerging global Cold War. "Dependence" signified femininity and failed masculinity, weakness and vulnerability. It belied the portrait of an autonomous island nation increasingly ready to take its place in the modern democratic world, a view that American policy makers and Muñoz Marín's PPD were eager to propagate as worldwide pressures for decolonization made Puerto Rico's status increasingly embarrassing. Nonetheless, Puerto Rico's strategic location, its close economic ties to U.S. industry, and its cultural ties to Latin America, where the United States was seeking to consolidate its own influence, all made independence risky from the perspective of U.S. policy makers. The 1944 remarks of Representative Fred Crawford of Michigan, an influential participant in the debates about Puerto Rico's status, reveal that even before the end of World War II, U.S. officials were cognizant of Puerto Rico's significance in anticipated postwar conflicts with the Soviet Union. As he put it, "Puerto Rico cannot be independent because the United States has to maintain an army and a navy in the island to defend the territory against the Russian menace, which after this war will try to dismember this continent to take possession of South America."[23] These concerns only grew more intense in the postwar years.

The solution to this dilemma was to shift the terms of the debate from "independence" to "self-determination." Self-determination could accommodate a wide variety of political processes and outcomes, and unlike independence, it might be reconciled with Puerto Rico's continued dependence on the United States. Indeed, its focus on *process* rather than *outcome* shaped the postwar universe of political possibilities for Puerto Ricans. Meshing nicely with an older political maturity model that "would grant to the people of Puerto Rico a constantly increasing measure of real control over their local affairs" while putting off "independence" indefinitely, it became crucial to representations of the United States as a decolonizing power.[24] In October 1945 President Truman came out forcefully for self-determination, proclaiming that "[it] is the settled policy of this Government to promote the political[,] social and economic development of people who have not yet attained full self-government and eventually to make it possible for them to determine their own form of government." He asked Congress to move forward on identifying feasible options, authorizing a plebiscite, and enacting a solution to the status problem.[25]

Following this, PPD leaders and the Truman administration showcased a new developmentalist narrative, one in which Puerto Rico was making steady progress toward "true freedom," marked by increasing local self-government, modernization, and economic growth. This progress was traced through a number of discrete markers—the appointment of the first indigenous governor in 1946; the passage of an elective governor bill in 1947 and the inauguration of Luis Muñoz Marín as governor in 1948; the enactment in 1950 of Public Law 600 (PL 600), which enabled Puerto Ricans to write their own constitution (while also leaving substantially untouched the institutional framework that granted the U.S. government authority over trade, defense, foreign affairs, currency, and a host of other matters); and, in 1952, the ratification of that constitution by both the Puerto Rican people and the U.S. Congress and the creation of the Commonwealth of Puerto Rico, also known as the Estado Libre Asociado, or Free Associated State. Puerto Rico's emergence in 1952 as a U.S. "dominion," according to this story, not only marked the end of this nation's history as an imperial power but also proved the superiority of the American way of decolonization. No longer a "stepchild," the Commonwealth of Puerto Rico was the United States' adult partner in making the postwar order.[26]

This narrative required resignifying U.S.-insular relations as ties not of paternalism but of fraternalism. To this end, U.S. and Puerto Rican officials offered a repetitious, almost compulsive recitation of the steps by which U.S. control had fostered the ability of Puerto Ricans to govern themselves. Recasting a history of imperialism as a genealogy of ever-increasing self-rule, U.S. legislators described the years after the invasion as a prologue to self-determination, when Puerto Ricans were offered a series of lessons in the art of self-government.[27] Each of the postwar reforms then became further development and proof of insular political maturity. Thus in 1946, when Jesus T. Piñero was appointed the first Puerto Rican to serve as governor, Secretary of the Interior J. A. Krug spoke of his hopes that the Puerto Rican people would "continue . . . to stride forward along the road toward full political maturity." Half a year later, supporting the elective governor bill, former governor James Beverly testified that the people of Puerto Rico had been "politically mature . . . for some time."[28] Muñoz Marín went a bit further, framing the Puerto Rican constitution as not simply "another step in self-government but . . . self-government within the American Union by the free agreement of the Puerto Rican people and in a new manner." It did not increase "in any substantial way the real political freedom of the people of Puerto Rico," because, he argued, islanders were already practicing democracy. The passage of the constitution simply made "the law catch up with the facts so that the United States . . . cannot at all be accused again by communists or by mistaken people of good faith who are not communists in Latin-America and in the world of holding a colonial possession in Puerto Rico."[29] Reforming Puerto Rico's status crafted a "third way" to a "new state," substituting a "common citizenship" for the economic suicide of nationalism or the cultural suicide of statehood. With such reforms, U.S. officials agreed, Puerto Rico could take its "due and proper place as another adult member of our political family."[30]

Substantial tensions remained in these characterizations of a new relationship between the United States and its "former" colony. Decolonization signified the maturity and masculinization of former dependencies. But since Puerto Rico's continued economic dependence remained front and center in arguments for self-determination rather than complete independence, gendered tropes of fraternity could not map precisely onto the new political arrangements.[31] Puerto Rican and U.S. officials sought to grapple with this contradiction by using the conceit of the "compact" to trace the new lineaments of Puerto Rico's economic and political partnership with the United States. A clause in the preamble to PL 600 stating it was "adopted in the nature of a compact" was meant to convey that this act of Congress created a "voluntary association" based on "mutual consent and esteem," a "partnership mutually acceptable" to both entities.[32] Muñoz Marín offered a stirring declaration of the meanings of such a shift:

> There could be no more exciting way than this of abolishing the colonial system . . . no more brotherly way, no freer way . . . no clearer way for Puerto Rico to know that the decision of her political destiny is in her own hands, without her having pressure put on her or being resisted, without her being either hurried or put off, without her being obliged to make her choice under adverse economic conditions, and without anyone interfering

> with her judgment as to when economic conditions have ceased to be adverse. This is offering a brother the key to one's house, so that he may freely depart or freely remain.[33]

In his mixing of metaphors—free brothers on the one hand, woman in control of her destiny on the other—he showcased the ability of the compact to reconcile Puerto Rico's economic dependence with its supposed political sovereignty. But his words also suggest how it functioned like other contracts that masked inequality between partners with the legal fiction of free consent—such as labor contracts and, above all, the marriage contract. Like these, the creation of the Commonwealth purported to detach the economic from the political so that Puerto Rico's substantial economic dependence on the United States did not prohibit its citizens from consenting to their continued governance, much as the economic dependence of U.S. women on their husbands was widely believed to be compatible with their political freedom. A "grown-up" Puerto Rico might be masculinized—a "brother" to whom you entrust the key to your home—but it also remained feminized: a wife whose "dominion" was restricted to domestic concerns and who remained both financially dependent and unable to contract with others.[34] Even though creation of the Commonwealth left Puerto Rico a territory under Congress's plenary control, when President Truman formally approved the Constitution of the Commonwealth of Puerto Rico, he could assert that the Puerto Rican people's decision to "reaffir[m] their union with the United States" was evidence that America stood for "the right of free peoples everywhere." Puerto Rico remained the quintessential state of exception, still belonging to but not a part of the United States, its people's semi-citizenship disguised by the rhetoric of decolonization.[35]

"Forced to Sacrifice Their Dignity in Order to Live"
Debating U.S. Colonialism

The effort to reframe Puerto Rico's continued subordination to the United States as self-determination was challenged not only by the Nationalist Party, which worked hard to disrupt the process leading to the creation of the Commonwealth, but also by its supporters in North America. ALPRI members questioned the self-determination narrative at every step. They opposed the elective governor bill, the creation of the Commonwealth, and a variety of plebiscites, arguing that only independence with reparations would provide the territorial, military, political, and economic sovereignty necessary to "contract on equal terms" with the United States. Drawing attention to the injustice of proposals that would require Puerto Rico to "barter away its birthright of full freedom" in return for economic development, they condemned the "dependent independence and . . . dominated dominion status" that would result from any reforms short of full independence.[36] This position, they claimed, was the only patriotic one possible. As Reynolds argued, only by admitting "individual and corporate responsibility for every act of our government—a sense of responsibility without which democracy is nothing but a lie," could American citizens "begin to free ourselves from the racial and national arrogance that is making our nation a curse in the earth."[37]

These sentiments were brought to an international stage when the UN debated Puerto Rico's status. The question of what role the United Nations would have in monitoring, and perhaps liberating, so-called dependent territories in the postwar years was contentious from the moment the new international agency was envisioned, and in important ways Puerto Rico served as a test case for UN policies and procedures. Independence advocates had looked to the United Nations from its very beginnings. In March 1945 ALPRI appealed to Secretary of State Edward Stettinius, head of the U.S. delegation to the San Francisco conference at which the UN charter was written, urging him to press for granting independence to Puerto Rico before the meeting convened in April. In 1946 Reynolds and Smith spent many hours observing UN committee meetings, and in July of that year ALPRI submitted a lengthy brief asserting that U.S. policy toward Puerto Rico violated the UN Charter. By January 1947 the United Nations had agreed to grant the Nationalist Party "observer" status, and the NP designated as its representatives party member Oscar Collazo and ALPRI activist Thelma Mielke. Mielke went to Geneva, where she attended meetings of the Special Committee on Information, charged with working out the UN's policies and procedures on dependent territories. These efforts appear to have yielded little, since under pressure from the colonial powers, the committee refused twice to grant a requested hearing to the Nationalist representatives. Nonetheless, as a "permanent observer" Mielke was able to caucus with sympathetic members, provide information about the "true picture" of conditions in Puerto Rico, and gain insight into committee politics.[38]

Muñoz Marín and the Truman and Eisenhower administrations also treated the United Nations as an important arbiter of Puerto Rico's status in the court of world opinion. The agency's charter stipulated that "administering" powers must report on "economic, social and educational conditions" for so-called non-self-governing territories.[39] Barely a month after the creation of the Commonwealth, Puerto Rican and U.S. officials began planning to notify the UN that, since Puerto Rico was now self-governing, the United States would cease reporting on it. Negotiations over how to phrase the announcement were prolonged, as insular and federal authorities disagreed over such weighty matters as whether or not Puerto Rico remained a "territory" and if the "compact" required that further adjustments to the island's status could be accomplished only by mutual consent.[40] Perhaps because of these questions, the official notice of the decision to stop reporting was not submitted until January 19, 1953, the last full day of Truman's term in office.

Despite continuing conflict among and between U.S. and Puerto Rican officials, when they presented the case to the United Nations, any uncertainty about the nature of the compact was buried beneath assertions that this was an unprecedented arrangement that revealed a new way forward for dependent peoples who, in partnership with the capitalist world, were seeking economic, social, and political development. Since PPD leaders originated this interpretation of Puerto Rico's "new state," it is no surprise that they were its foremost defenders in the United Nations. At Muñoz Marín's suggestion, the State Department made Puerto Rico's resident commissioner, Antonio Fernós-Isern, a member of the U.S. delegation in order to "enhance American prestige" in Africa, Asia, and Latin America. Fernós-Isern introduced the U.S. position in August 1953, proclaiming that "any semblance of a colonial relationship was eliminated" with the creation of the Commonwealth. As he explained, "As of July 25, 1952, the jurisdiction of the Federal Government in Puerto Rico is based on a bilateral compact to which it is a party and into which the people of Puerto Rico have entered of their own volition. The Puerto Rican state of today has been created by the will of the people, in the exercise of their natural rights. . . . Puerto Rico is today in the most profoundly democratic sense of the word a free people voluntarily associated with the United States of America."[41] Addressing the UN later that year, he presented the compact as something magical, a legal and political instrument with transformative powers: "Provisions of law which originally were enacted by unilateral action of the Congress of the United States . . . now became, by virtue of the compact, bilateral stipulations forming the association between Puerto Rico and the United States." Through this "new form of political relationship," he asserted, "the last vestige of colonialism has disappeared in Puerto Rico."[42]

U.S. officials were just as determined—if, perhaps, more disingenuous—to affirm the inviolability of the new relationship. For example, diplomat Mason Sears defined "compact" in his comments preceding Fernós-Isern's initial statement: "A compact, as you know, is far stronger than a treaty. A treaty usually can be denounced by either side, whereas a compact cannot be denounced by either party unless it has the permission of the other." When delegate Frances P. Bolton responded to criticism of the U.S. position, she highlighted two "facts": that the Commonwealth was grounded in the "sovereignty" of the Puerto Rican people, and that "there exists a bilateral compact of association between the people of Puerto Rico and the United States which has been accepted by both and which in accordance with judicial decisions may not be amended without common consent." The "judicial decisions" to which Bolton referred were in fact a lone district court ruling that Congress had given up its plenary powers when it approved PL 600, but U.S. representatives presented the question as much more settled than it actually was.[43]

Both PPD leaders and U.S. officials had second thoughts about the wisdom of declaring Puerto Rico's sovereignty in the UN, anticipating domestic and international challenges.[44] Though a feared revolt from Congress did not materialize, the move was the subject of contentious debate at every level of the United Nations. Among advocates of Puerto Rican independence, the Nationalists and the more moderate Puerto Rican Independence Party unsuccessfully sought to testify, while ALPRI members contented themselves with submitting a brief, highlighting the Commonwealth's lack of sovereignty as well as the undemocratic process by which the constitution was adopted. They made particular note of political repression of the Nationalist Party (discussed later in this chapter), alleging that the referendum on the constitution took place while "the Island was being subjected to a rule close to that of martial law."[45]

These criticisms were taken seriously by some representatives of UN member states, most notably India, Mexico, and Guatemala, and used as weapons against the United States by the Soviet Union and its partners. In one discussion, for example, Indian delegate Lakshmi Menon zeroed in on Puerto Ricans' semi-citizenship, questioning whether Puerto Rico could be called self-governing since it had no real representation in Congress. (Equal legislative representation was one of the factors specified by the United Nations for demonstrating self-governance.) At another moment, Indian representatives rejected the U.S. assertion that self-governance was possible even without independence, asserting this was simply "a new form of colonialism."[46] Similarly, a Mexican diplomat denounced the decision to stop reporting on Puerto Rico's status as coldly calculated to increase U.S. prestige in Latin America. He expressed his hope that a time would come when "no peoples in the world were ever forced to sacrifice their dignity in order to live," to which Bolton riposted, "Poverty, hunger, and ignorance are not the ingredients with which a society of free people can be established and developed and its dignity maintained."[47]

Such a contested process was not what U.S. and Puerto Rican officials had had in mind. Although the State Department was relatively confident that the General Assembly would ultimately endorse the U.S. decision to end reporting,[48] the extended and acrimonious debate had aired doubts not only over whether or not Puerto Rico was self-governing, but also about the intentions of the United States. It was because these proceedings were as much about political theater as multilateral governance and cooperation that President Eisenhower decided to get into the act. At breakfast a week before the General Assembly was scheduled to take up the Puerto Rico question, Eisenhower suggested to his old friend UN ambassador Henry Cabot Lodge that a "dramatic" move might be in order. Lodge took the floor shortly before the General Assembly vote to announce, "I am authorized to say on behalf of the President that if at any time the Legislative Assembly of Puerto Rico adopts a resolution in favor of more complete or even absolute independence, he will immediately thereafter recommend to Congress that such independence be granted." Since the PPD-dominated legislature opposed independence, this was an empty promise, but its utterance at the United Nations had an electrifying effect. An exultant Lodge told Eisenhower: "Your idea about Puerto Rico turned out to be a ten-strike. . . . I . . . received an unprecedented burst of applause. . . . The effect will be tremendous in Latin America and in all colonial areas."[49]

The General Assembly did indeed vote to approve the U.S. decision to cease reporting on Puerto Rico, but some nations still expressed doubt that a dependent Puerto Rico could freely determine its future. Lakshmi Menon had the final word at the session:

> There can be no free, just or valid compact, association or agreement between two countries or territories except on a basis of equality. We believe that independence should precede any voluntary association. . . . An association of States under any form in which the inequality of status is not redeemed, would only camouflage the relics of a colonial past.

> This would be contrary to the Charter, which aims not at the creation or perpetuation of colonialism in some form or other, but its total and complete elimination from the political system and thought of the new world.[50]

Alluding to the objections voiced by Nationalists and their allies, Menon and a few other representatives of the global South thus called into question the entire project of presenting the Commonwealth of Puerto Rico as a "brother" in the postcolonial order, reminding the assembled nations that economic dependence and the inequality it expressed made true self-determination impossible. But at least at this early moment in a decolonizing world, U.S. economic power and Cold War pressures made hers a minority voice.

Still, the contentious debate at the United Nations signaled that Puerto Ricans' semi-citizenship, and their leaders' determination to stand outside the nation-state form that was reaching its zenith in the postwar years, could not be so easily resolved.[51] Lodge's announcement brought a storm of protest from Puerto Rican advocates of statehood, particularly members of Eisenhower's own Republican Party, who feared that the United States "does not want [Puerto Rico] and is ready to turn the island loose." Members of Puerto Rico's legislature also quickly rebuffed the idea of independence.[52] Eisenhower, encouraged by Lodge's exuberant assessment of the UN response, seized on the idea of granting Puerto Rico independence as an ideological weapon in the Cold War, but he was forced to retreat. As State Department officials reminded him, independence raised a troubling question for Puerto Ricans, a question that had, much earlier, been asked by Justice Edward Douglass White in one of the Insular Cases: Could the United States "sell American citizens?" Mass expatriation of U.S. citizens—even if the Puerto Rican legislature requested independence—had consequences that could not be easily resolved.[53] This question returned again to the paradoxical nature of citizenship for residents of Puerto Rico. PL 600 reaffirmed them as citizens of both Puerto Rico and the United States, but this remained more a semi-citizenship than dual citizenship. Increasingly moving back and forth between the island and the mainland, and in that mobility sometimes repeatedly experiencing enfranchisement and disenfranchisement, Puerto Ricans found no clear path to liberty along the "third way" that was laid out for them. Although the most obvious effects of the U.S. decision to cease reporting on Puerto Rico were to suggest that independence was not the only road to self-governance, and to disguise the role of economic inequality in constituting a postcolonial world, the hotly contested process also hinted that these were questions that would return to haunt the nation and its territory.[54]

"Imperialism Is the Real Violence"
Terrorism and the National Security State

The legislative and symbolic reframing of Puerto Rico's relationship to the United States was deeply entwined with the operations of the national security state. Although U.S. military officials moved to create and control a modern police authority soon after the invasion of the island, Puerto Rico's "surveillance state" was greatly consolidated and strengthened in response to the Nationalist ferment of the 1930s. The enmeshing of the federal and insular security apparatus was significant: as early as 1935 the FBI trained members of the Insular Police; its special agents collected information from a wide range of island authorities and informants; army and navy intelligence officers conducted political surveillance on Puerto Rican dissidents and mainstream political leaders alike; in 1942 the FBI organized and trained an internal security unit in the police force. The tangled relationship between island and federal police efforts was made obvious in the prosecution of Pedro Albizu Campos and other Nationalist leaders in the wake of the shooting by two NP members of a police officer. Charged with conspiring to overthrow the government of the United States, the defendants were first tried before a majority–Puerto Rican jury, whose members could not agree on a verdict. Their second trial, in which it was alleged that federal officials had handpicked a biased jury and then directed it to arrive at a guilty verdict, ended with their exile to a federal prison in Atlanta.[55]

In their insistence that the U.S. presence was nothing more than an illegal military occupation of the sovereign nation of Puerto Rico, and in their unyielding opposition to attempts to reframe the colonial relationship as an equal partnership, Nationalists represented a substantial threat to these policing efforts. Unsurprisingly, then, the intertwined national security states of Puerto Rico and the United States used the strategies of the second red scare to target NP members ever more intensely. In the postwar years, for example, after Albizu Campos returned to his homeland, Puerto Rican officials adapted anti-Communist strategies to control their Nationalist foes. In response to a 1948 student strike at the University of Puerto Rico that erupted when university officials suppressed the activities of NP supporters, the Puerto Rican legislature hurriedly enacted Law 53, popularly known as *la mordaza,* or the "gag law." Modeled on the Smith Act, the law made it a felony "to encourage, defend, counsel, or preach, voluntarily or knowingly, the need, desirability, or convenience of overturning, destroying, or paralyzing the Insular Government, or any of its political subdivisions, by way of force or violence; . . . as well as to organize or help organize any society, group, or assembly of persons who encourage, defend, counsel, or preach any such thing." Although this law would also be used against Communists and more moderate advocates of independence, its primary target was the NP.[56]

So began a rapidly spiraling cycle of violence, as Nationalists, under constant surveillance and harassment, turned to increasingly aggressive tactics, while Puerto Rican and federal authorities used an expanding arsenal of repressive techniques to stop them. But growing Nationalist militancy also responded to the reforms accomplished through the PPD-U.S. alliance. Along with other independence advocates, Nationalists were dismayed by the creation of the Commonwealth and, later, the UN's endorsement of Puerto Rico's decolonization. They recognized that these moves did as much to invalidate insular opposition movements as to sanction the island's continued domination by U.S. capital. Hobbled both by police repression and by the PPD's political acumen, NP members insisted, "We Puerto Ricans have the right to resist force with force."[57] Pointing to the symbolic and real violence that underlay the efforts to cast Puerto Rico as a showplace of democracy and development, they too employed violence in order to "make a demonstration" to Americans and the world that Puerto Rico remained unfree. In response, U.S. and Puerto Rican officials adroitly seized the opportunity to consolidate the national security state further by labeling them terrorists. Thus the conflict over Puerto Rico's status quickened a debate about the legitimacy of state and extra-state violence.

"Terrorism" had long been used to designate certain forms of political violence as illegitimate. In the 1930s and early 1940s "terror" mostly described "totalitarian" states' violence against individuals. In the wake of World War II, as some anticolonial movements turned to violence as a strategy for defeating the old imperial order, "terrorism" was redefined again. During these years the term came into wider use to suggest senseless and often random violence against innocent victims, intended to instill fear among both the general population and state officials. Certainly some groups—in Palestine and Malaya in the 1940s, and in Cyprus and Algeria in the 1950s—embraced violence as a psychological weapon, but the label "terrorism" functioned less to denote a set of strategies than to legitimate Western nation-states' deployment of political violence while limiting popular support for anticolonial movements. This explains the use of the term against members of the Nationalist Party. Their strategies (their targets were *always* government officials rather than civilians), and the overall rarity of their recourse to violence, made their independence movement quite distinct from these other groups. But by labeling Nationalists "terrorists," Puerto Rican and U.S. officials could rule their entire critique out of bounds.[58]

Descriptions of the NP as terrorist dated back at least to the 1930s, but during the 1950s this rhetoric became ubiquitous, especially as party members brought political violence to the continent. On October 30, 1950, after a predawn raid by Puerto Rican police on Nationalist supporters in Ponce erupted in gunfire, Nationalists launched an island-wide uprising, attacking federal offices and police stations, staging an assault on the governor's residence, and occupying several mountain towns. The revolt, which resulted in upwards of two dozen deaths, was soon put down by Insular Police and the National Guard, who not only engaged in pitched gun battles with NP supporters but also used "bazookas, tanks and planes" against rebels in Jayuya and Utuado.[59] This was more traditional armed resistance than terrorism, but before the smoke had cleared, party members Oscar Collazo and Griselio Torresola traveled from their homes in New York City to Washington to "make a demonstration" against colonialism and launched an armed assault on President Truman's temporary residence at Blair House. They did not reach him, but their attack had tragic consequences: Torresola and one of the president's guards were killed, two other Secret Service agents and Collazo were wounded, and Collazo was sentenced to death (later commuted to life imprisonment) for the crime.[60] It was little more than three years later when Lolita Lebrón and her compatriots opened fire on Congress, an act that sealed the Nationalists' reputation as terrorists.

These incidents had serious adverse consequences, including the exclusion of NP observers and the rejection of their petitions at the United Nations, thus depriving Nationalists of access to this international forum.[61] More important, they led to the detention of thousands of Puerto Ricans and, eventually, the imprisonment of almost all Nationalist leaders. After the 1950 insurrection, close to one thousand individuals, including Communists and moderate advocates of independence, were detained by insular authorities. Upwards of 150 were convicted and incarcerated under *la mordaza* and other laws.[62] In 1954 harassment and imprisonment were aimed at Puerto Ricans on the continent as well as on the island. Collazo, Lebrón, Flores Rodriguez, and Cancel Miranda were not freed until their pardon by President Jimmy Carter in 1979. Albizu Campos, convicted in 1950 on assault and conspiracy but released for health reasons in 1953, was reincarcerated in 1954 and remained in prison, in declining health, until 1964. He died in April 1965.

These outbreaks of violence were not random, but responses to specific U.S.-PPD maneuvers to "solve" Puerto Rico's colonial problem. The 1950 uprising was intended, in part, to disrupt the electoral process that would lead to the founding of the Commonwealth. The 1954 attack occurred three short months after the United Nations endorsed the decision to end reporting on Puerto Rico. It was also linked to growing concerns about Albizu Campos's health that will be discussed shortly; but its broader significance was that, with the purported decolonization of Puerto Rico and widespread support for Muñoz Marín's economic policies, opponents of U.S. rule were running out of options. Their turn to violence reflected the Nationalists' marginal position in the debates over Puerto Rico's status, but it also expressed their simultaneous and somewhat contradictory positions that the U.S. government would respond only to force, and that American imperial power could be made visible and challenged only through self-sacrifice.

If the uprising on the island was intended to meet force with force, Nationalists explained the violent attacks in Washington, D.C., as sacrificial acts. Oscar Collazo, Lolita Lebrón, and their associates maintained that they expected to be killed; all of them purchased one-way train tickets to Washington, presuming that they would have no need for return passage. Self-sacrifice would draw attention to their homeland's desperate straits, but it was necessitated by the overweening power and arrogance of the United States. As Collazo testified at his trial: "I am sure . . . that the American people, ninety per cent of the American people, don't know where Puerto Rico is; they don't know what is Puerto Rico; they don't know that Puerto Rico is a possession of the United States, even though it has been so for the last fifty-two years. . . . By coming to Washington and making some kind of demonstration in the capital of this nation, we would be in a better situation to make the American people understand the real situation in Puerto Rico."[63] Cancel Miranda told jury members that he had gone to Congress "to demonstrate to the world that the Puerto Ricans not only wanted their independence but also that he fights, that he defends, and that he would offer his life for the independence of his country."[64] Cancel Miranda's willingness to fight for the freedom of his country was a matter of masculine honor, but it also was a testament to the U.S. government's power to perpetuate a "fraud and falsehood" on the whole world. And, he acknowledged, it might well result in his death. Juan Bernardo Lebrón (no relation to Lolita), also on trial for conspiracy in connection with the 1954 shooting, scoffed at U.S. pretensions that Nationalists endangered the security of the nation: "Here we are, a few little Puerto Ricans, and here is the great powerful government of the United States—and the United States is afraid that we will overthrow them!"[65]

Lolita Lebrón laid bare the inequities that prompted NP "terror" even more vividly, identifying her own suffering as a woman with the suffering of her country. A twenty-one-year-old Lebrón had come, alone, to New York City in 1940, leaving her young daughter in her mother's care on the island. A skilled needleworker, she found employment in the textile industry, but her outspokenness on behalf of workers made for much job insecurity. She joined the NP out of anger over the discrimination and abusive treatment accorded Puerto Rican migrants to the city. Lebrón married and had another child, but by the late 1940s her marriage broke up, in part because her husband objected to her political activities, and she was forced to send her son back to Puerto Rico. Shortly before she testified in her second trial, she learned that he had died, a victim of drowning.[66]

Lebrón's courtroom testimony was infused by her sorrow over this loss, but it also expressed a specific logic of anticolonial struggle. Situating her decision to go to Washington in a broader national and international context, she described how she had ruminated on the words of George Washington and Abraham Lincoln as she walked the grounds of the United Nations. And she located herself within the political economy of American empire: "I was going to my work every day, but I keep on that machine, the machine have taken my life, more than my life. I kept on . . . thinking I should do something for the freedom of my country. I could not live." Lebrón "could not live" both because she did not make enough money to support her son and because of her homeland's plight, two issues that were connected for her: "My son believed in the freedom of my life. . . . He wanted me, he wanted my country to be free." She asked why it was that the powerful representatives of the United States—members of Congress, prosecutors, judges—did not want to hear her speak the "beautiful words" of freedom:

> Why am I here, because I want the freedom of my country and the indictment says that we want by force and violence to bring up the independence of my country, and every time our country brings up the question of independence our mouths have to be closed. That is not freedom that

> is really the truth. . . . But don't you worry. A woman is going to write in prison—this woman is going to write in prison, because I am going to tell you, somebody else is wrong, more wrong than me.

Finally, she insisted that she and her people hated violence, that she had been badly misunderstood:

> I am not the woman you think I am. I say I have a heart who has been crucified. . . . I have lost a lot of things and with terrible suffering. That you would not be able to take, maybe, Mr. Lumbard [the district attorney]. Maybe not many of the people here will take what I have taken. . . . I have paid so hard, and for this moment, to come here to tell you, we want this country to live, this belongs to our new world. . . . We don't want wars. We want to live. We want this country to live. We want the world to live.[67]

Lebrón's testimony, which her lawyer claimed moved even the hard-nosed judge to tears, encapsulated a history of a people struggling against a behemoth for their freedom.[68] In her cry "I am not the woman you think I am" was the Nationalist defense against the accusation of terrorism.

Nationalists employed both of these gendered discourses—the first emphasizing masculinist defenses of honor, the second highlighting the feminine, suffering, exploited nation—to explain their use of violence against the United States. Both of these were very different from the stance struck by Muñoz Marín, which scholars have associated with the verb *bregar.* Ubiquitous in Puerto Rican culture, *bregar* conveys a range of meanings, but in the political context, one of its most important is a sense of "survival, negotiation, slipping from one position to another to achieve a difficult balance between potentially conflictual elements. . . . It entails struggle without a frontal clash. It implies a pact or a dialogue between parties." Arcadio Díaz-Quiñones argues that Muñoz Marín was a master of *bregar,* negotiating with both U.S. officials and the Puerto Rican people to achieve reform that asserted Puerto Rican dignity without subverting the colonial order. He did so by simultaneously inhabiting a paternalist role toward the Puerto Rican masses, whom he promised to rescue from economic and political dependency, and articulating a fraternalist framework for understanding the new Puerto Rican–U.S. relationship. This was a masculinist stance, then, but it was one of compromise and conciliation, not belligerence and bravado, and it concealed inequality rather than naming it. It "avoid[ed] the violence of radical rupture." Nationalists, by contrast, contended that radical rupture was necessary.[69]

If Nationalists used masculinist rhetorics to speak back to Muñoz Marín's strategies of negotiation, their rhetorics grounded in feminine weakness and suffering succeeded in mobilizing North American pacifists on their behalf despite their use of violence as a political tactic. The NP's defenders highlighted the inequalities between Nationalists and their colonial oppressors, insisting that the episodic violence of the former was less troubling than the structural violence of imperialism. Their efforts, particularly important for keeping the cause of independence alive after the NP was decimated by the imprisonment of its leaders, were, ironically, facilitated by U.S. responses to Nationalist violence. For her promotion of the NP cause, North American activist Ruth Reynolds was convicted and imprisoned under the gag law, and *this* embodiment of the national security state propelled national and international movements in defense of her as well as her Nationalist allies.

Reynolds had first traveled to Puerto Rico in 1945 and had returned to investigate the 1948 student strike at the University of Puerto Rico. She stayed on, writing a book on government repression of the strike and being drawn ever more closely into Nationalist circles. Although she insisted that she never joined the NP, she frequently attended party gatherings and conferences, and her closest associates were members. Just before the 1950 uprising, Reynolds was riding home from an Albizu Campos speech with three friends when insular authorities stopped their car. A search of the trunk revealed several small firearms and Molotov cocktails. The young men were arrested, but Reynolds was merely questioned and released. Then, the day after the shooting at Blair House, she was swept up in the police dragnet. Held in Puerto Rican prisons for nine months before being brought to trial, Reynolds was accused on two counts of violating *la mordaza.* She was acquitted of participating in the Nationalist insurrection but convicted of promoting the overthrow of the insular government. Reynolds had been present at a gathering where Albizu Campos exhorted the crowd: "All those who feel themselves Nationalists; that is true Nationalists, rise. Raise your right hand all who are ready to sacrifice their lives and give up their fortunes defending the cause; all those who are ready to die for the movement that must continue over the bones of Albizu Campos." She adamantly denied taking this "oath," but on conflicting evidence was sentenced to serve two to six years. After filing an appeal and making bail in June 1952, Reynolds returned to the mainland, where she sought to raise funds for her own legal defense. In 1954 the Puerto Rican Supreme Court set aside her conviction, ruling that even had she taken the oath, neither this "nor her affiliation with the Nationalist Party nor her attendance at particular meetings . . . can be classified as criminal acts."[70]

Reynolds's arrest provided the impetus for the emergence of a more radical assault on U.S. policy. Her close connections to Nationalists divided ALPRI, which disbanded, but other activists committed themselves to the cause. Dave Dellinger, A. J. Muste, Julius Eichel, Ernest and Marion Bromley, and others, most of whom were associated with the War Resisters League or the "revolutionary pacifist" group Peacemakers, joined with some ALPRI members to form the Ruth Reynolds Defense Committee. They raised money, arranged for the radical lawyer Conrad Lynn to represent her, publicized her case both in the United States and internationally, and lobbied for her release from "behind America's own iron curtain."[71] From advocating for Reynolds, they moved on to work in solidarity with the Puerto Rican Nationalist movement. Many of them agitated against the impending execution of Oscar Collazo, participating in a worldwide campaign that succeeded when President Truman commuted his sentence to life in prison on July 24, 1952—not coincidentally, the day of the Commonwealth's founding. Some also joined Americans for Puerto Rico's Independence, a group that Reynolds helped organize shortly after her return; later, many of them were founding members of the Committee for Justice to Puerto Ricans (CJPR), which was created in the wake of the 1954 attack. Some remained active in Puerto Rico solidarity work into the 1960s and even the 1970s; others went on to organize against U.S. imperial policies in Cuba and Vietnam.[72]

It is one of the paradoxes of history that, at the height of the red scare, these internationalists and "absolute" pacifists were defending a nationalist organization that used violence to oppose U.S. power. This was a tricky balancing act, and it led to long debates within the groups, as well as difficulty in attracting supporters, particularly in 1954. Nonetheless, North American activists argued for support of and engagement with the Puerto Rican independence struggle in a variety of ways. One common strategy was to invoke "American" traditions of dissent and revolution, positing that Nationalists such as Collazo were not terrorists but "true patriots" and "heirs of the American Declaration of Independence." They maintained that "if George Washington was a hero," then "Oscar Collazo is not a scoundrel."[73] Another was to emphasize the impact of the domestic Cold War on civil liberties, suggesting that in the "hysteria" of the contemporary anti-Communist crusade, it was especially important to guard the due process rights of those accused of subversion. They particularly emphasized this line of argument in the wake of the 1954 shootings, when outrage against the attack made a civil libertarian stance the only viable defense. It allowed activists to sidestep the question of whether Nationalist violence was justifiable while criticizing the excesses of the national security state.[74]

Above all, these activists situated NP violence as a response to the massive violence of U.S. occupation. Defenders of incarcerated Nationalists asserted that they were political prisoners who had been responding to "the continuous aggression of the United States" against the Puerto Rican people. Peacemakers, for example, sent three members to "witness" at Ruth Reynolds's trial in 1951. While there, they urged island residents to embrace nonviolence as a way of resistance, but they also acknowledged that "imperialism [is] the real violence" and denounced the "long, continuous domination and exploitation" that had produced the more superficial violence of the 1950 uprising. Reynolds was fond of telling U.S. officials and fellow activists alike that "during the Party's entire history the acts of violence with which our Government has credited it can be counted on the fingers of one hand (an exceedingly poor record for an organization supposedly concentrating on nothing else)." This she contrasted with a half century's record of "force and violence as . . . national policy."[75]

Even after the 1954 attack, some of these solidarity workers tried to teach Americans about the violence of U.S. empire. In New York City, members of Peacemakers picketed the Foley Square courthouse where Nationalists were being sentenced, distributing a flyer that rebuked the U.S. government for "condemning the violence of Puerto Rican Nationalists while practicing violence herself," and urging, "We believe that, instead of sending Puerto Rican patriots to prison, the American government should TAKE ITS ARMY OUT OF PUERTO RICO." Reynolds was dismayed and infuriated by the shooting in Congress, but she did not waver in her belief that "empire is in itself the basic violence, and that to oppress with violence is worse than to resist oppression with violence." This stance fueled her testimony before the grand jury that the NP did not engage in terrorism. When asked how she could defend an "unwarranted attack on innocent men," her answer was "Innocent? My God!" For pacifists who accepted the Nationalists' argument that the United States had illegally occupied Puerto Rico for the past fifty-six years, and that Congress was the body most responsible for this continuing occupation, a violent assault on the House of Representatives was not exactly excusable, but it was understandable. They put front and center Puerto Rico's suffering and its weakness relative to the United States, insisting that it was the Nationalists who were the victims.[76]

The Cold War accorded these arguments a special resonance as U.S. militarization of Puerto Rico grew in intensity. During World War II, the U.S. Navy and Army had built large installations there. Immediately after the war, the navy appropriated three-fourths of the island of Vieques for munitions storage and training exercises, causing the displacement of much of its population and severe social and economic dislocation. By the early 1950s, Ramey Air Force Base (originally Borinquen Field) had been transferred to the Strategic Air Command; it was home to some of the most advanced weapons of the Cold War, including surveillance aircraft and nuclear-equipped B-36 bombers that could reach into the Soviet Union.[77] As Puerto Rico's military significance expanded from an outpost overlooking the Panama Canal to an important staging ground for the atomic-age Cold War, Nationalists drew attention to U.S. nuclear capacity there. In the months before the 1950 uprising, Albizu Campos toured the island accusing the United States of making Puerto Rico its "atomic base and the base for [its] most advanced weapons. . . . Ostensibly, they are inviting the enemy to attack Puerto Rico, which has come to be the Pearl Harbor of the Atlantic." Warning that the island was being transformed into an atomic arsenal that could be used against all of Latin America, he railed against U.S. officials' "cynical" belief that "because they possess the atom bomb they can sit on the heads of all human beings. Theirs is a power which respects nothing but brute force." Pacifists, not surprisingly, found such rhetoric compelling, and they joined with Nationalist Party members to charge that "the Puerto Rican people have become a target for death" (fig. 9).[78]

In sum, "terrorism" and "real violence" were the terms used to debate the legitimacy of Puerto Rico's state of exception. For U.S. officials and their PPD allies, the allegation that Nationalists were terrorists was meant to justify the full weight of national security measures that equated resistance to U.S. policy in Puerto Rico with the attempt to overthrow the entire U.S. government. On the other side, radical pacifists and NP members used gendered languages of power and oppression to reveal the structural violence that enabled and even necessitated the suspension of the rights to liberty and self-governance. In no sense were the meanings of these terms self-evident. Rather, in the global Cold War moment, the ferment over Puerto Rico provided an opportunity to dispute what sorts of violence would be recognized or erased, validated or condemned. This was a debate that routinely fused and confused violence

FIGURE 9. In 1959, Reynolds and her compatriots in the radical pacifist movement demonstrated against the military occupation of Puerto Rico. (Photo courtesy of the Ruth M. Reynolds Papers, Archives of the Puerto Rican Diaspora, Centro de Estudios Puertorriqueños, Hunter College, CUNY)

against persons and violence against states, individual bodies and political bodies. And it was a debate that finally pivoted on the contested meanings of Puerto Rican embodiment. In particular, Pedro Albizu Campos's body—and the psyche it housed—became a synecdoche for the struggle for independence itself. Stories about his body furnished yet another arena for arguing over terror, state violence, and the legitimacy of America's Cold War empire.

"Lynching at the Height of the Atomic Age"
Minds, Bodies, and the State of Exception

U.S. journalists and officials elaborated on the political consequences of embodiment in endless stories about Albizu Campos. Discussions about the circumstances of his birth were an important medium for conveying the illegitimacy and irrationality of Puerto Rican desires for independence. These accounts proffered a tragic mulatto story that implicated the United States in the emergence of nationalism but ultimately held the NP leader responsible for its excesses. The basic facts are relatively undisputed: Albizu Campos was born in 1891, the child of Juana Campos and Alejandro Albizu y Romero. But in this typical account of his formative experiences from a 1954 story in *Life,* his parents' identity is less important than is their class, race, and sexual impropriety: "The Harvard-educated son of a Spanish sugar man and his Negro mistress, Campos was treated as a Negro in the U.S. army during World War I and emerged teeming with hatred for the United States."[79] For U.S. commentators, these racial origins and their consequences were key to understanding the rest of Albizu Campos's career, as his experience of racial categorization in the army allegedly "twisted" and "warped" his life, generated his burning contempt for all things American, and set him on the road to violence.[80]

This racial narrative superficially acknowledged the damaging effects of segregation in the United States but displaced blame for those effects onto Albizu Campos himself. While it might seem to question the United States for its unfair treatment of the young soldier, the recent desegregation of the armed forces blunted this critique; Albizu Campos, who unaccountably could not forget the slight of long ago, was mired in the past. Never referring to the nuances and specificities of racialized systems of respectability in Puerto Rico, this account also presumed a binary racial order that proved troublesome for "mulattos" like Albizu Campos but was not necessarily wrong in itself.[81] The harm resulted instead from Albizu Campos's inappropriate identification with his white father rather than his black mother, and his extreme and irrational response to a supposed insult to his honor. Thus this story also implicitly rejected the NP position that violence was an appropriate defense of masculinist honor.

As with most myths, there may be some truth in this narrative. Albizu y Romero did not legally recognize Pedro Campos as his son until 1914, after he had matriculated at Harvard. The young man may well have resented that the U.S. military did not affirm the shift in social status that such recognition conferred. Nonetheless, by identifying this moment as the "turning point" in a life thenceforth dedicated to violence and destruction, this story disregarded the very real inequalities and injustices enacted through U.S. imperialism in Puerto Rico and signified the Nationalist movement itself as racialized Other, a stereotyped expression of Latin emotionalism and pride. Albizu Campos's racially embodied self placed him and his movement outside the bounds not simply of racial order but of legitimate political discourse and action, outside the bounds of reason itself.[82]

Albizu Campos's supposed irrationality implicated his followers as well. Accusations that Nationalist attackers were "insane," "psychotic," "crazy," "lunatic," "psychopathic," and the like were lodged in 1950 and 1954 at every level of public debate.[83] Muñoz Marín memorably called the NP a "serpent of madness in the body of Puerto Rico," observing that Nationalists "live in a completely unreal world, and the trouble is that occasionally they escape from the unreal world and kill somebody."[84] This madness, it was sometimes intimated, derived from Albizu Campos's "hypnotic influence" over his followers. The universal translation by his opponents of Albizu Campos's moniker "el Maestro" as "the master" instead of the more appropriate "teacher" or "leader" undergirded the implication that the party leader had the ability to compel women and men to commit acts they would never contemplate were they in full possession of their faculties.[85]

These allegations of insanity impugned not only NP strategies but also the very desire for independence. Puerto Rico's political and economic "progress" became evidence of the irrationality of the Nationalist enterprise. Mason Barr, in charge of Caribbean policy at the Department of the Interior, wrote that the Blair House attack was "particularly puzzling because it occurred at a time when the last vestigial remnants of colonialism are being eliminated. These actions cannot be explained on any rational basis, and the answer lies in the field of abnormal psychology." Editorial writers at the *Washington Post* similarly observed that Oscar Collazo's "fanaticism" and "delusions" were "the more preposterous in the light of . . . a recognition by the island's more stable leaders and the bulk of Puerto Ricans that complete independence would be . . . ruinous." In the wake of the Capitol shootings, the *Post* continued this theme, heading a story on Puerto Rican attitudes toward independence "Sane Puerto Ricans Spurn U.S. Break." Another commentator chimed in that "the Nationalist movement in Puerto Rico is about as lunatic a movement as could exist in this world. Puerto Rico is not bound to the United States by iron chains or by any compulsion other than the will of its people." Casting the United States as the guarantor of Puerto Rican democracy and prosperity and Muñoz Marín as its rational and mature partner, these narratives rendered the desire for independence incomprehensible (fig. 10).[86]

This language was so universal that even anti-imperialist activists used the same rhetoric, if only in an attempt to challenge it. The writer and activist Waldo Frank, a member of the Committee for Justice to Puerto Ricans, which was organized to ensure a fair trial for those arrested after the 1954 attack,

FIGURE 10. Luis Muñoz Marín and Dwight D. Eisenhower are pictured as partners guiding Puerto Rico to a more "sane" future. Here, Muñoz Marín has come "to offer his apologies" for the shooting in Congress. (Photographer, Mark Kauffman. Time & Life Pictures/Getty Images)

penned a column for *The Nation* in which he analyzed the "fantastic lunacy" of the attack on Congress. While he acknowledged both economic and political progress on the island, he warned against "writing off the Congress affair as the mere froth of crackpots, signifying nothing." Frank suggested that the "madmen" who carried out the assault were expressing the "unconscious . . . resentments and hate" of the "sane majority" in Puerto Rico who loathed the imposition of U.S. values and culture on their country. Linking the events in Washington to the informal U.S. empire in Latin America and to the struggle between the Soviet Union and the United States for the hearts and minds of peoples of the developing South, he concluded, "In a psychotic world, madness must speak truth."[87]

These allegations about Nationalist insanity were also articulated—and challenged—through a parallel discourse about Nationalist bodies as diseased. Again, specific stories about Albizu Campos translated into general denunciations of nationalism. But this narrative is more difficult to prise apart, for the etiology of Albizu Campos's illness was very much contested. And, unlike accusations of madness—which mostly traveled only one way—this story of diseased bodies could be used as a weapon against supporters of the Commonwealth and U.S. empire.

Since his first imprisonment, when Albizu Campos was transferred to Columbus Hospital after a heart attack, his health was made a political subject, with federal officials accusing him of malingering,[88] and supporters decrying government persecution of a sick man. During his incarceration after the 1950 uprising, however, the issue took on greater urgency. In 1951 Albizu Campos charged that the U.S. government was targeting him with atomic rays, causing debilitating physical injuries. Puerto Rican officials countered that his bodily infirmities were simply a symptom of his mental illness. In this debate, Albizu Campos's body, and the bodies of other Puerto Rican prisoners, became signs of the legitimacy or illegitimacy of Puerto Rico's relations with the United States, and of U.S. relations with the world.

Nationalist accusations of medical experimentation were not new. Albizu Campos first came to worldwide attention in 1932, when he charged Dr. Cornelius Rhoads, a North American physician working on the island for the Rockefeller Foundation, with killing Puerto Ricans by "injecting" them with cancer.[89] This was just the first of many accusations by islanders that U.S.-sponsored medical initiatives, including birth control efforts and vaccination campaigns, were genocidal strategies intended "to kill all of us." These charges may not have persuaded most Puerto Ricans, but they had at least some credibility in the postwar years, as Puerto Rico became a "social laboratory" for demonstrating the uses of modern science for developing the third world, including body-disciplining techniques like birth control and sterilization.[90] When the atomic age dawned, these long-standing concerns with the destructive force of U.S. technologies erupted with even greater intensity.

In May 1951 Albizu Campos complained to the warden of the San Juan District Jail (known as La Princesa) that he was being attacked in his cell by "electronic rays" as part of a U.S. military experiment. Prison officials had him examined by a team of doctors and psychiatrists, who diagnosed him as psychotic, paranoid, and suffering a "persecution mania." Their response was to remove him from solitary confinement and place him in a larger cell. Albizu Campos denied that he was hallucinating, pointing to a variety of physical symptoms, including headache, high blood pressure, weight loss, edema, burns, and fever (fig. 11). Government officials insisted that many of these symptoms were self-inflicted. In 1952 the Nationalist Party presented a petition to the United Nations requesting an investigation into the "cruel and inhuman treatment" that was endangering Albizu Campos's life. Members charged the U.S. government with trying to "weaken him, to burn him, to make him desperate, to provoke a cerebral attack or a heart attack," to murder him "without anyone assuming the responsibility." By mid-1952 Albizu Campos was refusing to allow doctors to examine him, arguing that his problems were "only incidentally . . . medical. . . . It is . . . a case of nuclear physics." This was, he concluded, "lynching at the height of the atomic era."[91]

Puerto Rican officials were concerned that what they viewed as mental illness might interfere with their efforts to prosecute Albizu Campos further, but these worries came to naught, for two months after his accusations surfaced, he was convicted on additional charges and sentenced to fifty-four more years, bringing his total sentence on charges related to the 1950 uprising to almost eighty years. In September 1953, however, Muñoz Marín was forced to issue a pardon. Media reports that Albizu Campos's health was worsening, a flood of inquiries and protests from Latin America, and the government's concern that he might die a martyr in prison all contributed to this decision. Muñoz Marín seized on the opportunity to make the pardon an object lesson in the irrationality of nationalism and the liberal spirit of the Puerto Rican government, releasing to the press an exchange of letters between himself and José Figueres, president-elect of Costa Rica. Figueres, citing Latin American "misunderstanding"

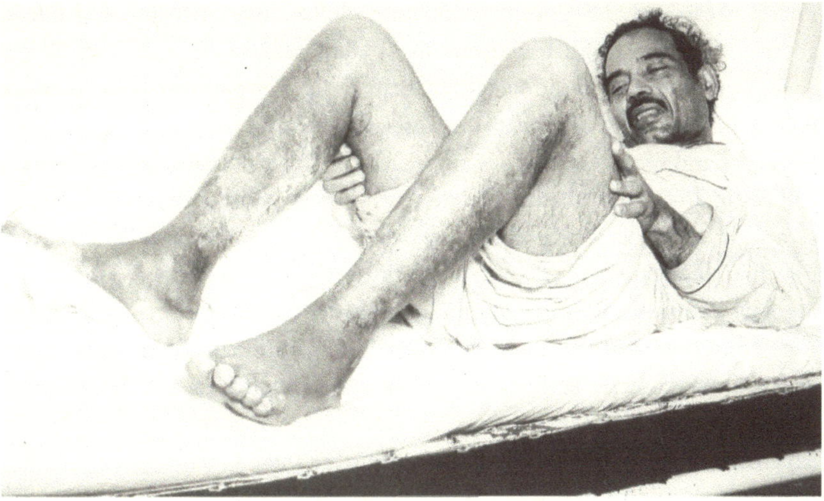

Figure 11. This photo of Albizu Campos in prison shows swelling and burns on his legs. (Photo courtesy of the Archivo Fotográfico, Archivo General y Biblioteca Nacional de Puerto Rico)

about Puerto Rico's political status and misapprehension of Albizu Campos as a "heroic" figure, urged Muñoz Marín to pardon on humanitarian grounds this most deluded of "a small band of self-deluded men, who pretend to 'free' Puerto Rico by means of terrorist attempts." The governor's response similarly emphasized not only Albizu Campos's alleged delusions but also the "unrealistic" nature of the movement he headed, and connected the Nationalists' current accusations to two decades of "fantastic ideas," beginning with his publication of the infamous Rhoades letter. Insisting that Albizu Campos was not a political prisoner, and that there were neither political prisoners nor "political crimes" in the Commonwealth of Puerto Rico, he issued a pardon on the basis of "advanced age" and "state of health," which could be revoked only if the Nationalist leader "conspire[d] against the public safety, attempting to subvert by violence or terror the established constitutional order and to trample on the will of the Puerto Rican people, as democratically expressed at the polls." By labeling Albizu Campos crazy and essentially placing him under house arrest through constant surveillance, Muñoz Marín sought to cement the portrayal of nationalism as irrational, terroristic, and undemocratic, and the Commonwealth as the defender of civil liberties and democracy.[92]

The release of Albizu Campos seemed to solve a political problem for the

Puerto Rican and U.S. governments, but it did not assuage Nationalists' fears about U.S. abuse of nuclear technology. The "attacks," he reported, did not abate, and visitors to his home told of seeing blue, silver, or rose-colored rays of light in his bedroom. For the Nationalists who surrounded him, as well as Ruth Reynolds and her circle, this news was credible in part because other prisoners had complained of similar incidents. During the summer of 1952, while incarcerated at La Princesa, Reynolds and other women prisoners told authorities that they had experienced electric shocks, temporary paralysis, "vibrations," mental confusion and "oppression," and other mysterious ailments. They, too, were convinced that these afflictions resulted from illicit experimentation by the U.S. government, perhaps via laser beams or nuclear rays. That belief may be more comprehensible in light of recent evidence of government-sanctioned experimentation on prisoners and others during these years, including the use of both irradiation and psychotropic drugs. That Albizu Campos's old nemesis Cornelius Rhoades was at this very moment director of the Sloan-Kettering Institute, which conducted human radiation experiments for the Atomic Energy Commission, also fed suspicion that Puerto Rican political prisoners were victims of government experimentation. In any case, this common experience of torture, together with little improvement in Albizu Campos's health, fed anxiety among Nationalists and their allies and convinced them that something must be done to save his life.[93]

In the winter of 1953–54, friends of Albizu Campos worked furiously to protect him. In Puerto Rico, this ranged from providing personal care to documenting his injuries. In New York, Ruth Reynolds, Dave Dellinger, and others sought to determine whether Albizu Campos was suffering from radiation sickness, sending a Geiger counter to San Juan and appealing to prominent scientists to investigate. On February 24 Dellinger wrote to Albert Einstein, asking for his opinion on the matter. Dellinger confessed that he had "considerable reservations" about Albizu Campos's allegations but thought it important to find out whether such an attack was possible. He was delayed in mailing the letter, however, as a postscript made clear: "The violence in Congress erupted between the time I wrote this letter and the time I got it out. About all I can say is that this probably underlines the urgency of the situation. Apparently those who made the attack are amongst those who accept Albizu's charges implicitly."[94]

When Lolita Lebrón led her compatriots in the attack on the House of Representatives, her immediate motive was to draw attention to the atomic torture of Pedro Albizu Campos. Lebrón had been intimately involved with the efforts to save Albizu Campos's life. In August 1953 she was arrested along with other members of the Women's Committee for the Freedom of Puerto Rican Political Prisoners who were demonstrating outside the UN to demand his release. She huddled with party members to strategize about how to draw attention to his medical condition, wrote articles for the NP newspaper, attended fund-raising meetings, and spent late nights working on a petition to the United Nations. And in February 1954, at a party meeting at which Lebrón was appointed "general delegate" (essentially Albizu Campos's representative) of the Nationalist Party in the United States, the primary topic of conversation was the "health and welfare of our political prisoners," particularly Albizu Campos's "critical condition."[95]

Lebrón's elevation to the highest NP position on the continent was decreed by Albizu Campos, and it was the subject of much speculation at the time and since. Was this evidence that the party leader directly ordered the attack on Congress? Did he view Lebrón, a party activist but one with little official leadership experience, as easier to manipulate than Julio Pinto Gandía, the longtime New York delegate? Or, as some hinted, was this simply a maneuver to distance Gandía from any criminal activity? These questions may never be definitively answered, but substantial evidence of turmoil within the NP at this time suggests that the conviction that Albizu Campos was the victim of atomic torture led directly to the March 1 shooting. Reflecting late in her life, Ruth Reynolds recalled that during the Nationalists' trial, an FBI informer who had infiltrated the party testified that Albizu Campos had sent a message for the New York organization: "He didn't want to hear any more excuses. He wanted to read [it] in the newspapers. . . . That if any of them had been suffering from such burning as he was suffering . . . he . . . would have swept the place with gun fire." Reynolds was dubious that the party leader had issued a direct order, but she acknowledged that his impatience might well have played a role. "The issue we were all discussing at that time is what are we going to do in relation to Don Pedro's body? What can be done? And Lolita was in on these discussions and so was . . . Rafael Cancel. . . . Let's say, for example, Pinto Gandía was deposed as delegate because there was no action coming out of New York. . . . Lolita is put in his place. Lolita, what's she going to think? Don Pedro is dissatisfied with this way of doing things. We've got to do something else."[96]

Two pieces of writing authored by Lebrón suggest that these issues were indeed on her mind. The first, found in her purse immediately after she was apprehended, was a note that read:

> Before God and the world my blood claims for the independence of Puerto Rico. My life I give for the freedom of my country. This is a cry for victory in our struggle for independence. Which for more than a half century has tried to conquer that land that belongs to Puerto Rico. I state that the United States of America are betraying the sacred principles of mankind in their continuous subjugation of my country, violating [our] rights to be a free nation and a free people in *their barbarous torture of our apostle of independence,* Don Pedro Albizu Campos. I take responsibility for everything.[97]

The second was penned after Lebrón had served three years of her sentence in the federal women's prison in Alderson, West Virginia. While incarcerated, she had begun having religious visions. After one of these visions, in which the ceiling of her prison cell "burst into flames," she composed a long document titled "A Message from God in the Atomic Age," denouncing U.S. nuclear policy. After sending part of it to President Eisenhower, she was transferred to a federal psychiatric hospital in Washington, where she was confined for eight months. While there she, too, complained of medical experimentation and torture.[98]

Lebrón's critique of the United States as an atomic power, like Albizu Campos's accusations of nuclear terrorism against his body and his homeland, like the very idea that Puerto Rico could not be free until it was independent, all became evidence of the irrationality and "political insanity" of the entire Nationalist project. In fact, by drawing attention to *their* experiences of terror and victimization, Lebrón, Albizu Campos, and Reynolds inadvertently contributed to their own marginalization. Their bodies—unruly, frail, disabled—and their allegedly illogical minds came to signal their incapacity to engage in meaningful action and their lack of self-sovereignty. Their political irrelevance rested on what had come before: a concerted effort by Puerto Rican and U.S. authorities to redefine Puerto Rico as "free" even as it remained dependent on the United States for markets, capital, and aid, and the Commonwealth as the rational response to that dependence. To reframe this "dependence" as "independence"—"a part of the independence of the United States," as Muñoz Marín put it—government officials had also to counter the insistence that Puerto Rico was *not* free, that "free association" was colonialism by another name. They accomplished this, in part, by displacing onto the Nationalist Party negative and traditionally feminized and racialized attributes: irrationality, emotionality, and physical vulnerability.

Ironically, they were abetted by Albizu Campos's willingness to put women in leadership positions. Certainly, most of the power in the NP resided in the hands of men. And there is much contention about his reasons for entrusting certain women—including his wife, Laura Meneses de Albizu Campos, who lived in exile in Cuba, from where she directed much of the party's efforts to get international support, and Blanca Canales Torresola, who led the 1950 uprising in the mountain town of Jayuya, as well as Lolita Lebrón and Ruth Reynolds—with significant responsibilities. His opponents alleged that he could easily manipulate—or, more to the point, seduce—weak women. Or it may have been because he had a mystical view of women as mothers of the nation, as his public response to news of the 1954 attack reveals: "A Puerto Rican heroine of sublime beauty has again pointed out for the history of all nations that woman represents the nation and that the idea of an enslaved mother is inconceivable. . . . Lolita Lebron and her countrymen . . . have given notice to the United States, made bold with its atomic bombs, that they must respect the independence of all nations."[99] Or perhaps it was just that he believed he had to use all the soldiers he had in a war against the most powerful nation on earth. Whatever the reason, when Lebrón led the assault on Congress, she was made to epitomize the "craziness" and ultimate impotency of the Nationalist attack on U.S. power. In her first trial, on charges of assault with a dangerous weapon and assault with intent to kill, Lebrón was convicted only on the first charge, apparently because the bullets from her gun all lodged in the ceiling. Her three comrades were convicted on both counts, and were sentenced to longer jail terms as a result.[100] Although the U.S. and Puerto Rican governments accomplished their goal of incapacitating the Nationalist Party—after a second trial on sedition charges, combined with the prosecutions in the wake of the 1950 uprising, virtually all of the party's leadership was imprisoned—the fascination with Lebrón that surrounded the trials also figured Nationalist failure.

Perhaps this was an inevitable outcome. U.S. officials had a great deal riding on their success in managing what they heralded as the decolonization and development of Puerto Rico, as did the Puerto Rican leaders who joined them. Not only was Puerto Rico a keystone in U.S. Latin American policy and an important symbol of American support for "democracy"—Nationalists were being rounded up, after all, at the very moment when the CIA was accomplishing the overthrow of a popularly elected government in Guatemala—but also it was essential to U.S. military supremacy in the atomic age. But even when—perhaps especially when—the Nationalist threat was put down through violence and imprisonment, the contradictions that made Puerto Rico America's most obvious "state" of exception remained.

Those contradictions made for some strange bedfellows, bringing together women and men who embraced violence as protest against injustice with women and men who dedicated their lives to nonviolent resistance. This was not an easy alliance. Lolita Lebrón and Ruth Reynolds did not become friends until much later in life. During her incarceration Lebrón conceived her own style of Christian pacifism, and after her release she continued her anti-militarist activism in the struggle to reclaim Vieques Island from the U.S. Navy; but in the early 1950s, she found Reynolds's pacifism irrelevant and annoying. Still, they agreed, as Reynolds put it, that "no government that takes its authority from anything except the will of the governed can possibly be valid," and that the Puerto Rican people had not yet been able to express their will.[101] The Cold War–era resolution of the "Puerto Rican paradox"—an island called free but in fact a possession, a territory neither foreign nor domestic, a people both citizens of a country that did not exist and semi-citizens of the United States—would be only temporary. The repressed would return in the 1960s with the FALN, the Young Lords' Party, and other pro-independence groups, all of whom named semi-citizenship on the continent and the island for the structural violence that it was. Furthermore, while that resolution might have worked to partly silence Reynolds's and Lebrón's criticisms of state violence and its expression in the national security state, there existed other opportunities for articulating such a critique. Fredric Wertham, too, sought to draw attention to the ways in which discourses of national security subjected American citizens to violence. His efforts to change the very meanings of "security" are the subject of the next chapter.

CHAPTER FIVE.

"The Show of Violence"

Social Citizenship, Democracy, and the Remaking of National Security

IN MAY 1955 THE AMERICAN CIVIL LIBERTIES UNION WEIGHED IN ON THE continuing debate over juvenile delinquency in American society. The group warned members of the U.S. Senate that while the problem of youth crime was indeed "alarming," the growing demand for comic book censorship posed an even greater danger to the nation. As long as it could not be shown that the circulation of comic books created a clear and present danger to America's youth, the risk that they might negatively influence some children had to be tolerated, for "risk is an indelible mark of democracy and a society of freedom." This reasoning irked the psychiatrist Fredric Wertham, whose recently published *Seduction of the Innocent* figured as exhibit number one in the case for legislation regulating the comics. After reading the ACLU's statement, he mused: "I believe that whoever wrote this . . . has missed what democracy is. For democracy is based not on risk but on security."[1]

Wertham's invocation of "security" as justification for censorship appears supremely consonant with the domestic Cold War's subjugation of civil liberties, and most scholars have remembered him as a sort of Joe McCarthy of popular culture, a zealot who created widespread hysteria and sought to crush freedom of speech.[2] These comparisons are not wholly without merit: what became his overriding concern—some might even say obsession—with comic books resonated with McCarthy's one-note condemnations of Communists and fellow travelers. Furthermore, like McCarthy, he tended to manipulate (perhaps even manufacture) evidence to achieve his aims.

But Fredric Wertham was no Joe McCarthy. While he accepted that security might require the sacrifice of liberty, he took the time to ask what sorts of security democracy required and whose liberty was at stake. His answers challenged the terms of Cold War discourse, including its displacement of the dangers to America, its narrow definition of freedom, and its valorization of state-sanctioned violence. Wertham sought to shift the focus from totalitarian violence supposedly directed at the United States from outside to the systemic violence produced by capitalism, racial inequality, and male supremacy. His comic book crusade was just one aspect of a lifetime commitment to redefining national security so as to encompass the rights of all Americans to be protected from the everyday violence that eroded the nation from within.[3]

This version of national security owed much to Wertham's experience as a practitioner of social psychiatry. At a time when most prominent social scientists looked to individual personality to explain national character, and when mainstream psychiatrists blamed social ills on family dynamics, he offered a different calculus for the integration of the individual and the social. Emphasizing that Americans bore collective responsibility for the inequities that damaged individual lives, he insisted that government guarantee democracy by providing citizens with necessary material, social, legal, and psychic supports.[4] In this sense, his anti-violence campaign resonated with what the British economist T. H. Marshall was simultaneously defining as "social citizenship." Marshall focused on the state's responsibility to provide educational, financial, and social resources that would make it possible to "live the life of a civilized being according to the standards prevailing in the society."[5] For Wertham, living the life of a civilized being included being protected from the violence of poverty, racism, and incarceration, as well as from physical violence and what we might call a violence of the imagination that bred authoritarian rather than democratic citizens. His understanding of national security predicated individual security on the social security of a state committed to combating structural violence in all its forms.[6]

Nonetheless, Wertham's most lasting contribution was to feed the panic about juvenile delinquency. He helped create a state of exception that suspended the rights and liberties of both adult and child readers, often in the name of fighting Communist infiltration and subversion. Ironically, his intent was to make visible a different emergency: the one produced by a nation-state that was mesmerized by violence. What Wertham called the "show of violence" hid the real operations of a state that systematically suspended the rights of some citizens—the poor, people of color, women, and children—in order to protect the freedoms and privileges of the powerful. He opposed a Cold War culture that propagandized the need for a state oriented toward violence, inculcated and embodied masculine aggressiveness and toughness, and taught American children to value the "superman" rather than the "ordinary man or woman."[7] But his efforts to unmask these aspects of national security failed.

"Better to Be Subversive Than Subservient"
Social Psychiatry, Inequality, and Democracy

Fredric Wertham (born Friedrich Wertheimer in 1895) was the son of a middle-class assimilated Jewish family in Nuremberg. After training as a psychiatrist in Germany, he emigrated to the United States in 1922, where as chief resident at the Phipps Psychiatric Clinic at Johns Hopkins, he began a career focused on treating those traditionally underserved by psychiatry.[8] In 1927 he married the artist Florence Hesketh, became an American citizen, and changed his last name. Five years later Wertham moved to New York City, where he directed psychiatric clinics first at Bellevue and then at Queens Hospital, and also became director of the New York Court of General Sessions clinic. These positions furthered his interest in forensic psychiatry, and by the 1940s Wertham had become a respected expert on forensic medicine.[9]

Wertham did not restrict his practice to impoverished clients—in Baltimore he had treated Zelda Fitzgerald—but he called himself "the poor man's Sigmund Freud"[10] and his career was marked first and foremost by his commitment to public psychiatry. He spent many years unsuccessfully lobbying Mayor Fiorello La Guardia to create a publicly funded psychiatric clinic that would be free to all New York residents. Nor was Wertham able to persuade liberal philanthropists to support his efforts to build such a clinic in Harlem, the site, he argued, of the greatest need. Finally, in 1946, Wertham and his friends, author Richard Wright and journalist Earl Brown, decided to do it themselves. They founded the Lafargue Clinic in the basement of Harlem's St. Philip's Episcopal Church with a volunteer staff.

The Lafargue Clinic was widely heralded in the nation's press as a response to the problems plaguing urban centers like Harlem, where wartime migration, overcrowding, and poverty fostered mental illness but few services were available. The clinic, which treated upwards of 1,400 patients over its thirteen-year history, was open two evenings a week. Its interracial staff of psychiatrists, psychologists, and social workers treated adults and children for the price (often waived) of twenty-five cents a visit. It had long waiting lists from the start, and clients came to its doors through church and neighborhood networks, court referrals and government offices, and word-of-mouth endorsement by family and friends. Clinic staff provided individual and group psychotherapy, intervened on clients' behalf with welfare officials and schools, offered referrals to other institutions when necessary, and often simply provided a sympathetic ear. Lafargue's day-to-day operations were directed by Wertham and his colleague at Queens Hospital Dr. Hilde Mosse, but its board of directors was composed of Harlem residents, including Earl Brown, author Ralph Ellison, Pastor Shelton Hale Bishop (whose church housed the clinic), and Marion Hernandez of Planned Parenthood. The clinic provided important training and experience for African American mental health practitioners (fig. 12).[11]

In part, Lafargue was Wertham's protest against a privatized psychiatry that was concerned not with citizens but with paying patients. "Psychotherapy," he proclaimed with heavy irony, "should not be limited to the wealthy alone. . . . Discrimination and poverty cause as much mental confusion and neurosis as the bewilderment of possessing several million dollars." He expressed impatience with a system that provided talking therapy to the rich and, if anything, institutionalization to the poor, betraying a certain hostility toward a society built on the profit motive. Criticism of capitalism was not the keynote of Wertham's public career, but it was an important subtext. For example, at a 1947 conference titled "The Future of American Capitalist Democracy," Wertham noted that "the fundamental principle that guides people is that capital must have its dividend. . . . If that works, it is wonderful. It has been a pretty bloody affair since 1914." He urged that social scientists "should really tell what happens to people these days" under capitalism. The same year, he favorably (if very naïvely) compared the Soviet approach to psychiatry to that in America. Lauding the Soviets for treating mental illness as a matter of public health and praising their practice of sending "thousands and thousands of patients [to] collective farms" for work therapy, he noted sarcastically that such a system was impossible in the United States because work must be done for profit and nobody could figure out who should profit from the work of the mentally ill. If not unequivocally anticapitalist, Wertham ardently believed that "psychoanalysis and psychotherapy are not the private property of the rich but the common property of the people."[12]

FIGURE 12. Fredric Wertham and an interracial staff counsel a young Lafargue Clinic patient, circa 1955. (Photographer unknown; Courtesy of the Museum of the City of New York)

The idea of a clinic that made mental health care available to all regardless of their ability to pay appealed both to conservative commentators alarmed by rising crime rates and to those with more progressive ideas about psychotherapy and race relations. The former simply heralded the clinic as a "new weapon against crime" and emphasized its utility in fighting Harlem's high juvenile delinquency rate,[13] but many drew attention to the ways in which racism and poverty contributed to mental ill health. For example, S. I. Hayakawa, then a college instructor in Chicago, penned a *Chicago Defender* column in which he highlighted the clinic's role in the fight against juvenile delinquency: "The uncertain status of the adolescent in our culture produces dangerous enough tensions in the most privileged of our American communities—but in the Negro community where the ordinary tensions are enormously aggravated by poverty, by the lack of privacy that goes with slum housing, by the spiritually corrosive discovery of the facts of Jim Crow, the tensions are furious." Many profiles of the clinic similarly asserted that African Americans' "underprivileged status" could set in motion an escalating pattern of frustration, neurosis, and crime. In a sense, such accounts could be read as justifying an individualist approach to solving broad social problems: the clinic enabled "Negroes temporarily swamped by the Jim Crow conditions of Harlem" to avoid frustration by helping them adjust to those conditions.[14]

But, as readers of Hayakawa's column learned, Wertham was not really interested in adjustment; instead, his aim was to inspire in his clients "the will to live in a hostile world."[15] Although he was not above referring to "frustrations" and "neuroses," Wertham went further to claim that racial discrimination was "one of the most serious if not the most serious cause" of mental disorders and that mental ill health maintained systems of racial and class inequality, rendering poor people and people of color helpless to change either their own situation or the society that victimized them. As Wertham told a reporter for *People's Voice*, Lafargue staff did not want to "help adjust people to a vicious environment. We give them the best in psychiatric care to help build strong citizens, fighters against this debilitating ghetto!" Or, as the journalist Robert Bendiner wrote in describing Wertham's position, "he often tells people that it is 'far better to be subversive than subservient.'"[16] Lafargue, then, was not merely a stopgap measure in a privatized health system that discriminated against the poor and people of color. It was, more important, an institution for strengthening American democracy.[17]

Forensic Medicine and Structural Violence

In many ways, the concerns that brought Wertham to found the Lafargue Clinic were the same that fueled his interest in forensic medicine: How could social institutions prevent mental illness, and particularly the expression of that illness in violence? What did high rates of disease and crime reveal about the very culture itself? In his writings about forensic medicine as well as those about Lafargue, Wertham focused on two issues. On the one hand, he sought to explain how social forces interacted with individual emotional disorder to produce an explosion of violence. On the other, he indicted the state for abandoning its role in preventing that explosion. Each of these concerns was a vital aspect of his brand of social psychiatry.

Wertham sounded these notes in several books that situated individual violence in its social context. In *Dark Legend: A Study in Murder,* he presented the case of seventeen-year-old Gino, who stabbed his widowed mother thirty-two times, killing her in her bed, while his younger siblings cowered in the next room. Wertham confessed himself "fascinated" by the "paradox" of a boy who seemed "normal," "direct and simple and honest," but had committed a murder of immense brutality and claimed to be happy about it. His testimony that Gino was legally insane led to the youth's commitment to a criminal asylum, and Wertham spent many months treating him in order to understand this paradox.[18]

Wertham read Gino's story in relation to two other stories of matricide in Western culture: the Greek myth of Orestes and *Hamlet,* each the story of a youth who avenges his father's loss of honor by murdering his adulterous mother. This method of tracing literary parallels focused on family dynamics might have led readers to expect a traditional psychoanalytic interpretation, but while he did acknowledge Gino's incestuous feelings, he blamed the murder on social attitudes. Matricide was "the disease of a patriarchal society," and Gino's disordered thinking reflected "the picture of the mother which our society has created . . . that of an almost sacred person detached from the practical life of the world and existing merely to attend to the wishes and needs of her children, and to obey the authority of her husband." Gino's widowed mother was the opposite of this picture, the "active mother . . . who joins the practical life of the world, who steps outside the home, who enters the struggle of earning a living." This matricide, then, was an expression in part of Gino's attachment to a "glorified role of subordinate passivity" for women. In Wertham's opinion, this was "an outmoded conception which has no place in our modern society, in which women have earned the right to be people—not just wives and mothers." In addition, Gino's use of violence to express his hostility both reflected his immersion in a culture that offered violence as a solution to problems and revealed how poverty and social alienation limited his options. His life of unceasing work left him no other resources for relieving his tension. Gino could imagine no way out but murder.[19]

These themes were elaborated in Wertham's next book, *The Show of Violence,* in which he also developed an argument to which he would return again and again: that social institutions—particularly government and the psychiatric profession—failed miserably in preventing violence. This account of his role in seven New York City murder prosecutions purported to explain the science behind the insanity plea, but it also advanced the argument that psychiatrists have a "duty to determine the point where individual guilt resolves itself into social responsibility." Wertham distinguished between those responsible for their crimes (for example, several individuals who faked insanity to escape punishment) and those who turned to violence because of contemporary society's insensitivity to the vulnerable. Once again, family dynamics played a role, but poverty and "social isolation" often "tipped the scales" toward murder. And, again, the persistence of outmoded gender norms led to violence, as in the tale of a young and exhausted widow who brutally attacked her two children, killing one. Her boyfriend had refused to marry her because he could not support them, and welfare authorities ignored her pleas to remove the children from the home so that she could "get a rest." This was a woman, Wertham wrote, who "was left to shift for herself under circumstances that were too much for her," forced to choose between motherhood and self-expression. The "real issue," he claimed, "is the dignity of woman as an individual." The mother, he suggested, was just as much a victim as her children, rebuffed by a society and a state that would not help her.[20]

If Wertham displayed remarkable sympathy for some of the perpetrators of these crimes, he betrayed a profound distrust of psychiatric experts and state authorities. Both of these stances were on display in his discussion of the infamous sexual predator Albert Fish, who was executed in the mid-1930s for the murder of a ten-year-old girl. Wertham had served as an expert witness for the defense, arguing that Fish was legally insane and therefore not responsible for his actions. Instead, he insisted, the legal and psychiatric systems were to blame for the untold number of children Fish had likely also molested, tortured, and perhaps killed. He noted that Fish had been arrested at least eight times prior to his detention for murder; that even after the murder he had twice been institutionalized for psychiatric observation and then set free; and that he "was 'picked up' innumerable times, usually for the impairment of the morals of minors. Yet the attention of the authorities to this man, whom his family, many neighbors, and many past employers knew to be constantly after children, was neither penetrating nor persistent. Nobody ever made any attempt to pick up the pieces or put them together. . . . This was true although he made no secret of his interests or of his predilections."[21]

Albert Fish had been given leave to victimize children because his victims were of so little concern to the broader society. Wertham reported that Fish, who was white, had made it a practice to target "colored children especially, because the authorities didn't pay much attention when they were hurt or missing." Observing that most of Fish's victims "belonged to the poorer classes of the population. Many of them were Negroes. All of them were unprotected by the present setup," he argued that the failure of New York's psychiatric and government institutions to stop Fish was an indication of "all the callousness and unconcern of those whose duty it was to protect the children of the community." Executing Fish was like "burning witches," a futile gesture at the wrong target. It was a show of violence, but it did nothing to make the community more secure.[22]

Murder, Wertham concluded in the book's final chapter, was really a question of social institutions, not individual pathology, and it was simply one of the numerous forms of violence produced by the structural inequalities of modern society. These inequalities included the "masculine" leanings of both psychiatry and law that forced women into acts of infanticide, and the lack of concern with the fate of the "little people" who made up the "vast majority of murder victims," among whom were the poor, the outcast, the "colored," and the "dispossessed." Then he went further, arguing that what society recognized as murder was part of a much broader array of preventable deaths: deaths from starvation in India under British rule; from industrial accidents in American mines; from illness among the Navajo and Mexicans in the American Southwest and the poor in Brazil. He particularly singled out high death rates among African Americans from tuberculosis, homicide, maternal and infant mortality, and execution. The lack of concern about *these* deaths, Wertham asserted, reveals "the value society puts on the lives of its different groups and shows that the official belief that in our society human life is sacrosanct is unfortunately not true."[23] There would come a time, he concluded, "when there will be a name for these differences, and that name will be *murder*. . . . It is not a matter of episodic violence, but of a continuous violation of the principle of the dignity and value of human life."[24]

In his writings about forensic psychiatry, then, Fredric Wertham sought to demonstrate that individual acts of violence were far less significant than the state-sanctioned structural violence that went not merely unanswered but unrecognized. But the "show" of violence—the horror of inexplicable, individual eruptive acts—tended to distract Americans from the everyday violence all around them. Furthermore, it fostered a focus on the interior life of the perpetrator rather than the social disorder that produced his or her inability to cope, or the inequalities and hierarchies that made some ready victims. Finally, he suggested, state "justice"—arrest, incarceration, execution—was also a show of violence. It promised security and safety while offering only pretend solutions and ignoring systemic problems. These concerns with the ubiquity of violence and its misapprehension also animated Wertham's anti–comic book campaign.

"Everything Is Permitted"
Comic Book Violence and the Seductions of Sadism

Comic books had a pernicious effect on national security, Wertham claimed, creating a citizenry that embraced force and fascism and enabling state violence against the most vulnerable Americans. He introduced these arguments in a 1948 article and spent more than a decade expanding on them, attaining the height of his influence with the 1954 publication of *Seduction of the Innocent.* Much of his ire was directed toward psychological experts who argued that comic books offered an appropriate space within which children could "work out" their "natural" hostility. Wertham disputed that humans are naturally aggressive, and he accused these experts (whom he termed a "defense team" for the comic book industry) of setting children up, helping to instill in them the desire for violence and then condemning as "abnormal" those children who took these lessons too strongly to heart. On the contrary, he insisted, comic books corrupted the ethical sense of "normal" children, cultivating the "special perversion" of sadism. Comics were both a reflection and an engine of a culture of violence in postwar America, and they required state control.[25]

Born in the 1930s and expanding through the war years, the comic book industry was not small change in postwar America. By 1954, when *Seduction* was published, *monthly* sales of 650 titles reached 150 million copies. Since it was estimated that each comic book was shared by three or four readers, actual circulation was much higher, and readership was not confined to children. A 1945 survey reported that 41 percent of men and 28 percent of women aged eighteen to thirty were "regular" comics readers; five years later, 54 percent of those reading comic books were over twenty years old, even though children still read more comic books than adults.[26]

By the early 1950s, the superhero comics that had originally fueled the industry's growth competed with war, jungle, western, romance, crime, and horror comics, and these genres were increasingly infused with violence and sex. Crime comic books, for example, detailed assaults, blackmail, poisoning, murder, and executions, all under cover of slogans such as "crime does not pay," and horror comics also featured liberal amounts of violence. Female bodies were drawn in increasingly erotic ways, with exaggerated, sometimes grotesque depictions of breasts (known as "headlights") and poses that accentuated vulnerability. An unconscious woman held in the clutches of an ape or a villain, or alternatively a rescuing hero, back arched, breasts pointed toward the sky, legs stretched out to their full length, was a favorite convention. To a great degree, the increasing measure of sex and violence in comic books reflected changes in postwar popular literature more broadly, but because children had widespread access to comics, Wertham focused his critique on them.[27]

Although Wertham's objections to comic books ranged broadly from their impairment of reading skills to their fraudulent ads to their teaching of criminal methods, his most constant refrain was that they made children unable "even in their imagination to view a non-violent life." He especially targeted crime comics, which, he argued, created a generation of children schooled in fascism. The comic book approach to the world glorified individual power and force above the rule of law, respect for others, and empathy, creating ethical confusion among an entire generation of American children. As Wertham summed up the ethics of comic books: "It is not a question of right, but of winning. Close your heart against compassion. Brutality does it. The stronger is in the right. Greatest hardness. Follow your opponent till he is crushed." These were the words, he told his readers, of Adolf Hitler as he instructed his generals on the eve of the invasion of Poland, and they constituted the gist of the comic book narrative that was consumed by American children many millions of times each year.[28]

It is no accident that Wertham quoted Hitler rather than Lenin or Stalin in his condemnation of comic books. *Seduction* was published at the height of the domestic Cold War, but Wertham was concerned not with totalitarian robots but with budding fascists "fed on the Nietzsche-Nazi myth of the exceptional man who is beyond good and evil." He followed in the footsteps of earlier critics who connected comics and fascism. As early as 1941 Sterling North wrote that comic books provided American children with a "pre-Fascist pattern."[29] After the war, the iconoclastic folklorist and cultural critic Gershon Legman, with whom Wertham corresponded, also lambasted the comics for "giving every American child a complete course in paranoid megalomania such as no German child ever had, a total conviction of the morality of force such as no Nazi could even aspire to."[30] Wertham's own catalogue of the impact of comics on their readers anticipated and paralleled the arguments set forth in the

Frankfurt School's influential volume *The Authoritarian Personality*, published in 1950 but informed by revulsion against the rise of European fascism in the 1930s. Unthinking submission to authorities, intolerance for nonconformists, preoccupation with power, cynicism and hostility, unusual attention to sexual matters: personality characteristics like these explained popular support for authoritarianism, and Wertham charged that all of them were glorified in comic books. While some other detractors of the comic book industry framed their concerns more explicitly in Cold War terms—the anti-Communist writer Norbert Muhlen, for example, suggested that comic books might offer a "prep school for totalitarian society"—Wertham's complaints were deeply inflected by his thinking about fascism.[31]

Comic books, he argued, did not simply present violent images; they "seduced" children into admiring violence and losing their respect for the rule of law. In his view, crime comics (which he defined very broadly to include superhero, jungle, romance, horror, and war genres) prompted children to "identify themselves with the strong man," whether that strong man was the criminal who used force to break the law or the hero who used force to uphold it. Superhero comics in particular offered children "the fantasy of the superior being who is a law unto himself," an "exceptional" man whose awe-inspiring endeavors to mete out justice destabilized the rule of law. The result was that readers might either imagine themselves "supermen . . . or [become] submissive and receptive to the blandishments of strong men who will solve all their social problems for them—by force."[32]

Not only did the superhero undermine respect for ordinary authorities, but also he (or she) required "an endless stream of ever new submen," making comics a primer for prejudice. Comic book narratives encouraged readers to see only "two kinds of people . . . the tall, blond . . . superman and the inferior people: natives, primitives, savages, 'ape men,' Negroes, Jews, Indians, Italians, Slavs, Chinese and Japanese, immigrants of every description, people with irregular features, swarthy skins, physical deformities, Oriental features." Such images tutored young people in racism, convincing them that there are "regular men who have the right to live, and submen who deserve to be killed" while undermining their faith in legal authorities. As a result, comic books were at odds with America's Cold War interests: "The United States is spending at present millions of dollars to persuade the world . . . that race hatred is not an integral part of American life. At the same time, millions of American comic books are exported all over the world which give the impression that the United States is instilling race hatred in young children." But of greater concern was that they actually provoked racial violence, fomenting a growing number of physical attacks on children simply because of the color of their skin.[33] Translating Nazi ideals into a U.S. idiom, comic books undermined the nation's ability to end the persistent racial inequality that damaged not just its credibility in the Cold War but also democracy itself.

The racial inequality justified in comic books had a corollary in their "sexism." By this term Wertham meant to convey both the ubiquitous presence of erotic images and the ways those images promoted gender inequality. Comic books, he argued, taught children that men's brutality toward women was at once normal and desirable, presenting a masculine ideal that put women and girls at risk. "Everything," he wrote, "is permitted to men in comic books." The "most characteristic" act of brutality in a comic book was "to smack a girl in the face with your hand. Whatever else may happen, afterwards, no man is ever blamed for this. On the contrary, such behavior . . . enhances the strength and prestige of the boy or man who does it." Wertham contended that these gender dynamics characterized the entire genre of crime comics: "The situation is boy meets girl, boy beats girl." As a result, readers of the comics experienced a "moral disarmament [and] a blunting of the finer feelings of conscience, of mercy, of sympathy for other people's suffering and of respect for women as women and not merely as sex objects to be bandied around or as luxury prizes to be fought over."[34] The portrayal of men's brutality toward women as normal, he suggested, helped seduce American children into accepting authoritarian modes of thinking.

Indeed, it was their graphic and explicit "admixture of sensuality with cruelty" that made comic books so effective at drawing children into a reverence for violence. Wertham charged that comics were schools for sadism, offering ritualized sadomasochistic imagery that warped children's sexual as well as their ethical development. The "graphic description of sexual flagellation on the buttocks" or scenes of bound and chained near-naked women offered readers "every opportunity to develop . . . psychopathic tendencies." The most "typical" comic book images endorsed eroticized violence against women: "The villain (a foreigner, of course) has the half-nude girl in his power. As an appetizer, she is hit in the face. Then: 'I know that you shall love me and shall be loyal after you have taken a dozen or so lashes across your beautiful back!' She is taken to the cellar, bound by the wrists to a tall post, her breasts conspicuously drawn, and pleads for mercy. The man stands behind her with a coiled whip in hand."

Such imagery could move children toward a variety of perversions including male masochism, female sadism, and homosexuality. But its most likely impact was the creation of a generation of male sadists.[35]

Wertham sought to substantiate these concerns by offering examples from his clinical work as evidence that comic books actually fostered violence against women. He proposed that violent fantasies led directly to violence. One young boy, for example, described his reaction to crime comics: "When you see a girl and you see her headlights and she is beaten up, that makes you hot and bothered! If she will take a beating from a man she will take anything from him." A group of boys with whom Wertham worked agreed that the "torture" in comic books was bad, but admitted that they liked to see it. "I asked the boys whether any of them, if they actually had a little girl in a lonely place, would really like to tie her up, beat her and torture her. I wondered whether any of them would admit to that and asked for a show of hands. Everybody smiled—and every hand went up." Presumably, these boys were on the path already trodden by one "twelve-year-old sex delinquent" whom Wertham had treated. He admitted to getting "sexually excited" when he read comic books in which "men tie [women] around to chairs and then they beat them." Other youth allegedly influenced by comic book stories beat and robbed a prostitute, forced an eight-year-old boy into sexual acts, were accused of attempted rape, and tortured a little girl.[36] Comic book violence, then, cultivated sadistic desires and ended in sadistic acts.

Even Wertham's much-ridiculed analysis of the Batman comic books as homosexual stories reflected his belief that comic books eroticized force and seduced children to believe that authoritarianism and inequality were desirable. Certainly he emphasized that the Batman stories were "like a wish dream of two homosexuals living together," as this oft-quoted passage demonstrates: "At home [Batman and Robin] lead an idyllic life. They are Bruce Wayne and 'Dick' Grayson. . . . They live in sumptuous quarters, with beautiful flowers in large vases and have a butler, Alfred. Batman is sometimes shown in a dressing gown. . . . Robin is a handsome ephebic boy . . . devoted to nothing on earth or in interplanetary space as much as to Bruce Wayne. He often stands with his legs spread, the genital region discreetly evident. . . . If [a girl] is after Bruce Wayne, she will have no chance against Dick."[37] But key to his critique was his reading of Batman and Robin's relationship as a reiteration of the Ganymede-Zeus myth, in which Zeus abducted a beautiful boy to be his lover. This was a story structured on hierarchies—god versus mortal, maturity versus youth—and for

Wertham those hierarchies were at least as disturbing as was homosexual desire itself. Batman, he argued, was a pedophile, and the Batman stories suggested to adolescents that they could "be loved by someone like Batman or Superman," mature, powerful men who would support, protect, and control them. To dramatize the danger, Wertham quoted one gay man who described himself as a young boy: "I found my liking, my sexual desires, in comic books. I think I put myself in the position of Robin. . . . I felt I'd like to be loved by someone like Batman or Superman." Reading about "Batman and his boy," real boys began to fantasize about life with a superman. But, as Wertham reiterated, "the normal concept for a boy is to wish to become a man, not a superman, and to live with a girl rather than with a superheroic he-man."[38] The "wish dream" of homosexuality fostered the wish for the exceptional man who was not subject to the law but a law unto himself.

For Wertham, then, "sadism" encapsulated the ways in which comic books made all sorts of inequality and violence something to be desired. All his concerns came together in the case of the "Brooklyn thrill-killers," which drew local and national attention shortly after *Seduction* was published. These were four Jewish adolescents "from good homes" who went on a three-week rampage in their Williamsburg neighborhood, beating men they believed to be vagrants, torturing them by burning them with cigarettes or setting them afire, and using a whip to lash women whom they encountered on the street. Police took them into custody in mid-August 1954 on suspicion of beating to death steeplejack Reinhold Ulrickson, but to the detectives' surprise, one of the boys confessed to another murder, heretofore unsuspected: the drowning of a "park vagrant" later identified as Willie Menter, a thirty-four-year-old African American father of two who worked at a bag factory (fig. 13). Announcing the charges against them the next day, the district attorney confessed, "I can't understand what would make boys do such terrible things." It seemed that their only reason was "the thrill they got." His perplexity was echoed by numerous commentators who sought to explain what was presumably inexplicable violence. Why would middle-class boys with loving and concerned parents and good school records go out "bum-hunting?" What could possibly have induced these intelligent, privileged boys to torture and murder? What explained their violence against those they perceived as their inferiors: women and poor, old, or African American men?[39]

For answers, the media quickly focused attention on eighteen-year-old Jack Koslow, the supposed leader of the "gang." Journalists described him in terms

FIGURE 13. Robert Trachtenberg (at left, in white jacket), Jack Koslow (in plaid shirt), Melvin Mittman (center), and Jerome Lieberman (third from right) point to the body of Willie Menter in this newspaper photo. The caption called the boys "ruthless" and "sadistic." (Bettman/CORBIS)

that bordered on the monstrous. Marya Mannes, for example, proclaimed that "it was no effort to see evil in Jack." She described the malevolence of his inner life as written on his body: the eerie "dead green whiteness" of his skin, his "delicately ugly" features, his hands, "white and thin and smooth as a girl's," the way his "narrow head hangs forward from his body like a condor's." Many others agreed that he was the "really sick boy" of the group. An intellectually gifted if mentally disturbed youth, he was the "directing brain," the one who bore all the responsibility.[40]

Koslow embodied many of the features of the authoritarian personality. He was a self-admitted fascist and white supremacist. Although a Jew, he purported to worship Adolf Hitler, mounting Nazi paraphernalia on his bedroom walls and, journalists reported, growing a mustache in imitation of his idol. Trying to justify the rampage, Koslow explained that he had an "abstract hatred for bums," elaborating: "I despise them. They are parasites on society and should all be removed." They were cockroaches that he felt compelled to "squash." Wertham interviewed Koslow in jail and concluded that he "fancied himself a superman," a member of "an elite, who would be very intelligent and rule everybody else. He believed in the greatest physical ruthlessness against dissidents and all those he considered inferior."[41]

Koslow's propensity toward senseless violence could be explained as "sickness" or "evil," but his "hold" over the other boys—Melvin Mittman, a strapping seventeen-year-old known as the group's "muscle man," and Jerome Lieberman and Robert Trachtenberg, aged seventeen and fifteen, respectively—was equally troubling, the subject of sustained speculation. Koslow and Mittman, in particular, were described as "a loyal and devoted pair"; the two, Mannes noted, "seemed to function as mind and body, Koslow doing the planning and direction, Mittman . . . the rough stuff." Many accounts either hinted at or directly asserted that the "bond" among all the boys was homosexual in nature. It was widely reported that none of the boys was much interested in sex. The implications of this "fact" were made clear by one journalist who asserted that Koslow, "born queer and bad," had "seduced three girl-shy susceptibles into his abnormal harem."[42]

Still, for most commentators, homosexuality was not a sufficient explanation for the brutality and torture that the youths had wreaked upon Brooklyn. Mittman, Lieberman, and Trachtenberg could only be comprehended as weak young men who were not just easily dominated but fascinated by a leader like Koslow, and who compensated for their own weakness by brutalizing those who were even more helpless. As Mittman admitted, he liked to punch homeless men, explaining, "It makes me feel big and strong." In the end, what bound the boys together, many commentators agreed, was the "need to assert superiority, to 'Be Somebody.'" And that was something they found through their shared "compulsion to watch other people in agony."[43]

The case of the Brooklyn thrill-killers stood out among other reports of violence in the midst of a moral panic over juvenile delinquency not only because they came from middle-class families but also because they seemed to take pleasure—some insisted sexual pleasure—in violence and pain. Wertham, who was widely quoted on the matter, attributed this to their reading habits: "Paramount as a direct, causative contributing factor in these acts of violence was what [they] read." Mittman, a fan of crime and superhero comics, "tried to prove himself a superman by meting out the violence with which Superman solves problems." Koslow had confessed to reading crime and superman comics as a child, graduating to horror comics and, finally, to "the type of pornographic horror literature which is closely allied to comic books." In particular, Wertham alleged that Koslow had read fourteen volumes of *Nights of Horror,* a serial publication that offered sadomasochistic stories illustrated by line drawings. Many of its narratives featured women who were victimized by men—beaten, whipped, raped, and murdered. Frequently, the tales were related from the point of view of a male hero who sought valiantly to save the female victims, a plot device that provided a thin cover for the explicit descriptions of violence in the stories. Wertham contended that he had compared the youths' rampage with scenes in *Nights of Horror,* and "the parallelism is complete." Their crimes mirrored the tortures in the publication. Furthermore, it was because comics indoctrinated children in "race prejudice against colored people" that the boys had aimed much of their violence against black men.[44]

Despite his horror at this outbreak of sadistic violence, Wertham was sympathetic toward the four boys, and especially Koslow. Their immersion in the world of crime comics and pornographic literature, he claimed, was "irrefutable" evidence of the power of such material to seduce children to violence. These were youths whose mental and emotional difficulties were inflamed by what they read, and who were then scapegoated for the failings of society and the state. The conviction of Koslow and Mittman on first-degree murder charges enraged him: "It is deeply shocking to me . . . that the two boys have to spend the rest of their lives in jail while the profiteers of this instigating material are not even fined two dollars." He advocated instead passing a law that banned the sale of crime comics and pornographic literature to children.[45]

While much of the tabloid coverage focused on the individual emotional disorders of these youth, other journalists were heavily influenced by Wertham's thinking. Even though they tended not to share his somewhat single-minded focus on crime comics as the tipping point that pushed young people to such frightening acts, they endorsed his concern with the culture of violence in postwar America. In a series of newspaper columns, for example, Max Lerner echoed the analysis that Wertham had advanced in *The Show of Violence.* Koslow, Mittman, and the rest "were weak boys with fires of rage burning in them, wanting to express their aggressions somehow, either in doing something violent or in watching something violent done. Thus and only thus, in the show of violence, could they overcome their pervading sense of weakness, and feel themselves to be effective human beings." But it was not only these disturbed boys who found meaning in the show of violence: "We . . . use savage punishments for savage crimes" in order to "get revenge or else to stifle the uneasy pangs of our own conscience, since we know so little about what causes such crimes among our young people or how to deal with them. And so in our blindness we strike out angrily, to give ourselves the sense of doing something."[46] Criminals, government officials, and the public found relief in the show of violence, but real understanding, real security, and real justice remained out of reach. It was the show of violence by the state for which Wertham reserved his greatest wrath.

The "Unsocial" State

For Wertham the question was not *whether* the state would respond to the comic book problem but *how.* He claimed that children who imbibed comics' message of force and violence were punished by the state all the time. In fact, it was because state authorities and expert apologists for the comic book industry had abdicated their responsibility to protect children from a culture of violence that young Americans found themselves in trouble with the law. Wertham styled himself a "defense counsel for the children who were condemned and punished by the very adults who permitted them to be tempted and seduced." He contended that the child—"unprotected" and "endangered"—was subject to the "armed might of the law," while "the material interests of the adult" were "punctiliously safeguard[ed]." Decrying the unfairness of this situation, Wertham argued that juvenile delinquency was in fact "continuously recreated by adults," whose protection of a comic book industry that "violate[d] children's minds" was akin to permitting the rape of a young girl. His studies of the comic book industry, he concluded, had shown that "it is not a question of the comic books but of the mentality from which comic books spring, and that it was not the mentality of children but the mentality of adults. What I found was not an individual condition of children, but a social condition of adults."[47]

The story of fourteen-year old "Willie," which was featured in *Seduction* and opened the *Reader's Digest* condensed version of the book, encapsulated Wertham's sense that the refusal to regulate comic books constituted a form of "cruelty to children [by] those in high estate, in courts and welfare agencies."[48] "Willie" was in fact a young black teenager named Robert Peebles. In 1950 he was arrested after a spectator at a Dodgers-Giants game died from a gunshot wound to the head. A team of eighty police officers, believing that the bullet was fired from outside the ballpark, searched the surrounding African American neighborhood, questioning more than 1,200 adults and youth before they detained Robert, who lived with his aunt on a street adjacent to the Polo Grounds. They found two .22-caliber rifles and a .22-caliber pistol in Robert's apartment. Even when it turned out that the dead man had been struck by a bullet fired from a .45-caliber automatic weapon, they continued to focus on Robert as their suspect. At first he denied possessing such a firearm, but after several days in detention he confessed that he had fired a .45-caliber gun into the air from the roof of his apartment building and then thrown it away. This confession, it appears, came after police told him that if he admitted to the crime, they would release his aunt from jail, where she was also being held on charges of illegal possession of firearms. Because the weapon was never recovered, Robert could not be tried on charges related to the death, but he received an indeterminate sentence at the State Training School for Boys at Warwick on the basis of his possession of the other firearms.[49]

Wertham placed the blame for this unintended death not on "Willie," nor on his fifty-three-year-old aunt, who had been condemned by the local African American newspaper for her alleged neglect of the boy, but on state inaction on comic books. He had known Willie and his aunt for years, ever since she brought the boy to the Lafargue Clinic at age eight when he experienced problems in school. She was "an intelligent, warm, hard-working woman," a domestic worker who had cared for the boy after his parents separated and had done her best to see he received a good education. But Willie was a "rabid" reader of comic books, and while his aunt had tried to curb his reading, she'd had "no chance of succeeding": they were everywhere, and in any case, misguided welfare workers had "told her she should let Willie read all the comic books he wanted." Those comic books featured "pictures of brutality and shooting and . . . endless glamorous advertisements for guns and knives."[50]

Long before Willie was detained for the shooting, Wertham confided, Lafargue staff had debated how to help him. After his arrest, the psychiatrists and social workers asked themselves: "Can one be satisfied with the explanation that he comes from a broken family and lives in an underprivileged neighborhood? Can one scientifically disregard what occupied this boy's mind for hours every day? . . . Can we get anywhere by saying that he must have been disordered in the first place or he would not have been so fascinated by comic books?" In Willie's case, Wertham concluded, there "was a constellation of many factors" drawing him along the path to juvenile delinquency, but comic books "tipped the scales." Still, the police, the courts, and the public "looked for the cause of this extraordinary event . . . in one little boy and took it out on him, along with a public slap at his aunt. . . . With Willie under lock and key, the community felt that its conscience was clear."[51] A poor African American boy had been incarcerated, while those who were most to blame—comic book publishers, their defenders, and a negligent state—escaped notice.

Restricting children's access to comic books was a technique of child protection clearly within the purview of the modern state, and it was more immediately achievable than eradicating racism or poverty. Wertham argued for state control as a "simple sanitary law." As with child labor laws, such regulation was necessary to protect young people's health, and as with child labor laws, the industrialists who profited from the exploitation of children mounted an intense offensive against the prospect of government control. Wertham frequently compared the effect of comic books to that of tuberculosis—just because not everyone who was exposed got sick, that was no reason to ignore the potency of the tubercle bacillus—but this metaphor did not capture his conviction that in the case of comic books, state intervention was necessitated by the power of capital. The "ruthless economic power of the comic-book industry" was "concentrated" against "the most defenseless members of society, the children," as well as their parents, who were powerless to stem the tide. Furthermore, the industry had paid off experts who defended it vigorously, confusing parents and contributing to their "paralysis."[52] In this unequal battle, Wertham argued, the state had a responsibility to intervene if democracy was to be preserved.[53]

Wertham vociferously rejected the criticism that barring the sale of such materials to children was arbitrary censorship. He claimed that he had a long history of defending the rights of adults to read what they chose. In 1948, for example, he appeared as a defense witness in an obscenity action against the publishers of the sex-themed novel *The Gilded Hearse.* There he compared the novel favorably to a comic book, arguing that the latter—saturated with sadism and widely available to children—was a corrupting influence while the former, which featured sex but not violence and had a relatively limited adult audience, was not.[54] In general, he denounced a double standard that endorsed the "protection" of adults but not children, citing "such fantastic incongruities as the arrest of a girl in a nightclub for obscenity because she wrestles with a stuffed gorilla, when any six-year-old, for ten cents, can pore for hours or days over jungle books where real gorillas do much more exciting things with half-undressed girls than just wrestling." Censoring adult reading matter was often "undemocratic" or "totalitarian," but denouncing efforts to protect children from dangerous images was a "perversion of the very idea of civil liberties."[55]

Outlawing the display or sale of crime comics to children, he maintained, was necessary in a capitalist system that denied them the rights of self-government.

Other proposed remedies—rating systems, self-censorship, or bringing pressure on distributors—were wholly insufficient to offset the industry's economic power: "How does one bring pressure on a hundred-million-dollar business without a law? And how can children bring pressure?" A law prohibiting the sale of crime comics to those under fifteen years of age would correct a legal system that was consistently weighted "against the interests of children" and that displayed no concern for their "rights and happiness." Deriding the false cry for free speech as "tyranny by a handful of unscrupulous people," he sought to clarify the relationship between freedom, security, and democracy: "I do not advocate censorship, which is imposing the will of the few on the many, but just the opposite, a step to real democracy: the protection of the many against the few. That can only be done by law."[56]

It is unsurprising that *Seduction of the Innocent,* in which Wertham framed his critique of the state more narrowly around comic books, became his best-known work. This was a book that, despite his intentions, could be assimilated neatly into relatively conservative approaches to social problems. Publications that highlighted the broader context within which he understood the state's responsibilities to its most vulnerable citizens met with less success. This was particularly true of *The Circle of Guilt,* a book occasioned by Wertham's involvement in yet another juvenile homicide. On May 1, 1955, readers of New York City newspapers learned that, as one headline put it, "Strangers on Bikes Slay Boy in Street." According to these early reports, fifteen-year-old William "Billy" Blankenship, a "good student from a good family," was surrounded by bicycle-riding gang members and shot without provocation. Soon, the police had a confessed gunman in custody: Frank Santana, a seventeen-year-old dropout who belonged to the Navajos, a Puerto Rican gang in the Bronx. This murder of a "model" boy—whose father, in an ironic twist, was a community activist who "tried to do something practical about juvenile delinquency"—invited national attention. Coming less than a year after the trial of Puerto Rican Nationalists for the attack on Congress, and in the midst of growing tension about migration from the island, it initiated another wave of hysteria about juvenile gang violence in New York. City police stepped up their patrols in Puerto Rican neighborhoods, Mayor Robert Wagner poured money into juvenile delinquency programs, and municipal judges cracked down on young offenders while exhibiting a "grisly array" of seized weapons to frighten parents into being "the bosses at home." Santana's family reported death threats, as did police officers charged with rounding up gang members.[57]

As the case came to trial, however, the story became more complex. Prosecutors and defense counsel recommended that Santana, who had been indicted on first-degree murder charges, which carried the possibility of execution, be permitted to plead guilty to second-degree murder. In a tearful statement before the judge, Billy Blankenship's father supported this plea deal, arguing that "the defendant is the product of our social environment and structure; that his background is a complete social responsibility and that all society should be made to share its proper part for its guilt in this crime." After Blankenship had left the courtroom, the district attorney justified the deal by announcing that, contrary to earlier stories, the dead boy was not the model student he appeared to be. In fact, he too belonged to a gang, and he had gone "a long distance from home that day, spoiling for a fight." Billy Blankenship, he declared, was the aggressor in the encounter and had "contributed to his own tragedy." Although Billy's father reacted strongly to these allegations, charging that he had been "tricked" by the district attorney's office and that his son's death had become a "political football," the plea stood, and Frank Santana received the maximum sentence: twenty-five years to life in prison.[58]

Wertham became involved in Santana's case when the defendant's lawyers asked him to interview the young man in jail, where he was awaiting trial. There, he encountered a boy who expressed no hostility but who exhibited "extraordinary indifference" and apathy. Frank had morals, he said, but "no purpose."[59] Wertham and his colleagues at Lafargue, with whom he discussed the case, thought that a "constellation" of factors had led Santana to this juncture, but that "one could treat this boy." But he received no treatment, and when Santana was sent off to prison, Wertham determined to do what he could to rectify this injustice. This included not only publishing *The Circle of Guilt* but also lobbying New York and Puerto Rican officials on Santana's behalf. Signaling his willingness to build bridges with any group he thought shared his commitment to a progressive politics, he also collaborated with Joyce Cowley of the Socialist Workers' Party to publish a pamphlet on the case, hoping that this might prompt a wider movement in Santana's support (fig. 14).[60]

As Wertham told it, this was the story of a young boy buffeted by circumstances he barely understood. Frank Santana and his brothers had come to New York from Puerto Rico in 1951 to join their widowed mother, a garment worker who had migrated the year before. Soon, however, his mother became ill and had to stop working. They lived in a small but immaculately kept two-room apartment with shared bath and kitchen. Santana did well in junior high,

this boy, I'd lose my job! Don't you see? I have a family to think of!"

Frank Santana in the custody of a police officer at the time of his conviction.

Neither William Blankenship, who joined a gang that beat up Puerto Ricans, nor Frank Santana, who bought a gun because he was afraid of that gang, were the "criminals" in this case. The racist antagonism that made Blankenship push Pedro, and the fear that made Santana grab for the gun, were both the result of race tensions and prejudice in the adult community where they lived.

A case like this would ordinarily end for everyone but Santana and his family when the cell door closed behind him and he started serving his term of 25 years to life. But Dr. Wertham, who never had an opportunity to tell a jury what he learned about Santana, decided to bring the facts before a wider jury. He wrote **Circle of Guilt**, a book which not only gives an honest presentation of

15

FIGURE 14. In the pamphlet "The Santana Case," authored by Joyce Cowley of the Socialist Workers' Party, Frank Santana is portrayed as a young boy endangered by racism, and Fredric Wertham is praised for presenting a "demand for action" on Santana's behalf. (Library of Congress)

but in high school he began a history of truancy after he was denied the radio and television training he requested and was instead assigned "electricity," in which he had no interest. Santana confided his suspicions about why this had happened: "Sometime in school the teachers said, 'You Puerto Ricans go back where you belong.' . . . You know how some teachers are. When you ask them something they come yelling at you." Santana was a well-behaved, polite, but sad boy who—hiding his truancy from his mother—spent his days at movie theaters and his evenings with other Puerto Rican boys from his neighborhood, playing stickball. His stickball club, named the Navajos, became a gang in order to protect members from the Italian American Golden Guineas. As one white acquaintance of Santana's family told Wertham: "Make no mistake about it, this is an area where they *have* to have a gang. . . . The Puerto Ricans can't go here or there. . . . If it weren't for the feeling of the whites against the Puerto Ricans, that gang trouble wouldn't exist at all in this area!"[61]

Racism led directly to Frank Santana's encounter with Billy Blankenship. According to Santana, several days earlier a group of Golden Guineas had threatened him, and he got a handgun for self-protection. Then, on April 30, he and other Navajos were accosted by Billy Blankenship, who belonged to the Red Wings, a "brother club" to the Golden Guineas, whose only activity, a school official reported, was "beating up Puerto Ricans." Blankenship pushed the leader of the Navajos, a boy known as "Superman." Superman was carrying Santana's gun, and he pulled it out but did not fire it. For some unknown reason, Santana grabbed the gun; it went off—accidentally, he claimed—and Billy Blankenship fell down dead.[62]

Wertham did not completely exonerate Frank Santana, but he traced a much broader "circle of guilt" for Blankenship's murder. Generally, professionals writing about juvenile delinquency in the 1950s identified youth crime as a "subcultural" response to economic frustrations and social marginalization at the same time that they branded "broken" family dynamics as a font of young people's disorder. In *Delinquent Boys: The Culture of the Gang,* for example, Albert Cohen contended that gangs were a reaction to the class stratification of American society, observing that gang membership provided alternative forms of masculine status and recognition to boys struggling to overcome their early identification with feminine figures in mother-dominated American families.[63] Wertham differed from these professionals particularly in his rejection of family-centered analyses. He explicitly rejected mother-blaming and the "it's-all-up-to-the-family argument," warning of "the danger . . . that psychiatrists let themselves be used as an instrument for localizing the blame exclusively within the individual person or within the individual family." He looked beyond the family to indict "society [and] the State itself" as "unsocial."[64]

Notably, the circle of guilt for Blankenship's death encompassed U.S. foreign policy. Wertham offered his readers a history lesson, contending that the subjugation of Puerto Rico within its colonial relationship to the United States marked Frank as an "unplaced" person. He contended that Puerto Rico was still "more 'associated' than free. . . . Whereas Puerto Rico is in name not a colony, it is not unlike one in operation." Meditating on the violence in Congress that had arisen from this injustice, he noted, "It has been said . . . that 'every once in a while real bullets come out of the unreal world and kill real people.'" Though he did not identify Luis Muñoz Marín as the speaker, he rejected this analysis: "As far as I can see . . . bullets always come from an all-too-real world."[65]

The oppression that plagued Puerto Ricans on the island was mirrored and even exacerbated in New York, where they experienced intense hostility, prejudice, and discrimination in housing, education, and employment. The patterns of juvenile delinquency, particularly in gangs organized along racial lines, replicated these racial hatreds, but Wertham pointed out that these had their origin in "adult life, adult values and adult tensions," for "children do not infect neighborhoods with race prejudice; the neighborhoods infect the children with it." Local, national, and international inequalities, then, were critical for understanding the eruption of individual acts of violence. As Wertham asserted, "The connections between the wages of a needle worker in Puerto Rico and a gun in the hands of a boy on the sidewalks of New York may not be apparent; but they do exist."[66]

As important as consideration of U.S. colonialism and racism to understanding this crime was the recognition that "there is nothing as likely to make [children] delinquent as the realization that they are regarded as second-rate citizens." Children had "fundamental rights . . . to health, to education, and to protection," Wertham claimed, but these rights went undefended. One reason was that juvenile delinquency was actually in the economic interests of a large sector of the adult population—newspaper publishers, social scientists, and charitable organizations as well as drug dealers, gun merchants, and pornographers. Reprising his critique of the ACLU's definition of democracy as "risk," he argued that to control delinquency and restore democracy, adults who violated children's rights must be restrained. It was true, he admitted, that youth crime had many causes, but this did not mean that any particular strategy, such as controlling comic books, need be discarded. Rather, regulating the "creeps comics" with which Santana was fascinated was one concrete step that could be taken to protect children more generally from seduction, exploitation, and violence. And it was "violence, the threat of violence and the fear of violence" that was pervasive in Santana's everyday life, "at school or on the street," as well as in mass media. It was no surprise at all that, in this unremitting culture of violence, this young Puerto Rican boy would carry a gun for protection. "If we follow all the clues," Wertham told his readers, "the circle of guilt enlarges in every case."[67]

Perhaps if many of Wertham's professional colleagues had not already dismissed him as obsessed with comic books, his campaign on Frank Santana's behalf would have had more impact. But perhaps not, since his emphasis on social responsibility was so far out of sync with the individualist currents of Cold War–era American social and political discourse. In the 1950s, even those who argued for "understanding" toward juvenile delinquents hesitated to condemn the state for creating the violence they enacted. There were relatively few reviews of Wertham's book; the occasional positive appraisal still condemned his emotionality, while Michael Maccoby of the *New Republic* called the book "dangerous," ignoring everything it contained except for the very brief chapter on comic books. In *The Nation,* author and New York City magistrate Morris Ploscowe reviewed the book together with a reprint of Robert Lindner's *Rebel Without a Cause.* Reflecting the tenor of the times, he found Wertham's analysis "superficial" in comparison to Lindner's "major contribution" in his case study of a psychopath named Harold whose troubles with the law and society stemmed from "his observation as a small child of an act of sexual intercourse between his parents."[68] These indifferent or negative reviews were matched by the popular response, and Wertham complained of his difficulty in rousing New York's Puerto Rican community to action. Despite the fact that in 1969 New York's Court of Appeals agreed that Santana should have the opportunity to demonstrate that pretrial publicity had unfairly forced him into his guilty plea, he served his complete minimum sentence of twenty-five years. After his release, he bitterly criticized Wertham's book, maintaining that the doctor had exploited him by telling his story without his permission and sharing none of the profits.[69]

Whatever motivations Wertham might have had for writing this book—and among them was, undoubtedly, a wish for self-promotion and recognition—they included the desire to achieve justice for boys like Frank Santana and Robert Peebles, who, he believed, were scapegoats for a society unwilling to "look at itself." He insisted that analyses of American culture that focused on individual adjustment or family dysfunction must give way to a redefinition of democracy as a system that mobilized the state to protect the rights of the poor, the dark-skinned, the female, and the young against the so-called liberties of the wealthy and powerful. Asserting that "freedom is not something that one can have, but is something that one must do," he advocated collective commitment to a social state that would create the conditions for real security and real freedom—freedom from violence of all sorts, including the state-sanctioned violence of colonialism, racism, and incarceration. The social state would also express an ethical stance toward all of its citizens, guarding children's rights to health, education, protection from exploitation, and fair treatment by the justice system, as well as assisting their parents in their quest for dignified work and decent housing. Most important, the social state would seek to train children to *non*violence, nurturing both male and female citizens who valued cooperation and empathy over brute force, and creating a more democratic nation in the process. Wertham implored Americans to "set the children free!" from the violence that spoiled their futures. But his vision of freedom, it turned out, would play little role in the anti–comic book campaigns that he incited.[70]

"Parents, Wake Up!" Grassroots Activism and Cold War Culture

Overall, the responses to Fredric Wertham's anti-violence campaign were complex and varied. Although *The Circle of Guilt* received relatively little attention, *Seduction of the Innocent* was widely and, generally, positively reviewed, and many commentators praised it as a wake-up call for parents. Some reviewers leavened their praise with complaints about Wertham's emotional prose, his self-aggrandizement, and his tolerance for censorship, or accused him of oversimplifying the effect of comic books on their readers. Despite Wertham's formal insistence that comic books were only one factor contributing to youth crime, as much a symptom as a cause of societal ills, his own tendency to concentrate on them gave heft to this critique. And what one reviewer called his almost "pathological" disdain for other social scientists and policy makers certainly had much to do with his ultimate marginalization within professional circles.[71]

Nevertheless, analyses that emphasize Wertham's professional isolation miss his broader social and political influence. Fredric Wertham did not "almost singlehandedly" destroy the American comic book industry in the 1950s, as many comics fans have claimed, but he did help foment a social movement to regulate the industry. Wertham launched his anti-comics crusade in March 1948. By April, Detroit's police commissioner was calling for legislation outlawing crime comics, particularly those that featured brutality against women, children, or racial minorities. Soon a number of other municipalities were discussing and enacting similar laws, partly in response to a U.S. Supreme Court decision that required specificity in laws regulating the "circulation of objectionable printed matter." Another burst of lawmaking followed on the heels of the publication of *Seduction.* By 1955, one-third of the states and at least sixty municipalities were considering legislation to control comic books. Although few states actually passed any laws, a number of localities did enact regulations. These ranged from strengthening traditional obscenity statutes, to outlawing the sale of crime and horror comic books, to creating boards of review. In addition, the problem received attention at the federal level when several Senate subcommittees held hearings investigating the influence of comic books. All of this forced the comic book industry to adopt a code that effectively banned some of the images to which Wertham objected.[72]

But Wertham's role went beyond that of publicizing the alleged dangers of comics. Despite his protest that he was not an activist but merely a doctor offering a diagnosis, Wertham worked to organize social agitation. He was deluged with letters from parents who had read his articles and his book or heard him on the radio, and from local and state officials who wanted his assistance in framing anti-comics legislation. Wertham provided information and advice when he could, sending other Lafargue doctors to speak to local women's clubs and PTAs, mailing out statistics and reprints, or suggesting legal language. He worked particularly closely with Harold Kennedy, Los Angeles County Counsel, to draft an anti–comic book law, and had extensive correspondence with a number of women community activists, offering them encouragement, advice, and exhortation. These relationships sustained him in his work. As he told one journalist, "On the one hand, I am really isolated, as far as psychiatrists and mental hygiene organizations are concerned; on the other hand, I feel like the voice of the people when I get the mail every day and am swamped with letters from parents, teachers, librarians, lawyers, and children, from all over the country, wanting to do something."[73]

Wertham's relationships with women activists in particular were likely facilitated by his willingness to defend mothers from critics who blamed them for children gone wrong. This theme, which was reiterated again and again in Wertham's writings, found its most dramatic articulation in the story that closes *Seduction of the Innocent.* A young mother had come to him for help when her son was arrested for possession of a knife. As Wertham related: "I . . . told her we would do whatever we could. Then I added, 'I know what you have done for this boy. Don't think that it's your fault.' At that she looked up, all alert. 'It must be my fault,' she said. 'I heard that in the lectures. And the judge said it, too.' " He hastily interrupted to reassure her: "You are a good mother, and you've given this boy a good home. But the influence of a good home is frustrated if it is not supported by the other influences children are exposed to—the comic books, the crime programs and all that. . . . So don't worry about yourself. It's not your fault." But this mother needed yet more support: "When she was halfway through the door she turned slowly. 'Doctor,' she said in a low voice. 'I'm sorry to take your time. But please—tell me again. . . . Tell me again. . . . Tell me again that it isn't my fault.' And I did."[74] Closing the book with these words, Wertham emphasized again the powerlessness of parents, especially mothers, in a society that found the origins of violence in dysfunctional families and ignored a legal system that privileged the rights of publishers to profits over the rights of children to protection.

Still, he encouraged mothers "as voters, as citizens, and as money-spenders" to demand a state that served social needs, and women's groups responded to his entreaties. Although numerous men's and mixed-sex organizations battled crime comics, women's groups were especially active in these efforts. Notable among them was the General Federation of Women's Clubs (GFWC), the nation's largest women's organization. With a membership mostly composed of middle-class and upper-middle-class white women, the GFWC had a long tradition of activism on cultural issues. Though at first reluctant to advocate legislation, in the wake of *Seduction*'s publication, GFWC leaders vastly expanded their efforts to enact local, state, and federal legislation to ban the sale of crime comics and "indecent magazines."[75]

Wertham's ability to mobilize middle-class women can be traced to his skill at manipulating the symbolism of motherhood in ways that were likely to appeal to them. His insistence that mothers were not to blame for their children's crimes stood in stark contrast to more widespread sentiments that deemed bad mothering itself a danger to the nation. Mothers failed both in their absence from the home—a concern as married women's labor force participation rates rose in the postwar years—and in their invasive overprotectiveness, decried by critics of "momism" for undermining male autonomy. Conservative commentators accused mothers of raising boys to be either too soft or too hard—homosexuals and sex maniacs, traitors and juvenile delinquents—but rarely just right.[76] Wertham rejected these "pseudo-Freudian" explanations that found the causes of juvenile delinquency in "neurotic," overprotective, or inattentive mothers in favor of praise for "harassed" and embattled mothers whose efforts to protect their children were stymied by the comic book industry and its defense team. Women who enlisted in his anti-comics campaign on the grounds that children needed protection from forces outside the home challenged this view of the all-powerful mother. By emphasizing the influence of the mass media, they defended all mothers against the charge that they were to blame for the problem of boys gone wrong. What, after all, could any one mother do when confronted with an industry with sales of half a billion dollars each year? But united in the GFWC, they could make a difference.[77]

In the South, Midwest, and West, clubwomen met with a good deal of success in their anti–comic book organizing, but they went far beyond Wertham's call for a public health measure that would ban the sale of crime comics to children under fifteen. Some used informal pressure on retailers to drive "objectionable literature" from the shelves of newsstands, drugstores, and groceries. In Kansas, for example, they checked newsstands on a regular basis and conducted "Big Bonfire rallies," burning books to dramatize their opposition to immoral literature. And by 1955, clubwomen in Colorado had persuaded the Safeway grocery chain to stop selling comic books and paperback novels in its 137 stores in the Rocky Mountain region.[78]

Other clubs focused on legislative action, demanding stricter obscenity laws that encompassed a broad range of publications and applied to adults as well as children. In 1954 and 1955, clubs in a dozen states worked on strengthening local laws. They succeeded in passing legislation in communities as diverse as Monroeville, Alabama; San Leandro, California; and Houston, Texas. A 1956 Florida campaign that combined all of these strategies received national attention. In Coral Gables, clubwomen investigated Dade County newsstands and found forty "objectionable publications," including some subtitled "Entertainment for Men" (a reference to *Playboy*). Expressing their shock that "any youth . . . could learn the art of seduction, how to rape a girl, how to assault with a deadly weapon and the techniques of sadistic torture," they organized forty-six civic groups into a Decent Literature Council, pressured city officials to enforce existing laws, and secured promises from newsdealers to stop selling sixteen blacklisted magazines. Then they successfully lobbied for a state law that strengthened the penalties for distributing pornographic materials.[79]

As this account suggests, while Wertham's framing of the problem of crime comics proved attractive to clubwomen, their analysis of the problem and its solutions often departed from his own. They quickly expanded their campaign to include the sorts of "pornographic" materials with which Wertham was concerned hardly at all, especially "girlie" magazines featuring "sexy photography [and] lurid stories, all geared to the sexually inquisitive mind." Their focus on this sort of "immoral" literature suggests that while clubwomen may also have been concerned about a culture of violence, much of their activism stemmed from resistance to changing sexual norms. Lurid literature, they argued, corrupted young people, teaching them to "accept nudity, immoral situations, risqué stories as the normal way of life in this country." Thus, though Wertham and GFWC members agreed that the 1955 adoption of the comic book code did not solve the problem of "objectionable literature," their diagnoses were starkly different. Wertham complained that the code did almost nothing to get rid of the sadism that, he thought, still permeated comic books; clubwomen shifted their attention to the dangers of sex itself.[80]

Clubwomen were not the only Americans whose comic book activism strayed from the path that Wertham had envisioned. He had studiously avoided the sorts of Cold War rhetoric that accused comic books of fomenting "totalitarianism," but others traced both indirect and direct lines between crime comics—and "immoral" literature more generally—and the Communist threat. Although Richard Clendenen, executive director of the Senate Subcommittee to Investigate Juvenile Delinquency, concluded that it was the desire for profits, not a Communist conspiracy, that lay behind the proliferation of comic books, activists and concerned citizens around the country reckoned differently. One pamphlet published by Minnesota juvenile judges, for example, lambasted the ACLU for opposing a 1953 amendment to the state's obscenity statutes. Noting that the ACLU had been named a Communist front group by numerous government and civic organizations, it asked, "How long and how often can the American people be duped?" exhorting: "Parents, wake up! The objective of communism is to despoil your children, to rob them of their respect for law and the teachings of morality, to enslave them with sex and narcotics. When that happens, the seeds of communism will fall on fertile ground."[81]

Many of Wertham's correspondents sounded similar warnings. After reading *Seduction,* one Washington, D.C., man wrote: "This is planned and deliberate subversion by means of psychological 'brain-washing.' I don't mean to sound dramatic, or to have brought upon me the much-repeated and tiresome phrase, 'seeing Reds under the bed.' But I do think that there is much more behind the staggering volume of cheap literature and lurid comic books than profit and profit alone." A woman living in New York City voiced remarkably similar thoughts, identifying herself as "a liberal who does not see a Communist under every bush. . . . But I became convinced after watching TV one night that there is a real plot going on to poison the minds of our youth: to debauch us from within. . . . Has anyone approached our lawmakers with the idea of comic books as a source of subversion?" This association between comic books and Communism even persuaded one boy to give up "weird" (horror or science-fiction) comics because, as he put it, "they could get us kids to believe anything . . . and if we started to believe anything, we would soon be believing what the communists wanted us to believe in."[82]

Others made different linkages between comic books and the Cold War, emphasizing that the race hatred and violence that saturated American comic books seemed to substantiate Communist characterizations of American culture, undermining the nation's reputation in Europe and the developing world. This was a point that Wertham briefly made himself, but it became the keynote of some condemnations. In fact, some Communist publications in eastern Europe did offer this critique, as one German professor wrote Wertham from Stuttgart: "It is difficult to see what comic books have got to do with democracy and indeed the enemies of the West in their propaganda against democracy make use of this strange predilection for the gruesome." Former ambassador to India Chester Bowles noted that "the Communist propagandists themselves could not possibly devise a more persuasive way" than comic books to convince "color sensitive Indians that Americans . . . are indoctrinating our children with bitter racial prejudice from the time they learn to read." According to one Senate subcommittee investigating comic books, the Soviets and their allies claimed that American "imperialists" used such "trash literature" to "condition a generation of young automatons who will be ready to march and kill in the future wars of aggression planned by the capitalists."[83]

Ironically, this was precisely Wertham's point: that comic books *were* preparing young American boys to "become good stormtroopers, paratroopers, commandos and cannon-fodder." A few others echoed this position. Marya Mannes hinted that the violence in American culture generally, and in comic books specifically, had given rise to the violence of McCarthyism and belied

Americans' claims to be "the friendliest people in the world."[84] Very occasionally a correspondent wrote Wertham to endorse his view that comics constituted "a calculated effort" by "big war-mongers to inculcate brutality in the minds of our children."[85] Still, he was much more likely to hear from those who feared comics' propaganda value to the Soviets than from those who shared his concerns about the absence of security and equal citizenship for the nation's most vulnerable. This is not to say that Americans were not concerned about violence. The moral panic over juvenile delinquency that occupied citizens as well as senators during the 1950s tells us that they were. But it seems that the violence they feared was displaced onto others: Communists who somehow manipulated American comic books in order to accomplish the "moral disarmament" of the United States; "abnormal" boys whose consumption of media violence turned them into juvenile delinquents; African American and Puerto Rican youth who were all too quick to pull the trigger. The structural violence *against* those boys, or the violence that the United States exported through its foreign policy—the violence that Wertham was most concerned about—became lost in the rush to blame mothers, or Communists, or shoddy research.

Near the end of *Seduction of the Innocent,* Wertham recounted an exchange he purportedly had with a member of a New York State committee studying the problem of comic books, who himself was describing a conversation with a comics defender. The legislator told Wertham, "The general counsel of the Association of Comics Magazine Publishers said to me, 'Somewhere right now a little boy has a gun and reads crime comics. That boy will be president some day,'" and asked what Wertham had to say to that. "All I can say," he answered, "is that that is precisely what I would like to prevent."[86] This brief vignette starkly captures Wertham's views about the dangers that comic books posed to the nation, and it clearly illustrates his distance from most other contributors to the debates about juvenile delinquency and American culture in the early Cold War years. Wertham feared for the future of the nation if its leaders were raised to be sadists. But most cultural commentators advocated a "Cold War cult of masculine toughness" to counteract American men's dangerous softness, and deemed the U.S. government's capacity for increasingly sophisticated and deadly forms of violence the only hope for preventing Armageddon. They bemoaned the problems of "conformity," "other-directedness," and passivity and prescribed in their stead a virile individualism that substituted a hard-edged realism for flaccid sentimentality. As the psychoanalyst Robert Lindner pronounced, humanity was *constituted* through the "drive to master, to overcome," and it was because mass society did not permit the expression of "socially channelized aggression" that American teenagers had become psychopaths. Wertham, by contrast, rejected the idea that humans were naturally aggressive, and he valued cooperation above the pursuit of individual freedom.[87] In this context, Wertham's cautionary tales about masculine brutality, sadistic citizens, and an unsocial state were not likely to gain much traction.

In the end, what most distinguished Wertham from other cultural critics was his understanding of the state's responsibility to ensure the individual and collective security of its citizens. This was a responsibility that had first to be met by preventing violence. Speaking in 1949 about the racial inequities in the criminal justice system that had resulted in convictions and death sentences for the Trenton Six (African American men falsely accused of murder in New Jersey), Wertham observed: "It isn't possible to discuss any program of democracy or peace on earth without discussion of violence. At present there is a condemnation of people who advocate the overthrow of the Government by violence. What the powers that be are really worried about are the people who advocate the overthrow of violence by government."[88] Against a rhetoric that insisted, against much evidence to the contrary, on the most powerful nation's vulnerability to totalitarian violence and terror, he recast the relationship between security and democracy, seeking to include all the nation's citizens, including its most vulnerable, within the law's protection. His vision paralleled the logic of the Cold War state of exception, which premised national security on restricting individual rights, all in the name of guarding the liberty that made the United States exceptional. But it inverted that logic as well, making national security social by identifying it with the protection of even the most disadvantaged citizens' rights to live a civilized life, and suggesting that it was violence, not liberty, that constituted American exceptionalism. It is perhaps, then, little surprise that Fredric Wertham's critique of Cold War culture was so easily misconstrued.

CONCLUSION.

Exceptions, Exceptionalism, and U.S. Citizenship

DURING THE EARLY COLD WAR YEARS, THE IMPACT OF THE NATIONAL security state on those vulnerable individuals whose membership in the U.S. polity was *least* secure sometimes awoke a broader public to the contradictions of American citizenship. Fought in the name of guarding the rights and freedoms imagined to give meaning to national belonging, the Cold War had the unsettling effect of calling attention to their fragility. The claim that democracy at home and liberty abroad required exceptional measures for their protection threatened to undermine the hoary faith that America itself was exceptional. The cost of asserting the supremacy of democratic capitalism against totalitarian Communism was that some Americans expected the United States to pay its debts to its citizens.

In recent years, historians grappling with the massive cultural change and political rebellion of the 1960s have strained against the confines of a historical memory that insists on conformity in the 1950s. How could a consensus on the superiority of the American way and all it entailed have crumbled so quickly? They have drawn attention to the rumblings—and sometimes the major eruption—of discontent in the 1950s, most notably the rise of a mass civil rights movement, but also the articulation of disquiet about other-directed men and unhappy housewives, the increasing popularity of rock and roll and the seemingly sudden arrival of the Beat generation, the "rediscovery" of poverty, and a burgeoning sexual revolution. Emphasizing the continuities across the postwar years as well as the differences, they seek to explain the 1960s not merely as a reaction against the buttoned-down decade that preceded it, but as a flowering of dissent that already had deep roots.

Those roots were nourished by the belief in American exceptionalism that underwrote the ideology and practices of the early Cold War–era national security state. The radical movements of the 1960s were criticized by their detractors as anti-American, but certainly one of the fonts of the social, political, and cultural dissent of the decade was the insistence that America's ideals of freedom, rights, and democracy ought to fully encompass all of its citizens. The pamphlet trumpeting Students for a Democratic Society's Port Huron Statement had emblazoned on its front page the New Left's debt to American ideals, proclaiming as a goal "the establishment of a democracy of individual participation, governed by two central aims: that the individual share in those social decisions determining the quality and direction of his life; that society be organized to encourage independence in men and provide the media for their common participation."[1] The insistence that American society be restructured so as to foster the freedom, protect the rights, and facilitate the participation of every citizen undergirded a host of movements that fought to expand democracy in America, even if they also came to question many of the nation's bedrock principles. The demand for full citizenship that animated movements for civil rights and racial liberation, for gender and sexual equality, for economic justice and responsive government took form long before the sixties, and it quickly morphed in previously unimagined directions, but its explosion in that decade owed a great deal to the realization that the caretakers of the burgeoning national security state had to be pushed into living up to American ideals.

The Cold War is an increasingly distant memory, but the contradictions that its state of emergency made visible—both the specific struggles detailed in this volume and the more general exclusions that always ground liberal democracy—remain vital questions for debate in the twenty-first century. For example, Puerto Ricans continue to seek a solution to the status question, which has been revisited time and again in the past half century or so. In a controversial two-part referendum in November 2012, a majority of voters rejected the status quo of the Commonwealth, reflecting not only dissatisfaction with their continued position as semi-citizens but also unhappiness with policies that have maintained

Puerto Rico's level of poverty (at less than one-half the per capita income of Mississippi, the poorest state) and contributed to massive unemployment and skyrocketing violence. Of those who indicated a preference, most voters supported statehood, while only 5 percent chose independence, and almost half a million expressed no opinion on what should replace the Commonwealth. Statehood had never before commanded the backing of a majority of voters, but the confusion over the plebiscite's results, along with congressional concern over the potential economic burdens, political transformations, and partisan reconfigurations that statehood might bring, has led most observers to conclude that Puerto Rico's status will not soon be resolved. Although President Barack Obama had proclaimed before the plebiscite that if Puerto Ricans expressed themselves in support of statehood, he would ask Congress to act, he now demurred. "This administration, as you know, is committed to the principle that the question of political status is a matter of self-determination for the people of Puerto Rico," an administration official declared. Because the vote was "unclear," Obama, who had earlier been the first sitting president since 1961 to conduct an official visit to the island, called for additional study.[2] Thus, as it was in the 1950s, the continued denial of full civil and political rights to residents of Puerto Rico was justified by the appeal to "self-determination."

Questions about the loyalty of African Americans take on a different tenor now, but the perception that black people in America have divided loyalties that impede their ability to participate as citizens is still to be heard in accusations that African Americans voted en masse for Barack Obama as a matter of identity rather than from a reasoned reflection on their political interests. Furthermore, the economic citizenship of black women and men can be said in some senses to be less, not more, secure than during the 1950s. Annie Lee Moss staked her claim to the right to a decent job on the eve of the eruption of a mass civil rights movement, one that demanded both government protection of that right and the removal of myriad barriers to African American equality. Sixty years later, the claim by some that the United States had entered a "postracial" age—a claim materialized in a creeping abandonment of the institutional frameworks created to ameliorate the legacy of racial slavery, including affirmative action, a more equitable welfare system, the antipoverty programs of the Great Society, even the Voting Rights Act—ignored the evidence of continuing and growing racial (and class) disparities in political and economic access in the twenty-first century. The Great Recession revealed how tenuous any economic advance among blacks could be, as unemployment rates roughly double those of whites, combined with the catastrophic effects of confinement to the subprime mortgage market, checked any progress that had been made. Certainly there has been substantial change: poverty rates among blacks were halved from 1959 to 2011. Nonetheless, as recently as 2012, the median household income for African Americans remained 58 percent that of whites, essentially the same rate as forty years earlier, and median household wealth inequality rose in 2009 to an all-time high, with white households having twenty times the wealth of African Americans and eighteen times that of Hispanics.[3] These disparities can be even more marked for women: in 2010, among unmarried women aged thirty-six to forty-nine, whites had a median wealth of $42,600, while that for women of color was only $5.[4] These sorts of statistics, as well as the myriad ways that people of color continue to struggle with marginalization, have led many scholars to question whether citizenship provides an answer to the problem of "racial capitalism." As the historian and theorist Nikhil Pal Singh notes, "formal citizenship rights have not delivered economic opportunity and political empowerment for a significant proportion of U.S. blacks."[5]

The sorts of social citizenship that Fredric Wertham called for are similarly unrealized in the twenty-first century. If the general trend in U.S. history has been toward a decline in the prevalence of violence, it nevertheless remains the case that people of color are disproportionately victims of violent crime, and this is particularly true for young men like those about whom Wertham was most concerned. In the first decade of the twenty-first century, almost half of all homicide victims in the United States were African American men, and homicide was the leading cause of death among young black men.[6] Far from being offered the sorts of social goods that would ameliorate these conditions, young men of color also continue to find themselves disproportionately victims of state violence, with a direct and adverse impact on their status as citizens. The United States has distinguished itself by having the highest incarceration rates in the world; since 1952, the number of individuals imprisoned at any one time has grown by approximately a factor of eight. In 2010, African American men were imprisoned at a rate almost seven times that of non-Hispanic white men, and almost 8 percent of American blacks were disenfranchised because of a felony conviction, in part a result of racial disparities in crime prosecution and sentencing practices.[7] Wertham's warnings that the state is more notable as an agent of violence than a protector of its citizens are perhaps more germane than ever; it is not quite ironic, but it is chilling, that calls for the regulation of violent films, television shows, and video games, which Wertham might have approved, have more traction in debates about violence in America than do demands for gun control, which he also supported.

Furthermore, in the new post-9/11 state of emergency, government policies have led a number of Americans to interrogate anew the meanings of freedom and democracy in a nation obsessed with security. For example, the reasoning grounding the Supreme Court's ruling that Ellen Knauff had no right to know the reasons for her exclusion still stands as a fundamental principle of American jurisprudence. Noncitizens outside the borders of the United States continue to be denied due process rights in their dealings with the nation, a refusal that matters a great deal when U.S. intelligence agencies practice extraordinary rendition and the military detains individuals for indeterminate periods in overseas prisons.[8] More broadly, national security remains a legitimate justification for government secrecy, including vastly expanded surreptitious surveillance of U.S. citizens, the holding of secret deportation hearings, and the refusal to disclose evidence or even to name individuals who are held by the U.S. government. Although some of the most egregious practices instituted by President George W. Bush as crucial to the survival of the United States were discarded by the Obama administration, even a president who promised a "new standard of openness" on the day of his inauguration continued to cite national security as grounds for ubiquitous government secrecy policies. And again that insistence on secrecy brought forth comment on the contradictions of American democracy. In a case in which the Obama administration refused to respond to Freedom of Information Act requests from journalists and others regarding its tactic of targeting suspected terrorists with drone attacks, including U.S. citizens, federal judge Colleen McMahon declared that she felt like Alice in Wonderland: "I can find no way around the thicket of laws and precedents that effectively allow the Executive Branch of our Government to proclaim as perfectly lawful certain actions that seem on their face incompatible with our Constitution and laws, while keeping the reasons for their conclusion a secret." Bemoaning the "paradoxical situation" that led to her ruling as "a veritable Catch-22," she sounded very much like those judges who wanted to keep Ellen Knauff in the country but despaired of finding the power to do so.[9]

If Cold War psychology called into question the ability of Communists to be real Americans, the "War on Terror" that followed on the 2001 attacks made possible a new set of distinctions between the nation's purported enemies and its loyal citizens. Although in their early responses President Bush and members of his administration were careful to assert that the United States was not at war with "Islam" and to condemn acts of hatred against Arab Americans, their later claims that the enemy was "Islamic fascists" and "radical Islam," as well as continued recourse to racial and religious profiling in security policies, did little to abate suspicion of Muslims—or those perceived to be Muslim—in America. In one sense, the rhetoric of tolerance and respect for "normal" Muslims that informs most official declarations of War on Terror policy reflects the changes in American culture accomplished by the radical movements of the 1960s.[10] The sorts of crude psychological analysis that characterized Cold War–era diagnoses of Communists and Puerto Rican Nationalists have fallen out of vogue, and while the wholesale disavowal of entire groups of U.S. citizens on the basis of their beliefs may yet be common among some sectors of society, bald statements of bigotry are mostly, though not always, seen as impolitic when uttered by government representatives.

Nonetheless, there are some strong structural similarities between analyses of the Cold War's Communist enemy and the War on Terror's Islamist one, most notably the assertion that each is unalterably opposed to Western values of individualism and freedom and committed to the complete destruction of Western civilization. And, just as in the Cold War, the identification of Islam as fundamentally Other—in this case foreign, irrational, ahistorical, and anti-modern—has had its domestic impacts as well. In the year after the September 2001 attacks, hate crimes against those perceived to be Muslim increased by 1,600 percent, and though they subsequently dropped, they declined to a rate that was still roughly five times their pre-9/11 level. Harassment, employment discrimination, vandalism, and zoning discrimination continued to rise, a dozen years and more after the attacks. And the civil rights and civil liberties of Muslim Americans have been grossly violated. The revelation that New York City police spied on mosques as well as Muslim businesses and students even outside their jurisdiction, employing "mosque crawlers" and "rakers" to keep track of Muslims and map their movements, is only one example of the ways that America's Muslim citizens are treated differently in the wake of 9/11. Together with the campaign against the building of an Islamic community center in lower Manhattan on the basis that a "ground zero mosque" would "desecrate" the memory of the victims of the World Trade Center attacks, and Representative Michele Bachmann's accusations that Islamists had infiltrated the federal government, it suggests that the belief that Muslims are highly suspect as American citizens may be more widespread than is acknowledged by proclamations of religious tolerance.

Notwithstanding countless comparisons, the War on Terror is not simply the Cold War reinvented. Some may wish to see it that way, another iteration of the endless war of ideas between freedom and totalitarianism. As George W. Bush told the nation shortly after the 9/11 attacks, "They hate our freedoms—our freedom of religion, our freedom of speech, our freedom to vote and assemble and disagree with each other. . . . This is not, however, just America's fight. And what is at stake is not just America's freedom. This is the world's fight. This is civilization's fight. This is the fight of all who believe in progress and pluralism, tolerance and freedom."[11] For Bush and his supporters, this new global conflict offered an opportunity for the United States to rediscover its world-historical function as the defender of liberal individualism (especially for women), freedom, and progress against a corporatist and authoritarian foe. But many others have pointed out the vast differences, including the fact that the enemy in this latter-day struggle "for the soul of mankind" is not another powerful state but a relatively resource-poor network linked across borders but often riven by competition.[12] If, in that way, the "terrorists" whose enmity has provided the opportunity to shore up the national security state are similar to the Puerto Rican militants who felt its force at mid-century, one of the differences is seen in how the vulnerability of the United States is—or is not—figured. During the Cold War, the expansion of national security policy signaled American strength as much as it did American susceptibility, with the result that the Puerto Rican threat was both heavily penalized and ridiculed. Today, when the nation's military power is unmatched by that of rival states, the abridgment of civil liberties in the name of national security may depend more on persuading citizens of national weakness than on performing strength.

Despite these important differences, the similarities between the regimes of citizenship established during the Cold War and the War on Terror, and the relationship between those regimes and U.S. nationalism, run deep. In both periods, it is the need to protect a purported American exceptionalism, an exceptionalism that is necessary to the survival of "civilization," that requires crafting exceptions to the protections that constitute not just national belonging but the very substance of civilization itself.[13] The assertion of those exceptions *as exceptional* seeks to mask the fact that they have always been present and necessary to the constitution of state sovereignty. But, paradoxically, the state of exception also makes them visible. It is in *that* Catch-22 that the possibility for a critical citizenship resides.

NOTES

Abbreviations

DDEL	Dwight D. Eisenhower Library, Abilene, Kans.
HST	Harry S. Truman Presidential Library and Archives, Independence, Mo.
NARA	National Archives and Records Administration, Washington, D.C.
NARA II	National Archives and Records Administration, College Park, Md.
NARA-NY	National Archives and Records Administration, New York, N.Y.
RG	Record Group

Introduction

1. Stouffer, *Communism, Conformity, and Civil Liberties,* 13.
2. Ibid., 39–46.
3. Ibid., 227.
4. Ibid., 216, 223.
5. *United States ex rel. Knauff v. Shaughnessy.*
6. The literature on Cold War–era anti-Communism is vast. For an introduction, see Schrecker, *Many Are the Crimes;* Caute, *Great Fear;* Leffler, *Preponderance of Power;* and Storrs, *Second Red Scare.* On the discourse of national security, see Leffler, "National Security"; Rosenberg, "Commentary"; and Hogan, *Cross of Iron,* 1–22.
7. Sherry, *In the Shadow of War,* 174.
8. X, "Sources of Soviet Conduct," 581; May, *Homeward Bound,* 198–99, 15–16.

9. For examples, see De Hart, "Containment at Home"; Spigel, *Make Room for TV;* Lewis, *Prescription for Heterosexuality.*
10. For works that depart from the model of domestic containment, see the essays in Meyerowitz, *Not June Cleaver;* Meyerowitz, "Sex, Gender"; McEnaney, *Civil Defense Begins at Home;* Lynn, *Progressive Women;* Murray, *Progressive Housewife;* Gore, *Radicalism at the Crossroads.*
11. McEnaney, "Cold War Mobilization," 440. Critiques of the notion of Cold War consensus have been proliferating for several decades, and McEnaney provides an excellent overview of this literature. For a thorough delineation of the multiple axes of contradiction characterizing Cold War political culture, see Jacobson and González, *What Have They Built You to Do?,* 33–38.
12. Storrs, *Second Red Scare;* Rogin, *Ronald Reagan;* Heale, *American Anticommunism;* Powers, *Not Without Honor;* Heale, *McCarthy's Americans;* Jenkins, *Cold War at Home.*
13. Agamben, *Homo Sacer,* 13. I have chosen to use masculine pronouns here to emphasize how profoundly masculine this power has been. See Pateman, "Fraternal Social Contract."
14. Agamben, *State of Exception,* 3.
15. For an introduction to Agamben's thought, see Murray, *Giorgio Agamben.*
16. Carruthers, *Cold War Captives,* 5; see also Stephanson, "Liberty or Death"; Fousek, *To Lead the Free World.*
17. Sherry, *In the Shadow of War;* Leffler, *Preponderance of Power;* McCoy, *Policing America's Empire.*
18. "A Report to the National Security Council—NSC 68," April 12, 1950, 7, President's Secretary's Files, HST (available at www.trumanlibrary.org).
19. Rodgers, *Contested Truths,* 215.
20. On citizenship and "worth stories," see Smith, *Stories of Peoplehood.*
21. Smith, *Civic Ideals;* Novak, "Legal Transformation."
22. Shklar, *American Citizenship,* 1.
23. Cohen, *Semi-Citizenship,* 13, 3; Fousek, *To Lead the Free World.*
24. Kerber, "The Stateless as the Citizen's Other"; Glenn, *Unequal Freedom.*
25. For important key texts in the relationship between race, gender, and political discourses, see Scott, "Gender"; Higginbotham, "African-American Women's History"; Rosenberg, "Gender."
26. Smith, *Stories of Peoplehood.*

1. Internal Security, National Security

1. "A Report to the National Security Council—NSC 68," April 12, 1950, 7–8, President's Secretary's Files, HST (available at www.trumanlibrary.org).
2. Herman, *Romance of American Psychology;* Lewis, *Prescription for Heterosexuality;* Meyerowitz, "How Common Culture." For an overview of representations of Communists, see Schrecker, *Many Are the Crimes.*
3. Of course, the "nonfiction" character of some of these works was a matter of dispute, especially in the case of the memoirs. For example, Charles Alan Wright titled his review

of Whittaker Chambers's *Witness* "A Long Work of Fiction." On cultural representations of Cold War citizenship, see Jacobson and González, *What Have They Built You to Do?;* Whitfield, *Culture of the Cold War;* Corber, *In the Name* and *Cold War Femme;* Cohan, *Masked Men;* Rogin, *Ronald Reagan;* Nelson, *Pursuing Privacy;* Hendershot, *Anti-Communism and Popular Culture;* Doherty, *Cold War, Cool Medium.*

4. Because they serve a somewhat different purpose, I have not analyzed works by "professional" informants such as those by Philbrick, Cvetic, and Harvey Matusow. On the informant in the Cold War era, see Lichtman and Cohen, *Deadly Farce;* Navasky, *Naming Names.* For a contemporary critique of the "ex-Communist," see Arendt, "Ex-Communists." On anti-Communist writing, see Fleming, *Anti-Communist Manifestos;* Seed, "Ex-Communist Memoirs." On Cold War–era confessional culture, see Nelson, *Pursuing Privacy.*
5. Lichtblau, "A Recruiter Confesses."
6. Seed, "Ex-Communist Memoirs," 606.
7. Crossman, *The God That Failed,* 4; Bentley, *Out of Bondage,* 16, 30; Richard Wright in Crossman, *The God That Failed,* 118. On Bentley, see Olmsted, *Red Spy Queen;* Wilson, "Elizabeth Bentley"; Kessler, *Clever Girl.*
8. Chambers, *Witness,* 11, 196; Tanenhaus, *Whittaker Chambers.*
9. Chambers, *Witness,* 9–10, 17.
10. Crossman, *The God That Failed,* 6; Bentley, *Out of Bondage,* 16, 42–43; Koestler quoted in Crossman, *The God That Failed,* 15. The theme of Communism as akin to a religious faith figured in many reviews of these books as well.
11. Bentley, *Out of Bondage,* 285; Budenz, *This Is My Story.*
12. Massing, *This Deception,* 26, 31, 312.
13. Bentley, *Out of Bondage,* 3; Chambers, *Witness,* 148–49.
14. Bentley, *Out of Bondage,* 311, 99, 134, 101–2.
15. Arthur Koestler in Crossman, *The God That Failed,* 15, 32, 75. The language of "seduction" and "flirtation" also figures in Granville Hicks's review of the book. See Hicks, "Appeal of Communism."
16. Bentley, *Out of Bondage,* 279; Richard Wright in Crossman, *The God That Failed,* 156–57, 162; Chambers, *Witness,* 46; Massing, *This Deception,* 219, 335. Veronica Wilson takes a different approach to the theme of loneliness in "Now You Are Alone."
17. Massing, *This Deception,* 83, 276, 155; Bentley, *Out of Bondage,* 167; Stephen Spender in Crossman, *The God That Failed,* 255; for Koestler, see ibid., 68; Chambers, *Witness,* 420.
18. Chambers, *Witness,* 60, 193, 196, 26; Bentley, *Out of Bondage,* 70, 32; Wright in Crossman, *The God That Failed,* 136; Massing, *This Deception,* 215; Bentley, *Out of Bondage,* 36; Crossman, *The God That Failed,* 10–11.
19. Massing, *This Deception,* 184; Bentley, *Out of Bondage,* 29, 281; Spender in Crossman, *The God That Failed,* 271; Budenz, *Men without Faces,* 13–14.
20. Bentley, *Out of Bondage,* 198, 206, 221. In *Red Spy Queen,* Kathryn Olmsted claims that counterintelligence cables back up Bentley's story, but Price denied Bentley's allegations that she was an underground Communist. See Mary Price Adamson, Oral History Interview, April 19, 1976, Interview G-0001, Southern Oral History Program Collection,

Southern Historical Collection, Wilson Library, University of North Carolina at Chapel Hill (available at http://docsouth.unc.edu).

21. Chambers, *Witness,* 325; Budenz, *Men without Faces,* 112–15.
22. Bentley, *Out of Bondage,* 256; Chambers, *Witness,* 33, 420; Budenz, *Men without Faces,* 17, 9; Hoover, *Masters of Deceit,* 102.
23. Lichtblau, "A Recruiter Confesses," 57; Schlesinger, "Dim Views of the Red Star"; Miller and Miller, review of *Witness;* "This Deception," *New Yorker,* March 31, 1951, 90; John Oakes, "Elizabeth Bentley's Own Story," *New York Times,* September 23, 1951; Pilat, "Repudiation"; Baehr, "Misused Idealism"; Miller, "Memoirs"; Morris, "Chambers's Litmus Paper Test"; Alsop, "Miss Bentley's Bondage"; John Oakes, "Caught in the Network," *New York Times,* September 23, 1951.
24. Ernst and Loth, *Report,* 5, 28, 127; Almond, *Appeals of Communism,* 258. Almond was later a chair of the American Political Science Association. His collaborators on the project included Herbert Krugman, whose research was the basis for his doctoral dissertation in sociology at Columbia University, and who later became chair of the American Association for Public Opinion Research; Howard Wriggins, a political scientist who was later ambassador to Sri Lanka; and Elsbeth Lewin, later the executive editor of *World Politics.*
25. Ernst and Loth, *Report,* 77.
26. Almond, *Appeals of Communism,* 264–65, 286, 277, 288–89.
27. Ernst and Loth, *Report,* 3, 64, 92, 169; Almond, *Appeals of Communism,* 154–56, 159.
28. Almond, *Appeals of Communism,* 268–72, 278–79, emphasis added.
29. Ibid., 289–92.
30. Krugman, "The Role of Hostility." The "hostility syndrome" bears a marked likeness to Erich Fromm's analysis of sadomasochism (discussed later in this chapter), and indeed Krugman noted that the hostility syndrome was intended to "avoid some of the complexities of the concept of sadomasochism"—complexities he did not specify.
31. Johnson, *Lavender Scare;* Braukman, *Communists and Perverts;* Dean, *Imperial Brotherhood;* D'Emilio, "Homosexual Menace"; Terry, "Momism"; Shibusawa, "Lavender Scare."
32. Ernst and Loth, *Report,* 112–13.
33. Arendt, *Origins of Totalitarianism;* Fromm, *Escape from Freedom;* Jay, *Dialectical Imagination;* Baehr, *Hannah Arendt,* 36–37, 45; Schlesinger, *Vital Center.*
34. Fromm, *Escape from Freedom,* 4, 17, 59, 21.
35. In the 1930s, Fromm conceptualized sadomasochism as a sexual perversion, but he largely abandoned that analysis in *Escape from Freedom,* a decision that was criticized by his Frankfurt School colleagues. Jay, *Dialectical Imagination,* 127–29; Slane, *Not So Foreign Affair.*
36. Fromm, *Escape from Freedom,* 141, 157, 162–63. *Escape from Freedom* was published in 1941, and Fromm was more concerned with explaining the specific authoritarianism of fascism than a more broadly defined totalitarianism. His work, however, was taken up by others who wrote in the later 1940s and 1950s about the Soviet Union.
37. Arendt, *Origins of Totalitarianism,* 317, 307. Here Arendt uses "class" in the sense of unifying interest.
38. Ibid., 475–77. This language appears in a new chapter in the 1958 edition of the book.

39. Ibid., 322–24.
40. Ibid., 478, 417, 437, 473–74, 457, 462.
41. Ibid., 437, 465–66, 455–56, 438, 478, 441. Arendt later clarified that while this was the aim of totalitarianism, these outcomes were not yet possible.
42. Fromm, *Escape from Freedom*, 183–84, 203, 253.
43. Cuordileone, *Manhood*, 97; McLaughlin, "Critical Theory Meets America."
44. Schlesinger's book was published several years before *The Origins of Totalitarianism*, but he had read Arendt's 1948 *Partisan Review* article on the concentration camp. On the convergences between Arendt and Schlesinger, see Corber, *In the Name*, 19–26.
45. Schlesinger, *Vital Center*, 54, 161, 87–88, 104, 54. Although Arendt explicitly argued against a view of the camp as an expression of sadomasochism, Schlesinger cited her in support of this analysis. On the gender and sexual dynamics of his text, see Cuordileone, "Politics."
46. Schlesinger, *Vital Center*, 169, 163, 170, 38, 37; Arendt, *Origins of Totalitarianism*, 465. Schlesinger echoed Arendt's argument that totalitarian rulers sought not to achieve "personal . . . aggrandizement" but to "save mankind." Schlesinger, *Vital Center*, 88.
47. Ibid., 248, 253, 256.
48. Fromm, *Escape from Freedom*, 151–64.
49. Schlesinger, *Vital Center*, 55; Ernst and Loth, *Report*, 119; Hoover, *Masters of Deceit*, 176.
50. On Arendt's conception of worldlessness, see Gottsegen, *Political Thought of Hannah Arendt*, 5–6; Villa, *Politics, Philosophy, Terror*, 190–91.
51. Quoted in Schrecker, *Many Are the Crimes*, 139; Hoover, *Masters of Deceit*, vi.
52. *Dennis v. United States*, 577–78; "Opening Statement on Behalf of the Government," quoted in Schrecker, *Age of McCarthyism*, 174. On the Smith Act, see Belknap, *Cold War Political Justice*.
53. Internal Security Act of 1950, 987; Communist Control Act of 1954, 775; Wiecek, "Legal Foundations," 429; Rohr, "Communists and the First Amendment."
54. Eisenhower, "Annual Message to Congress"; "Expatriation Act of 1954."
55. George F. Kennan, "'Where Do You Stand on Communism?,'" *New York Times*, May 27, 1951, quoted by Frankfurter in *Dennis v. United States*, 554–55. Frankfurter concurred that the Smith Act convictions should be upheld as a matter of law, but he questioned the "wisdom" of the law and the prosecution.
56. *Congressional Record* 100 (1954): 11279; "Expatriation Act of 1954," esp. 1190, 1198. On expatriation and subsequent limits imposed by the Supreme Court, see Jones, "Expatriation." According to Samuel Stouffer, 77 percent of a national cross-section of Americans stated that Communists should be deprived of U.S. citizenship. Stouffer, *Communism*, 43.
57. In fact, in 1958 the Supreme Court declared punitive expatriation "cruel and unusual punishment" under certain circumstances; see *Trop v. Dulles*, 356 U.S. 86 (1958). It was not until *Afroyim v. Rusk*, 387 U.S. 253 (1967), that Congress was denied the power of forcible expatriation. Voluntary expatriation still stands, although the question of what evidence is necessary to demonstrate voluntary expatriation is somewhat unsettled. The Expatriation Act's insistence that membership in the Communist Party constitutes an act of voluntary expatriation has never been tested in the courts.
58. *Congressional Record* 100 (1954): 11282.

59. Olmsted, "Blond Queens"; Wilson, "Elizabeth Bentley"; Mitchell and Mitchell, *The Spy Who Seduced America.* This image remained persuasive at least into the 1960s; it was at the heart of the 1963 film *The Manchurian Candidate.* See Jacobson and González, *What Have They Built You to Do?* As the example of Elizabeth Bentley suggests, journalists frequently ignored the "reality" to situate accused women within such stereotypes.
60. Brennan, "Popular Images," 58–63; Antler, "Bond of Sisterhood," 205–7; Olmsted, "Blond Queens"; Radosh and Milton, *Rosenberg File,* 358, 378–79.
61. In this light, it is interesting that Tony Kushner chose to emphasize Ethel Rosenberg's maternal feeling and Roy Cohn's manipulation of it in his indictment of the national security state. See Kushner, *Angels in America.*

2. The Case of the War Bride

1. Strictly speaking, Knauff's planned removal was an "exclusion" rather than a "deportation" because she had never been formally admitted to the United States. At the time, however, "deportation" was widely used to describe efforts to transport her back to Europe.
2. "On Application for Stay," May 17, 1950, HR 8093 folder, RG 233, Records of the U.S. House of Representatives, NARA; press release, May 17, 1950, folder 10, box 164, Papers of Robert Houghwout Jackson (hereafter Jackson Papers); copy of letter by Emanuel Celler, May 16, 1950, ibid.; "Ellen Knauff Deportation Stayed at Last Minute by Order of Justice Jackson," *St. Louis Post Dispatch,* May 17, 1950; "Writ Saves War Bride at Plane," *Washington Daily News* clipping, May 17, 1950, folder 10, box 164, Jackson Papers; "Reprieve"; "Reprieve for Ellen."
3. "Ellen Blames Plight on Jealous German," *New York Post,* March 3, 1950; "And Today, Ellen Sits on Ellis Island," *New York Post,* March 5, 1950; "The Ellen Knauff Case," July 1951, reel 262, Archives of the American Civil Liberties Union, 1950–1990, Legal Case Files, series 4 (hereafter ACLU Papers).
4. May, *Homeward Bound;* "A Wrong to Right," *St. Louis Post-Dispatch,* February 5, 1950.
5. Honig, *Democracy and the Foreigner,* 95.
6. As will be explained later in this chapter, because "excluded" aliens had never been admitted to the territory of the United States, whatever due process protections they received were not a matter of constitutional right but were extended as a matter of courtesy.
7. In fact the divorce was not finalized, and Ellen had to return to Czechoslovakia to obtain a new divorce in 1947 in order to marry again. See Judgment, February 2, 1947, U.S. Citizenship and Immigration Services, Ellen Raphael [Knauff] Hartley file (hereafter Knauff CIS file), in author's possession, GEN2007000277, 1825.
8. In the Czech language, women's surnames are feminized; hence on marrying Boxhorn, she took the name Boxhornova. Knauff, *Ellen Knauff Story,* 11–13, 16–19, 39–40; Applicant's Brief, Board of Immigration Appeals (BIA), HR 893 folder, RG 233, NARA; Agent Report, Subject: Knauff, Kurt Walter, July 26, 1951, Ellen Knauff folder (2 of 2), box 177, Records of the Army Staff, Investigative Records Repository, RG 319, NARA II (hereafter IRR). The War Brides Act, allowing the racially eligible spouses and children of American military personnel to use an expedited process to enter the United States,

was due to expire at the end of the year, which prompted Knauff to travel to the United States at this time. In fact the law was renewed before the deadline.

9. Bredbenner, *Nationality of Her Own*, 98–105; Gardner, *Qualities of a Citizen*, 122–56. These laws applied only to women who were themselves "racially eligible" for citizenship or married men who were. On race and immigration policy, see Ngai, *Impossible Subjects*. Knauff was doubly denationalized, as Jews were deprived of their German citizenship in 1941, and it was not restored until 1949.
10. Zeiger, *Entangling Alliances;* Shukert and Scibetta, *War Brides;* Virden, *Good-Bye, Piccadilly;* Goodman, "Only the Best British Brides."
11. Letter from G. Washburn, May 7, 1946, S2122—Continued folder, box 121, RG 46, NARA; Dorothea A. Appel to Senator Richard Russell, May 7, 1946, ibid.; Mrs. Elsie Gilbert to Senator Russell, [May 1946], ibid.; Mrs. J. H. McCall to Senator Russell, May 6, 1946, ibid.; The Girls of Grand Rapids to Senator Russell, May 6, 1946, ibid.; Alyce Mary Rinz to Representative Klein, May 21, 1946, H.R. 6279 folder, box [label missing], RG 233, NARA. On concerns about the wisdom and sustainability of wartime marriages, see Bossard, "The Hazards of War Marriages"; Wayne, "G.I. Divorce Dangers"; Tenenbaum, "Fate of Wartime Marriages"; Zeiger, *Entangling Alliances*, 130. On GI benefits and sexual citizenship, see Canaday, *Straight State*, esp. 137–73.
12. This sense of Grant as soldier, not spouse, is highlighted when military officials, who have imprisoned him in a cabin as a stowaway and female impersonator, realize who he is and apologize for the mix-up, addressing him repeatedly as "Lieutenant." Immediately thereafter Grant retakes "possession" of his wife from the authorities who have so far prevented him from exercising his marital rights.
13. Zeiger, *Entangling Alliances*, 140–50; for an interesting reading of another war bride film, see 160–62.
14. Ibid., 128–30.
15. On U.S. refugee policy during and after the war, see Bon Tempo, *Americans at the Gate*, 13–18; Daniels, *Guarding the Golden Door*, 73–80, 98–110; Dinnerstein, *America and the Survivors*, 4–6, 163–83; Zucker, *In Search of Refuge;* Genizi, *America's Fair Share*, 18–37; Kurt R. Grossman, "The Jewish DP Problem: Its Origin, Scope, and Liquidation" (Institute of Jewish Affairs, 1951), box 16, Harry N. Rosenfield Papers, HST. Difficult travel conditions in wartime account in part, but not entirely, for the low numbers.
16. "United States ex rel. Ellen Knauff vs. Shaughnessy," undated, HR 893 folder, RG 233, NARA; Bon Tempo, *Americans at the Gate*, 20; Hull, *Without Justice for All*, 19. Regulations quoted in *United States ex rel. Knauff v. Shaughnessy* (hereafter *Knauff v. Shaughnessy*).
17. Biddiscombe, "Dangerous Liaisons"; Willoughby, "Sexual Behavior."
18. Tom Clark to Joseph Nunan, Kn folder, box 51, Tom C. Clark Papers, HST.
19. William C. Hacker, memorandum for the Officer in Charge, May 21, 1948, Ellen Knauff folder (1 of 2), box 117, IRR; George R. Eckman, memo re Ellen Boxhornova, June 25, 1948, ibid.; W. R. Rainford to Director of Intelligence, July 6, 1948, ibid.; L. R. Forney to Commander-in-Chief, European Command, July 14, 1948, ibid.; memorandum, A. D. Mead Jr. to Director, Central Intelligence Agency, August 3, 1948, ibid.; transcript of Victor Kadane interview, February 6, 1951, ibid. Hacker also stated in 1951 that he

had received similar information from "a reliable and confidential source which can not be disclosed." See transcript of William C. Hacker interview, March 12, 1951, Ellen Knauff folder (2 of 2), IRR.

20. W. F. Kelly, memo re Mrs. Kurt W. Knauff, August 11, 1948, Knauff CIS file, 1913; report on Ellen Boxhornova, Director FBI to attorney general, August 6, 1948, doc. 100-356886-1, Ellen Knauff FBI file (in author's possession). This document is completely redacted, except for the recommendation.
21. Gunther Jacobson to William Langer, January 31, 1950, HR 893 folder, RG 233, NARA; Gunther Jacobson to Franklin D. Roosevelt Jr., January 31, 1950, E. Knauff Case—Correspondence—W. G. Jacobson folder, box 3, Franklin D. Roosevelt Jr. Papers (hereafter Roosevelt Jr. Papers); unsigned memo to Senator, February 6, 1950, S 2979 folder, RG 46, NARA; U.S. Congress, House, Committee on the Judiciary, *Exclusion of Ellen Knauff;* Watson B. Miller to Frank Fellows, July 12, 1948, folder 10, box 164, Jackson Papers; press release, May 17, 1950 (copy of Emanuel Celler to J. Howard McGrath, May 16, 1950), ibid.; "Statement of the Immigration and Naturalization Subcommittee of the Senate Committee on the Judiciary," undated, S 2979 folder, RG 46, NARA. Immigration officials finally shared evidence with the chairmen of the House and Senate immigration committees in July 1951.
22. McGrath became attorney general after Tom Clark was appointed to the Supreme Court. On Knauff's 1951 release, see hearing transcript, H.R. Committee on the Judiciary, Subcommittee No. 1, February 12, 1951, 20, HR 893 folder, RG 233, NARA.
23. Nonetheless, Lavickova and Kadane both claimed to fear reprisals from the Czech government, and they refused to answer questions about their residence, occupation, or employers because of their concerns about their personal as well as national security. Furthermore, Knauff's attorney was forbidden to cross-examine them, again on national security claims.
24. Record of Hearing before a Board of Special Inquiry, March 26, 1951, HR 893 folder, RG 233, NARA; "Mrs. Knauff Is Called a Spy: Immigration Unit Bars Her," *New York Times,* March 27, 1951; "Mrs. Knauff Is Barred from U.S. as Czech Spy, [*Baltimore Sun*] clipping, Ellen Knauff folder (1 of 2), box 117, IRR; "Veteran's Wife Barred from US as Ex-Spy," *New York Herald Tribune* clipping, March 27, 1951, ibid.; "GI's War Bride Barred as Spy for Red Czechs," [March 27, 1951], clipping, Ellen Knauff folder (2 of 2), IRR.
25. "The Knauff Case Ruling," *St. Louis Post-Dispatch,* March 28, 1951. See also "The Knauff Case," *New York Herald Tribune* (Paris edition), March 31, 1951, clipping, Ellen Knauff folder (1 of 2), box 117, IRR.
26. Letter from Howard McGrath, November 2, 1951, in Knauff, *Ellen Knauff Story,* appendix.
27. See Weisselberg, "Exclusion and Detention," for a discussion of the legal ramifications of Knauff's case.
28. Hull, *Without Justice for All,* 53–57; Neuman, *Strangers to the Constitution,* 4–15; Ngai, *Impossible Subjects,* 4–6; Schuck, *Citizens,* 27–38; *Knauff v. Shaughnessy,* 544, emphasis added.
29. *Knauff v. Shaughnessy,* 546–47. In fact, Proclamation 2523 required that the attorney general *and* the secretary of state agree to exclude an alien under its provisions, but only

the attorney general had acted in Knauff's case. To avoid this difficulty in this and like cases, President Truman issued a new proclamation (2850) on August 17, 1949, allowing the attorney general to order exclusions without the secretary of state's concurrence. On the concerns leading to the proclamation, see Stephen J. Spingarn, memorandum on proposed proclamation, July 26, 1949, National Defense—Deportation and Exclusion of Aliens folder, box 34, Stephen J. Spingarn Papers, HST.

30. *Knauff v. Shaughnessy,* 549. This argument is discussed at greater length later in this chapter.
31. Ibid., 551–52. The description of the twice-married thirty-five-year-old Knauff as a "girl" seems intended to emphasize her vulnerability and innocence.
32. Dudziak, "Law, Power, and 'Rumors of War' "; Schubert, *Dispassionate Justice.*
33. Memo on *U.S ex rel. Ellen Knauff v. Watkins,* undated, folder 5, box 161, Jackson Papers.
34. The case was ultimately dismissed as moot when Ellen was temporarily released to Kurt's custody.
35. Handwritten draft beginning "Ellen Knauff must leave," undated, folder 10, box 164, Jackson Papers.
36. "Deportation Case in Hands of Court," *New York Times,* March 7, 1950; "Appeals Court Grants Stay of Deportation to Ellen Knauff," *St. Louis Post-Dispatch,* February 28, 1950; Knauff, *Ellen Knauff Story,* 112–13.
37. N. Conroy to A. Rosen, March 11, 1954, doc. 100-356886-119, Knauff FBI file; A. H. Belmont to Mr. Boardman, March 16, 1954, doc. 100-356886-120, ibid.; Kelly to A. H. Belmont, March 17, 1954, [no doc. number], ibid.; SAC, NY, to Director FBI, July 22, 1955, doc. 100-356886-129, ibid. See also C. E. Hennrich to A. H. Belmont, February 7, 1951, doc. 100-356886-64, ibid.; C. E. Hennrich to A. H. Belmont, November 2, 1951, doc. 100-356886-102, ibid. Note that a clerical error led to the creation of two documents numbered 102.
38. Representative Francis Walter introduced a similar bill the following session, but it met a comparable fate. In any case, the opposition of Senator Pat McCarran would have doomed any bill that was approved by the House. Gunther Jacobson to Franklin D. Roosevelt Jr., January 31, 1950, Civil Liberties: E. Knauff Case—Correspondence, W. J. Jacobson folder, box 3, Roosevelt Jr. Papers; Anthony Akers to Roosevelt, February 23, 1950, ibid.; Roosevelt to J. Howard McGrath, February 8, 1950, Civil Liberties, E. Knauff Case, Statements and Press Releases folder, ibid.; Roosevelt to McGrath, February 21, 1950, ibid.; press release, February 28, 1950, ibid.; Ed [Harris] to Irv [Dilliard], February 8, 1950, Ellen Knauff Correspondence, 1950 folder, box 28, Irving Dilliard Papers (hereafter Dilliard Papers); Ed Harris to Irving [Dilliard], March 18, 1950, ibid.; F. D. Roosevelt Jr., "Civil Liberties and the 'War Bride' Case," *Congressional Record* 96 (1950): A1704; F. D. Roosevelt Jr., "A Scandalous Situation: The Knauff Case," *Congressional Record* 96 (1950): A3961; "The Case of the 'War Bride,' " *New York Times,* March 4, 1950.
39. Memo from Harry S. Truman to Attorney General McGrath, May 19, 1950, Loyalty, Communism and Civil Rights folder (1 of 3), box 36, Spingarn Papers, HST; Stephen Spingarn, memorandum for the files, May 20, 1950, ibid.; Stephen J. Spingarn to Mr. Hopkins, September 29, 1950, Justice Department folder (10 of 10), box 22, Confidential Subject Files, 1945–53, White House Central Files, HST; David Bell to Charles S.

Murphy, March 12, 1951, Internal Security folder, box 27, Charles S. Murphy Files, Staff Member and Office Files, HST.

40. Stephen Spingarn to attorney general, June 21, 1950, Justice Department folder (10 of 10), box 22, White House Central Files, HST; memorandum for the President re: Ellen Knauff case, [July 14, 1950], ibid.; "Summary of Material in Department of Justice Files," September 12, 1950, ibid.; Stephen Spingarn, memorandum for Peyton Ford, September 25, 1950, ibid.; [Spingarn] to [George] Elsey, October 19, 1950, ibid.; [Elsey], memorandum on the Ellen Knauff case, November 19, 1950, ibid.; A. H. Belmont to D. M. Ladd, October 4, 1950, doc. 100-356886-47, Knauff FBI file; D. M. Ladd to Director, October 9, 1950, doc. 100-356886-47X, ibid.

41. Record of hearing before a Board of Special Inquiry, March 26, 1951, HR 893 folder, RG 233, NARA.

42. Decision of the Board of Immigration Appeals, U.S. Department of Justice, reprinted in Knauff, *Ellen Knauff Story*, appendix; Harold F. Reis to attorney general, March 28, 1951, Knauff CIS file, 754–65.

43. Ed Harris to Irving [Dilliard], March 8, 1950, Ellen Knauff Correspondence, 1950 folder, box 28, Dilliard Papers; Brandt to Mr. Reese, March 8, 1950, ibid.; Ed Harris to Mr. Reese, March 10, 1950, ibid.; V. P. Keay to A. H. Belmont, March 28, 1950, doc. 100-356886-25, Knauff FBI file; Gunther Jacobson to Joseph Pulitzer, May 20, 1950, reel 57, Joseph Pulitzer Papers, 1897–1958 (hereafter Pulitzer Papers); Ed Harris to Mr. Reese, May 24, 1950, ibid.; memo for Charles Ross, June 15, 1950, Justice Department folder (10 of 10), box 22, Confidential Subject Files, 1945–53, White House Central Files, HST; attorney general to Irving Dilliard, October 3, 1950, DI 52 folder, box 86, J. Howard McGrath Papers, HST; Ellen Knauff to Ed Harris, May 28, 1950, Ellen Knauff folder, box 3, Edward A. Harris Papers (hereafter Harris Papers); Dick Greer to Ed Harris, March 9 [no year], ibid.; Irving Dilliard to Robert Jackson, May 17, 1950, folder 10, box 164, Jackson Papers; Dilliard to Jacob Billikopf, May 18, 1950, folder 5, ibid. In addition, the paper published a broadside about the case, and its publisher contributed hundreds of dollars to pay Knauff's legal expenses. See Gunther Jacobson to Joseph Pulitzer, May 20, 1950, reel 57, Pulitzer Papers.

44. Knauff to Ed Harris, October 9, 1950, Ellen Knauff file, box 3, Harris Papers; Mikulas Ferjencik to Harris, undated, ibid.; U.S. Congress, House, *Exclusion of Ellen Knauff*, 10–11.

45. May, *Homeward Bound;* Canaday, *Straight State;* Cott, *Public Vows;* Kessler-Harris, *In Pursuit of Equity;* Lewis, *Prescription for Heterosexuality.*

46. Relator-Appellant's Brief, *US ex rel. Knauff vs. Watkins,* U.S. Court of Appeals (2d cir.), reel 262, ACLU Papers, 40; "Petition for Writ of Certiorari," *Knauff v. Watkins,* Supreme Court of the United States (October term, 1948), ibid., 7; "Appellant's Brief," *Knauff v. Shaughnessy,* Supreme Court of the United States (October term, 1949), ibid., 6–7; "Petitioner-Appellant's Reply Memorandum," *Knauff vs. Shaughnessy,* Supreme Court of the United States (October term, 1949, No. 54), *Supreme Court Records & Briefs,* 6; *Knauff v. Shaughnessy,* 548–52; "Record of Hearing before a Board of Special Inquiry," 75, HR 893 folder, RG 233, NARA; "The Perplexing Case of Ellen Knauff," *St. Louis Post-Dispatch,* February 5, 1950; "Veteran Fights on Against Red Tape," *New York Times,* January 10, 1951; Zeiger, *Entangling Alliances,* 132.

47. "The Perplexing Case of Ellen Knauff"; "And Today, Ellen Sits on Ellis Island"; Ellen Knauff to Ed Harris, February 26, 1950, Ellen Knauff folder, box 3, Harris Papers; Kurt W. Knauff to William C. Langer, July 12, 1950, doc. 2244, HR 7614 folder, RG 46, NARA.
48. L. B. Nichols to Mr. Tolson, January 9, 1951, doc. 100-356886-52, Knauff FBI file; A. H. Belmont to D. M. Ladd, January 10, 1951, doc. 100-356886-53, ibid.; July 26, 1951, agent report re Kurt Walter Knauff, Ellen Knauff folder (2 of 2), box 117, IRR; Thomas E. Phillips, memo for Mr. Crowley, February 11, 1952, reel 57, Pulitzer Papers.
49. Knauff, *Ellen Knauff Story,* 3–4.
50. "A Wrong to Right"; Knauff, *Ellen Knauff Story,* 51, 77, 205.
51. Ibid., 156, 178–80, 194. A copy of her original letter to Howard McGrath, dated January 22, 1951, is in HR 893 folder, RG 233, NARA.
52. Knauff, *Ellen Knauff Story,* 54–55; Knauff to Ed Harris, May 29, 1950, Ellen Knauff file, box 3, Harris Papers; U.S. Congress, House, *Exclusion of Ellen Knauff,* 13. See also "Ellen Blames Plight on Jealous German"; *Knauff v. Watkins,* "Transcript of Record," 11, reel 262, ACLU Papers; hearing transcript, February 12, 1951, Subcommittee No. 1 of the Committee on the Judiciary, HR 893 folder, RG 233, NARA.
53. "Will No One Call a Halt?," *St. Louis Post-Dispatch,* February 26, 1950; "Justice Jackson Stops an Outrage," *St. Louis Post-Dispatch,* May 17, 1950; "The G.I.'s Bride," *Omaha World-Herald* clipping, February 19, 1950, folder 5, box 161, Jackson Papers; "The Case of the 'War Bride,'" *New York Times,* March 4, 1950; Max Lerner, "One Is Not Zero," *New York Post,* May 18, 1950; "Give the Facts," *New York World-Telegram and Sun,* May 18, 1950; undated handwritten draft, folder 10, box 164, Jackson Papers.
54. Knauff, *Ellen Knauff Story,* 8, 29.
55. Ibid., 3–4.
56. "Lost Perspective," *Christian Science Monitor,* November 6, 1951 clipping, folder 10, box 164, Jackson Papers; Knauff, *Ellen Knauff Story,* 226, 234.
57. Kalven, *Worthy Tradition,* 440, notes how the Knauff case was linked to themes of "Home and Motherhood." On the longer history of marriage and loyalty, see Kerber, *No Constitutional Right;* Cott, *Public Vows,* 191–93.
58. While the immigrant, then, may be the individual who desires America, the citizen is, additionally, the individual who is desired. On the immigrant as the desiring subject, see Berlant, *Queen of America,* 195; Somerville, "Notes toward a Queer History."
59. Gardner, *Qualities of a Citizen,* 215; Honig, *Democracy and the Foreigner,* xxii–xxiii and passim; Canaday, *Straight State,* 214–54.
60. Ngai, *Impossible Subjects,* 54–55, 88, 202–24.
61. Mrs. J. J. Jones to Franklin D. Roosevelt Jr., April 27, 1950, Civil Liberties: E. Knauff Case—Correspondence folder, box 3, Roosevelt Jr. Papers; Mrs. L. Cooper to Dear Sir, undated, ibid.; report by Louis C. Salz on Frederich [*sic*] Bauer, April 19, 1951, Ellen Knauff folder (2 of 2), box 117, IRR; Ellen [Knauff] to Wilma and Fred, April 13, 1951, Ellen Knauff folder (1 of 2), ibid. Wilma and Fred are apparently the pseudonymous Clara and Hans in *The Ellen Knauff Story.* On Mezei, see Weisselberg, "Exclusion and Detention," 964–66; Hull, *Without Justice for All,* 54–56.
62. "Reprieve"; "The Perplexing Case of Ellen Knauff"; "Supreme Court Order Stays

Deportation of German War Bride," clipping, May 17, 1950, folder 10, box 164, Jackson Papers; "Mrs. Knauff Leaves Ellis Island after Winning Fight to Enter US," *New York Times,* November 3, 1951; "The Woman Who Wouldn't Give Up," *New York Post,* November 2, 1951.

63. Borgwardt, *New Deal,* 53. On the longer history of human rights, see Hunt, *Inventing Human Rights;* Lauren, *Evolution of International Human Rights.*
64. Patrick Murphy Malin and Arthur Garfield Hays to William Langer, May 19, 1950, OGL no. 19, folder 9, box 467, William Langer Papers (hereafter Langer Papers); "The Case of the 'War Bride' "; Ralph Busser to Franklin D. Roosevelt Jr., February 17, 1950, Civil Liberties: E. Knauff Case, Correspondence folder, box 3, Roosevelt Jr. Papers.
65. "The Letter Killeth," *New York Times,* January 28, 1950; teletype re: Thomas Hennings's statement, undated (doc. 100-356886), Knauff FBI file; "The Case of the 'War Bride' "; "The Knauff Affair," *New York Times,* March 30, 1950; "The Case of Ellen Knauff," *St. Louis Post-Dispatch,* January 18, 1950; "For a Review of the Ellen Knauff Case," *St. Louis Post-Dispatch,* March 23, 1950; "Views of a Star Chamber Case" (reprinting editorials from the *Christian Science Monitor* and the *New York Times*), *St. Louis Post-Dispatch,* April 4, 1950; Edward N. Lehman to William Langer, February 26, 1950, folder 9, box 467, Langer Papers; John N. Johns to Justice Robert H. Jackson, January 17, [1950], folder 5, box 161, Jackson Papers; Ralph C. Busser to Franklin D. Roosevelt Jr., February 17, 1950, Civil Liberties: E. Knauff Case, Correspondence folder, box 3, Roosevelt Jr. Papers; Franklin D. Roosevelt Jr. to Stephen B. Fish, June 6, 1950, ibid.; Ellen Knauff to Irving Dilliard, October 3, 1950, folder 1009, box 28, Dilliard Papers; Arthur Garfield Hays, "Introduction," in Knauff, *Ellen Knauff Story,* xiii.
66. "Give the Facts"; "The Injustice Department's Triumph," *New York Post,* May 17, 1950; Edward Lehman to William Langer, February 26, 1950, folder 9, box 467, Langer Papers; Patrick Murphy Malin and Arthur Garfield Hays to William Langer, May 19, 1950, ibid.; "The Case of the 'War Bride' "; "A Wrong to Right"; Margaret M. Noel to Pat McCarran, May 26, 1950, S2979 folder, doc. 1772, RG 46, NARA; Franklin D. Roosevelt Jr. to Stephen Fish, June 6, 1950, Civil Liberties: E. Knauff Case, Correspondence folder, box 3, Roosevelt Jr. Papers; "The Knauff Case."
67. Marquis Childs, "Security and Dictatorship," *St. Louis Post-Dispatch,* February 20, 1950; "A Wrong to Right." See also Margaret M. Noel to Pat McCarran, May 26, 1950, S2979 folder, doc. 1772, RG 46, NARA; "The Knauff Scandal"; I. F. Stone, "Strange Case of the FBI and the War Bride," *Daily Compass,* January 18, 1950.
68. "Ellen Proves the Point," *New York Post,* May 5, 1950; circular letter from Patrick Murphy Malin and Arthur Garfield Hays, undated, S3372 folder, RG 46, NARA; Edwin Weinstock to Editor, *St. Louis Post-Dispatch,* April 12, 1950; see also "The Knauff Affair"; press release, November 2, 1951, reel 262, ACLU Papers; Patrick Murphy Malin statement, ibid.; Ellen Knauff to Irving Dilliard, March 3, 1950, folder 1009, box 28, Dilliard Papers; Ellen Knauff to Francis E. Walter, April 4, 1950, HR 893 folder, RG 233, NARA; "Mrs. Knauff's Day in Court," *New York Post,* April 4, 1950.
69. "The Woman Who Wouldn't Give Up"; "Justice Wins in the End," *St. Louis Post-Dispatch,* November 4, 1950; see also "One Is Not Zero."

70. "In the Matter of the Petition of Ellen Knauff" [transcript of 1953 naturalization hearing], Knauff CIS file, 904–52, 1572–1704; William Libowitz, "Findings of Fact," July 28, 1954, ibid., 889–903; "Mrs. Knauff, Barred Three Years, Passes Test for U.S. Citizenship," *St. Louis Post-Dispatch,* December 15, 1951; "Mrs. Knauff Walks Out of Hearing on Bid to Obtain U.S. Citizenship," *New York Times,* July 3, 1952; "Ellen Knauff Walks Out on Citizen Quiz," clipping, Ellen Knauff folder (1 of 2), box 117, IRR; EML to AR, memorandum re Ellen Knauff case, August 5, 1953, reel 262, ACLU Papers; Kelly to Director, March 16, 1954, doc. 100-356886-121, Knauff FBI file; W. A. Branigan to A. H. Belmont, March 19, 1954, doc. 100-356886-122, ibid.; SAC, NY, to Director, April 27, 1954, doc. 100-356886-125, ibid.; SAC, NY, to Director FBI, July 22, 1955, doc. 100-356886-129, ibid.; Harry A. Mattingly, "Findings of Fact" [1963], Knauff CIS file, 1451–61; Lewis, "Security and Liberty," 72.
71. L. B. Nichols to Tolson re: Ellen Boxhornova, January 9, 1951, doc. 100-356886-52, Knauff FBI file. On women immigrants as tricksters, see Kerber, "The Stateless as the Citizen's Other," 30.
72. Affidavit by Ellen Knauff, March 5, 1950, HR 893 folder, RG 233, NARA; Ellen Knauff to Irving Dilliard, October 3, 1950, folder 1009, box 28, Dilliard Papers; Begeman, "What Ellen Knauff Won," 14.
73. "Abrupt and Brutal," *Washington Post* clipping [January 18, 1950], with J. Edgar Hoover's notation, doc. 100-356886-17, Knauff FBI file.

3. The Right to Earn a Living

1. U.S. Congress, Senate, Permanent Subcommittee on Investigations of the Committee on Government Operations, *Army Signal Corps—Subversion and Espionage,* pt. 1, 333.
2. For the views of popular conservative commentators, see George S. Schuyler, "Views—Reviews," *Pittsburgh Courier,* August 21, 1954; "Stone Cold Dead"; Coulter, *Treason.* Within the scholarly literature on McCarthy, Moss's story is generally told as a not-so-amusing anecdote demonstrating McCarthy's recklessness and vindictiveness. See, for example, Reeves, *Life and Times of Joe McCarthy,* 548–50, 567–69; Oshinsky, *A Conspiracy So Immense,* 402–3; Donald A. Ritchie, "Introduction," in U.S. Senate, Permanent Subcommittee on Investigations, *Executive Sessions of the Senate Permanent Subcommittee* (hereafter *Executive Sessions*) 5: xiv–xvi (made public January 2003). For a conservative scholarly treatment, see Herman, *Joseph McCarthy,* which includes an appendix on the Moss case; see also Evans, *Blacklisted by History.*
3. Myrdal, *American Dilemma,* 1–3 and passim.
4. Borstelmann, *The Cold War and the Color Line,* 78; Dudziak, *Cold War Civil Rights;* Plummer, *Window on Freedom;* Jackson, *Gunnar Myrdal and America's Conscience;* Southern, *Gunnar Myrdal and Black-White Relations.* For the view that racial liberalism was less potent in local politics, see Hirsch, "Massive Resistance in the Urban North"; and Sugrue, "Crabgrass-Roots Politics."
5. Anderson, *Eyes Off the Prize;* Horne, *Black Liberation / Red Scare;* Lewis, *The White South and the Red Menace;* Cobb, "Antidote to Revolution." On civility, see Chafe, *Civilities and Civil Rights.*

6. On economic citizenship in the postwar years, see Cohen, *Consumers' Republic;* Jacobs, *Pocketbook Politics.* On African American economic citizenship in particular, see MacLean, *Freedom Is Not Enough;* Kessler-Harris, *In Pursuit of Equity;* Feldstein, *Motherhood in Black and White.* On the importance of the right to work in conceptions of U.S. citizenship, see Shklar, *American Citizenship;* Boris, "The Right to Work Is the Right to Live!" On the limitations of a focus on economic rights, see Singh, *Black Is a Country.*
7. U.S. President's Committee on Civil Rights, *To Secure These Rights,* 89; Landis, *Segregation in Washington,* 88; Patterson, *We Charge Genocide,* 178–79.
8. Schrecker, *Many Are the Crimes;* Storrs, *Second Red Scare;* Caute, *Great Fear;* Bontecou, *Federal Loyalty-Security Program;* Brown, *Loyalty and Security;* Gellhorn, *Security, Loyalty, and Science;* Bernstein, *Loyalties.*
9. Biographical information about Moss is compiled from several sources, including materials contained in her official personnel folder, in author's possession; Carleton Kent, "Meet Mrs. Moss, a Target of Senator McCarthy," *Chicago Sun-Times,* April 5, 1954; Eleanor Bontecou, "What's in a Name?," manuscript [1955], Moss, Annie LA6-3919 folder, box 813, Cobb, Howard, Hayes & Windsor Papers (hereafter Cobb Papers). See also James L. Hicks, "Who Is Annie Lee Moss?," *Washington Afro-American,* February 27, 1954.
10. This was the national figure; rates for Southern women would likely be lower. U.S. Census Bureau, "Median Years of School." Moss must have made an impression, for when her case commanded attention in the 1950s, her high school principal sent her a letter of support and encouragement.
11. On North Carolina's tobacco industry, see Korstad, *Civil Rights Unionism.* Moss worked at Liggett and Thompson. By the time she left, some black workers in the factory had been organized by the AFL-affiliated Tobacco Workers International Union, although it did not include women workers.
12. Crew, "Melding the Old and the New," 216.
13. U.S. Census Bureau, *Full-Time, Year-Round Black Workers;* U.S. Census Bureau, *Race and Hispanic Origin.* For purposes of comparison, in 1955 the median income for full-time, year-round female workers of all races was $2,735; the median income for full-time, year-round black female workers was $1,468.
14. Bontecou, "What's in a Name?"; report cards from Randall High School, box 813, Cobb Papers. The home Moss purchased was located at 1244 Evarts Street, N.E. On postwar Washington, see Green, *Secret City;* Crew, "Melding the Old and the New," 221–25; on alley dwellings, see Borchert, *Alley Life in Washington;* on Brookland, see Feeley, *Brookland.*
15. Records relating to loyalty-security hearings for federal employees were not retained on a systematic basis, and some of the transcripts of Moss's hearings have been lost. This summary has been patched together from a number of sources including the materials in Moss's official personnel folder; Executive Secretary, Loyalty Review Board, to Chief, Investigations Division, January 4, 1952, Annie Lee Moss Case File, Records of the Permanent Subcommittee on Investigations, RG 46, NARA (hereafter PSI); Herbert Hawkins to Francis P. Carr, February 26, 1954, ibid.; typescript, "Annie Lee Moss Case," August 2, 1954, ibid.; Herbert Hawkins to Francis P. Carr, September 14, 1954, ibid.; Charles E. Wilson to Secretary of the Army, January 18, 1955, ibid.; T. A. Flynn to Mrs.

Annie Lee Moss, May 26, 1948, Ann Moss file, Investigative Name Files, Records of House Un-American Activities Committee, RG 233, NARA (hereafter HUAC Records); E. L. Fisher to Mrs. Annie Lee Moss, June 23, 1948, ibid.; John G. Connell Jr. to Mrs. Annie Lee Moss, July 23, 1951, ibid.; John W. Martyn to Mrs. Annie Lee Moss, October 23, 1951, ibid.; Mary S. Markward testimony, Moss Security Hearing [1954], Securities Activities Control Board Exhibit, FBI records relating to Mary Stalcup Markward, in possession of Heming Nelson, Washington, D.C. (hereafter Markward FBI file); General Accounting Office Loyalty Board Hearing transcript, June 22, 1948 (doc. 121-2900-31), Annie Lee Moss FBI file, in author's possession. As an army employee, Moss actually came under the provisions not only of the executive orders creating the loyalty-security programs but also Public Law 733, which governed military security investigations.

16. Markward FBI file.
17. On the lavender scare, see Johnson, *Lavender Scare;* Dean, *Imperial Brotherhood;* Braukman, *Communists and Perverts.*
18. Pederson, *Communist Party in Maryland;* U.S. Congress, House, Committee on Un-American Activities, *Communism in the District of Columbia–Maryland Area;* Heming Nelson, "Pointing the Way in the Hunt for Communists," *Washington Post,* July 5, 1999; Frank R. Kent Jr., "FBI Agent Now Housewife in Quiet Chesterbrook, Va.," *Washington Post,* July 7, 1951; "CP Expels 'FBI Agent,'" *Washington Post,* February 8, 1951; "Hearings before the Committee on Un-American Activities," February 15, 1951, HUAC Records.
19. Conversation with Heming Nelson, Washington, D.C., November 2005; Herndon, "Secret Agent in Apron Strings."
20. Pedersen, "Perfect Witness."
21. T. A. Flynn to Mrs. Annie Lee Moss, May 26, 1948, Ann Moss file, Investigative Name Files, HUAC Records; C. E. Owens to Louis J. Russell, January 27, 1952, ibid.; L. B. Nichols to Mr. Tolson, November 4, 1953, doc. 121-2900-9X, Moss FBI file.
22. L. B. Nichols to Tolson, November 4, 1953, doc. 121-2900-9, ibid. FBI officials did share some of the information in their files with Democratic senator Henry Jackson and Democratic committee counsel Robert F. Kennedy, but they regretted doing so. In response to Assistant Director Lou Nichols's written comment that the fallout from sharing information "made me realize that some times in trying to be helpful, you build up nothing but trouble for yourself," J. Edgar Hoover scrawled, "This is all too true." L. B. Nichols to Mr. Tolson, February 24, 1954, doc. 121-2900-20, ibid.; L. B. Nichols to Mr. Tolson, March 30, 1954, doc. 121-2900-30, ibid.
23. Du Bois, *Souls of Black Folk,* 45. On the entanglements of race and nation that made the concept of black loyalty so contested, see Singh, *Black Is a Country.*
24. Hutchinson, *Blacks and Reds;* Naison, *Communists in Harlem;* Kelley, *Hammer and Hoe;* Woods, *Black Struggle, Red Scare;* Record, *Race and Radicalism;* Bontecou, *Federal Loyalty-Security Program,* 139; Horne, *Black Liberation / Red Scare,* 219; Arnesen, "No 'Graver Danger.'"
25. "Stenographic Transcript of Hearings before the Committee on the Judiciary, U.S. Senate, Internal Security Subcommittee, Executive Session, May 15, 1953," Records of the Senate Internal Security Subcommittee, RG 46, NARA. John Earl Haynes notes the fluctuations in African American CP membership in "Reconsidering Two Questions."

26. During the Truman administration, for example, approximately five hundred federal workers were fired for disloyalty, while about five times that many resigned in the face of charges. Caute, *Great Fear;* Schrecker, *Many Are the Crimes,* 298; Bernstein, *Loyalties.*
27. Rung, "United Public Workers of America"; Bernstein, *Loyalties.*
28. Bernstein, *Loyalties,* esp. 175; Crew, "Melding the Old and the New."
29. Bernstein, *Loyalties,* 180; Abram Flaxer to Harry S. Truman, November 24, 1948, "The Truman Administration's Loyalty Program," Harry S. Truman Library and Museum website, www.trumanlibrary.org.
30. Bontecou, *Federal Loyalty-Security Program,* 137–40; Gellhorn, *Security, Loyalty, and Science,* 152–54; Schrecker, *Many Are the Crimes,* 281–82.
31. Bernstein, *Loyalties,* 176–78; "Blood and Loyalty," *Washington Post,* December 2, 1948.
32. Barth, *Loyalty of Free Men;* Schrecker, *Many Are the Crimes,* 274, 281–82; Bontecou, *Federal Loyalty-Security Program,* 119, 133, 226.
33. "The Case of Marie Richardson Harris: The Victim of a Modern Witch Hunt," in author's possession; "Mary Stalcup Markward," draft, February 19, 1951, Investigative Name File, ser. 2, HUAC Records; U.S. Congress, House, Committee on Un-American Activities, *Communist Political Subversion, Part 1,* 6732–33, 7934; "Former Agent Says Accused Joined Reds," *Washington Post,* February 22, 1952; "U.S. Winds Up Case against Suspected Red," *Washington Post,* February 27, 1952; "Jury Due to Get Case of Woman Accused of Hiding Red Ties," *Washington Post,* February 28, 1952; "Woman Who Denied Red Tie Given 2 Years," *Washington Post,* March 8, 1952; Horne, *Communist Front?,* 259; Gellman, *Death Blow to Jim Crow,* 260–61. Harris's supporters suspected that she had been singled out because her brother was an official in the American Peace Crusade and may have been a CP member.
34. Perucci, "Red Mask of Sanity," 22, 30–32.
35. Duberman, *Paul Robeson;* Cobb, "Antidote to Revolution," 222–30; Smith, "Paul Robeson–Jackie Robinson Saga"; U.S. Congress, House, Committee on Un-American Activities, *Hearings Regarding Communist Infiltration,* 427–28, 455, 476. All quotes from the hearings are from this text. Robeson's responses to this controversy can be traced in Foner, *Paul Robeson Speaks,* 201–30.
36. Tony Perucci notes that "black witnesses . . . could . . . secure their citizenship by disavowing [Robeson] in order to affirm their loyalty to the United States." Perucci, "Red Mask of Sanity," 37.
37. "'Black Stalin' Aim Is Laid to Robeson," *New York Times,* July 15, 1949; "Dr. Bunche and Mr. Robeson," *New York Times,* July 19, 1949. Manning Johnson also charged that Robeson aspired to be a "Black Stalin," a master of African Americans as well as a Soviet slave. On Johnson, see Cobb, "Antidote to Revolution," 266–67.
38. So, for example, when Coleman Young referred to his military service as proof of his loyalty in his 1952 testimony before HUAC, he was excoriated by the white press for his brash attitude toward the committee but lauded by many in the black community. See Halpern, "I'm Fighting for Freedom."
39. *Executive Sessions,* 2:973–98; U.S. Congress, Senate, Permanent Subcommittee on

Investigations of the Committee on Government Operations, *State Department Information Program: Information Centers,* 75, 79–80.

40. U.S. Congress, House, Committee on Un-American Activities, *Communism in the District of Columbia, Part 2,* 3234–35.
41. Caute, *Great Fear,* esp. 147–52.
42. Memorandum for John W. Martyn from John G. Connell Jr., September 15, 1953, Misc-Conf folder, box 6, entry 100, Records of the Office of the Secretary of the Army, RG 335, NARA II; "Accuser of Army Guard Threatened," September 3, 1953, *New York Daily News* clipping, box 4, ibid.; U.S. Congress, Senate, Permanent Subcommittee on Investigations of the Committee on Government Operations, *Communist Infiltration,* 39–40.
43. *Executive Sessions,* 2:1625–1757; U.S. Congress, Senate, *Communist Infiltration,* 3, 4–9, 23–30; memorandum for Martyn from Connell, September 5, 1953, box 6, entry 100, RG 335, NARA II. In fact, Powell had a reputation at the paper as a staunch anti-Communist. See Ritchie, "Introduction."
44. U.S. Congress, Senate, *State Department Information Program,* 1224. This exchange occurred in executive committee, but it was essentially re-created in the public session that followed.
45. U.S. Congress, Senate, *State Department Information Program,* 473–74, 480, emphasis added.
46. Weigand, "Red Menace"; Olmsted, "Blond Queens"; Olmsted, *Red Spy Queen;* Wilson, "Elizabeth Bentley and Cold War Representation"; Antler, "Bond of Sisterhood."
47. Herndon, "Secret Agent in Apron Strings," 31.
48. Gerson, "Is Family Devotion Now Subversive?" For an account that questions the importance of maternalist strategies to radical and activist women, see Murray, *Progressive Housewife.*
49. Cox, "Programs of Negro Civil Rights Organizations." On Sampson, see Laville and Lucas, "The American Way"; Horne, *Communist Front?,* 172–73; Dudziak, *Cold War Civil Rights,* 105; Anderson, *Eyes Off the Prize,* 203–6; Carruthers, *Cold War Captives,* 128–32. On black musicians' tours for the State Department, see Von Eschen, *Satchmo Blows Up the World.*
50. Gore, *Radicalism at the Crossroads;* McDuffie, *Sojourning for Freedom;* Davies, *Left of Karl Marx;* Washington, "Alice Childress, Lorraine Hansberry, and Claudia Jones."
51. Eve Edstrom, "Mrs. Moss Confused, but Feels No Anger," *Washington Post,* March 14, 1954. For evidence of Moss's activism, see "Visit of Santa Assured in 4 Southwest Projects," *Washington Afro-American,* December 4, 1948; "200 Pay Woody L. Taylor Tribute at Testimonial," *Washington Afro-American,* November 18, 1950; "Tenants Honor Southwest Housing Project Manager," *Washington Afro-American,* August 19, 1950; Bontecou, "What's in a Name?" I am indebted to Mary Helen Washington for urging me to contemplate the different ways African American women's citizenship work was understood by distinct audiences.
52. This does not mean, of course, that liberal reformers did not seek to demonstrate their loyalty by distinguishing their own organizational work from that of Communists and fellow travelers. See Anderson, *Eyes Off the Prize;* Berg, "Black Civil Rights"; Biondi, *To Stand and Fight.*

53. "Mrs. Sampson's Speech, University of Helsinki, January 14, 1952," box 11, folder 231, Edith Sampson Papers; Laville and Lucas, "The American Way"; Anderson, *Eyes Off the Prize.*
54. Foner, *Paul Robeson Speaks,* 201–11; Anderson, *Eyes Off the Prize,* 206; Laville and Lucas, "The American Way," 572.
55. Transcript, General Accounting Office Loyalty Board Hearing, June 22, 1948 (doc. 121-2900-31), Moss FBI file, 7.
56. This would have been the convention of the Communist Political Association. The pamphlet by Wilkerson was likely "The Negro People and the Communists" (New York: Workers Library Publishers, 1944). My thanks to Trevor Joy Sangrey for her assistance in identifying it.
57. Transcript, General Accounting Office Loyalty Board Hearing, June 22, 1948, 6–8, 12.
58. Testimony of Annie Lee Moss, February 22, 1954, 24, 29, 34, HUAC Executive Session Transcripts, HUAC Records; U.S. Congress, Senate, *Army Signal Corps,* 446, 447, 449–51.
59. "UFWA to Protect Jobs of Negroes after War," *Washington Post,* October 26, 1944; "Testimony of Annie Lee Moss," February 22, 1954, Executive Session Transcripts, HUAC Records; U.S. Congress, Senate, *Army Signal Corps.*
60. "Hearings before the Committee on Un-American Activities," February 15, 1951, Executive Session Transcripts, HUAC Records; "Stenographic Transcript of Hearings before the Committee on the Judiciary," 93; U.S. Congress, House, *Communism in the District of Columbia–Maryland Area;* transcript, General Accounting Office Loyalty Board Hearing, June 22, 1948. FBI agents questioned her claim about accompanying a white neighborhood acquaintance to the meeting, concluding that there were no white individuals living on the block Moss identified as the neighbor's. See C. H. Stanley to A. Rosen, April 1, 1954 (doc. 121-2900-90), Moss FBI file.
61. "Stenographic Transcript of Hearings before the Committee on the Judiciary, U. S. Senate, Internal Security Subcommittee, Executive Session, May 15, 1953," 94–95, Records of the Senate Internal Security Subcommittee, RG 46, NARA; Mary Stalcup Markward testimony, February 19, 1954, House Committee on Un-American Activities, Executive Session Transcripts, HUAC Records.
62. Bontecou, "What's in a Name?"; Edstrom, "Mrs. Moss Confused, but Feels No Anger." On Christianity and Communism, see Kelley, *Hammer and Hoe.*
63. It should be noted that by 1954, FBI agents concluded that there was no evidence that Moss had ever been an "active" Communist.
64. L. B. Nichols to Mr. Tolson, February 15, 1954 (doc. number illegible), Moss FBI file; Senator Joseph McCarthy to Philip Young, February 4, 1954, case file 47-8 (Annie Lee Moss), PSI; "Testimony of Annie Lee Moss Taken during Interrogatory on February 16, 1954," ibid.; Markward interrogatory, February 16, 1954, ibid.; memorandum for the Chief Signal Officer, February 10 1954, Mom-Moz folder, box 390, RG 335, NARA II. HUAC had received a similar tip about Moss in 1952 but declined to pursue it. See C. E. Owens to Louis J. Russell, January 27, 1952, "Ann Moss" Investigative Name File, HUAC Records. For overviews of McCarthy's conflict with the army, see Reeves, *Life and Times of Joe McCarthy;* Oshinsky, *A Conspiracy So Immense.*

65. C. E. Owens to Thomas W. Beale, February 17, 1954, Mary Stalcup Markward folder, Investigative Name File, ser. 2, HUAC Records; testimony of Mary Stalcup Markward, February 19, 1954, ibid.; testimony of Annie Lee Moss, February 22, 1954, HUAC Executive Session Transcripts, HUAC Records. Because of her illness, Moss did not testify before HUAC until February 22, one day before the McCarthy committee opened its hearings on her case. HUAC's decision not to pursue the case appears to have been based in large part on the fact that Moss had no access to "top secret" messages, despite McCarthy's allegations. See "Memo re: Velde Subcommittee Hearing on Annie Lee Moss," February 25, 1954, Mom-Moz folder, box 390, RG 335, NARA II. For media discussion of the HUAC testimony, see "McCarthy Says Red Decodes Secrets, but Army Denies It," *New York Times*, February 24, 1954. McCarthy went from the session at which Moss appeared to the famous "chicken luncheon," at which Secretary of the Army Robert T. Stevens apparently capitulated to the senator's demands that he be given free rein in questioning army witnesses.
66. "200 Pay Woody L. Taylor Tribute at Testimonial"; "Negro Nominated for Job in Capital," *New York Times*, February 13, 1955; "George Hayes, 74, a Rights Lawyer," *New York Times*, December 21, 1968; George E. C. Hayes to Senator McCarthy, March 5, 1954, case file 47-8 (Annie Lee Moss), PSI; "Attorney Begs Sen. McCarthy to Give Mrs. Moss a Chance," *Washington Daily News*, March 6, 1954; "Mrs. Moss Gets Hearing," *Washington Daily News*, March 9, 1954; "Joe Takes a By-Pass," *Chicago Defender*, March 20, 1954.
67. L. B. Nichols to Mr. Tolson, February 15, 1954 (doc. number illegible), Moss FBI file; L. B. Nichols to Mr. Tolson, February 24, 1954 (doc. 121-2900-20), ibid.; L. B. Nichols to Mr. Tolson, March 30, 1954 (doc. 121-2900-39), ibid.; Robert F. Kennedy to Senator Stuart Symington, March 9, 1954, folder 2455, Stuart Symington Papers (hereafter Symington Papers). J. Edgar Hoover had approved revealing to Senator Jackson the evidence against Moss "on a personal and confidential basis." Jackson apparently shared the information with Robert F. Kennedy, who told Symington that, while Moss didn't deserve being "completely ruined," she had probably been connected to the Communist Party before 1945. The point is that Democratic senators—even more so than Republicans—were privy to evidence that the charges against Moss had some substance.
68. If Moss's memory in her HUAC testimony is correct—that "Hall" had delivered the newspaper to her in 1943—then it most likely had not been CP member Robert Hall, who was in Alabama at the time. In the wake of the hearing, FBI agents spent a good deal of time seeking to discover who had delivered the newspaper; they suspected that it was not Robert Hall but another CP member, whose name has been redacted from FBI investigative reports. See C. H. Stanley to Mr. Rosen, March 21, 1954 (doc. 121-2900-29), Moss FBI file; C. H. Stanley to Mr. Rosen, March 22, 1954 (doc. 121-2900-31), ibid.
69. An examination of Washington, D.C., city directories (1948 and 1954) and telephone directories (December 1952 and September 1954) reveals that they list several women with similar names, including Mrs. Anna L. Moss, Mrs. Addie Moss, Annie Moss, and Mrs. Abbie Lee Moss. See also Moss FBI file, which records a detailed investigation into the "mistaken identity" story, especially C. D. DeLoach to Mr. Tolson, March 16, 1954 (doc. 121-2900-67); and report, March 22, 1954 (doc. 121-2900-81).

70. For example, see M. C. Donaldson to Symington, March 22, 1954, folder 2465, Symington Papers, for reference to a Fulton Lewis broadcast debunking the idea that there were three Annie Lee Mosses in the phone book.
71. Symington's exchange with Moss might be profitably contrasted with the testimony of African American labor activist Yates Holmes before the PSI just a few months later. Whereas Holmes seems to have expected Symington to be sympathetic to his concerns that allegations that he was subversive might endanger his job as a sandblaster—"Senator Symington, you understand my position. I work for a living. My job is at stake"—Symington seemed quite put out to learn that Holmes earned $22 a day: "Do you call that a second-class citizen?" *Executive Sessions,* 5:397–401.
72. Rosteck, *"See It Now" Confronts McCarthyism,* 162; Friendly, *Due to Circumstances Beyond Our Control.* Apparently footage of the hearings also appeared on *Open Hearing,* an ABC news show hosted by John Daly, on March 11. At this time, however, ABC was a minor player in the television market, and Murrow's was the most significant coverage.
73. General Ralph Zwicker was Peress's commanding officer and thus another target of McCarthy's investigations. My description of the Murrow program relies on the script of the March 16, 1954, *See It Now* broadcast, "Annie Lee Moss before the McCarthy Committee," reel 40, Edward R. Murrow Papers, 1927–1965 (hereafter Murrow Papers). Thomas Rosteck offers a compelling interpretation of the broadcast as an example of "proletarian discourse" in *"See It Now" Confronts McCarthyism,* 142–74. See also Doherty, *Cold War, Cool Medium,* 180–84.
74. Perhaps not surprisingly, since Symington pronounced it oddly as "espē"ənij."
75. Unfortunately, of upwards of 22,000 letters received by CBS in response to Murrow's McCarthy programs, only a few dozen have been preserved. In addition, McClellan's papers are unprocessed and difficult to use. This discussion therefore draws mainly on correspondence contained in the Symington Papers. For the "pillorying" language, see Mercer R. Roach to Symington, March 13, 1954, folder 2458, Symington Papers; Anne B. Hemmeter to Symington, March 17, 1954, folder 2460, ibid. This language also appeared in "Senators Rap Hounding of Negro Woman Witness," *Daily Worker,* March 12, 1954.
76. Arthur R. Ramey to Symington, March 16, 1954, folder 2459, Symington Papers; Eleanor G. Williams to Symington, March 17, 1954, folder 2461, ibid.; Mrs. Gladys F. Compton to Senator Fulbright, March 16, 1954, folder F19-B-5, John L. McClellan Collection (hereafter McClellan Collection); Shirley Been to McClellan, March 16, 1954, folder F16-C-2, ibid.
77. Erwin W. Smith to Symington, March 12, 1954, folder 2457, Symington Papers; Frances Boudreaux to Symington, March 17, 1954, ibid.; Pleasant Gray to Symington, March 17, 1954, folder 2460, ibid.; Theodore F. Baer to Symington, March 20, 1954, folder 2464, ibid.; George T. Hally to Symington, March 22, 1954, folder 2465, ibid.; Mrs. Homer D. Myers to McClellan, March 17, 1954, folder F16-C-2, McClellan Collection.
78. I. F. Stone to Symington, undated, folder 2455, Symington Papers; Walter B. Simon to Symington, March 16, 1954, folder 2459, ibid.; Mildred R. Levy to Symington, undated, folder 2460, ibid.; Mrs. Walter J. Orlikoski to Symington, March 18, 1954, folder 2463, ibid.; Louis Potsdamer to Symington, March 21, 1954, folder 2464, ibid.; G. E. Munger

to Symington, undated, folder 2645, ibid.; Blanche S. Hamilton to McClellan, March 17, 1954, folder F19-B-5, McClellan Collection; Ernest Angell to Edward R. Murrow, March 19, 1954, reel 41, Murrow Papers. Even Secretary of Defense Charles Wilson chimed in, telling a reporter, "I would think myself that we ought to make up our minds about that poor woman." "Wilson Discounts His 'Risk' Problem," *New York Times,* October 5, 1954.

79. "Committee v. Chairman"; Marya Mannes, "The People vs. McCarthy," *The Reporter,* April 27, 1954, 26; John Crosby, "The Aroma of Decency," *New York Herald Tribune* clipping, March 19, 1954, folder 2463, Symington Papers; see also Irwin Holloway to Edward R. Murrow, March 17, 1954, folder 2460, ibid.
80. Mr. and Mrs. Maurice Harris to Senator Symington, March 15, 1954, folder 2458, ibid.; Nisson A. Finkelstein to Symington, March 16, 1954, folder 2459, ibid.; Mrs. Ruth Carbone to Symington, March 17, 1954, folder 2460, ibid.; Mrs. John R. Carey to Symington, undated, folder 2463, ibid.; Marguerite Kehr to Symington, March 22, 1954, folder 2645, ibid.; Paul Butler to McClellan, March 26, 1954, folder F19-B-5, McClellan Collection; Marion R. Innerst (?) to McClellan, March 20, 1954, ibid.; Edith Pascal to McClellan, March 20, 1954, ibid.; Louis R. Hochberg to McClellan, March 13, 1954, folder F16-C-2, ibid.
81. Winifred Scott to Symington, March 12, 1954, folder 2457, Symington Papers. See also Doris Jackson to Symington, March 12, 1954, folder 2456, ibid.; Pauline Grand to Symington, undated, folder 2458, ibid.; Muriel Greenhill to Symington, March 16, 1954, folder 2459, ibid., Mrs. Irene Eck to Symington, March 17, 1954, folder 2460, ibid.; Theodore F. Baer to Symington, March 20, 1954, folder 2464, ibid., I. Davidson and S. James Davidson to Symington, March 23, 1954, folder 2645, ibid., Jessica Myers to McClellan, March 17, 1954, folder 15-C-2, McClellan Collection.
82. Crosby, "The Aroma of Decency."
83. Anne B. Hemmeter to Symington, March 17, 1954, folder 2460, Symington Papers.
84. For examples, see "Never a Red, Says Mrs. Moss," *Pittsburgh Courier,* March 6, 1954; "Sen. McCarthy Fails to Crack Mrs. Moss," *Pittsburgh Courier,* March 20, 1954; "Who Is Annie Lee Moss?"; "McCarthy Walks Out on Mrs. Annie Moss," *Washington Afro-American,* March 13, 1954; "Eisenhower Must Stop McCarthy," *Washington Afro-American,* March 20, 1954; "G-Worker Called a Communist by Sen. McCarthy," *Washington Afro-American,* August 7, 1954; "Mrs. Annie Lee Moss: Loyal or Subversive? $64 Question," *Washington Afro-American* clipping, folder 2474, Symington Papers; "McCarthy-Army Red Feud Rages around Ill Widow," *Chicago Defender,* March 6, 1954; "Moss Case Flops; Exit McCarthy," *Chicago Defender,* March 20, 1954; "The Truth Prevails," *Chicago Defender,* March 27, 1954. NAACP officials also saw McCarthy's attack on Moss as evidence of his "bigotry." See "National Grapevine," *Chicago Defender,* March 13, 1954; Walter White to Symington, telegram, March 12, 1954, folder 2456, Symington Papers; transcript, Ethel Payne, interview by Kathleen Currie, September 8, 1987, 40, Women in Journalism, Washington Press Club Foundation Oral History Project, Washington, D.C. Rarely, similar stories appeared in the mainstream press, notably Edstrom, "Mrs. Moss Confused, but Feels No Anger"; Kent, "Meet Mrs. Moss, a Target of Sen. McCarthy."

85. "Committee v. Chairman"; "McCarthy Walks Out on Mrs. Annie Moss." In its February 27, 1954, issue the *Afro-American* had used the same photo with the caption "I am not now and never have been a Communist."

86. On the SACB ruling, see Eve Edstrom, "U.S. Baring Secret Files on Mrs. Moss to Reds," *Washington Post,* May 23, 1958; "Recommended Decision of Board Member Francis A. Cherry on Second Remand Proceeding," September 19, 1958, *William P. Rogers, Jr., Attorney General of the United States, Petitioner, v. The Communist Party of the United States of America, Respondent,* Moss—1958 folder, box 298, Symington Papers; "Modified Report of the Board on Second Remand," *Rogers v. The Communist Party of the United States,* Moss—1959 folder, ibid.; *Communist Party of U.S. v. Subversive Activities Control Board,* 254 F.2d 314 (1958); *Communist Party v. Control Board,* 367 U.S. 1 (1961).

87. A January 5, 1959, article in the *Le Mars (Iowa) Globe-Post* echoed the last comment more baldly, observing, "It looked as if there might be a Nigger in Annie's Woodpile." See also Wilhelmina Logan to Symington, March 11, 1954, folder 2456, Symington Papers; E. B. Thompson to Symington, March 18, 1954, folder 2462, ibid.; "Annie" to Symington, August 6, 1954, folder 2471, ibid.; Mrs. Albert Brown to McClellan, April 6, 1954, folder F19-B-5, McClellan Collection; postcard postmarked Berwyn, Ill., undated, ibid. Folders 2465–75 of the Symington Papers are full of negative letters.

88. "Stone Cold Dead." For other examples, see Alice Widener, "FBI Files Prove Annie Was a Red," *USA: An American Magazine of Fact and Opinion,* November 7, 1958, Moss folder, box 127, Alfred Kohlberg Papers; "Depends on the Way"; Jerry Greene, "U.S. Admits Ex-Red Stays in Army Job," [New York] *Daily News* clipping, reel 40, Murrow Papers; "Who Promoted Moss" clipping, undated, reel 41, ibid.; Edward J. Mowery, "Reds Call Annie Lee Moss a Red" clipping, undated, ibid.; Fulton Lewis Jr., "McCarthy Was Correct" clipping, undated, ibid.; William V. Shannon, "The Heirs," *New York Post* clipping, December 4, 1958, Moss—1958 folder, box 298, Symington Papers; Joseph W. Donohue to Symington, November 17, 1958, ibid.; Rose Grenwald to Symington (including *Los Angeles Times* clipping), December 15, 1958, ibid.; "New Chapter in the Case of Annie Lee Moss," *U.S. News & World Report* clipping, December 26, 1958, ibid.; Westbrook Pegler to Symington (two letters), undated, Moss—1960 folder, ibid.; Symington to Westbrook Pegler, October 10, 1960, ibid.; Westbrook Pegler, "Fair Enough," *Odessa (Tex.) American,* November 8, 1960; William F. Buckley Jr., "New Book Revives Old Myths," *Syracuse Herald-American,* October 3, 1965.

89. Doris Jackson to Symington, March 12, 1954, folder 2456, Symington Papers; Erwin W. Smith to Symington, March 12, 1954, folder 2457, ibid.; Winifred Scott to Symington, March 12, 1954, ibid.; Mercer R. Roach to Symington, March 13, 1954, folder 2458, ibid.; Jerry Marconi to Symington, March 16, 1954, folder 2459, ibid.; Arthur R. Ramey to Symington, March 16, 1954, ibid.; Donald W. Carruthers to Symington, March 20, 1954, folder 2464, ibid.; "National Grapevine," *Chicago Defender,* March 13, 1954; transcript, Ethel Payne, interview by Kathleen Currie, 39; Crosby, "The Aroma of Decency." On Symington's racial politics, see transcript, Christine McCreary, interview by Donald A. Ritchie, May 19, 1998, 11–24, Oral History Project, U.S. Senate Historical Office, Washington, D.C.; on McClellan, see Woods, *Black Struggle, Red Scare.*

90. In fact this was not new information. Reeves, *Life and Times of Joe McCarthy,* 643–48.
91. John G. Connell Jr. to Annie Lee Moss, August 4, 1954, doc. 121-2900-108, Moss FBI file (preferring new charges); James C. Cook to Annie Lee Moss, January 19, 1955, box 813, Cobb Papers; Anthony Leviero, "Mrs. Moss Restored to a Job by Wilson," *New York Times,* January 20, 1955; John A. Giles, "Wilson Reinstates Mrs. Moss, Once Called Red by McCarthy," [*Washington Star*] clipping, January 10, 1955, Moss FBI file (doc. number illegible); minutes, cabinet meeting of January 7, 1955 folder, Dwight D. Eisenhower Papers, Ann Whitman File, Cabinet Series, box 4, DDEL; "Mrs. Moss' Job," *New York Times,* January 22, 1955.
92. This is affirmed by a reading of the extant transcripts of Moss's testimony before loyalty boards and HUAC, which demonstrate her extraordinarily literal responses to questioning; one imagines that she was an extremely frustrating witness. Thomas Doherty makes a similar argument, suggesting that Moss donned a "Sambo mask" to fool her inquisitors. See Doherty, *Cold War, Cool Medium,* 184.
93. Bontecou, "What's in a Name?"; conversation with Bill Dickens, St. Louis, November 1, 2010.

4. "A Dependent Independence and a Dominated Dominion"

1. On the arrests, see, for example, "8 More Seized in Roundup of Puerto Ricans," *Chicago Daily Tribune,* March 5, 1954; "Puerto Rico Hits at Terror," *Chicago Daily Tribune,* March 7, 1954; "Federal Jury Summons 20 Puerto Ricans," *Chicago Daily Tribune,* March 9, 1954; "FBI Seizes 11 Puerto Ricans; Six in Chicago," *Chicago Daily Tribune,* May 27, 1954; "15 Puerto Ricans on Trial," *New York Times,* November 6, 1954; "3 Nationalists Sentenced," *New York Times,* January 5, 1955. According to Manuel Roig-Franzia, Lebrón related that Cancel Miranda was already in Washington, but he remembers it otherwise. See Manuel Roig-Franzia, "A Terrorist in the House," *Washington Post,* February 22, 2004; Cancel Miranda, "They Never Caged My Mind."
2. Press release, January 11, 1954, folder 2, box 19, Ruth M. Reynolds Papers (hereafter Reynolds Papers); Paralitici, "Imprisonment and Colonial Domination," 77.
3. Dietz, *Economic History,* 143–58; Escobar, *Encountering Development;* Cohen, *Semi-Citizenship.* On connections between postwar and sixties solidarity movements, see Friedman, "Empire at Home"; Gosse, *Where the Boys Are.*
4. Costigliola, "Nuclear Family."
5. Transcript, Voice of America recording, Puerto Rico—Political Parties—Nationalist Party folder (pt. 2), box 355, Office of the Territories, RG 126, NARA II.
6. Román, *Other American Colonies,* 33–44; Cabranes, "Citizenship and the American Empire," 428. For an excellent overview of Puerto Rican history, see Ayala and Bernabe, *Puerto Rico in the American Century.* See also Trías Monge, *Puerto Rico;* Findlay, *Imposing Decency.* On other aspects of U.S. empire, see for example Kramer, *Blood of Government;* McCoy and Scarano, *Colonial Crucible.*
7. *Downes v. Bidwell,* 341–42. On the meanings and impact of the Insular Cases, see the essays in Burnett and Marshall, *Foreign in a Domestic Sense;* Sparrow, *Insular Cases;* Erman, "Meanings of Citizenship."

8. Quoted in Cabranes, "Citizenship and the American Empire," 467. The resident commissioner was granted the privilege of "representing" Puerto Rico in the House of Representatives. He could sit on committees and speak on the floor, but he had no vote. Leibowitz, *Defining Status*, 140–42; Sparrow, *Insular Cases*, 200–204.
9. Ayala and Bernabe, *Puerto Rico in the American Century*, 95–112; Lewis, *Puerto Rico*, 87–97; Trías Monge, *Puerto Rico*, 88–98.
10. Ayala and Bernabe, *Puerto Rico in the American Century*, 105–7; Power, "Pedro Albizu Campos"; Maldonado, *Luis Muñoz Marín;* Villaronga, *Toward a Discourse of Consent.*
11. Malavet, *America's Colony*, 33–35.
12. Power, "Pedro Albizu Campos"; Ayala and Bernabe, *Puerto Rico in the American Century*, 110–12; Bosque-Pérez, "Political Persecution"; Estades-Font, "Critical Year of 1936"; Rodríguez Beruff, "From Winship to Leahy."
13. For examples of earlier efforts, see Roger Baldwin to Vito Marcantonio, October 1, 1937, Civil Liberties—Campos folder, box 46, Vito Marcantonio Papers; minutes, January 30, 1940, Committee for Fair Play to Puerto Rico, Puerto Rico, General Correspondence folder (pt. 4), box 55, ibid.; resolutions on Puerto Rico, Women's International League for Peace and Freedom, Puerto Rico, [April 30, 1940], General Correspondence folder (pt. 9), box 54, ibid.; Petition relating to Concurrent Resolution, [1943], ibid.; Oswald Garrison Villard to Franklin D. Roosevelt, May 26, 1930, Government—Status—Independence—Legislation—General folder, box 863, RG 126, NARA II; William Sentner to Franklin D. Roosevelt, October 12, 1943, Government—Status—Independence—For—General folder, ibid.; Pierina Arnold to Franklin D. Roosevelt, October 21, 1943, ibid. See also Rodríguez Fraticelli, "U.S. Solidarity with Puerto Rico."
14. Ruth Reynolds Oral History, folder 2, box 45, Reynolds Papers.
15. Reynolds Oral History, folders 1 and 2, ibid. On the Harlem Ashram, see Dekar, *Creating the Beloved Community;* Fox, "Passage from India"; Kosek, *Acts of Conscience*, 183–86; Farmer, *Lay Bare the Heart.*
16. Reynolds Oral History, folder 2, box 45, Reynolds Papers; "Pedro Albizu Campos: The Man of Faith, the Man of Inflexible Principle, the Man of Compassion," folder 1, box 16, ibid.; Ruth Reynolds to A. J. Muste, February 21, 1949, folder 7, box 18, ibid.
17. Reynolds Oral History, folder 3, box 45, ibid.
18. [Illegible] to the Socialist Party of New York, January 23, 1944, folder 7, box 22, ibid.; "WHAT! Firecrackers on January 26?," flyer, ibid.; Reynolds Oral History, folder 2, box 45, ibid.; Pearl S. Buck to Dear Friend, March 22, 1945, folder 5, box 18, ibid.; "Statement of Position of The American League for Puerto Rico's Independence," folder 4, ibid. Conflict over ALPRI's stance can be traced in the Reynolds Papers, esp. box 18.
19. ALPRI collapsed in 1950 (see the discussion later in this chapter), but Reynolds organized a number of successor groups that worked for Puerto Rican independence into the 1970s.
20. Muñoz Marín emphasized that Puerto Rico's position behind the U.S. tariff "wall," as well as Puerto Ricans' exemption from the federal income tax, were essential to the island's development.
21. Petrullo, *Puerto Rican Paradox*, 27–28. On ideologies of race and sexuality, see Findlay, *Imposing Decency* and "Love in the Tropics"; Briggs, *Reproducing Empire.*

22. Text of address by Luis Muñoz Marín, July 4, 1948, Government—Status—Statehood—General folder, box 865, RG 126, NARA II; Briggs, *Reproducing Empire.*
23. Quoted in Bhana, *The United States,* 75. On Puerto Rico's regional significance, see Macpherson, "Toward Decolonization"; Sheinin, "The Caribbean and the Cold War"; Langley, *The United States and the Caribbean.*
24. Harold Ickes to Millard Tydings, July 14, 1943, Government—Status—Statehood—General folder, box 865, RG 126, NARA II. For discussions of the United States and decolonization in other contexts, see Westad, *Global Cold War;* Kramer, *Blood of Government;* McCoy, *Policing America's Empire;* Neptune, *Caliban and the Yankees;* Parker, *Brother's Keeper.*
25. "President Truman's Message to Congress Regarding Puerto Rican Political Status," October 16, 1945, Government—Status—Statehood—General folder, box 865, RG 126, NARA II.
26. Office of Puerto Rico Press Survey no. 14, Government—Status—General folder (pt. 5), box 862, ibid.
27. Findlay, "Love in the Tropics." On the trope of political maturity, see, for example, Rosenberg, "Gender."
28. Press release, September 3, 1946, folder 6, box 18, Reynolds Papers; U.S. Congress, House, Committee on Public Lands, Subcommittee on Territorial and Insular Possessions, *Election of Governor,* 30. For additional examples of this sort of argument, see U.S. Congress, Senate, Report 1779, *Providing for the Organization,* 6; Henry Hirshberg to B. W. Thoron, memo, November 13, 1944, Government—Status—Independence—For—General folder, box 863, RG 126, NARA II; Remarks by Oscar L. Chapman, January 2, 1949, Government—Status—General folder (pt. 5), box 862, ibid.; Harry Truman to Luis Muñoz Marín, December 21, 1948, folder 30, ser. 1, sec. 5, Archivo Histórico de la Fundación Luis Muñoz Marín (hereafter AFLMM); U.S. Congress, House, *Approving the Constitution,* 1–2.
29. Washington Press Club Luncheon, May 6, 1952, folder 4, box 4, ser. 9, sec. 5, AFLMM. See also, for example, "Puerto Rico Constitution," Monday, March 13, 1950, U.S. Senate, Hearings before the Committee on Interior and Insular Affairs, 11, folder 167, subseries 24, ser. 8, ibid.
30. "The Political Status of Puerto Rico," folder 219, subseries 34, ser. 8, sec. 5, ibid.; press release, September 3, 1946, folder 6, box 18, Reynolds Papers. The degree to which the Department of the Interior, the State Department, and Puerto Rican officials collaborated on framing this process was remarkable. The process can be traced in materials in the AFLMM, esp. ser. 1, sec. 5.
31. Beyond materials already cited, on the relationship between gender, maturity, and colonialism, see Gouda, "Gender and 'Hyper-Masculinity'"; Patil, *Negotiating Decolonization;* Bergeron, *Fragments of Development;* Scott, *Gender and Development;* Muñoz-Pogossian, "Gendered Language."
32. U.S. Congress, Senate, Report 1779, *Providing for the Organization,* 9; Harry S. Truman, "Statement by the President," June 6, 1950, Puerto Rico—Constitution, 1949–52 folder, box 27, Philleo Nash Files, HST; "Statement of Governor Luis Muñoz Marín," [1952],

folder 219, subseries 37, ser. 8, sec. 5, AFLMM; Fernós Isern, "Mind of Puerto Rico"; A. Fernós-Isern to Julius Krug, March 10, 1947, Government—Status—General folder (pt. 4), box 862, RG 126, NARA II.

33. Text of address by Luis Muñoz Marín, July 4, 1948, Government—Status—Statehood—General folder, box 865, ibid.

34. Feminist scholars have shown that, even in the mid-twentieth century, marriage rationalized gender inequality by sustaining a vision of contract as consensual and voluntary while also masking social, economic, and often political dependence. See Cott, *Public Vows;* Kessler-Harris, *In Pursuit of Equity.* For an earlier period, see Stanley, *From Bondage to Contract.* Eileen Findlay demonstrates that the PPD's economic policies during these years encouraged wives' economic dependence on male breadwinners. See Findlay, *We Are Left without a Father Here.*

35. Truman, "Statement by the President."

36. "Additional Testimony of the American League for Puerto Rico's Independence," April 26, 1945, folder 4, box 18, Reynolds Papers; typescript beginning "Honored Members of the Committee on Territories," [July 1945], ibid.; "Testimony of the American League for Puerto Rico's Independence on the Tydings Bill," March 7, 1945, ibid.; press release, July 21, 1945, ibid.; ALPRI to Harry S. Truman, September 5, 1945, Government—Status—Independence—For—General folder, box 863, RG 126, NARA II.

37. Reynolds, *Campus in Bondage,* 286–87.

38. Jay Holmes Smith to Edward Stettinius, March 23, 1945, folder 5, box 18, Reynolds Papers; typescript containing translations of August and September 1947 correspondence between Nationalist Party and UN, folder 2, box 27, ibid.; Theresa Mielke and Oscar Collazo to Trygve Lie, September 2, 1948, ibid.; Victor Hoo to Sir/Madam, September 16, 1948, ibid.; Thelma Mielke to Oscar Collazo, September 20, 1948, folder 2, box 20, ibid.; report, September 3, 1948, folder 8, box 29, ibid.

39. Borgwardt, *New Deal,* 186–89; El-Ayouty, *The United Nations and Decolonization.*

40. Muñoz Marín's papers painstakingly document these negotiations. See, for example, "Summary Report of Meeting with Governor Muñoz Marín by Benjamin Gerig," June 30, 1953, folder 10, subseries 3, ser. 8, sec. 5, AFLMM; see also Bhana, *The United States,* 168–74. For an overview of the process by a participant, see Trías Monge, *Puerto Rico,* 121–24. For examples of intergovernmental conflict, see James P. Davis to Muñoz Marín, September 25, 1952, folder 163, subseries 24, ser. 8, sec. 5, AFLMM; Muñoz Marín to Secretary of the Interior, January 17, 1953, folder 11, subseries 3, ibid.

41. Muñoz Marín to Henry Cabot Lodge, May 25, 1953, personal collection of Antonio Fernós, in author's possession; "Puerto Rico's New Political Status," *Department of State Bulletin,* September 21, 1953, 395. See also Luis Muñoz Marín to President of the United States, January 17, 1953, OCB 091 Puerto Rico folder (December 1953), box 54, White House Office, NSC Staff, Operations Coordinating Board, OCB Central File Series, DDEL.

42. "Statement by Dr. Fernos-Isern," *Department of State Bulletin,* December 7, 1953, 799, 802. PPD leaders strongly believed that the compact extended the logic of federalism to Puerto Rico and therefore fundamentally changed the island's relationship to the United States.

43. *Department of State Bulletin,* September 21, 1953, 392; "November 3 Statement by Mrs. Bolton," ibid., 802. The district court's decision in the case, *Mora v. Torres,* had been approved by the Court of Appeals, but on other grounds. On the significance of this case, see Torruella, "¿Hacia dónde vas Puerto Rico?" Apparently the ramifications of the *Mora* case were considered at the highest level. A copy of the decision is to be found in OCB191 Puerto Rico folder, [December 1953], box 54, White House Office, National Security Council Staff Papers, 1948–1962, OCB Central File Series, DDEL. Despite *Mora,* subsequent events made it clear that Congress had not yielded its plenary powers.
44. For federal officials' anxieties, see "Memorandum by the Adviser, United Nations Planning Staff," U.S. Department of State, *Foreign Relations of the United States, 1952–1954* (hereafter *FRUS*), 3:1438–40; "Memorandum by the Assistant Secretary of State for United Nations Affairs (Hickerson) to the Secretary of State," ibid., 1440–41. For PPD leaders, see ibid., 122, 124.
45. Brief, September 9, 1952, box 19, folder 1, Reynolds Papers; "Puerto Rico Does Not Possess the Factors Indicative of the Attainment of Independence," September 23, 1952, ibid.; El-Ayouty, *The United Nations and Decolonization,* 196; Sady, *The United Nations and Dependent Peoples,* 98; "In the Matter of the Relation of the Government of Puerto Rico."
46. "India Disputes US over Puerto Rico," *New York Times,* September 1, 1953; "Puerto Rico Issue Sent to Assembly," *New York Times,* September 2, 1953; Sady, *The United Nations and Dependent Peoples,* 100.
47. "The Secretary of State to the Embassy in Mexico," *FRUS,* 1952–1954, 3:1469–70; "November 3 Statement by Mrs. Bolton," *Department of State Bulletin,* December 7, 1953, 802; "Statement by Frances P. Bolton," *Report on the Eighth Session of the General Assembly of the United Nations,* Committee on Foreign Affairs, H.R. Rep. No. 83-1695 (1954), 242. The debate about Puerto Rico's status was also complicated by its ramifications for a broader conflict over whether the UN or colonial powers were "competent" to determine when to end reporting. On Puerto Rico's role in this debate, see El-Ayouty, *The United Nations and Decolonization,* 198.
48. "Memorandum by the Director of the Office of Dependent Area Affairs (Gerig) to the Assistant Secretary of State for United Nations Affairs (Murphy)," *FRUS,* 1952–1954, 3:1473–74.
49. State Department officials, including Secretary of State John Foster Dulles, strongly opposed the idea. See [Dulles], telephone conversation with Amb. Lodge, November 20, 1953, Telephone Memoranda, 11/1/53–12/31/53 folder 2, box 2, Telephone Conversations series, John Foster Dulles Papers, DDEL; Henry Cabot Lodge Jr. to "General," November 28, 1953, Lodge, Henry Cabot, 1952–53 (2) folder, box 23, Administrative Series, Ann Whitman File, ibid.; Lodge to Eisenhower, November 28, 1953, ibid.; press release no. 1833, November 27, 1953, ibid.; Lodge to Eisenhower, December 10, 1953, Lodge, Henry Cabot 1952–53 (1) folder, ibid.; *FRUS,* 1952–1954, 3:1473–76.
50. United Nations General Assembly, 459th Plenary Meeting, Official Records, November 27, 1953 (New York, 1954), 321.
51. On the relationship between decolonization and the hegemony of the nation-state form, see Kelly and Kaplan, *Represented Communities.* A number of postcolonial scholars of

Puerto Rico and its diaspora have questioned the hegemony of the nation-state and the value of Puerto Rican nationalism. See Grosfoguel, *Colonial Subjects;* Negrón-Muntaner, *None of the Above;* Soto-Crespo, *Mainland Passage.*

52. Louis Raul Esteves to Eisenhower, January 1, 195[4], McKay, Douglas (3) folder, box 26, Administrative Series, Ann Whitman File, DDEL; Helen Weaver to Miss Life, January 14, 1954, ibid.; Eisenhower to Luis Raul Esteves, January 12, 1954, Puerto Rico folder, box 45, International Series, ibid.; William Langer to Sherman Adams, January 8, 1954, 147-F Puerto Rico (1) folder, box 755, Central Files, Official File, ibid.; [Sherman Adams] to William Langer, January 23, 1954, ibid.; Concurrent Resolution, January 18, 1954, folder 1, box 7, ser. 9, sec. 5, AFLMM.
53. Bernard Shanley to John Foster Dulles, December 16, 1953, OCB091 Puerto Rico folder, December 1953, box 54, White House Office, NSC Staff, OCB Central File Series, DDEL; extract, OCB minutes, December 22, 1953, ibid.; Walter Radius to Mr. Staats, December 23, 1953, ibid.; H. C. Lodge Jr. to Sherman Adams, December 21, 1953, Dept. of State folder (11/23/53–12/23/53)(1), box 68, Confidential Files, Subject Series, White House Central Files, DDEL; Orme Lewis to Bernard Shanley, January 13, 1954, Puerto Rican Independence folder, box 61, ibid.; Mr. Phleger to [Dulles], January 14, 1954, ibid.; "Subject: Present Commonwealth Status of Puerto Rico," ibid.; "Memorandum on the Constitutional Aspects of the Status of the Commonwealth of Puerto Rico," ibid.; Herbert Brownell Jr., memorandum for Bernard M. Shanley, February 2, 1954, ibid.; "Memorandum for Mr. Bernard M. Shanley on Status of Puerto Rico," February 3, 1954, ibid.
54. On the distinction between "independence" and "self-government," see "Attainment of Self-Government by the Commonwealth of Puerto Rico," March 31, 1953, personal collection of Antonio Fernós, in author's possession.
55. "Joint Report by the Interdepartmental Intelligence Conference and Interdepartmental Committee on Internal Security to the National Security Council Regarding the Recent Outbreak of Violence by Puerto Rican Nationalists," January 17, 1951, reproduced in Fernós, "Documentos secretos," 18; Bosque-Pérez and Colón Morera, *Puerto Rico under Colonial Rule,* esp. essays by Estades-Font and Paralitici; Rodríguez Fraticelli, "U.S. Solidarity with Puerto Rico." On U.S. empire and the construction of a "surveillance state," see McCoy, *Policing America's Empire.*
56. Acosta-Lespier, "The Smith Act Goes to San Juan"; Helfeld, *Discrimination for Political Beliefs.* The law was repealed in 1957, after the Supreme Court of Puerto Rico restricted its reach.
57. Pedro Albizu Campos FBI file, vol. 12, frame 60, "The FBI Files on Puerto Ricans" (hereafter Albizu Campos FBI file). This and other quotations from Albizu Campos's speeches and press conferences are from FBI or Puerto Rico Police recordings, transcriptions, and translations. Given this provenance, they must be read cautiously. Nonetheless, these transcripts constitute a very useful archive of Albizu Campos's speeches.
58. For useful surveys of the history of terrorism, see Law, *Terrorism,* esp. chap. 11; Hoffman, *Inside Terrorism,* esp. chap. 1. On terrorism as discourse, see Zulaika and Douglass, *Terror and Taboo.*
59. "1 Killed, 5 Shot In San Juan as Revolt Flares," *Washington Post,* November 1, 1950, clipping

in Law & Order—Nationalist Party—Press Clips folder, box 933, CCF 1907–51, RG 126, NARA II; "Puerto Rico"; "Call Troops in Puerto Rican Revolt," *Chicago Tribune,* October 31, 1950; "Revolt Flares in Puerto Rico; Soon Quelled with 23 Dead," *New York Times,* October 31, 1950; "Rebels Pour Out of Puerto Rico's Hills to Give Up," *Chicago Tribune,* November 3, 1950; J. Edgar Hoover to James Davis, Withdrawn Item tab 1, October 30, 1950, box 355, Classified Files 1951–71, RG 126, NARA II; Hoover to Davis, October 31, 1950, ibid. U.S. military police were deployed to help defend the governor's residence, but Muñoz Marín's request for federal troops to help round up Nationalist Party members was denied. See "Joint Report by the Interdepartmental Intelligence Conference," in Fernós, "Documentos secretos," 20. For overviews of the uprising, see Helfeld, *Discrimination for Political Beliefs,* 33–58; Seijo Bruno, *La insurrección nacionalista.*

60. Hunter and Bainbridge, *American Gunfight;* Donovan, *Assassins,* 169–215; Donovan, "A Demonstration at Blair House"; McCann, *Terrorism on American Soil,* 86–92.
61. Thelma Mielke to Trygve Lie, October 31, 1950, folder 2, box 27, Reynolds Papers; Executive Assistant to the Secretary-General to Mielke, November 2, 1950, ibid.; J. B. Orrick to Mielke, November 6, 1950, ibid.; State Department telegram from [Dean] Acheson, November 2, 1950, Puerto Rico—Political Parties—Nationalist Party folder (pt. 2), box 355, Confidential Files 1951–71, RG 126, NARA II; E.W. to James Davis, November 6, 1950, ibid.; James Davis to W. Wentworth Linebarger, November 7, 1950, ibid.; Frank J. Dailey, "Memo re Diplomatic Exchange between Cuba and Puerto Rico," [November 1950], ibid.; "Island Rebels Ask UN to Investigate," *New York Times,* November 3, 1950; "Puerto Rico's UN Plea Brushed Off," *Times-Herald* clipping, November 3, 1950, Law & Order—Nationalist Party—Press Clips folder, box 933, CCF 1907–51, RG 126, NARA II.
62. "Puerto Rico Police Round Up 400 Nationalists, Communists," *Washington Post,* November 5, 1950; "91 Puerto Ricans Rounded Up Here," *New York Times,* March 9, 1954; "Anti-US Plot Is Laid To 17 Puerto Ricans," *New York Times,* May 27, 1954; "Puerto Ricans Get Maximum Terms," *New York Times,* July 9, 1954; "Puerto Ricans Guilty of Sedition," *New York Times,* October 13, 1954; "3 Terrorists Convicted," *New York Times,* December 24, 1954; Paralitici, "Imprisonment and Colonial Domination," 77; Helfeld, *Discrimination for Political Beliefs.*
63. Typescript, Oscar Collazo testimony, folder 2, box 28, Reynolds Papers; *Collazo v. United States,* 576.
64. Stenographic transcript, 1652–53, box 1797, Criminal Case Files, U.S. District Court, Southern District of New York, RG 21, NARA-NY.
65. "Deposition of Juan Bernardo Lebrón, in Support of Motion to Dismiss the Indictment," folder C144-167 [3], box 1795, ibid.
66. Ribes Tovar, *Lolita Lebrón;* Vilar, *Message from God.*
67. Stenographic transcript, 1413–1525, box 1797, RG 21, NARA-NY; Ribes Tovar, *Lolita Lebrón.*
68. Lynn, *There Is a Fountain,* 136.
69. Díaz-Quiñones, *El arte de bregar;* Findlay, *We Are Left without a Father Here.* I am indebted to Eileen Findlay for sharing with me her forthcoming work and her deep understanding of *bregar.*

70. "Rebel Chiefs and Commies Caught in Net," *Times-Herald* clipping, November 3, 1950, Law & Order—Nationalist Party—Press Clips folder, box 933, CCF 1907–51, RG 126, NARA II; Wayne Morse to James P. Davis, May 2, 1951, Puerto Rico—Political Affairs—Political Parties—Nationalist Party folder (pt. 3), box 355, ibid.; Ruth Reynolds to Helen [Tysell], June 21, 1951, folder 3, box 9, Reynolds Papers; Alberto Arrillaga to Lyle Tatum, October 26, 1951, folder 6, box 24, ibid.; "Notes on Civil Liberties in Connection with the Cases of Puerto Rican Nationalists," folder 4, box 20, ibid. Reynolds claimed that one reason for her arrest was to prevent her from publishing her study of the response to the 1948 student strike. The book was finally published in 1989, the year she died.
71. Press release, November 6, 1950, folder 4, box 18, Reynolds Papers; Jay Holmes Smith to Whom It May Concern, February 19, 1951, folder 3, ibid.; Reynolds Oral History, folder 5, box 46, ibid. Puerto Rican solidarity efforts have been overlooked by historians of radical pacifism. On 1950s-era radical pacifism, see Mollin, *Radical Pacifism;* Bennett, *Radical Pacifism;* Tracy, *Direct Action;* Hunt, *David Dellinger.*
72. Religious activists from the Fellowship of Reconciliation and the Catholic Worker movement also participated in these activities, which are amply documented in Reynolds's files. On the Ruth Reynolds Defense Committee, see, for example, "The Case of Ruth M. Reynolds," folder 3, box 24, Reynolds Papers; Carl Colodne to Ruth Reynolds, October 12, 1951, folder 7, box 2, ibid. On opposition to the Collazo execution, see, for example, Thelma Mielke to Dear Friend, [1952], folder 2, box 20, ibid.; Committee to Save the Life of Oscar Collazo, flyer, folder 1, ibid.; James P. Davis to Victor Gutierrez Franqui, April 3, 1952, Puerto Rico—Political Affairs—Political Parties—Nationalist Party folder (pt. 3), box 355, CF 1951–71, RG 126, NARA II. The Defense Committee was particularly important because Reynolds's family apparently contributed no money for her legal defense, urging her instead to accept a deal that would require her to leave Puerto Rico and live under their supervision. See Francis Heisler to John E. Tysell, May 1, 1951, folder 4, box 24, Reynolds Papers. On Americans for Puerto Rico's Independence, see press release, July 25, 1952, folder 1, box 19, ibid.; minutes, July 23, 1952, folder 2, ibid. On the CJPR, see A. J. Muste to Dave Dellinger, March 23, 1954, folder 5, box 20, ibid.; "Statement of Purpose," folder 4, ibid.
73. "Help Save a Life," folder 1, box 20, ibid.; "Who Conspires: The Government or the People," folder 4, ibid.; Thelma Mielke to Dear Friend, [1952], folder 2, ibid.; Frances Cowell et al. to Truman, July 22, 1952, ibid.; A. J. Muste and Bill Sutherland to Truman, July 16, 1952, folder 7, box 23, ibid.
74. For examples, see "Statement of Purpose," folder 4, box 20, ibid.; Waldo Frank and Norman Mailer to Dear Friend, [1954], ibid. This sort of argument was also sometimes used by anti-Communist pacifists who contended that if liberals and pacifists did not come to the aid of Puerto Rican Nationalists, Communists were all too ready to step up. See, for example, Muste, "The Communists Gain"; "Memo to the Hesitant," folder 4, box 20, Reynolds Papers.
75. A. J. Muste and Bill Sutherland to Truman, July 16, 1952, folder 7, box 23, ibid.; "A. J. Muste Reports on Puerto Rican Nationalist Party," *The Peacemaker,* August 4, 1951, clipping, ibid.; "Peacemakers' Manifesto to the People of Puerto Rico," folder 8, ibid.;

"The United States Government Conspires Again against the Nationalist Party of Puerto Rico," folder 1, box 12, ibid.

76. "Responsible Pacifism and the Puerto Rican Conflict," ibid.; "Help Fight the Puerto Rican Conspiracy Case!," ibid; Ruth Reynolds, untitled typescript for *The Peacemaker,* May 5, 1954, ibid.; "Hear Ye! Hear Ye!," flyer, folder 1, box 24, ibid.

77. On Puerto Rico's militarization, see Garcia Muñiz, "U.S. Military Installations in Puerto Rico"; Ayala and Carro-Figueroa, "Expropriation and Displacement." Information on the history of Ramey Air Force Base is found at www.rameyafb.org.

78. J. Edgar Hoover to James P. Davis, July 10, 1950, Withdrawn Item tab 2A, box 355, Classified Files 1951–71, RG 126, NARA II; Albizu Campos FBI file, vol. 12, frames 85–86, 91; Julius Eichel to Truman, October 31, 1950, folder 7, box 18, Reynolds Papers; Ruth Reynolds to Marc [Vito Marcantonio], [1950], folder 2, box 9, ibid.; "Peacemakers' Manifesto to the People of Puerto Rico"; "Who Conspires: The Government or the People"; "A. J. Muste Reports on Puerto Rican Nationalist Party"; Muste, "The Communists Gain."

79. ". . . A Sad Day for Two Peoples," 19.

80. "Why Puerto Rico Boils Over"; "Puerto Rico Revolt"; "Insurrection"; Peter Edson, "A Warped Life," *Washington Daily News* clipping, [December 1950], Albizu Campos FBI file, vol. 8, frames 18–19; "A Dangerous Person"; "'Sublime Heroism' Cited in Shooting," *New York Times,* March 3, 1954; "Plots against U.S." For the repetition of this story in a letter, see Jane Nicole de Mariani to Truman, November 23, 1950, Puerto Rico—Political Parties—Nationalist Party folder (pt. 2), box 355, RG 126, NARA II. The real story of Albizu Campos's military service was somewhat more complicated. See Ayala and Carro-Figueroa, "Expropriation and Displacement"; Seijo Bruno, *La insurrección nacionalista.*

81. For exceptions that condemn military policy while still asserting that this episode was the "turning point" in Albizu Campos's life, see Bill O'Reilly, "The Apotheosis of Hate," *Palabras Neighbors,* Albizu Campos FBI file, vol. 8, frames 28–35; Shellaby, "Background to Violence."

82. Duany, *Puerto Rican Nation,* 236–60; Findlay, *Imposing Decency.*

83. The rhetoric of madness is frequently leveled at those alleged to be terrorists. Nonetheless, the ubiquity of descriptors focusing on the mental health of Nationalists is striking, especially when compared to other ways of marking terrorism as out of bounds, for example, as an outcome of barbarism or ideology. Postwar analyses of the irrationality of terrorism likely reflected the primacy of psychological modes of understanding human behavior in these years. For examples of the incessant journalistic use of these terms, see "Roots of Tragedy"; "2 Die, 3 Shot in Truman Attack," *New York Daily News,* November 2, 1950; "Assassin's Mania," *Washington Post,* November 3, 1950; "F.B.I. and Police Dig for Plot Roots Here," *New York Times,* March 3, 1954; "Bloody Session"; Frank, "Puerto Rico and Psychosis," 210. For examples in correspondence and official pronouncements, see "Declaraciones del Gobernador de Puerto Rico trasmitidas por la radio con motive de los sucesos del 30 de Octubre de 1950," folder 3, box 2, ser. 9, sec. 5, AFLMM; Mason Barr to Jane Nicole de Mariani, December 11, 1950, Puerto Rico—Political Parties—Nationalist Party folder (pt. 2), box 355, RG 126, NARA II;

Oscar Chapman to Eduardo R. Pons, December 5, 1950, ibid.; James Davis to William Dale, November 7, 1950, ibid.; Leonardo Vargas to Truman, November 7, 1950, file 1-n, Public Opinion Mail, President's Personal Files, HST; Pedro Piza to Truman, November 2, 1950, ibid.; "Resolution by the Association of City and Town Mayors," 17-R Attack on Congressmen folder (pt. 1), box 322, General Files, White House Central Files, DDEL; Sherman Adams to Federico Cordero, March 12, 1954, ibid.; Ellsworth Bunker to Eisenhower, March [8], 1954, ibid.; Maciano Villaronga and Francisco Collazo to Eisenhower, March 4, 1954, 17-R Attack on Congressmen folder (pt. 2), ibid.; William Arnold to John Dailey, March 26, 1954, Puerto Rico—Political Affairs—Political Parties—Nationalist Party folder (pt. 4), box 355, RG 126, NARA II.

84. "Terrorists' Chief Held in San Juan after Gun Battle," *New York Times,* March 7, 1954; "Puerto Rico Head Calls It Lunacy," *New York Times,* March 2, 1954.

85. For example, J. Edgar Hoover to Robert Cutler, March 3, 1954, Puerto Rican Matters folder (pt. 2), box 4, White House Office, Office of the Special Assistant for National Security Affairs (hereafter OSANSA), FBI Series, DDEL.

86. The *Post* editors did, however, note that Collazo had not been found "psychotic." Mason Barr to Pierre Pinet, November 15, 1950, Puerto Rico—Political Parties—Nationalist Party folder (pt. 2), box 355, RG 126, NARA II; "Commutation," *Washington Post,* July 27, 1952; "Roots of Tragedy"; "Assassination Attempt"; "Puerto Rico Revolt"; "Sane Puerto Ricans Spurn U.S. Break," *Washington Post,* March 7, 1954; "Aftermath in Puerto Rico," *New York Times,* March 7, 1954; "Bloody Session." It is worth noting that many Puerto Ricans in the United States and on the island agreed with such characterizations, in part because of their fears that all Puerto Ricans would be presumed to share Nationalist "craziness."

87. Frank, "Puerto Rico and Psychosis"; see also A. J. Muste, memo on Puerto Rico, folder 3, box 18, Reynolds Papers.

88. Director, FBI, to the attorney general, November 3, 1950, "P" folder, box 146, Subject File 1940–53, President's Secretary's Files, HST.

89. Rhoads had written but not mailed a letter in which he claimed to have killed eight Puerto Ricans and "transplant[ed] cancer into several more." When the letter came to light, he claimed that it was a joke. On the Rhoads letter, see Duany, *Puerto Rican Nation,* 236–60; Findlay, *Imposing Decency;* Lederer, "Porto Ricochet"; Aponte Vázquez, *Unsolved Case;* Malavet, *America's Colony,* 151–52.

90. Director, FBI, to the attorney general, November 3, 1950; Briggs, *Reproducing Empire,* 76–77 and passim.

91. J. Edgar Hoover to U. E. Baughman, June 7, 1951, Albizu Campos FBI file, vol. 8, frames 46–52; memo re Pedro Albizu Campos, October 8, 1953, ibid., vol. 11, frames 20–25; Petition and Brief, folder 7, box 27, Reynolds Papers.

92. Statement for USIA, October 1, 1953, Puerto Rico—Political Affairs—Political Parties—Nationalist Party folder (pt. 3), box 355, RG 126, NARA II; Mason Barr to Victor Gutierrez Franqui, June 13, 1951, ibid.; Julius Eichel to "Sis," December 3, 1953, folder 3, box 19, Reynolds Papers; Albizu Campos FBI file, vol. 11, frames 2–3. For an alternative translation of Muñoz Marín's letter, see ibid., frames 66–67.

93. Doris Torresola to Juan Bravo (copy), July 3, 1952, folder 6, box 28, Reynolds Papers; Doris Torresola on "Prison Conditions Surrounding the Trial in July–August 1952," August 29, 1953, ibid.; "Memorandum on Experiences Phenomenal, Mostly in the Princesa Hotel," folder 1, box 16, ibid.; Reynolds Oral History, folders 5–6, box 46, ibid. Reynolds herself heard voices and suffered from hallucinations, and she continued to experience "attacks" in her legs as late as 1973. She firmly believed that they were the result of federal government experiments. Today many Puerto Ricans recount without hesitation that Albizu Campos was tortured while in prison. See Aponte Vázquez, *Unsolved Case;* Lederer, "Cold War and Beyond"; Goliszek, *In the Name of Science;* Foster, *Project MKULTRA Compendium.*
94. Thelma Mielke, "Report of a Visit to Pedro Albizu-Campos," folder 2, box 31, Reynolds Papers; memorandum, February 12, 1954, ibid.; David Dellinger to Albert Einstein, February 24, 1954, folder 3, ibid.; meeting minutes, February 1, 1954, folder 5, ibid.; sworn statement by Herminia Rijos, January 30, 1954, folder 3, box 28, ibid.; Dave [Dellinger] to Reynolds, February 15, [1954], folder 6, box 3, ibid.; Reynolds to Dr. Buttrick, February 15, 1954, folder 4, box 9, ibid.; Sidney Aberman, David Dellinger, Ruth Reynolds, and Harold Wurp to Dr. Franklin Miller, February 17, 1954, ibid.; Reynolds to Herbert Jehle, February 18, 1954, ibid.; Reynolds to Dr. Victor Patschkiss, February 18, 1954, ibid.
95. Stenographic transcript, 1462–66, 1646–47, 1711–12, box 1797, RG 21, NARA-NY; "Statement Issued by the Women's Committee for the Freedom of Puerto Rican Political Prisoners," folder 6, box 20, Reynolds Papers; press release of the Women's Committee for the Release of the Political Prisoners of Puerto Rico, ibid.
96. Reynolds Oral History, folders 10, 11, box 46, Reynolds Papers. Despite her closeness to many Nationalists, Reynolds maintained that she was not informed about this or other strategic decisions. This account, therefore, is based on her memory of her observations of the time and cannot be taken as definitive. For the FBI's account of the planning for the attack, which had Albizu Campos giving the orders, see "Memo re Nationalist Party of Puerto Rico," March 5, 1954, Puerto Rican Matters folder (pt. 2), box 4, White House Office, OSANSA, FBI Series, DDEL.
97. "Five Congressmen Shot in House by 3 Puerto Rican Nationalists; Bullets Spray from Gallery," *New York Times,* March 2, 1954, emphasis added. Slightly different text is reproduced in a memo titled "Nationalist Party of Puerto Rico," August 29, 1957, Lolita Lebrón FBI file (file 62-7721-6555), in author's possession.
98. Vilar, *Message from God,* 4–5, 259–62. I have not been able to find the letter itself. For a later example of Lebrón's warnings of the dangers of the atomic age, see Director FBI to SAC, NY, October 21, 1957, transmitting a translation of a Lebrón letter to *El Diario de Nueva York,* September 9, 1957, folder 3-HQ-41, box 8, Records of the FBI, NARA II (unprocessed collection, in possession of author in response to FOIA request). Lebrón's accounts of her torture in the hospital bear a marked resemblance to the descriptions of other Nationalist prisoners: hearing voices, suffering radiation burns and edema. In prison she also experienced paralysis. At St. Elizabeth Hospital she apparently received electroshock treatment. See Vilar, *Message from God,* 260, 264; Ribes Tovar, *Lolita Lebrón.*
99. J. Edgar Hoover to Robert Cutler, March 3, 1954, Puerto Rican Matters folder (pt. 1), box 4, White House Office, OSANSA, FBI Series, DDEL.

100. "Woman Terrorist Freed of 'Intent,'" *New York Times,* June 18, 1954; "Puerto Ricans Get Maximum Terms," *New York Times,* July 9, 1954.

101. Reynolds Oral History, folder 11, Reynolds Papers; Reynolds, *Campus in Bondage,* 286.

5. "The Show of Violence"

1. American Civil Liberties Union, *Censorship of Comic Books,* 10; [Wertham], note on *Censorship of Comic Books,* folder 8, box 114, Fredric Wertham Papers (hereafter Wertham Papers).
2. An exception to this trend is Beaty, *Fredric Wertham.* Numerous scholars have treated Wertham's comic book crusade. Two important works are Nyberg, *Seal of Approval;* and Gilbert, *Cycle of Outrage.*
3. My thinking on this subject is informed by the work of Joseph Masco, who has argued for a rearticulation of national security that defines it "not simply as a question of how to protect the territorial borders of the state, but also as one of making a diverse citizenry feel politically, economically, culturally, and territorially secure within their nation." Masco, *Nuclear Borderlands,* 214.
4. On psychology in the postwar years, see Herman, *Romance of American Psychology;* Scott, *Contempt and Pity;* Meyerowitz, "How Common Culture."
5. Marshall, *Citizenship and Social Class,* 11.
6. On social citizenship, see Marshall, *Citizenship and Social Class;* Fraser and Gordon, "Genealogy of Dependency."
7. Wertham, *Seduction,* 98.
8. The Phipps Clinic opened in 1913 under the direction of Adolf Meyer, who reserved half of the clinic's resources for impoverished patients from the surrounding neighborhood. See Worthington, "When Psychiatry Was Very Young."
9. On Wertham's background, see Mendes, "Deeper Science"; Gilbert, *Cycle of Outrage,* 94–95; Beaty, *Fredric Wertham,* 16–17.
10. [Wertham] to Mr. Godwin, March 28, 1955, folder 5, box 123, Wertham Papers. Wertham explained to Godwin that his nickname "the poor man's Sigmund Freud" indicates "to some extent what I stand for. . . . The bare fact is that psychotherapy is practically restricted to those who can afford it and denied to those who haven't enough money. This is not only socially reprehensible but scientifically wrong."
11. Kenneth and Mamie Clark's Northside Center was also established in Harlem in the same year, but it treated only children. On the Lafargue Clinic, see Doyle, "Where the Need Is Greatest" and "A Fine New Child"; "Clinic for Sick Minds."
12. Wertham made his comments about Soviet psychiatry at a meeting at the home of Corliss Lamont. Robert Bendiner, "Psychiatry for the Needy," *Tomorrow,* April 1948, clipping, folder 1, box 53, Wertham Papers; James L. Tuck, "Here's Hope for Harlem," *New York Herald Tribune,* January 26, 1947, clipping, folder 8, ibid.; "The Future of American Capitalist Democracy," Fifth Annual Spring Conference, Williams College, May 1947, folder 1, box 181, ibid.; transcript, May 1947 meeting sponsored by Mr. and Mrs. Lamont, folder 2, ibid.; Martin, "Doctor's Dream in Harlem."

13. Tuck, "Here's Hope for Harlem"; Helen Strauss, "Lafarge [*sic*] Clinic Gives Harlem Free Expert Psychiatric Aid," *New York Herald Tribune,* August 11, 1946, clipping, folder 6, box 53, Wertham Papers.
14. S. I. Hayakawa, "Second Thoughts," *Chicago Defender,* January 11, 1947, reprint, ibid.; "Psychiatry in Harlem"; Norman M. Lobsenz, "Human Salvage in Harlem," *Coronet,* March 1948, reprint, folder 6, box 53, ibid.; Martin, "Doctor's Dream in Harlem"; Hayakawa, quoting Richard Wright, "Psychiatry Comes to Harlem," *Free World,* September 1946, clipping, folder 9, box 53, ibid.
15. This was one of Wertham's most oft-quoted phrases. See also Lobsenz, "Human Salvage in Harlem"; Tuck, "Here's Hope for Harlem."
16. "Harlem Pioneers with Mental Clinic," *Headlines and Pictures,* July 1946, reprint, folder 3, box 53, Wertham Papers; Bendiner, "Psychiatry for the Needy." Wertham's position eclipsed at the same time that it reflected the "pity" that characterized liberal social scientific understandings of race in the postwar years. See Scott, *Contempt and Pity;* Mendes, "Deeper Science."
17. Wertham was active in a variety of efforts to challenge racial inequality in the United States. He appeared as an expert witness for efforts to dismantle segregated educational systems, including one of the cases that came to be known collectively as *Brown v. Board of Education.*
18. Wertham, *Dark Legend,* 11.
19. Ibid., 116, 73, 86–90.
20. Wertham, *Show of Violence,* 18, 181, 233, 235–38.
21. Fish was not arrested for the murder of Grace Budd until six years after its occurrence. Ibid., 81.
22. Ibid., 73, 91–94.
23. Ibid., 265.
24. Ibid., 264–66.
25. Wertham, *Seduction,* 178. On the international crusade to control comic books during these years, see Gilbert, *Cycle of Outrage;* Nyberg, *Seal of Approval;* Hajdu, *Ten-Cent Plague;* Barker, *Haunt of Fears;* Lent, *Pulp Demons;* Springhall, *Youth, Popular Culture, and Moral Panics;* Adams, *The Trouble with Normal.*
26. Wertham, *Seduction,* 53; Wright, *Comic Book Nation,* 57; see also Feder, *Comic Book Regulation,* 2–3.
27. Wright, *Comic Book Nation,* 127–34; Benton, *Comic Book in America,* 119–23; Savage, *Comic Books and America,* 12, 124–25n16. On changes in postwar culture, see Berrett, "Gresham's Law of Culture," 4; Peterson, *Magazines in the Twentieth Century;* Ehrenreich, *Hearts of Men;* Meyerowitz, "Women, Cheesecake, and Borderline Material"; Davis, *Two-Bit Culture;* Fraterrigo, *Playboy.*
28. Wertham, *Seduction,* 95–96, 99.
29. Ibid., 97; North quoted in Hajdu, *Ten-Cent Plague,* 40, 44. See Beaty, *Fredric Wertham,* 115–18, for a more complete discussion of earlier critics.
30. Legman, *Love and Death,* 42. Legman's colorful and explicit argument that violence in American culture (sadism) was merely a substitute for the sexuality that was repressed

by censorship, which he self-published, invited the attention of postal authorities, and he ultimately fled the United States for France. For his correspondence with Wertham dated December 30, 1947, see folder 5, box 123, Wertham Papers; for March 16, 1948, see folder 12, box 109, ibid. Much of his analysis of comic books in *Love and Death* was first rehearsed by Legman at a symposium organized by Wertham. See Legman, "Comic Books and the Public."

31. Muhlen, "Comic Books and Other Horrors," 80.
32. Wertham, *Seduction,* 116, 97, 34.
33. Ibid., 34, 96–98, 100–103. A similar critique of racism in comic books can be found in Wagner, *Parade of Pleasure,* 98–99. On Wertham's racial analysis, see Barker, *Haunt of Fears,* 66–67; Gilbert, *Cycle of Outrage,* 98–101; Nyberg, *Seal of Approval,* 94–95.
34. Wertham, *Seduction,* 175, 187, 110, 185, 91.
35. Ibid., 178–83. Here Wertham was influenced by Erich Fromm's writings about sadomasochism.
36. Ibid., 178, 183–85, 192, 247; Wertham, "The Comics . . . Very Funny." He made a similar argument about "pornographic literature directed to children" in "Sex Crimes Can Be Prevented." In his 1966 book *A Sign for Cain,* he proclaimed that children who had read comic books in the 1950s were, in the 1960s, the parents of battered children. Wertham, *A Sign for Cain,* 197.
37. Wertham, *Seduction,* 190–91.
38. Ibid., 189–92, 233; see also Terry, *American Obsession,* 321.
39. "4 Teen-Agers Seized in Death by Kicking," *New York Times,* August 18, 1954; Emanuel Perlmutter, "Court Debate," *New York Times,* August 19, 1954; George K. Wynne, "Talked Good, Like They Was Pretty Educated," *Official Detective Stories,* November 1954, folder 10, box 16, Wertham Papers. For an interesting analysis of the changing racial dynamics of responses to youth crime that begins with this case, see Walker, "When Gangs Were White."
40. Marya Mannes, "The 'Night of Horror' in Brooklyn," *The Reporter,* January 27, 1955; Max Lerner, "Portrait of a Tragedy," *New York Post,* December 3, 1954, clipping, folder 11, box 22, Wertham Papers; Thomas Conway, "Kid Evil and His Harem," *Headquarters Detective,* January 1955, folder 10, box 16, ibid.; "4 Teen-Age Killers Are Indicted in First Degree in River Murder," *New York Times,* August 27, 1954.
41. "Teen-Age Killers Identify Body of 2nd Victim, Taken from River," *New York Times,* August 20, 1954; "A Puny 'Super-boy,' Killer-Pack's Chief," [*New York Daily Mirror*], August 19, 1954, clipping, folder 11, box 22, Wertham Papers; Mannes, " 'Night of Horror' in Brooklyn"; Wynne, "Talked Good"; Conway, "Kid Evil"; Wertham to Fitzpatrick, January 5, 1955, folder 8, box 16, Wertham Papers; Wertham to Harry Slochower, November 1, 1956, folder 8, box 22, ibid.
42. Mannes, " 'Night of Horror' in Brooklyn"; Conway, "Kid Evil."
43. "Brooklyn Murder Is Laid to Koslow," *New York Times,* December 3, 1954; Mannes, " 'Night of Horror' in Brooklyn"; Max Lerner, "What Kind of Thrill?," *New York Post,* December 1, 1954, clipping, folder 11, box 22, Wertham Papers.
44. Wertham to Fitzpatrick, January 5, 1955; Wertham to Slochower, November 1, 1956;

Mannes, "'Night of Horror' in Brooklyn"; *Report of the New York State Joint Legislative Committee,* 14–17. On *Nights of Horror,* see Friedman, "Sadists and Sissies"; Yoe, *Secret Identity.* Yoe contends that Joe Shuster, the original artist for the Superman comics, illustrated *Nights of Horror,* a plot twist that might not have surprised Wertham. New York City officials suppressed the publication, in an action that was ultimately upheld by the U.S. Supreme Court.

45. [Wertham] to Jack Koslow, December 15, 1954, folder 8, box 22, Wertham Papers; Wertham to Fitzpatrick, January 5, 1955, folder 8, box 16, ibid. Koslow and Mittman were originally sentenced to life in prison; an appeals court overturned the verdict, and they pleaded guilty to manslaughter charges, for which they received a sentence of ten to twenty years. See "'Thrill Killers' Get 10 to 20 Years' Jail," *New York Times,* July 2, 1958.
46. Mannes, "'Night of Horror' in Brooklyn"; Lerner, "What Kind of Thrill?"; Max Lerner, "The Verdict and the Guilt," *New York Post,* December 15, 1954, ibid. Lerner's columns on the case are reprinted in Lerner, *Unfinished Country,* 370–78.
47. Wertham, *Seduction,* 13, 148, 316, 149, 271–72, 394.
48. Wertham, "Comic Books—Blueprints"; Wertham, *Seduction,* 13.
49. "Mystery Bullet Kills Baseball Fan in Midst of Crowd at Polo Grounds," *New York Times,* July 5, 1950; "Youth Questioned in Death at Game," *New York Times,* July 6, 1950; "Search Extended in Mystery Death," *New York Times,* July 7, 1950; "Boy, 14, Admits Firing .45 Pistol at Time of Polo Grounds Killing," *New York Times,* July 8, 1950; "Pistol Search Continues," *New York Times,* July 9, 1950; "Boy Suspect Committed," *New York Times,* August 4, 1950. On the allegation that police used Robert's aunt's detention to elicit a confession, see Hilde L. Mosse to Wertham, July 15, 1950, folder 8, box 121, Wertham Papers; Vivienne Cheatham to Wertham, July 27, 1950, ibid. Peebles ultimately served a two-year sentence. See Jay Maeder, "Line of Fire Independence Day, 1950," *New York Daily News,* August 30, 1988.
50. "An Unsolved Problem," *New York Amsterdam News,* July 15, 1950, clipping, folder 8, box 121, Wertham Papers; Wertham, *Seduction,* 5–10, 234; Wertham, "What Parents Don't Know"; Wertham, "Comic Books—Blueprints."
51. Wertham, *Seduction,* 9–10, 7.
52. Ibid., 166; "Comic Books Are Bad" (1948), box 159, Wertham Papers; Wertham to Rev. Raymond Stephenson, April 18, 1954, folder 7, box 123, ibid.; Wertham, *Seduction,* 255, 390–93, 264, 283, 270, quoting Gilbert Seldes.
53. In his emphasis on economics, Wertham shared much with other critics of mass culture, as James Gilbert and Bart Beaty have argued. Nevertheless, while he clearly condemned comic books as "trash" and distinguished them from high culture, his emphasis on their allegedly violent effects was intended to move the debate about mass culture forward in a new way.
54. *John S. Sumner, Esq. vs. Creative Age Press, Inc.,* transcript of testimony, folder 10, box 159, Wertham Papers. See also Wertham, *Seduction,* 298–99. Note, however, his 1946 comment about *Forever Amber,* which Massachusetts officials had moved to suppress: "I am not against censorship in general. But a censorship which would forbid this book would be undemocratic and devoid of any scientific basis." Wertham to George P. Brett, December 8, 1946, folder 1, box 37, Wertham Papers.

55. Wertham, *Seduction,* 13–15, 326–27; Wertham to George P. Brett, December 8, 1946, folder 1, box 37, Wertham Papers.
56. Wertham, *Seduction,* 283, 316–26, 302. On tyranny, Wertham was quoting the author Virgilia Peterson.
57. "Strangers on Bikes Slay Boy in Street," *New York Times,* May 1, 1955; "Hoodlum, 17, Seized as Slayer of Boy, 15," *New York Times,* May 2, 1955; Henry Lee, "Boy Gangster Admits Killing," *New York Daily News,* May 2, 1955; "City Crushes Us, Says Dad of Gang-Slain Boy," *New York Daily News;* Jay Maeder, "Savage Land: Billy Blankenship, May–June 1955," *New York Daily News,* December 8, 2000; "Court Gives Show of Gang Weapons," *New York Times,* May 10, 1955; "Boy Gang Threats Reported in Bronx," *New York Times,* May 6, 1955; "2 Boys Indicted in Error Murder," *New York Times,* May 7, 1955; "Crime: Return to the Poconos." One of Santana's lawyers was Conrad Lynn, a longtime supporter of Puerto Rico's Nationalist Party who had defended Ruth Reynolds.
58. "Boy Killer Wins 2d-Degree Term," *New York Times,* June 9, 1955; "Prosecutor Denies 'Trick' Aided Killer," *New York Times,* June 10, 1955; "Boy Gets 25 Years as Youth's Killer," *New York Times,* July 16, 1955; Maeder, "Savage Land"; Fern Marja and Arthur Massolo, "Frank Santana: The Quiet One," *New York Post,* June 26, 1955, clipping, folder 6, box 101, Wertham Papers.
59. Wertham's assessment of Santana's "morals" reflected his own biases: "He . . . did not steal, did not go with the fag to make money." "Lafargue Conference Santana," May 24, 1955, folder 7, box 101, Wertham Papers.
60. Cowley published the story both in *The Militant* and as a stand-alone pamphlet. Joseph Monserrat to Wertham, November 21, 1956, folder 4, box 101, Wertham Papers; Wertham to [Gaetano] Masdsa, November 5, 1957, ibid.; Joyce Cowley to Wertham, February 10, 1957, ibid.; Cowley to Wertham, March 11, 1957, ibid.; Joyce Cowley, "The Santana Story—Poverty and Prejudice," *The Militant,* March 25, 1957, clipping, ibid.; Wertham to Luis Muñoz Marín, January 2, 1957, folder 6, ibid.; Cowley, *Santana Case.*
61. Wertham, *Circle of Guilt,* 32–33, 106.
62. Ibid., 151; "Where the Blame Lies." One account of the event attributes the initial aggression to the Navajos. See Beauford, *Rejected American,* 9–10, 17–21. Fred Beauford also suggests that this event was the inspiration for *West Side Story,* but that interpretation is not substantiated by other sources.
63. Actually, while all American boys had to overcome this identification with the feminine, he identifies this as a more fraught enterprise for middle-class boys and hence a more important path to masculinity than for working-class boys. Cohen, *Delinquent Boys,* 160–69; Gilbert, *Cycle of Outrage.*
64. Wertham, *Circle of Guilt,* 65, 82, 188.
65. Ibid., 191–92, 114–16.
66. Ibid., 150, 139, 154.
67. Ibid., 200 (quoting the director of the University of Maryland's Institute for Child Study), 155, 167, 152–53, 187, 195, 156.
68. Smythe, "Juvenile Tragedy"; Maccoby, "Violence and the Mass Media"; Ploscowe, "The Criminal as Patient." When he authored this review, Maccoby was engaged in graduate

work in anthropology at the University of Chicago. He was an early contributor to *New Left Review* and went on to train in psychoanalysis under Erich Fromm. In contrast, in a review titled "Salvation by Toughness," Max Lerner called the book "a thorough and moving discussion of the whole case." Lerner, *Unfinished Country,* 363–65.

69. Wertham to Masdsa, November 5, 1957; "The Santana Story: Poverty and Prejudice," *The Militant,* March 25, 1957; Bush, "Introduction," xviii; *People v. Santana;* Juan Gonzalez, "Exploitation in Gone-By Times Still as Repugnant," *Daily News,* February 17, 1993.
70. Wertham, *Circle of Guilt,* 202; Wertham, *Seduction,* 395, 390.
71. Edwin Lukas, *Survey,* November 1949, 626–27, clipping, folder 5, box 131, Wertham Papers.
72. Hajdu, *Ten-Cent Plague,* 92–94; *Winters v. New York;* Feder, *Comic Book Regulation,* 23–52; "Crime Comics and the Constitution"; Gilbert, *Cycle of Outrage.*
73. See, for example, "Statement of Harold W. Kennedy," September 27, 1954, folder 10, box 118, Wertham Papers; Kennedy to Wertham, May 17, 1956, ibid.; press release, February 26, 1959, folder 11, ibid.; Wertham to Rosemary Kiefer, August 18, 1948, folder 12, box 109, ibid.; Kiefer to Wertham, February 11, 1950, ibid.; Kiefer to Wertham, January 26, 1955, folder 5, box 124, ibid.; Wertham to [Esther] Goady, October 29, 1954, ibid.; Wertham to Mr. Katz, August 17, 1948, folder 7, box 116, ibid. James Gilbert emphasizes Wertham's "detached" position from many of these activities, noting that Wertham disagreed with the conservative politics of many who responded to his writings. I would argue that, despite his distaste for certain of the opinions voiced by letter writers (signaled, often, by his decision not to respond), and despite his refusal to create or affiliate with an anti-comics organization, he sought to shape the anti-comics crusade and other anti-violence efforts when he could. Gilbert, *Cycle of Outrage,* 104–6.
74. Wertham, *Seduction,* 395–97; see also, for examples, 224, 268, 367, 394.
75. Wertham to Goady, October 29, 1954, folder 5, box 124, Wertham Papers; see also Wertham to Mrs. Thomas, July 24, 1954, folder 2, box 129, ibid.; *General Federation Clubwoman,* October 1954, 10–11. On GFWC's earlier cultural activism, see Parker, *Purifying America;* Wheeler, *Against Obscenity.* For another analysis of clubwomen's anti-pornography activism, see Meyerowitz, "Women, Cheesecake, and Borderline Material."
76. See Rogin, *Ronald Reagan,* chap. 8; Terry, "Momism."
77. Wertham, *Seduction,* 167, 245, 253, 270; *General Federation Clubwoman,* September 1956, 10–11; *General Federation Clubwoman,* October 1957, 17–18.
78. *General Federation Clubwoman,* January 1955, 24–25; *General Federation Clubwoman,* October 1955, 10–11.
79. *General Federation Clubwoman,* December 1954, 16–17; *General Federation Clubwoman,* April 1955, 20–25; O. K. Armstrong, "How Coral Gables Cleaned Up Its Newsstands," *Parents Magazine,* December 1957, 50–51, 76, 78, excerpted as "Coral Gables against Obscenity," *Reader's Digest,* December 1957, 219–22.
80. Mrs. Walter F. Magee, "Our Scandalous Newsstands," *General Federation Clubwoman,* October 1957, 17; *General Federation Clubwoman,* October 1957, 18. Although Wertham did eventually turn his attention to pornography, he was concerned mostly with

bondage magazines. Still, his praise of clubwomen's efforts supports arguments that his growing obsession with comic books overwhelmed some of the finer points of his analysis of violence.

81. U.S. Congress, Senate, *Hearings before the Subcommittee to Investigate Juvenile Delinquency,* 59, 35.
82. Frank W. Greene Jr. to Wertham, September 23, 1954, folder 3, box 124, Wertham Papers; Phyllis A. Lewis to Wertham, April 5, 1955, folder 1, box 125, ibid.; Bob White to Wertham, December 25, 1954, folder 5, box 124, ibid. For more examples, see John Jones to Wertham, July 7, 1954, folder 2, ibid.; Mrs. Donald F. Nelson to Wertham, July 22, 1954, ibid.; Irvin Doress to editors, December 6, 1954, folder 5, ibid.; L. Pattillo to Wertham, July 23, 1948, folder 4, box 125, ibid.; Aileen McNerney to Wertham, May 16, 1954, folder 1, box 126, ibid.; Florence A. Davies to Wertham, May 21, 1954, folder 6, box 124, ibid.
83. Professor Dr. P. Gehring to Wertham, folder 2, box 126, ibid.; U.S. Congress, Senate, *Interim Report of the Subcommittee,* 27; Marya Mannes, "The Friendliest People in the World, Fundamentally," *The Reporter,* May 25, 1954, clipping, folder 7, box 119, Wertham Papers.
84. Wertham to H. H. Stansbury, November 16, 1948, folder 9, box 116, ibid.; Mannes, "Friendliest People."
85. Cynthia Sobsey to Wertham, November 16, 1954, folder 6, box 123, Wertham Papers.
86. Wertham, *Seduction,* 347.
87. Cuordileone, *Manhood,* 239; Lindner, *Must You Conform?,* 26, 112. On debates about Cold War masculinity, see, in addition to Cuordileone, Alpers, *Dictators,* esp. chap. 9; Schlesinger, *Vital Center.*
88. Quoted in "The Author," *Saturday Review of Literature,* May 7, 1949, 10.

Conclusion

1. "Port Huron Statement."
2. "During Rare Presidential Visit to Puerto Rico, Obama to Face Issues Other Than Statehood," *New York Times,* June 10, 2011; Jordan Fabian, "Puerto Rico's Status Vote Not Clear Says White House," ABC News, December 3, 2012, available at http://fusion.net.
3. DeNavas-Walt, Proctor, and Smith, *Income, Poverty, and Health Insurance Coverage; Twenty-to-One.* This was the highest disparity recorded since the government began tracking such data in 1984.
4. Chang, *Lifting as We Climb.*
5. Singh, *Black Is a Country,* 222.
6. Harrell, "Black Victims of Violent Crime."
7. "Trends in U.S. Corrections"; Uggen, Shannon, and Manza, "State-Level Estimates of Felon Disenfranchisement"; Thompson, "Why Mass Incarceration Matters"; Roberts, "Social and Moral Cost."
8. Roberts, "Social and Moral Cost."
9. Adam Liptak, "Secrecy of Memo on Drone Killing Is Upheld," *New York Times,* January 2,

2013, containing a link to Decision of J. McMahon, *New York Times v. U.S. Department of Justice.* Both the ACLU and the *New York Times* sued under the FOIA for information about the administration's targeted drone attacks, including one that allegedly resulted in the death of U.S. citizen Anwar al-Awlaki in Yemen.

10. Difo, "Enemies among Us." As Gargi Bhattacharyya points out, the racial politics of the War on Terror constitute "a racialization that builds on the insights of anti-racist critiques and the lessons of postcolonial theory." Bhattacharyya, *Dangerous Brown Men,* 90.
11. Quoted in Ritter, "Domestic Containment or Equal Standing?," 442–43.
12. Noon, "Cold War Revival"; Robin, "Remembrance of Empires Past"; Tirman, *The War on Terror and the Cold War.*
13. For a related argument, see Pease, "Re-thinking 'American Studies after U.S. Exceptionalism.'"

BIBLIOGRAPHY

Archival and Manuscript Collections

Alfred Kohlberg Papers. Hoover Institution Archives, Stanford University, Palo Alto, Calif.

Annie Lee Moss Official Personnel Folder (in author's possession)

Archives of the American Civil Liberties Union, 1950–1990, Legal Case Files, Series 4. Wilmington: Scholarly Resources, 1995.

Archivo Histórico de la Fundación Luis Muñoz Marín, San Juan

Cobb, Howard, Hayes & Windsor Papers. Unprocessed collection, Moorland- Spingarn Research Center, Howard University, Washington D.C.

Dwight D. Eisenhower Library, Abilene, Kans.

John Foster Dulles Papers

Papers of Dwight D. Eisenhower as President of the United States (Ann Whitman File)

White House Central Files

White House Office, National Security Council Staff Papers, Operations Coordinating Board Central File Series

White House Office, Office of the Special Assistant for National Security Affairs, FBI Series

White House Office, Office of the Staff Secretary, International Series

Edith Sampson Papers. Schlesinger Library, Radcliffe Institute for Advanced Study, Cambridge, Mass.

Edward A. Harris Papers. Syracuse University Library

Edward R. Murrow Papers, 1927–1965. Sanford: Microfilming Corporation of America, 1982.

Federal Bureau of Investigation files

Annie Lee Moss file (in author's possession)

Ellen Knauff file (in author's possession)

Lolita Lebrón file (in author's possession)

Mary Markward file (in Heming Nelson's possession)

Pedro Albizu Campos file, "The FBI Files on Puerto Ricans." Centro de Estudios Puertorriqueños, Hunter College of the City University of New York.

Franklin D. Roosevelt Jr. Papers. Franklin D. Roosevelt Library, Hyde Park, N.Y.

Fredric Wertham Papers. Library of Congress, Washington D.C.

Harry S. Truman Presidential Library and Archives, Independence, Mo.

Charles S. Murphy Files, 1945–1953

Harry N. Rosenfield Papers

J. Howard McGrath Papers

Philleo Nash Files

President's Personal Files

President's Secretary Files

Stephen J. Spingarn Papers

Tom C. Clark Papers

White House Central Files

Irving Dilliard Papers. Western Historical Manuscript Collection, State Historical Society of Missouri Research Center, St. Louis.

John L. McClellan Collection. Ouchita Baptist University, Arkadelphia, Ark.

Joseph Pulitzer Papers, 1897–1958. Washington D.C.: Library of Congress Microfilms, 1977.

National Archives and Records Administration, Washington, D.C. (NARA)

Record Group 46: Records of the U.S. Senate

Records of the Permanent Subcommittee on Investigations

Records of the Senate Internal Security Subcommittee

Record Group 233: Records of the House of Representatives

Records of the House Committee on Un-American Activities

Records of the Federal Bureau of Investigation, unprocessed collection

National Archives and Records Administration, College Park, Md. (NARA II)

Record Group 126: Office of the Territories

Record Group 319: Records of the Army Staff, Investigative Records Repository

Record Group 335: Records of the Office of the Secretary of the Army

National Archives and Records Administration, New York, N.Y. (NARA-NY)

Record Group 21: Criminal Case Files

Personal Collection of Antonio Fernós (in author's possession)

Robert Houghwout Jackson Papers. Library of Congress, Washington D.C.

Ruth M. Reynolds Papers. Archives of the Puerto Rican Diaspora, Centro de Estudios Puertorriqueños, Hunter College, City University of New York.

Stuart Symington Papers. Western Historical Manuscript Collection, University of Missouri, Columbia.

Supreme Court Records and Briefs. Library of Congress, Washington D.C.

U.S. Citizenship and Immigration Services

Ellen Raphael Hartley File (in author's possession)

Vito Marcantonio Papers. New York Public Library.

William Langer Papers. Department of Special Collections, Chester Fritz Library, University of North Dakota, Grand Forks.

Works Cited

Acosta-Lespier, Ivonne. "The Smith Act Goes to San Juan: La Mordaza, 1948–1957." In Bosque-Pérez and Colón Morera, *Puerto Rico under Colonial Rule,* 59–66.

Adams, Mary Louise. *The Trouble with Normal: Postwar Youth and the Making of Heterosexuality.* Toronto: University of Toronto Press, 1997.

Agamben, Giorgio. *Homo Sacer: Sovereign Power and Bare Life.* Translated by Daniel Heller-Roazen. Stanford: Stanford University Press, 1998.

———. *State of Exception.* Translated by Kevin Attell. Chicago: University of Chicago Press, 2005.

Almond, Gabriel A. *The Appeals of Communism.* Princeton: Princeton University Press, 1954.

Alpers, Benjamin L. *Dictators, Democracy, and American Public Culture: Envisioning the Totalitarian Enemy, 1920s–1950s.* Chapel Hill: University of North Carolina Press, 2003.

Alsop, Joseph. "Miss Bentley's Bondage." *The Commonweal,* November 9, 1951, 120–21.

American Civil Liberties Union. *Censorship of Comic Books: A Statement in Opposition on Civil Liberties Grounds.* New York: American Civil Liberties Union, 1955.

Anderson, Carol. *Eyes Off the Prize: The United Nations and the African American Struggle for Human Rights, 1944–1955.* Cambridge: Cambridge University Press, 2003.

"Annie Lee Moss before the McCarthy Committee." In *Edward R. Murrow Collection: The McCarthy Years,* produced by Edward R. Murrow and Fred Friendly. New York: Ambrose Video Publishing, 1991. Videocassette.

Antler, Joyce. "A Bond of Sisterhood: Ethel Rosenberg, Molly Goldberg, and Radical Jewish Women of the 1950s." In *Secret Agents: The Rosenberg Case, McCarthyism, and Fifties America,* edited by Marjorie Garber and Rebecca L. Walkowitz, 197–214. New York: Routledge, 1995.

Aponte Vázquez, Pedro. *The Unsolved Case of Dr. Cornelius P. Rhoades: An Indictment.* San Juan: René Publications, 2005.

Arendt, Hannah. "The Concentration Camps." *Partisan Review* 15, no. 7 (July 1948): 743–63.

———. *Essays in Understanding, 1930–1954.* Edited by Jerome Kohn. New York: Harcourt, Brace, 1994.

———. "The Ex-Communists." In *Essays in Understanding,* 391–400.

———. "On the Nature of Totalitarianism: An Essay in Understanding." In *Essays in Understanding,* 328–60.

———. *The Origins of Totalitarianism.* Revised ed., 1958; repr., New York: Harcourt, Brace, 1973. First published in 1951.

Armstrong, O. K. "How Coral Gables Cleaned Up Its Newsstands." *Parents Magazine,* December 1957, 50–51, 76, 78.

Arnesen, Eric. "No 'Graver Danger': Black Anticommunism, the Communist Party, and the Race Question." *Labor: Studies in Working-Class History of the Americas* 3, no. 4 (2006): 13–52.

"The Assassination Attempt." *New Republic,* November 13, 1950, 6.

Ayala, César J., and Rafael Bernabe. *Puerto Rico in the American Century: A History since 1898.* Chapel Hill: University of North Carolina Press, 2007.

Ayala, César J., and Viviana Carro-Figueroa. "Expropriation and Displacement of Civilians in Vieques, 1940–1950." In Bosque-Pérez and Colón Morera, *Puerto Rico under Colonial Rule,* 173–205.

Baehr, Harry W. "Misused Idealism and Perverted Faith." *New York Herald Tribune Book Review,* March 25, 1951, 4.

Baehr, Peter. *Hannah Arendt, Totalitarianism, and the Social Sciences.* Stanford: Stanford University Press, 2010.

Barker, Martin. *A Haunt of Fears: The Strange History of the British Horror Comics Campaign.* Jackson: University Press of Mississippi, 1992.

Barth, Alan. *The Loyalty of Free Men.* New York: Viking, 1951.

Bauman, Zygmunt. *Modernity and Ambivalence.* Ithaca: Cornell University Press, 1991.

Beaty, Bart. *Fredric Wertham and the Critique of Mass Culture.* Jackson: University Press of Mississippi, 2005.

Beauford, Fred. *The Rejected American.* Irvington, N.J.: Morton Books, 1999.

Begeman, Jean. "What Ellen Knauff Won." *New Republic,* January 7, 1952, 14–15.

Belknap, Michal R. *Cold War Political Justice: The Smith Act, the Communist Party, and American Civil Liberties.* Westport, Conn.: Greenwood Press, 1977.

Bennett, Scott H. *Radical Pacifism: The War Resisters League and Gandhian Nonviolence in America, 1915–1963.* Syracuse: Syracuse University Press, 2003.

Bentley, Elizabeth. *Out of Bondage: The Story of Elizabeth Bentley.* New York: Devin-Adair Company, 1951.

Benton, Mike. *The Comic Book in America: An Illustrated History.* Dallas: Taylor Publishing, 1989.

Berg, Manfred. "Black Civil Rights and Liberal Anticommunism: The NAACP in the Early Cold War." *Journal of American History* 94, no. 1 (2007): 75–96.

Bergeron, Suzanne. *Fragments of Development: Nation, Gender, and the Space of Modernity.* Ann Arbor: University of Michigan Press, 2004.

Berlant, Lauren. *The Queen of America Goes to Washington City: Essays on Sex and Citizenship.* Durham: Duke University Press, 1997.

Bernstein, Carl. *Loyalties: A Son's Memoir.* New York: Simon and Schuster, 1989.

Berrett, Jesse. "Gresham's Law of Culture: The Case of Mickey Spillane and Postwar America." In *Scorned Literature: Essays on the History and Criticism of Popular Mass-Produced Fiction in America,* edited by Lydia Cushman Schurman and Deidre Johnson, 1–15. Westport, Conn.: Greenwood Press, 2002.

Bhana, Surendra. *The United States and the Development of the Puerto Rican Status Question, 1936–1968.* Lawrence: University Press of Kansas, 1975.

Bhattacharyya, Gargi. *Dangerous Brown Men: Exploiting Sex, Violence and Feminism in the War on Terror.* London: Zed Books, 2008.

Biddiscombe, Perry. "Dangerous Liaisons: The Anti-Fraternization Movement in the U.S. Occupation Zones of Germany and Austria, 1945–1948." *Journal of Social History* 34, no. 3 (2001): 611–47.

Biondi, Martha. *To Stand and Fight: The Struggle for Civil Rights in Postwar New York City.* Cambridge: Harvard University Press, 2003.

"Bloody Session." *Newsweek,* March 8, 1954, 22.

Bolland, O. Nigel. "Labor Protests, Rebellions, and the Rise of Nationalism during Depression and War." In Palmié and Scarano, *The Caribbean,* 459–74.

Bontecou, Eleanor. *The Federal Loyalty-Security Program.* Ithaca: Cornell University Press, 1953.

Bon Tempo, Carl J. *Americans at the Gate: The United States and Refugees during the Cold War.* Princeton: Princeton University Press, 2008.

Borchert, James. *Alley Life in Washington: Family, Community, Religion, and Folklife in the City, 1850–1970.* Urbana: University of Illinois Press, 1980.

Borgwardt, Elizabeth. *A New Deal for the World: America's Vision for Human Rights.* Cambridge: Harvard University Press, 2005.

Boris, Eileen. "'The Right to Work Is the Right to Live!' Fair Employment and the Quest for Social Citizenship." In *Two Cultures of Rights: The Quest for Inclusion and Participation in Modern America and Germany,* edited by Manfred Berg and Martin H. Geyer, 121–141. Washington, D.C.: German Historical Institute, 2002.

Borstelmann, Thomas. *The Cold War and the Color Line: American Race Relations in the Global Arena.* Cambridge: Harvard University Press, 2001.

Bosque-Pérez, Ramón. "Political Persecution against Puerto Rican Anti-Colonial Activists in the Twentieth Century." In Bosque-Pérez and Colón Morera, *Puerto Rico under Colonial Rule,* 13–47.

Bosque-Pérez, Ramón, and José Javier Colón Morera, eds. *Puerto Rico under Colonial Rule: Political Persecution and the Quest for Human Rights.* Albany: State University of New York Press, 2006.

Bossard, James H. "The Hazards of War Marriages." *Science Digest,* July 1944, 1–4.

Braukman, Stacy. *Communists and Perverts under the Palms: The Johns Committee in Florida, 1956–1965.* Gainesville: University Press of Florida, 2012.

Bredbenner, Candice Lewis. *A Nationality of Her Own: Women, Marriage, and the Law of Citizenship.* Berkeley: University of California Press, 1998.

Brennan, Sheila M. "Popular Images of American Women in the 1950's and Their Impact on Ethel Rosenberg's Trial and Conviction." *Women's Rights Law Reporter* 14, no. 1 (Winter 1992): 43–63.

Brick, Howard. "The Disenchantment of America: Radical Echoes in 1950s Political Criticism." In Donohue, *Liberty and Justice for All?,* 157–84.

Briggs, Laura. *Reproducing Empire: Race, Sex, Science, and U.S. Imperialism in Puerto Rico.* Berkeley: University of California Press, 2002.

Brown, Ralph S., Jr. *Loyalty and Security: Employment Tests in the United States.* New York: Da Capo, 1972.

Budenz, Louis Francis. *Men without Faces: The Communist Conspiracy in the U.S.A.* New York: Harper and Brothers, 1948.

———. *This Is My Story.* New York: McGraw-Hill, 1947.

Burnett, Christina Duffy. "Empire and the Transformation of Citizenship." In McCoy and Scarano, *Colonial Crucible,* 332–41.

Burnett, Christina Duffy, and Burke Marshall. "Between the Foreign and the Domestic: The Doctrine of Territorial Incorporation, Invented and Reinvented." In Burnett and Marshall, *Foreign in a Domestic Sense,* 1–36.

Burnett, Christina Duffy, and Burke Marshall, eds. *Foreign in a Domestic Sense: Puerto Rico, American Expansion, and the Constitution.* Durham: Duke University Press, 2001.

Bush, William. "Introduction." In Wertham, *The Circle of Guilt.* Jackson: University Press of Mississippi, 2007.

Cabranes, José A. "Citizenship and the American Empire: Notes on the Legislative History of the United States Citizenship of Puerto Ricans." *University of Pennsylvania Law Review* 127, no. 2 (1978): 391–492.

Canaday, Margot. "Building a Straight State: Sexuality and Social Citizenship under the 1944 GI Bill." *Journal of American History* 90, no. 3 (2003): 935–57.

———. *The Straight State: Sexuality and Citizenship in Twentieth-Century America.* Princeton: Princeton University Press, 2009.

Cancel Miranda, Rafael. "They Never Caged My Mind." Translated by Sue Ashdown. *New York Latino Journal,* March 6, 2005. http://nylatinojournal.com.

Carruthers, Susan L. *Cold War Captives: Imprisonment, Escape, and Brainwashing.* Berkeley: University of California Press, 2009.

"The Case of Marie Richardson Harris: The Victim of a Modern Witch Hunt." Pamphlet. Ca. 1952. In author's possession.

Caute, David. *The Great Fear: The Anti-Communist Purge under Truman and Eisenhower.* New York: Simon and Schuster, 1978.

Chafe, William. *Civilities and Civil Rights: Greensboro, North Carolina, and the Black Struggle for Freedom.* New York: Oxford University Press, 1980.

Chambers, Whittaker. *Witness.* New York: Random House, 1952.

Chang, Mariko. *Lifting as We Climb: Women of Color, Wealth, and America's Future.* Oakland: Insight Center for Community Economic Development, Spring 2010.

"Clinic for Sick Minds." *Life,* February 23, 1948, 99–100.

Cobb, William A. J. "Antidote to Revolution: African American Anticommunism and the Struggle for Civil Rights, 1931–1954." Ph.D. diss., Rutgers University, 2003.

Cohan, Steven. *Masked Men: Masculinity and the Movies in the Fifties.* Bloomington: Indiana University Press, 1997.

Cohen, Albert K. *Delinquent Boys: The Culture of the Gang.* Glencoe: Free Press, 1955.

Cohen, Elizabeth F. *Semi-Citizenship in Democratic Politics.* Cambridge: Cambridge University Press, 2009.

Cohen, Lizabeth. *A Consumers' Republic: The Politics of Mass Consumption in Postwar America.* New York: Vintage, 2003.

Collazo v. United States, 196 F.2d 573 (1952).
"Committee v. Chairman." *Time,* March 22, 1954, 27.
Communist Control Act of 1954. U.S. Statutes at Large, Public Law 637, ch. 886, 775–80.
Corber, Robert J. *Cold War Femme: Lesbianism, National Identity, and Hollywood Cinema.* Durham: Duke University Press, 2011.
———. *In the Name of National Security: Hitchcock, Homophobia, and the Political Construction of Gender in Postwar America.* Durham: Duke University Press, 1993.
Costigliola, Frank. "The Nuclear Family: Tropes of Gender and Pathology in the Western Alliance." *Diplomatic History* 21, no. 2 (1997): 163–83.
Cott, Nancy F. *Public Vows: A History of Marriage and the Nation.* Cambridge: Harvard University Press, 2000.
Coulter, Ann. *Treason: Liberal Treachery from the Cold War to the War on Terrorism.* New York: Crown Forum, 2003.
Cowley, Joyce. *The Santana Case: Tragedy of a Puerto Rican Youth.* New York: Pioneer Publishers, 1957.
Cox, Oliver C. "The Programs of Negro Civil Rights Organizations." *Journal of Negro Education* 20, no. 3 (1951): 354–66.
Crew, Spencer R. "Melding the Old and the New: The Modern African American Community, 1930–1960." In *Urban Odyssey: A Multicultural History of Washington, D.C.,* edited by Francine Cary, 208–30. Washington, D.C.: Smithsonian Institution Press, 1996.
"Crime Comics and the Constitution." *Stanford Law Review* 7, no. 2 (March 1955): 237–60.
"Crime: Return to the Poconos." *Time,* May 16, 1955, 30.
Crossman, Richard, ed. *The God That Failed.* New York: Harper and Brothers, 1949.
Cuordileone, K. A. *Manhood and American Political Culture in the Cold War.* New York: Routledge, 2005.
———. "'Politics in an Age of Anxiety': Cold War Political Culture and the Crisis in American Masculinity, 1949–1960." *Journal of American History* 87, no. 2 (2000): 515–45.
"A Dangerous Person." *Time,* August 27, 1951, 39.
Daniels, Roger. *Guarding the Golden Door: American Immigration Policy and Immigrants since 1882.* New York: Hill and Wang, 2004.
Davies, Carole Boyce. *Left of Karl Marx: The Political Life of Black Communist Claudia Jones.* Durham: Duke University Press, 2008.
Davis, Kenneth C. *Two-Bit Culture: The Paperbacking of America.* Boston: Houghton Mifflin, 1984.
Dean, Robert D. *Imperial Brotherhood: Gender and the Making of Cold War Foreign Policy.* Amherst: University of Massachusetts Press, 2003.
De Hart, Jane Sherron. "Containment at Home: Gender, Sexuality, and National Identity in Cold War America." In *Rethinking Cold War Culture,* edited by Peter Kuznick and James Gilbert, 124–55. Washington, D.C.: Smithsonian Institution Press, 2001.
Dekar, Paul R. *Creating the Beloved Community: A Journey with the Fellowship of Reconciliation.* Telford, Pa.: Cascadia Publishing, 2005.

D'Emilio, John. "The Homosexual Menace: The Politics of Sexuality in Cold War America." In *Passion and Power: Sexuality in History*, edited by Kathy Peiss and Christina Simmons, 226–40. Philadelphia: Temple University Press, 1989.

DeNavas-Walt, Carmen, Bernadette D. Proctor, and Jessica C. Smith. *Income, Poverty, and Health Insurance Coverage in the United States: 2011.* U.S. Census Bureau, Current Population Reports, P60-243. Washington, D.C.: GPO, 2012.

Dennis v. United States, 341 U.S. 494 (1951).

"Depends on the Way You've Been Brought Up." *National Review*, December 20, 1958, 395.

Díaz-Quiñones, Arcadio. *El arte de bregar.* San Juan: Ediciones Callejón, 2000.

Dietz, James L. *Economic History of Puerto Rico: Institutional Change and Capitalist Development.* Princeton: Princeton University Press, 1986.

Difo, Germain. "Enemies among Us: Domestic Radicalization after September 11." *Perspectives* (American Security Project), October 2010. http://americansecurityproject.org.

Dinnerstein, Leonard. *America and the Survivors of the Holocaust.* New York: Columbia University Press, 1982.

Documents on the Constitutional History of Puerto Rico. Vol. 2. Washington, D.C.: Office of the Commonwealth of Puerto Rico, 1964.

Doherty, Thomas. *Cold War, Cool Medium: Television, McCarthyism, and American Culture.* New York: Columbia University Press, 2003.

Donohue, Kathleen G., ed. *Liberty and Justice for All? Rethinking Politics in Cold War America.* Amherst: University of Massachusetts Press, 2012.

Donovan, Robert J. *The Assassins.* London: Elek Books, 1956.

———. "A Demonstration at Blair House." *New Yorker*, July 19, 1952, 31–55.

Downes v. Bidwell, 182 U.S. 244 (1901).

Doyle, Dennis. " 'A Fine New Child': The Lafargue Mental Hygiene Clinic and Harlem's African American Communities, 1946–1958." *Journal of the History of Medicine and Allied Sciences* 64, no. 2 (2009): 173–212.

———. " 'Where the Need Is Greatest': Social Psychiatry and Race-Blind Universalism in Harlem's Lafargue Clinic, 1946–1958." *Bulletin of the History of Medicine* 83, no. 4 (2009): 745–74.

Duany, Jorge. *The Puerto Rican Nation on the Move: Identities on the Island and in the United States.* Chapel Hill: University of North Carolina Press, 2002.

Duberman, Martin. *Paul Robeson.* New York: Knopf, 1989.

Du Bois, W. E. B. *The Souls of Black Folk.* Edited by Nathan Hare and Alvin F. Poussaint. New York: New American Library, 1982.

Dudziak, Mary L. *Cold War Civil Rights: Race and the Image of American Democracy.* Princeton: Princeton University Press, 2000.

———. "Josephine Baker, Racial Protest, and the Cold War." *Journal of American History* 81, no. 2 (1994): 543–70.

———. "Law, Power, and 'Rumors of War': Robert Jackson Confronts Law and Security after Nuremberg." *Buffalo Law Review* 60 (2012): 367–85.

Dunlap, David W. *Abyssinian to Zion: A Guide to Manhattan's Houses of Worship.* New York: Columbia University Press, 2004.

Ehrenreich, Barbara. *The Hearts of Men: American Dreams and the Flight from Commitment.* Garden City, N.Y.: Anchor Press, 1983.

Eisenhower, Dwight D. "Annual Message to Congress on the State of the Union." January 7, 1954. http://www.eisenhower.archives.gov.

El-Ayouty, Yassin. *The United Nations and Decolonization: The Role of Afro-Asia.* The Hague: Martinus Nijhoff, 1971.

Erman, Sam. "Meanings of Citizenship in the U.S. Empire: Puerto Rico, Isabel Gonzalez, and the Supreme Court, 1898 to 1905." *Journal of American Ethnic History* 27, no. 4 (2008): 5–33.

Ernst, Morris L., and David Loth. *Report on the American Communist.* New York: Henry Holt, 1952.

Escobar, Arturo. *Encountering Development: The Making and Unmaking of the Third World.* Princeton: Princeton University Press, 1995.

Estades-Font, María E. "The Critical Year of 1936 through the Reports of the Military Intelligence Division." In Bosque-Pérez and Colón Morera, *Puerto Rico under Colonial Rule,* 49–66.

Evans, M. Stanton. *Blacklisted by History: The Untold Story of Senator Joe McCarthy and His Fight against America's Enemies.* New York: Three Rivers Press, 2007.

"Expatriation Act of 1954." *Congressional Record* 100 (1954): 11281–82.

Farmer, James. *Lay Bare the Heart: An Autobiography of the Civil Rights Movement.* 1985. Fort Worth: Texas Christian University Press, 2013.

Feder, Edward L. *Comic Book Regulation.* Berkeley: University of California, 1955.

Feeley, John J., Jr. *Brookland.* Charleston, S.C.: Arcadia Publishing, 2011.

Feldstein, Ruth. "'I Wanted the Whole World to See': Race, Gender, and Constructions of Motherhood in the Death of Emmett Till." In Meyerowitz, *Not June Cleaver,* 263–303.

———. *Motherhood in Black and White: Race and Sex in American Liberalism, 1930–1965.* Ithaca: Cornell University Press, 2000.

Fernós, Antonio, ed. "Documentos secretos de la intervención política norteamericana en Puerto Rico (1935–1987)." *Revista jurídica de la Universidad Interamericana de Puerto Rico* 31, no. 1 (1996): 1–147.

Fernós Isern, Antonio. "The Mind of Puerto Rico." In *Addresses of Antonio Fernós-Isern,* 5–22. Washington, D.C.: Office of Puerto Rico, 1947.

Findlay, Eileen J. *Imposing Decency: The Politics of Sexuality and Race in Puerto Rico, 1870–1920.* Durham: Duke University Press, 1999.

———. "Love in the Tropics: Marriage, Divorce, and the Construction of Benevolent Colonialism in Puerto Rico, 1898–1910." In *Close Encounters of Empire: Writing the Cultural History of U.S.-Latin American Relations,* edited by Gilbert M. Joseph, Catherine LeGrand, and Ricardo D. Salvatore, 139–72. Durham: Duke University Press, 1998.

———. *We Are Left without a Father Here: Masculinity, Domesticity, and Migration in Postwar Puerto Rico.* Forthcoming, Duke University Press.

Fleming, John V. *The Anti-Communist Manifestos: Four Books That Shaped the Cold War.* New York: Norton, 2009.

Foner, Philip S. *Paul Robeson Speaks: Writings, Speeches, Interviews, 1918–1974.* New York: Brunner/Mazel, 1978.

Foster, Stephen, ed. *The Project MKULTRA Compendium: The CIA's Program of Research in Behavioral Modification.* Privately printed, 2009.

Fousek, John. *To Lead the Free World: American Nationalism and the Cultural Roots of the Cold War.* Chapel Hill: University of North Carolina Press, 2000.

Fox, Richard G. "Passage from India." In *Between Resistance and Revolution: Cultural Politics and Social Protest,* edited by Richard G. Fox and Orin Starn, 65–82. New Brunswick: Rutgers University Press, 1997.

Frank, Waldo. "Puerto Rico and Psychosis." *The Nation,* March 13, 1954, 210–11.

Fraser, Nancy, and Linda Gordon. "A Genealogy of Dependency: Tracing a Keyword of the U.S. Welfare State." *Signs: Journal of Women in Culture and Society* 19, no. 2 (1994): 309–36.

Fraterrigo, Elizabeth. *"Playboy" and the Making of the Good Life in Modern America.* New York: Oxford University Press, 2009.

Friedman, Andrea. "The Empire at Home: Radical Pacifism and Puerto Rico in the 1950s." Paper presented at A New Insurgency: The Port Huron Statement in Its Time and Ours Conference, Ann Arbor, 2013.

———. "Sadists and Sissies: Anti-Pornography Campaigns in Cold War America." *Gender & History* 15, no. 2 (2003): 201–27.

Friendly, Fred R. *Due to Circumstances Beyond Our Control. . . .* New York: Random House, 1967.

Fromm, Erich. *Escape from Freedom.* 1941. New York: Henry Holt, 1994.

Garcia Muñiz, Humberto. "U.S. Military Installations in Puerto Rico: Controlling the Caribbean." In Meléndez and Meléndez, *Colonial Dilemma,* 53–65.

Gardner, Martha. *The Qualities of a Citizen: Women, Immigration, and Citizenship, 1870–1965.* Princeton: Princeton University Press, 2005.

Garrison, Dee. " 'Our Skirts Gave Them Courage': The Civil Defense Protest Movement in New York City, 1955–1961." In Meyerowitz, *Not June Cleaver,* 201–26.

Gellhorn, Walter. *Security, Loyalty, and Science.* Ithaca: Cornell University Press, 1950.

Gellman, Erik S. *Death Blow to Jim Crow: The National Negro Congress and the Rise of Militant Civil Rights.* Chapel Hill: University of North Carolina Press, 2012.

Geltzer, Joshua Alexander. "Of Suspension, Due Process, and Guantanamo: The Reach of the Fifth Amendment after Boumediene and the Relationship between Habeas Corpus and Due Process." *Journal of Constitutional Law* 14, no. 3 (2012): 719–80.

General Federation Clubwoman. 1954–1957.

Genizi, Haim. *America's Fair Share: The Admission and Resettlement of Displaced Persons, 1945–1952.* Detroit: Wayne State University Press, 1993.

Gerson, Deborah A. " 'Is Family Devotion Now Subversive?' Familialism against McCarthyism." In Meyerowitz, *Not June Cleaver,* 151–76.

Gilbert, James B. *A Cycle of Outrage: America's Reaction to the Juvenile Delinquent in the 1950s.* New York: Oxford University Press, 1986.

Gilmore, Glenda Elizabeth. *Gender and Jim Crow: Women and the Politics of White Supremacy in North Carolina, 1896–1920.* Chapel Hill: University of North Carolina Press, 1996.

Glenn, Evelyn Nakano. *Unequal Freedom: How Race and Gender Shaped American Citizenship and Labor.* Cambridge: Harvard University Press, 2002.

Goldstein, Eric L. *The Price of Whiteness: Jews, Race, and American Identity.* Princeton: Princeton University Press, 2006.

Goliszek, Andrew. *In the Name of Science: A History of Secret Programs, Medical Research, and Human Experimentation.* New York: St. Martin's Press, 2003.

Goodman, Giora. "'Only the Best British Brides': Regulating the Relationship between U.S. Servicemen and British Women in the Early Cold War." *Contemporary European History* 17, no. 4 (2008): 483–503.

Gore, Dayo F. *Radicalism at the Crossroads: African American Women Activists in the Cold War.* New York: New York University Press, 2011.

Gosse, Van. *Where the Boys Are: Cuba, Cold War America, and the Making of a New Left.* New York: Verso, 1993.

Gottsegen, Michael G. *The Political Thought of Hannah Arendt.* Albany: State University of New York Press, 1994.

Gouda, Frances. "Gender and 'Hyper-Masculinity' as Post-Colonial Modernity during Indonesia's Struggle for Independence, 1945 to 1949." In *Gender, Sexuality, and Colonial Modernities,* edited by Antoinette Burton, 161–74. New York: Routledge, 1999.

———. "Languages of Gender and Neurosis in the Indonesian Struggle for Independence, 1945–1949." *Indonesia* 64 (October 1997): 45–76.

Green, Constance McLaughlin. *The Secret City: A History of Race Relations in the Nation's Capital.* Princeton: Princeton University Press, 1967.

Grosfoguel, Ramón. *Colonial Subjects: Puerto Ricans in a Global Perspective.* Berkeley: University of California Press, 2003.

Hajdu, David. *The Ten-Cent Plague: The Great Comic-Book Scare and How It Changed America.* New York: Farrar, Straus and Giroux, 2008.

Halpern, Martin. "'I'm Fighting for Freedom': Coleman Young, HUAC, and the Detroit African American Community." *Journal of American Ethnic History* 17, no. 1 (Fall 1997): 19–38.

Harrell, Erika. "Black Victims of Violent Crime." *National Criminal Justice* (NCJ) 214258. Washington, D.C.: U.S. Department of Justice, 2007.

Hartmann, Susan M. "Women's Employment and the Domestic Ideal in the Early Cold War Years." In Meyerowitz, *Not June Cleaver,* 84–100.

Haynes, John Earl. "Reconsidering Two Questions: On Arnesen's 'No Graver Danger'; Black Anticommunism, the Communist Party, and the Race Question." *Labor: Studies in Working-Class History of the Americas* 3, no. 4 (2006): 53–57.

Heale, M. J. *American Anticommunism: Combating the Enemy Within, 1830–1970.* Baltimore: Johns Hopkins University Press, 1990.

———. *McCarthy's Americans: Red Scare Politics in State and Nation, 1935–1965.* London: Macmillan, 1998.

Helfeld, David M. *Discrimination for Political Beliefs and Associations.* San Juan: Revista del Colegio de Abogados de Puerto Rico, 1964.

Hendershot, Cyndy. *Anti-Communism and Popular Culture in Mid-Century America.* Jefferson, N.C.: McFarland & Company, 2003.

Herman, Arthur. *Joseph McCarthy: Reexamining the Life and Legacy of America's Most Hated Senator.* New York: Free Press, 2000.

Herman, Ellen. *The Romance of American Psychology: Political Culture in the Age of Experts.* Berkeley: University of California Press, 1995.

Herndon, Booton. "Secret Agent in Apron Strings." *Redbook,* February 1952, 30–31, 79–92.

Hicks, Granville. "The Appeal of Communism." *Commentary,* March 1950, 291–92.

Higginbotham, Evelyn Brooks. "African-American Women's History and the Metalanguage of Race." *Signs: Journal of Women in Culture and Society* 17, no. 2 (1992): 251–74.

Hine, Darlene Clark. "Rape and the Inner Lives of Black Women in the Middle West: Preliminary Thoughts on the Culture of Dissemblance." In *Unequal Sisters: A Multicultural Reader in U.S. Women's History,* edited by Ellen Carol DuBois and Vicki L. Ruiz, 292–97. New York: Routledge, 1990.

Hirsch, Arnold R. "Massive Resistance in the Urban North: Trumbull Park, Chicago, 1953–1966." *Journal of American History* 82, no. 2 (1995): 522–50.

Hoffman, Bruce. *Inside Terrorism.* New York: Columbia University Press, 1998.

Hogan, Michael J. *A Cross of Iron: Harry S. Truman and the Origins of the National Security State, 1945–1954.* Cambridge: Cambridge University Press, 1998.

Hoganson, Kristin L. *Fighting for American Manhood: How Gender Politics Provoked the Spanish-American and Philippine-American Wars.* New Haven: Yale University Press, 1998.

Honig, Bonnie. *Democracy and the Foreigner.* Princeton: Princeton University Press, 2001.

Hoover, J. Edgar. *Masters of Deceit: The Story of Communism in America and How to Fight It.* New York: Henry Holt, 1958.

Horne, Gerald. *Black Liberation/Red Scare: Ben Davis and the Communist Party.* Newark: University of Delaware Press, 1994.

———. *Communist Front? The Civil Rights Congress, 1946–1956.* Rutherford, N.J.: Fairleigh Dickinson University Press, 1988.

Hull, Elizabeth. *Without Justice for All: The Constitutional Rights of Aliens.* Westport, Conn.: Greenwood Press, 1985.

Hunt, Andrew E. *David Dellinger: The Life and Times of a Nonviolent Revolutionary.* New York: New York University Press, 2006.

Hunt, Lynn. *Inventing Human Rights: A History.* New York: W. W. Norton & Company, 2007.

Hunter, Stephen, and John Bainbridge. *American Gunfight: The Plot to Kill Harry Truman—and the Shoot-Out That Stopped It.* New York: Simon & Schuster, 2005.

Hutchinson, Earl Ofari. *Blacks and Reds: Race and Class in Conflict, 1919–1990.* East Lansing: Michigan State University Press, 1995.

I Was a Male War Bride. Dir. Howard Hawks. Twentieth Century Fox, 1949. DVD, 2004.

"In the Matter of the Relation of the Government of Puerto Rico to the United States of America." Excerpted in "Symposium: Is Puerto Rico Fully Self-Governing." *Journal of Human Relations* 2, no. 1 (1953): 88–111.

"Insurrection." *Time*, November 13, 1950, 38.

Internal Security Act of 1950. U.S. Statutes at Large, 81st Cong., 2nd sess., Ch. 1024, 987–1031.

Jackson, Walter A. *Gunnar Myrdal and America's Conscience: Social Engineering and Racial Liberalism, 1938–1987.* Chapel Hill: University of North Carolina Press, 1990.

Jacobs, Meg. *Pocketbook Politics: Economic Citizenship in Twentieth-Century America.* Princeton: Princeton University Press, 2005.

Jacobson, Matthew Frye. *Whiteness of a Different Color: European Immigrants and the Alchemy of Race.* Cambridge: Harvard University Press, 1998.

Jacobson, Matthew Frye, and Gaspar González. *What Have They Built You to Do? The Manchurian Candidate and Cold War America.* Minneapolis: University of Minnesota Press, 2006.

Jay, Martin. *The Dialectical Imagination: A History of the Frankfurt School and the Institute of Social Research, 1923–1950.* Berkeley: University of California Press, 1973.

Jenkins, Philip. *The Cold War at Home: The Red Scare in Pennsylvania, 1945–1960.* Chapel Hill: University of North Carolina Press, 1999.

Johnson, David K. *The Lavender Scare: The Cold War Persecution of Gays and Lesbians in the Federal Government.* Chicago: University of Chicago Press, 2004.

Jones, John Paul. "Expatriation." In *The Encyclopedia of American Civil Liberties*, edited by Paul Finkelman. New York: Routledge, 2006.

Kalven, Harry. *A Worthy Tradition: Freedom of Speech in America.* New York: Harper and Row, 1988.

Kelley, Robin D. G. *Hammer and Hoe: Alabama Communists during the Great Depression.* Chapel Hill: University of North Carolina Press, 1990.

Kelly, John D., and Martha Kaplan. *Represented Communities: Fiji and World Decolonization.* Chicago: University of Chicago Press, 2001.

Kerber, Linda K. *No Constitutional Right to Be Ladies: Women and the Obligations of Citizenship.* New York: Hill & Wang, 1998.

———. "The Stateless as the Citizen's Other: A View from the United States." *American Historical Review* 112, no. 1 (2007): 1–34.

Kessler, Lauren. *Clever Girl: Elizabeth Bentley, the Spy Who Ushered in the McCarthy Era.* New York: HarperCollins Publishers, 2003.

Kessler-Harris, Alice. *In Pursuit of Equity: Women, Men, and the Quest for Economic Citizenship in 20th-Century America.* New York: Oxford University Press, 2001.

Knauff, Ellen Raphael. *The Ellen Knauff Story.* New York: Norton, 1952.

"The Knauff Scandal." *The Nation*, May 27, 1950, 515–16.

Korstad, Robert Rodgers. *Civil Rights Unionism: Tobacco Workers and the Struggle for Democracy in the Mid-Twentieth-Century South.* Chapel Hill: University of North Carolina Press, 2003.

Kosek, J. K. *Acts of Conscience: Christian Nonviolence and Modern American Democracy.* New York: Columbia University Press, 2009.

Kramer, Paul A. *The Blood of Government: Race, Empire, the United States, and the Philippines.* Chapel Hill: University of North Carolina Press, 2006.

Krugman, Herbert E. "The Role of Hostility in the Appeal of Communism in the United States." *Psychiatry* 16 (August 1953): 253–61.

Kushner, Tony. *Angels in America: A Gay Fantasia on National Themes.* New York: Theatre Communications Group, 1995.

Landis, Kenesaw M. *Segregation in Washington: A Report of the National Committee on Segregation in the Nation's Capital.* Chicago, 1948.

Langley, Lester D. *The United States and the Caribbean in the Twentieth Century.* 4th ed. Athens: University of Georgia Press, 1989.

Lauren, Paul Gordon. *The Evolution of International Human Rights: Visions Seen.* 3rd ed. Philadelphia: University of Pennsylvania Press, 2011.

Laville, Helen, and Scott Lucas. "The American Way: Edith Sampson, the NAACP, and African American Identity in the Cold War." *Diplomatic History* 20, no. 4 (Fall 1996): 565–90.

Law, Randall D. *Terrorism: A History.* Malden, Mass.: Polity Press, 2009.

Lederer, Susan E. "The Cold War and Beyond: Covert and Deceptive American Medical Experimentation." In *Military Medical Ethics,* vol. 2, edited by Thomas E. Beam and Linette R. Sparacino, 507–31. Washington, D.C.: Borden Institute, 2003.

———. "'Porto Ricochet': Joking about Germs, Cancer, and Race Extermination in the 1930s." *American Literary History* 14, no. 4 (2002): 720–46.

Leffler, Melvyn P. *For the Soul of Mankind: The United States, the Soviet Union, and the Cold War.* New York: Hill and Wang, 2007.

———. "National Security." *Journal of American History* 77, no. 1 (1990): 143–52.

———. *A Preponderance of Power: National Security, the Truman Administration, and the Cold War.* Stanford: Stanford University Press, 1992.

Legman, Gershon. *Love and Death: A Study in Censorship.* New York: Hacker Art Books, 1963.

——— [Gerson]. "The Comic Books and the Public." *American Journal of Psychotherapy* 2, no. 3 (1948): 473–77.

Leibowitz, Arnold H. *Defining Status: A Comprehensive Analysis of United States Territorial Relations.* Boston: Martinus Nijhoff Publishers, 1989.

LeMay, Michael C. *Guarding the Gates: Immigration and National Security.* Westport, Conn.: Praeger Security International, 2006.

Lent, John A., ed. *Pulp Demons: International Dimensions of the Postwar Anti-Comics Campaign.* Madison, N.J.: Fairleigh Dickinson University Press, 1999.

Lerner, Max. *America as a Civilization: Life and Thought in the United States Today.* New York: Simon and Schuster, 1957.

———. *The Unfinished Country: A Book of American Symbols.* New York: Simon and Schuster, 1959.

Lewis, Anthony. "Security and Liberty: Preserving the Values of Freedom." In *The War on Our Freedoms: Civil Liberties in an Age of Terrorism,* edited by Richard C. Leone and Greg Anrig Jr., 47–73. New York: Public Affairs, 2003.

Lewis, Carolyn Herbst. *Prescription for Heterosexuality: Sexual Citizenship in the Cold War Era.* Chapel Hill: University of North Carolina Press, 2010.

Lewis, George. *The White South and the Red Menace: Segregationists, Anticommunism, and Massive Resistance, 1945–1965.* Gainesville: University Press of Florida, 2004.

Lewis, Gordon K. *Puerto Rico: Freedom and Power in the Caribbean.* New York: MR Press, 1963.

Lichtblau, John H. "A Recruiter Confesses." *Saturday Review of Literature,* April 14, 1951, 56–57.

Lichtman, Robert M., and Ronald D. Cohen. *Deadly Farce: Harvey Matusow and the Informer System in the McCarthy Era.* Urbana: University of Illinois Press, 2004.

Lindner, Robert. *Must You Conform?* 1956. New York: Grove Press, 1961.

Luibhéid, Eithne. *Entry Denied: Controlling Sexuality at the Border.* Minneapolis: University of Minnesota Press, 2002.

Lynn, Conrad. *There Is a Fountain: The Autobiography of a Civil Rights Lawyer.* Westport, Conn.: Lawrence Hill and Company, 1979.

Lynn, Susan. *Progressive Women in Conservative Times: Racial Justice, Peace, and Feminism, 1945 to the 1960s.* New Brunswick: Rutgers University Press, 1992.

Maccoby, Michael. "Violence and the Mass Media." *New Republic,* January 14, 1957, 19–20.

MacLean, Nancy. *Freedom Is Not Enough: The Opening of the American Workplace.* New York: Russell Sage Foundation, 2006.

Macpherson, Anne S. "Toward Decolonization: Impulses, Processes, and Consequences since the 1930s." In Palmié and Scarano, *The Caribbean,* 475–89.

Malavet, Pedro A. *America's Colony: The Political and Cultural Conflict between the United States and Puerto Rico.* New York: New York University Press, 2004.

Maldonado, A. W. *Luis Muñoz Marín: Puerto Rico's Democratic Revolution.* San Juan: La Editorial, Universidad de Puerto Rico, 2006.

Marshall, T. H. *Citizenship and Social Class, and Other Essays.* Cambridge: Cambridge University Press, 1950.

Martin, Ralph G. "Doctor's Dream in Harlem." *New Republic,* June 3, 1946, 798–800.

Masco, Joseph. *The Nuclear Borderlands: The Manhattan Project in Post–Cold War New Mexico.* Princeton: Princeton University Press, 2006.

Massing, Hede. *This Deception.* New York: Duell, Sloan and Pearce, 1951.

Matteo, Henry S. *Denationalization v. "The Right to Have Rights."* Lanham, Md.: University Press of America, 1997.

May, Elaine Tyler. *Homeward Bound: American Families in the Cold War Era.* Revised ed. New York: Basic Books, 2008.

McCann, Joseph T. *Terrorism on American Soil: A Concise History of Plots and Perpetrators from the Famous to the Forgotten.* Boulder, Colo.: Sentient Publications, 2006.

McCoy, Alfred W. *Policing America's Empire: The United States, the Philippines, and the Rise of the Surveillance State.* Madison: University of Wisconsin Press, 2009.

McCoy, Alfred W., and Francisco A. Scarano, eds. *Colonial Crucible: Empire in the Making of the Modern American State.* Madison: University of Wisconsin Press, 2009.

McDuffie, Erik S. *Sojourning for Freedom: Black Women, American Communism, and the Making of Black Left Feminism.* Durham: Duke University Press, 2011.

McEnaney, Laura. *Civil Defense Begins at Home: Militarization Meets Everyday Life in the Fifties.* Princeton: Princeton University Press, 2000.

———. "Cold War Mobilization and Domestic Politics: The United States." In *Cambridge*

History of the Cold War, vol. 1, edited by Melvyn P. Leffler and Odd Arne Westad, 420–41. New York: Cambridge University Press, 2010.

McLaughlin, Neil. "Critical Theory Meets America: Riesman, Fromm, and The Lonely Crowd." *American Sociologist* 32, no. 1 (Spring 2001): 5–26.

Meléndez, Edwin, and Edgardo Meléndez, eds. *Colonial Dilemma: Critical Perspectives on Contemporary Puerto Rico.* Boston: South End Press, 1993.

Mendes, Gabriel N. "A Deeper Science: Richard Wright, Dr. Fredric Wertham, and the Fight for Mental Healthcare in Harlem, NY, 1940–1960." Ph.D. diss., Brown University, 2010.

Meyerowitz, Joanne. "'How Common Culture Shapes the Separate Lives': Sexuality, Race, and Mid-Twentieth-Century Social Constructionist Thought." *Journal of American History* 96, no. 4 (2010): 1057–84.

———, ed. *Not June Cleaver: Women and Gender in Postwar America, 1945–1960.* Philadelphia: Temple University Press, 1994.

———. "Sex, Gender, and the Cold War Language of Reform." In *Rethinking Cold War Culture,* edited by Peter J. Kuznick and James Gilbert, 106–23. Washington, D.C.: Smithsonian Institution Press, 2001.

———. "Women, Cheesecake, and Borderline Material: Responses to Girlie Pictures in the Mid-Twentieth-Century U.S." *Journal of Women's History* 8, no. 3 (1996): 9–35.

Miller, James G., and Jessie L. Miller. Review of *Witness. University of Chicago Law Review* 20 (1953), 598–604.

Miller, Merle. "Memoirs from Sanctuary." *New Republic,* May 26, 1952, 19–20.

Mitchell, Marcia, and Thomas Mitchell. *The Spy Who Seduced America: Lies and Betrayal in the Heat of the Cold War; The Judith Coplon Story.* Montpelier, Vt.: Invisible Cities Press, 2002.

Mollin, Marian. *Radical Pacifism in Modern America: Egalitarianism and Protest.* Philadelphia: University of Pennsylvania Press, 2006.

Morris, Richard B. "Chambers's Litmus Paper Test." *Saturday Review of Literature,* May 24, 1952, 13.

Mosse, Hilde L. "Aggression and Violence in Fantasy and Fact." *American Journal of Psychotherapy* 2, no. 3 (July 1948): 477–83.

Muhlen, Norbert. "Comic Books and Other Horrors: Prep School for Totalitarian Society?" *Commentary,* January 1949, 80–87.

Muñoz-Pogossian, Betilde V. "Gendered Language and (Unequal) Power: Deconstructing U.S.–Latin American Relations in the Early Cold War." *International Politics* 45 (2008): 703–19.

Murray, Alex. *Giorgio Agamben.* Routledge Critical Thinkers. New York: Routledge, 2010.

Murray, Sylvie. *The Progressive Housewife: Community Activism in Suburban Queens, 1945–1965.* Philadelphia: University of Pennsylvania Press, 2003.

Muste, A. J. "The Communists Gain." *The Christian Century,* December 15, 1954, 1521–22.

Myrdal, Gunnar. *An American Dilemma: The Negro Problem and Modern Democracy.* New York: Harper and Brothers, 1944.

Naison, Mark. *Communists in Harlem during the Depression.* New York: Grove Press, 1984.

Navasky, Victor S. *Naming Names.* 3rd. ed. New York: Hill and Wang, 2003.

Negrón-Muntaner, Frances, ed. *None of the Above: Puerto Ricans in the Global Era.* New York: Palgrave Macmillan, 2007.

Nelson, Deborah. *Pursuing Privacy in Cold War America.* New York: Columbia University Press, 2002.

Neptune, Harvey R. *Caliban and the Yankees.* Chapel Hill: University of North Carolina Press, 2007.

Neuman, Gerald L. *Strangers to the Constitution: Immigrants, Borders, and Fundamental Law.* Princeton: Princeton University Press, 1996.

The New York Times Company v. U.S. Department of Justice, 11 CIV. 9336 CM (S.D.N.Y. Jan. 3, 2013).

Ngai, Mae. *Impossible Subjects: Illegal Aliens and the Making of Modern America.* Princeton: Princeton University Press, 2004.

Noon, David Hoogland. "Cold War Revival: Neoconservatives and Historical Memory in the War on Terror." *American Studies* 48, no. 3 (Fall 2007): 75–99.

Novak, William J. "The Legal Transformation of Citizenship in Nineteenth-Century America." In *The Democratic Experiment: New Directions in American Political History,* edited by Meg Jacobs, William J. Novak, and Julian E. Zelizer, 85–119. Princeton: Princeton University Press, 2003.

Nyberg, Amy Kiste. *Seal of Approval: The History of the Comics Code.* Jackson: University Press of Mississippi, 1998.

Olmsted, Kathryn S. "Blond Queens, Red Spiders, and Neurotic Old Maids: Gender and Espionage in the Early Cold War." *Intelligence and National Security* 19, no. 1 (2004): 78–94.

———. *Red Spy Queen: A Biography of Elizabeth Bentley.* Chapel Hill: University of North Carolina Press, 2002.

Oshinsky, David M. *A Conspiracy So Immense: The World of Joe McCarthy.* New York: Collier Macmillan, 1983.

Painter, Nell Irvin. "Hill, Thomas, and the Use of Racial Stereotype." In *Race-ing Justice, En-gendering Power: Essays on Anita Hill, Clarence Thomas, and the Construction of Social Reality,* edited by Toni Morrison, 200–214. New York: Pantheon Books, 1992.

Palmié, Stephan, and Francisco A. Scarano, eds. *The Caribbean: A History of the Region and Its Peoples.* Chicago: University of Chicago Press, 2011.

Paralitici, José (Ché). "Imprisonment and Colonial Domination, 1898–1958." In Bosque-Pérez and Colón Morera, *Puerto Rico under Colonial Rule,* 67–82.

Parker, Alison M. *Purifying America: Women, Cultural Reform, and Pro-Censorship Activism, 1873–1933.* Urbana: University of Illinois Press, 1997.

Parker, Jason C. *Brother's Keeper: The United States, Race, and Empire in the British Caribbean, 1937–1962.* New York: Oxford University Press, 2008.

Pateman, Carole. "The Fraternal Social Contract." In *Civil Society and the State: New European Perspectives,* edited by John Keane, 101–27. New York: Verso Books, 1988.

Patil, Vrushali. *Negotiating Decolonization in the United Nations: Politics of Space, Identity, and International Community.* New York: Routledge, 2008.

Patterson, William, ed. *We Charge Genocide: The Historic Petition to the United Nations for Relief from a Crime of the United States Government against the Negro People.* 2nd ed. New York: International Publishers, 1970.

Pease, Donald. "Re-thinking 'American Studies after U.S. Exceptionalism.'" *American Literary History* 21, no. 1 (2009): 19–26.

Pederson, Vernon L. *The Communist Party in Maryland, 1919–57.* Urbana: University of Illinois Press, 2001.

———. "Perfect Witness: Mary Stalcup Markward and the Dilemmas of Anticommunism." *American Communist History* 8, no. 1 (2009): 29–48.

People v. Santana, 25 N.Y. 2d 827 (1969).

Perucci, Tony. "The Red Mask of Sanity: Paul Robeson, HUAC, and the Sound of Cold War Performance." *Drama Review* 53, no. 4 (2009): 18–48.

Peterson, Theodore. *Magazines in the Twentieth Century.* Urbana: University of Illinois Press, 1964.

Petrullo, Vincenzo. *Puerto Rican Paradox.* Philadelphia: University of Pennsylvania Press, 1947.

Pfaff, Daniel W. *Joseph Pulitzer II and the "Post-Dispatch": A Newspaperman's Life.* University Park: Pennsylvania State University Press, 1991.

Philbrick, Herbert A. *I Led 3 Lives: Citizen, "Communist," Counterspy.* New York: Grosset and Dunlap, 1951.

Pilat, Oliver. "Repudiation of a Lost Decade." *Saturday Review of Literature,* December 1, 1951, 58.

Ploscowe, Morris. "The Criminal as Patient." *The Nation,* March 9, 1957, 220.

"Plots against U.S. by Terrorists." *U.S. News & World Report,* March 12, 1954, 21–25.

Plummer, Brenda Gayle, ed. *Window on Freedom: Race, Civil Rights, and Foreign Affairs, 1845–1988.* Chapel Hill: University of North Carolina Press, 2003.

"The Port Huron Statement." Reprint. New York: Students for a Democratic Society, 1964.

Power, Margaret. "Pedro Albizu Campos." In *Encyclopedia of Latino American History,* edited by D. H. Figueredo. New York: Facts on File, forthcoming.

Powers, Richard Gid. *Not Without Honor: The History of American Anticommunism.* New York: Free Press, 1995.

"Psychiatry in Harlem." *Time,* December 1, 1947, 50–52.

"Puerto Rico." *Time,* November 13, 1950, 38.

"Puerto Rico Revolt Endangers Truman." *Life,* November 13, 1950, 25–29.

Radosh, Ronald, and Joyce Milton. *The Rosenberg File.* 2nd ed. New Haven: Yale University Press, 1997.

Record, Wilson. *Race and Radicalism: The NAACP and the Communist Party in Conflict.* Ithaca: Cornell University Press, 1964.

Reeves, Thomas C. *The Life and Times of Joe McCarthy.* Lanham, Md.: Madison Books, 1997.

Renda, Mary A. *Taking Haiti: Military Occupation and the Culture of U.S. Imperialism, 1915–1940.* Chapel Hill: University of North Carolina Press, 2001.

Report of the New York State Joint Legislative Committee to Study the Publication of Comics. Albany: Williams Press, 1955.

"Reprieve." *Time,* May 29, 1950, 18.

"Reprieve for Ellen." *Newsweek,* May 29, 1950, 19.

Reynolds, Ruth M. *Campus in Bondage: A 1948 Microcosm of Puerto Rico in Bondage.* Edited by Carlos Rodríguez Fraticelli and Blanca Vázquez Erazo. New York: Centro de Estudios Puertorriqueños, 1989.

Ribes Tovar, Federico. *Lolita Lebrón: la prisionera.* New York: Plus Ultra Educational, 1974.

Ritter, Gretchen. "Domestic Containment or Equal Standing? Gender, Nationalism, and the War on Terror." *Journal of Policy History* 21, no. 4 (2009): 439–47.

Roberts, Dorothy E. "The Social and Moral Cost of Mass Incarceration in African American Communities." *Stanford Law Review* 56, no. 5 (2004): 1271–1305.

Robin, Corey. "Remembrance of Empires Past: 9/11 and the End of the Cold War." In *Cold War Triumphalism: The Misuse of History after the Fall of Communism,* edited by Ellen Schrecker, 274–97. New York: New Press, 2004.

Rodgers, Daniel T. *Contested Truths: Keywords in American Politics since Independence.* Cambridge: Harvard University Press, 1987.

Rodríguez Beruff, Jorge. "From Winship to Leahy: Crisis, War, and Transition in Puerto Rico." In McCoy and Scarano, *Colonial Crucible,* 431–40.

Rodríguez Fraticelli, Carlos. "U.S. Solidarity with Puerto Rico: Rockwell Kent, 1937." In Meléndez and Meléndez, *Colonial Dilemma,* 189–98.

Rogin, Michael Paul. *Ronald Reagan, the Movie: And Other Episodes in Political Demonology.* Berkeley: University of California Press, 1987.

Rohr, Marc. "Communists and the First Amendment: The Shaping of Freedom of Advocacy in the Cold War Era." *San Diego Law Review* 28, no. 1 (1991): 1–116.

Román, Ediberto. *The Other American Colonies: An International and Constitutional Law Examination of the United States' Nineteenth and Twentieth Century Island Conquests.* Durham: Carolina Academic Press, 2006.

"The Roots of Tragedy." *The Nation.* November 11, 1950, 423.

Rosado, Marisa. *Las llamas de la Aurora : Acercamiento a una biografía de Pedro Albizu Campos.* Biblioteca del Caribe. San Juan: Ediciones Puerto, 2006.

Rosenberg, Emily S. "Commentary: The Cold War and the Discourse of National Security." *Diplomatic History* 17, no. 2 (1993): 277–84.

———. "Gender." *Journal of American History* 77 (June 1990): 116–24.

Rosteck, Thomas. *"See It Now" Confronts McCarthyism: Television Documentary and the Politics of Representation.* Tuscaloosa: University of Alabama Press, 1994.

Rung, Margaret C. "United Public Workers of America / United Federal Workers of America." In *Encyclopedia of U.S. Labor and Working-Class History,* vol. 3, edited by Eric Arnesen, 1444–46. New York: Routledge, 2007.

". . . A Sad Day for Two Peoples." *Life,* March 15, 1954, 19–23.

Sady, Emil J. *The United Nations and Dependent Peoples.* Washington, D.C.: Brookings Institution, 1956.

Saldaña-Portillo, María Josefina. *The Revolutionary Imagination in the Americas and the Age of Development.* Durham: Duke University Press, 2003.

Santiago-Valles, Kelvin A. *"Subject People" and Colonial Discourses: Economic Transformation and Social Disorder in Puerto Rico, 1898–1947.* Albany: State University of New York Press, 1994.

Savage, William. *Comic Books and America, 1945–1954.* Norman: University of Oklahoma Press, 1990.

Schlesinger, Arthur, Jr. "Dim Views of the Red Star." *Saturday Review of Literature,* January 7, 1950, 11.

———. Introduction to "Whittaker Chambers & His *Witness*" (1952). Reprinted in *The Politics of Hope,* 183–95. Boston: Houghton Mifflin, 1963.

———. *The Vital Center: The Politics of Freedom.* Boston: Houghton Mifflin, 1949.

Schrecker, Ellen. *The Age of McCarthyism: A Brief History with Documents.* Boston: Bedford Books, 1994.

———. *Many Are the Crimes: McCarthyism in America.* Princeton: Princeton University Press, 1998.

Schubert, Glendon. *Dispassionate Justice: A Synthesis of the Judicial Opinions of Robert H. Jackson.* Indianapolis: Bobbs-Merrill, 1969.

Schuck, Peter H. *Citizens, Strangers, and In-Betweens: Essays on Immigration and Citizenship.* Boulder, Colo.: Westview Press, 1998.

Scott, Catherine V. *Gender and Development: Rethinking Modernization and Dependency Theory.* Boulder, Colo.: Lynne Rienner Publishers, 1995.

Scott, Daryl Michael. *Contempt and Pity: Social Policy and the Image of the Damaged Black Psyche, 1880–1996.* Chapel Hill: University of North Carolina Press, 1997.

Scott, Joan W. "Gender: A Useful Category of Historical Analysis." *American Historical Review* 91, no. 5 (1986): 1053–75.

Seed, David. "The Ex-Communist Memoirs of Howard Fast and His Contemporaries." *Prospects* 24 (1999): 605–24.

Seijo Bruno, Miñi. *La insurrección nacionalista en Puerto Rico, 1950.* San Juan: Editorial Edil, 1989.

Sheinin, David. "The Caribbean and the Cold War: Between Reform and Revolution." In Palmié and Scarano, *The Caribbean,* 491–503.

Shellaby, Robert K. "Background to Violence." *Christian Science Monitor,* November 4, 1950, 3.

Sheridan, Clare. "'Another White Race:' Mexican Americans and the Paradox of Whiteness in Jury Selection." *Law and History Review* 21, no. 1 (2003): 109–44.

Sherry, Michael S. *In the Shadow of War: The United States since the 1930s.* New Haven: Yale University Press, 1995.

Shibusawa, Naoko. "The Lavender Scare and Empire: Rethinking Cold War Antigay Politics." *Diplomatic History* 36, no. 4 (2012): 723–52.

Shklar, Judith. *American Citizenship: The Quest for Inclusion.* Cambridge: Harvard University Press, 1991.

Shukert, Elfrieda Berthiaume, and Barbara Smith Scibetta. *War Brides of World War II.* Novato, Calif.: Presidio Press, 1988.

Singh, Nikhil Pal. *Black Is a Country: Race and the Unfinished Struggle for Democracy.* Cambridge: Harvard University Press, 2004.

Sjoberg, Laura, and Caron E. Gentry, eds. *Women, Gender, and Terrorism.* Athens: University of Georgia Press, 2011.

Slane, Andrea. *A Not So Foreign Affair: Fascism, Sexuality, and the Cultural Rhetoric of American Democracy.* Durham: Duke University Press, 2001.

Smith, E. Timothy. *Opposition beyond the Water's Edge: Liberal Internationalists, Pacifists, and Containment, 1945–1953.* Westport, Conn.: Greenwood Press, 1999.

Smith, Marian L. "'Any Woman Who Is Now or May Hereafter Be Married . . .': Women and Naturalization, ca. 1802–1940." *Prologue* 30, no. 2 (Summer 1998), available at www.archives.gov.

Smith, Rogers M. *Civic Ideals: Conflicting Visions of Citizenship in U.S. History.* New Haven: Yale University Press, 1997.

———. *Stories of Peoplehood: The Politics and Morals of Political Membership.* Cambridge: Cambridge University Press, 2003.

Smith, Ronald A. "The Paul Robeson–Jackie Robinson Saga and a Political Collision." *Journal of Sport History* 6, no. 2 (1979): 5–27.

Smythe, Mabel M. "Juvenile Tragedy—Its Causes and Consequences." *Phylon Quarterly* 18, no. 2 (1957): 187.

Somerville, Siobhan B. "Notes toward a Queer History of Naturalization." *American Quarterly* 57, no. 3 (2005): 659–75.

Soto-Crespo, Ramón E. *Mainland Passage: The Cultural Anomaly of Puerto Rico.* Minneapolis: University of Minnesota Press, 2009.

Southern, David W. *Gunnar Myrdal and Black-White Relations: The Use and Abuse of an American Dilemma, 1944–1969.* Baton Rouge: Louisiana State University Press, 1987.

Sparrow, Bartholomew H. *The Insular Cases and the Emergence of American Empire.* Lawrence: University Press of Kansas, 2006.

Spigel, Lynn. *Make Room for TV: Television and the Family Ideal in Postwar America.* Chicago: University of Chicago Press, 1992.

Springhall, John. *Youth, Popular Culture, and Moral Panics: Penny Gaffs to Gangsta-Rap, 1830–1996.* New York: St. Martin's Press, 1998.

Stanley, Amy Dru. *From Bondage to Contract: Wage Labor, Marriage, and the Market in the Age of Slave Emancipation.* Cambridge: Cambridge University Press, 1998.

Starr, Douglas. "Revisiting a 1930s Scandal, AACR to Rename a Prize." *Science* 300 (April 25, 2003): 573–74.

Stephanson, Anders. "Liberty or Death: The Cold War as U.S. Ideology." In *Reviewing the Cold War: Approaches, Interpretations, Theory,* edited by Odd Arne Westad, 81–100. Portland, Ore.: Frank Cass Publishers, 2000.

"Stone Cold Dead." *National Review,* November 22, 1958, 326.

Storrs, Landon R. Y. *The Second Red Scare and the Unmaking of the New Deal Left.* Princeton: Princeton University Press, 2012.

Stouffer, Samuel A. *Communism, Conformity, and Civil Liberties: A Cross-Section of the Nation Speaks Its Mind.* 1955. New Brunswick: Transaction Publishers, 1992.

Sugrue, Thomas J. "Crabgrass-Roots Politics: Race, Rights, and the Reaction against Liberalism in the Urban North, 1940–1964." *Journal of American History* 82, no. 2 (1995): 551–78.

Tanenhaus, Sam. *Whittaker Chambers: A Biography.* New York: Random House, 1997.

Tenenbaum, Samuel. "The Fate of Wartime Marriages." *American Mercury,* November 1945, 530–36.

Terry, Jennifer. *An American Obsession: Science, Medicine, and Homosexuality in Modern Society.* Chicago: University of Chicago Press, 1999.

———. "'Momism' and the Making of Treasonous Homosexuals." In *Bad Mothers: The Politics of Blame in Twentieth-Century America,* edited by Molly Ladd-Taylor and Lauri Umansky, 169–90. New York: New York University Press, 1998.

Thomas, Lorrin. *Puerto Rican Citizen: History and Political Identity in Twentieth-Century New York City.* Chicago: University of Chicago Press, 2010.

Thompson, Heather Ann. "Why Mass Incarceration Matters: Rethinking Crisis, Decline, and Transformation in Postwar American History." *Journal of American History* 97, no. 3 (2010): 703–34.

Tirman, John. *The War on Terror and the Cold War: They're Not the Same.* Audit of the Conventional Wisdom. Cambridge: MIT Center for International Studies, April 2006. http://web.mit.edu/cis.

Torruella, Juan R. "¿Hacia dónde vas Puerto Rico?" Review of *Puerto Rico: The Trials of the Oldest Colony in the World,* by José Trías Monge. *Yale Law Journal* 107, no. 5 (March 1998): 1503–22.

Tracy, James. *Direct Action: Radical Pacifism from the Union Eight to the Chicago Seven.* Chicago: University of Chicago Press, 1996.

"Trends in U.S. Corrections." The Sentencing Project Fact Sheet (December 2012). www.sentencingproject.org.

Trías Monge, José. *Puerto Rico: The Trials of the Oldest Colony in the World.* New Haven: Yale University Press, 1997.

Truman, Harry S. "Statement by the President upon Signing Bill Approving the Constitution of the Commonwealth of Puerto Rico." July 3, 1952. The American Presidency Project. www.presidency.ucsb.edu.

Twenty-to-One: Wealth Gaps Rise to Record Highs between Whites, Blacks, and Hispanics. Washington, D.C.: Pew Research Center, 2011.

Uesugi, Sayoko. "Gender, Race, and the Cold War: Mary Price and the Progressive Party in North Carolina, 1945–1948." *North Carolina Historical Review* 77, no. 3 (2000): 269–311.

Uggen, Christopher, Sarah Shannon, and Jeff Manza. "State-Level Estimates of Felon Disenfranchisement in the United States, 2010." Washington, D.C.: The Sentencing Project, 2012. www.sentencingproject.org.

United States ex rel. Knauff v. Shaughnessy, 338 U.S. 537 (1950).

U.S. Census Bureau. *Full-Time, Year-Round Black Workers by Median Income and Sex: 1955–2011.* www.census.gov.

———. *Median Years of School Completed by Persons 20 Years Old and Over, by Age, Color, and Sex, for the United States, Urban and Rural: 1940.* www.census.gov.

———. *Race and Hispanic Origin of Householder-Families by Median and Mean Income: 1947–2009.* www.census.gov.

U.S. Congress. House. *Approving the Constitution of the Commonwealth of Puerto Rico Which Was Adopted by the People of Puerto Rico on March 3, 1952.* 82nd Cong., 2nd sess., April 30, 1952. H. Report 1832.

———. Committee on Immigration and Naturalization. Minutes. ProQuest Congressional Hearings Digital Collection.

———. Committee on the Judiciary. *Exclusion of Ellen Knauff.* 81st Cong., 2nd sess., March 27 and April 3, 1950.

———. Committee on Public Lands. Subcommittee on Territorial and Insular Possessions. *Election of Governor.* 80th Cong., 1st sess., May 19, 1947.

———. Committee on Un-American Activities. *Communism in the District of Columbia–Maryland Area: Testimony of Mary Stalcup Markward.* 82nd Cong., 1st sess., June 11, 1951.

———. Committee on Un-American Activities. *Communism in the District of Columbia, Part 2.* 81st Cong., 2nd sess., December 6, 11–13, 1950.

———. Committee on Un-American Activities. *Communist Political Subversion, Part 1.* 84th Cong., 2nd sess. vol. 4. Washington, D.C.: GPO, 1956.

———. Committee on Un-American Activities. *Hearings Regarding Communist Infiltration of Minority Groups.* 81st Cong., 1st sess., July 13, 14, 18, 1949.

———. Report Nos. 1073 and 1320. 79th Cong., 1st sess.

U.S. Congress. Senate. *Hearings before the Subcommittee to Investigate Juvenile Delinquency of the Committee on the Judiciary: Juvenile Delinquency (Comic Books).* 83rd Cong., 2nd sess. Washington, D.C.: GPO, 1954.

———. *Interim Report of the Subcommittee to Investigate Juvenile Delinquency to the Committee on the Judiciary: Comic Books and Juvenile Delinquency.* 84th Cong., 1st sess. Washington, D.C.: GPO, 1955.

———. Permanent Subcommittee on Investigations of the Committee on Government Operations. *Army Signal Corps—Subversion and Espionage.* 83rd Cong., 1st sess., March 11, 1954.

———. Permanent Subcommittee on Investigations of the Committee on Government Operations. *Communist Infiltration among Army Civilian Workers.* 83rd Cong., 1st sess., September 8 and 11, 1953.

———. Permanent Subcommittee on Investigations. *Executive Sessions of the Senate Permanent Subcommittee on Investigations of the Committee on Government Operations.* 83rd Cong., 1st and 2nd sess., 1954. Vols. 2 and 5. Washington, D.C.: GPO, 2003.

———. Permanent Subcommittee on Investigations of the Committee on Government Operations. *State Department Information Program: Information Centers.* 83rd Cong., 1st sess., July 1, 2, 7, 1953.

———. Report 1779. *Providing for the Organization of a Constitutional Government by the People of Puerto Rico.* 81st Cong., 2nd sess., June 6, 1950.

U.S. Department of State. *Department of State Bulletin.* Vols. 28–29. Washington, D.C.: GPO, 1953.

———. *Foreign Relations of the United States, 1952–1954.* Vol. 3. Washington, D.C.: GPO, 1979.

U.S. President's Committee on Civil Rights. *To Secure These Rights: The Report of the President's Committee on Civil Rights.* Washington, D.C., 1947.

Vilar, Irene. *A Message from God in the Atomic Age: A Memoir.* New York: Pantheon Books, 1996.

Villa, Dana R. *Politics, Philosophy, Terror: Essays on the Thought of Hannah Arendt.* Princeton: Princeton University Press, 1999.

Villaronga, Gabriel. *Toward a Discourse of Consent: Mass Mobilization and Colonial Politics in Puerto Rico, 1932–1948.* Westport, Conn.: Praeger Security International, 2004.

Virden, Jenel. *Good-Bye, Piccadilly: British War Brides in America.* Urbana: University of Illinois Press, 1996.

Von Eschen, Penny M. *Race against Empire: Black Americans and Anticolonialism, 1937–1957.* Ithaca: Cornell University Press, 1997.

———. *Satchmo Blows Up the World: Jazz Ambassadors Play the Cold War.* Cambridge: Harvard University Press, 2004.

Wagner, Geoffrey. *Parade of Pleasure: A Study of Popular Iconography in the USA.* New York: Library Publishers, 1955.

Wainhouse, David W. *Remnants of Empire: The United Nations and the End of Colonialism.* New York: Harper and Row, 1964.

Walker, Anders. "When Gangs Were White: Race, Rights, and Youth Crime in New York City, 1954–1964." *Saint Louis University Law Journal* 55, no. 4 (2011): 1369–78.

War Brides Act of 1945. H.R. 4857, Pub. L. 79-271, 59 Stat. 659.

Washington, Mary Helen. "Alice Childress, Lorraine Hansberry, and Claudia Jones: Black Women Write the Popular Front." In *Left of the Color Line: Race, Radicalism, and Twentieth-Century Literature of the United States,* edited by Bill V. Mullen and James Smethurst, 183–204. Chapel Hill: University of North Carolina Press, 2003.

Wayne, Harold M. "G.I. Divorce Dangers." *Colliers,* October 21, 1944, 13, 80–82.

Weigand, Kate. "The Red Menace, the Feminine Mystique, and the Ohio Un-American Activities Commission: Gender and Anti-Communism in Ohio, 1951–1954." *Journal of Women's History* 3, no. 3 (1992): 70–94.

Weisselberg, Charles D. "The Exclusion and Detention of Aliens: Lessons from the Lives of Ellen Knauff and Ignatz Mezei." *University of Pennsylvania Law Review* 143, no. 4 (April 1995): 933–1034.

Wells, Mildred White. *Unity in Diversity: The History of the General Federation of Women's Clubs.* Washington, D.C.: General Federation of Women's Clubs, 1953.

Wertham, Fredric. *The Circle of Guilt.* New York: Rinehart & Company, 1956.

———. "Comic Books—Blueprints for Delinquency." *Reader's Digest,* May 1954, 24–29.

———. "The Comics . . . Very Funny." *Saturday Review of Literature,* May 29, 1948, 6.

——— [Frederic]. *Dark Legend: A Study in Murder.* London: Victor Gollancz, 1947.

———. *Seduction of the Innocent.* 1954. New York: Main Road Books, 2004.

———. "Sex Crimes Can Be Prevented." *Ladies' Home Journal,* August 1961, 46–47.

———. *The Show of Violence.* New York: Doubleday, 1949.

———. *A Sign for Cain: An Exploration of Human Violence.* New York: Macmillan, 1966.

———. "What Parents Don't Know about Comic Books." *Ladies' Home Journal,* November 1953, 50–53.

Westad, Odd Arne. *The Global Cold War: Third World Interventions and the Making of Our Times.* Cambridge: Cambridge University Press, 2007.

Wheeler, Leigh Ann. *Against Obscenity: Reform and the Politics of Womanhood in America, 1873–1935*. Baltimore: Johns Hopkins University Press, 2007.

"Where the Blame Lies." *Newsweek,* October 15, 1946, 118–19.

Whitfield, Stephen J. *The Culture of the Cold War.* Baltimore: Johns Hopkins University Press, 1991.

"Why Puerto Rico Boils Over." *U.S. News & World Report,* November 10, 1950, 22.

Wiecek, William M. "The Legal Foundations of Domestic Anticommunism: The Background of *Dennis v. United States.*" *Supreme Court Review* 2001: 375–434.

Willoughby, John. "The Sexual Behavior of American GIs during the Early Years of the Occupation of Germany." *Journal of Military History* 62 (January 1998): 155–74.

Wilson, Veronica A. "Elizabeth Bentley and Cold War Representation: Some Masks Not Dropped." *Intelligence and National Security* 14, no. 2 (1999): 49–69.

———. "'Now You Are Alone': Anticommunism, Gender, and the Cold War Myths of Hede Massing and Whittaker Chambers." *Diplomatic History* 36, no. 4 (2012): 699–722.

Winters v. New York, 333 U.S. 507 (1948).

Woods, Jeff. *Black Struggle, Red Scare: Segregation and Anti-Communism in the South, 1948–1968.* Baton Rouge: Louisiana State University Press, 2004.

Worthington, Janet Farrar. "When Psychiatry Was Very Young." *Hopkins Medicine,* Winter 2008. www.hopkinsmedicine.org.

Wright, Bradford. *Comic Book Nation: The Transformation of Youth Culture in America.* Baltimore: Johns Hopkins University Press, 2001.

Wright, Charles Allen. "'A Long Work of Fiction.'" *Saturday Review,* May 24, 1952, 11–12.

X. "Sources of Soviet Conduct." *Foreign Affairs,* July 1947, 566–82.

Yoe, Craig. *Secret Identity: The Fetish Art of Superman's Co-Creator Joe Shuster.* New York: Abrams ComicArts, 2009.

Zeiger, Susan. *Entangling Alliances: Foreign War Brides and American Soldiers in the Twentieth Century.* New York: New York University Press, 2010.

Zucker, Bat-Ami. *In Search of Refuge: Jews and U.S. Consuls in Nazi Germany.* New York: Vallentine Mitchell, 2001.

Zulaika, Joseba, and William A. Douglass. *Terror and Taboo: The Follies, Fables, and Faces of Terrorism.* New York: Routledge, 1996.

INDEX

Page numbers in italics refer to illustrations.